OUTRAGEOUS
MISCONDUCT

OUTRAGEOUS MISCONDUCT

The Asbestos Industry on Trial

PAUL BRODEUR

PANTHEON BOOKS · NEW YORK

The material in this book appeared originally in *The New Yorker*,
in slightly different form.

Library of Congress Cataloging in Publication Data

Brodeur, Paul.
Outrageous misconduct.
Includes index.

1. Manville Corporation. 2. Asbestos industry.
3. Asbestos industry—Employees—Diseases and
hygiene. 4. Employers' liability. 5. Bankruptcy—
United States. I. Title.
HD9585.A66U63   1985   363.1'79   85-6558
ISBN 0-394-53320-8

Book design by Joe Marc Freedman

Manufactured in the United States of America

First Edition

To Ward Stephenson

CONTENTS

ACKNOWLEDGMENTS

The author wishes to express appreciation to William Shawn, the editor of *The New Yorker*, who provided him with the opportunity to undertake and complete this project, and space in the magazine to publish it; to Charles Patrick Crow, of *The New Yorker*, who edited the manuscript; to Martin J. Baron and Richard S. Sacks, whose prodigious research insured that the manuscript would be as free of error as possible; to Marcia Van Meter, who oversaw all the changes in the final proof; to Joseph H. Cooper, who provided valuable legal counsel; to Wendy Goldwyn, of Pantheon Books, who oversaw the production of the book; to Irving J. Selikoff, who has given encouragement over the years; and to the several dozen dedicated attorneys for both the plaintiff and the defense, who furnished the information and assistance which made this book possible.

ONE

A FAILURE TO WARN

When the Manville Corporation, the world's largest asbestos company, with twenty-five thousand employees and more than fifty factories and mines in the United States and Canada, filed a debtor's petition for reorganization and protection under Chapter 11 of the federal Bankruptcy Code, on August 26, 1982, it did so in order to force a halt to thousands of lawsuits that had been brought against it by workers who claimed that they had developed lung cancer and other diseases as a result of their exposure to asbestos in Manville's insulation products, and who were alleging that the company had failed to warn them of the dangers involved. The story made the front page of virtually every major newspaper in the country, because Manville (formerly the Johns-Manville Corporation) was not only the largest American industrial company ever to file under Chapter 11—at the time, it ranked 181st on *Fortune*'s list of the nation's 500 leading industrial corporations—but, with assets of more than $2 billion, was also one of the most financially healthy companies ever to take such action. In a full-page statement that appeared on August 27 in the New York *Times*, the Washington *Post*, the *Wall Street Journal*, and other leading papers, John A. McKinney, Manville's chairman and chief executive officer, announced that the company was "overwhelmed by 16,500 lawsuits related to the health effects of asbestos." McKinney said that lawsuits were being brought against Manville at a rate of 500 a month, and that the company could expect to be named as a defendant in at least 52,000 asbestos-disease lawsuits before the litigation ran its course. He estimated that at the present settlement cost of about $40,000 per case the lawsuits would create a potential liability of $2 billion, requiring Manville to set aside a reserve fund that would wipe out most of its net worth and cripple its operation. For these reasons, he declared, the company's board of directors had decided to file for relief in the hope of establishing an effective system for handling the asbestos claims under Chapter 11.

In his statement, McKinney took pains to point out those people whom he considered responsible for Manville's predicament. He began by blaming the federal government for refusing to admit responsibility for asbestos disease that had developed among Second World War shipyard workers, who made up half the plaintiffs in the lawsuits being brought against Manville. He criticized Congress for failing to enact a statutory compensation program for the victims of asbestos disease "so that the thousands of citizens and voters caught up in this problem will be spared the expensive, inefficient, and haphazard litigation system we have been saddled with." In addition, he castigated the insurance companies with which Manville had been doing business over the years for refusing to pay claims against product-liability policies totaling hundreds of millions of dollars. As for any responsibility that Manville might have incurred for the plight of the insulation workers, McKinney implied that the company was not at fault because "not until 1964 was it known that excessive exposure to asbestos fiber released from asbestos-containing insulation products can sometimes cause certain lung diseases." Since the mid-1970s, he said, Manville had disposed of some thirty-five hundred lawsuits by settlement or trial, and in a significant number of the cases that had gone to trial, he said, "juries have found that we were not at fault and acted responsibly in light of then existing medical knowledge."

In many ways, McKinney's statement was more revealing for its omissions than for what it contained. By neglecting to mention that Manville and its insurance carriers had settled out of court approximately thirty-four hundred of the thirty-five hundred lawsuits it had disposed of, and that it had paid out some $50 million in doing so, he ignored the extent to which his company had already acknowledged responsibility for the incidence of asbestos disease in the insulation workers. In claiming that insulation materials containing asbestos were not known to be dangerous until 1964—an assertion that had constituted Manville's chief legal defense for many years—he ignored the fact that this defense had been rejected by juries across the country, and had recently been struck down by the New Jersey Supreme Court. Far and away the most self-serving of the omissions in McKinney's statement, however, was his failure to go beyond a bare mention of the fact that punitive damages had been awarded against Manville.

Not only had juries found Manville liable for punitive damages in ten of some sixty-five asbestos lawsuits involving the company that had been tried in the United States during 1981 and the first half of 1982, but the average amount of punitive damages in the first six months of 1982 was about $600,000 a case. It is usually not possible to insure against punitive damages, which are assessed for outrageous and reckless misconduct, and McKinney could not have been unaware of their potential effect upon his company, for the simple reason that the likelihood of their being awarded in subsequent trials had been listed as a chief reason for Manville's financially uncertain future in a sworn affidavit that Manville's treasurer had submitted to the United States Bankruptcy Court of the Southern District of New York on the previous day. Moreover, in testimony given before the Senate Committee on Labor and Human Resources two years earlier, McKinney himself had underscored the devastating implications of punitive damages when, in order to substantiate his denial of the charge that employers had knowingly exposed workers to the hazards of excessive asbestos dust, he had pointed out that in all the litigation to date there had not been a single instance in which a jury or a trial judge had awarded punitive damages against any asbestos company. "I can think of no greater demonstration that the coverup charge is a complete fabrication," he declared at the time.

By and large, the newspaper stories that appeared on August 27 tended to describe Manville as a beleaguered giant reeling under the burden of mass litigation, and to portray McKinney as an embattled business manager fighting for his company's survival. Few of them reported the fact that juries had assessed punitive damages against Manville after hearing evidence that the company had engaged in a coverup of the asbestos hazard for nearly five decades. The *Times*, for example, not only neglected to tell its readers initially that punitive damages had been assessed but also ran an editorial that compared the suffering of diseased asbestos workers with the fiscal woes afflicting the asbestos companies. "Asbestos is a tragedy, most of all for the victims and their families but also for the companies, which are being made to pay the price for decisions made long ago," the editorial read. The editorial warned Congress to address the asbestos problem "before more victims die uncompensated and other companies follow Manville into the bankruptcy courts."

During the remainder of August and in the first part of September, the economic, legal, and political ramifications of Manville's Chapter 11 petition received daily attention in the press, which speculated at length on the dilemma it presented to Manville's stockholders and creditors, on the problems it posed for the bankruptcy court, and on the pressure it placed on Congress to enact legislation that would help Manville overcome its financial difficulties. Considerably less attention was given to a grim prediction made by Dr. Irving J. Selikoff, who was director of the Environmental Sciences Laboratory at the Mount Sinai School of Medicine, in New York, and was widely acknowledged as the world's leading expert on asbestos disease. Selikoff estimated that among the twenty-one million living American men and women who had been occupationally exposed to asbestos between 1940 and 1980 there would be between eight and ten thousand deaths from asbestos-related cancer each year for the next twenty years. As for the culpability of Manville and other leading asbestos companies in helping to create this immense human tragedy, it either went unreported or was mentioned only in passing. By the last week of September, when the story of Manville's Chapter 11 petition had dropped from the headlines, few people were aware that the bankruptcy filing was simply the latest episode in a fifty-year history of corporate malfeasance and inhumanity to man that is unparalleled in the annals of the private-enterprise system.

In a lineal sense, the legal troubles besetting the asbestos industry began on a sultry morning in August, 1961, when a man named Claude J. Tomplait walked into the law offices of Stephenson, Stephenson & Thompson in the East Texas town of Orange—so named for an orange grove that grew in the region in the early 1800s—and asked to speak with Ward Stephenson, who was the firm's senior partner. Tomplait, who was forty years old at the time, had worked as an asbestos insulator for half of his life, and was then living in Bridge City, which is eight miles southwest of Orange and about halfway to Port Arthur, where he was born and had grown up. Orange and Port Arthur are on the Sabine River, which divides Texas from Louisiana before it empties into the Gulf of Mexico, and, together with the city of Beaumont, which is about twenty-two miles west of Orange and about eighteen miles northwest of Port Arthur, they lie at the corners of a heavily industrialized area known as the Golden Triangle, which contains oil refineries, shipyards, steel-fabrication plants, and one of the largest concentrations of petrochemical factories in the world. During his twenty years as an asbestos insulator, Tomplait, who was a member of Local 112 of the International Association of Heat and Frost Insulators and Asbestos Workers, in Lake Charles, Louisiana, had been employed by dozens of insulation contractors on hundreds of jobs in more than fifteen states, but he had spent most of his time insulating steam pipes, boilers, turbines, and other high-temperature equipment in the shipyards, power plants, oil refineries, and petrochemical factories of the Golden Triangle. He was a short, slender man of Cajun descent, with an unassuming manner, and on the day he spoke with Stephenson he wore a somber expression because he had recently been given some bad news about his health.

Tomplait started out by telling Stephenson that for almost two years he had been short of breath, particularly when climbing stairs, and had felt a strange tightness in his chest. In March, during the course of a life-insurance medical examination, he said, Dr. John C. Greco, a physician in Bridge City, had called his attention to the fact that he had developed finger clubbing—a thickening of tissue at the fingertips that often occurs with asbestosis, a disabling lung disease caused by the inhalation of asbestos fibers. In late July, Dr. Greco sent Tomplait to Orange Memorial Hospital for chest X-rays, and when they revealed signs of scarring he tentatively diagnosed what his patient was suffering from as pulmonary dust disease. Greco then referred Tomplait to Dr. Tom R. Jones, a chest specialist in Houston, who, upon reviewing the X-rays and performing pulmonary-function tests, told Tomplait that he had developed pulmonary fibrosis—scarring of the lungs—probably as a result of inhaling asbestos fibers, and advised him to stop smoking and to avoid further contact with irritating dusts such as those of asbestos and silica. After recounting this medical history, Tomplait asked Stephenson if he would file a workmen's-compensation claim on his behalf with the Texas Industrial Accident Board, and when Stephenson agreed to do so Tomplait signed a power-of-attorney agreement with him.

Up to that point, Ward Stephenson, who was also forty years old, had never had occasion to take an occupational-disease case. However, he had had plenty of experience with workmen's-compensation claims, because serious industrial accidents—workers losing their fingers, hands, or arms to faulty equipment, or being blown to bits by exploding high-pressure pipe, or being electrocuted by improperly grounded welding machines or other electrical devices—were common in the shipyards, refineries, and factories of East Texas. In fact, Stephenson was then handling between seventy-five and a hundred industrial-injury claims a year, and had become known throughout Orange County as a specialist in the field, which is how Tomplait had come to hear of him. Married and the father of two small boys, he was a meticulously groomed man of medium height, with thinning, sandy hair and blue eyes, and he was noticeably self-conscious about a long, deep scar on his left cheek, which was a result of an operation some five years earlier for removal of a cancerous parotid gland—one of several glands that produce saliva. His physicians had told him that he had little chance of surviving the illness and he had only recently emerged from a long depression that had followed the surgery and the pessimistic prognosis, and had been exacerbated by the death of his father in 1958.

Stephenson had formed the law firm with his father, Kemper W. Stephenson, in 1947, after graduating from Southern Methodist University School of Law. Kemper W. Stephenson, who was himself the son of a lawyer was born in Center, Texas—a town 115 miles northwest of Orange. He was known as Mr. K.W., and he became district attorney in nearby Nacogdoches, where Ward was born on March 9, 1921. Shortly thereafter, the elder Stephenson moved his family to Orange and founded a law firm, together with Martin Dies, an attorney from Beaumont, and Dies's son, Martin, Jr. (known as Big Martin), who would later be elected to Congress and achieve notoriety as founder and chairman of the House Un-American Activities Committee. During the 1920s and 1930s, the firm of Dies, Stephenson & Dies, as it was then called, built its reputation by representing poor people and small property owners in land-title cases brought against wealthy landholders and big oil companies. After the Second World War, when the petrochemical industry moved into the Gulf Coast, and Orange County became heavily industrialized, it maintained its anti-establishment tradition by representing working-class people and labor unions, and by 1961, when Ward Stephenson took on Claude Tomplait as a client, it was known as one of the most aggressive and successful plaintiff firms in East Texas.

From his father, a diminutive man who was a devoted student of the law, a combative lawyer, and a stern mentor, Stephenson inherited perfectionism and an abiding anger at injustice. (One of the many stories told in Orange about the elder Stephenson describes a run-in he had with a local judge, who, irritated by what he considered to be excessive objections on K.W.'s part, told him, "If you do not shut up, Mr. Stephenson, I am going to put you in jail," to which Stephenson coolly replied, "I'd just as soon be put in jail as have to stay someplace I can't get justice.") As much as Ward and his father disliked injustice, however, they differed drastically in their approach to the law. K. W. Stephenson was a magnificent draftsman, with a penchant for logic and language, who would brief all of the theoretical aspects of a case before agreeing to take it. As a result, by the time he filed a petition he was usually prepared for trial. Ward was a poor draftsman, with a rambling and repetitious writing style, but he could be remarkably concise and improvisational in oral argument, and devastating on cross-examination, and he placed far greater emphasis upon investigating the facts of a case than upon theory and procedure.

From his mother, Margaret Kenna, who came from a family of Methodist ministers in Carthage (a town about sixty miles from Nacogdoches) and who is remembered in Orange as a woman of uncommon beauty, character, and kindness, Stephenson inherited a gentleness that enabled him to become deeply involved with the problems of the working people who were his clients. But like most human beings, he was a person of contradictions. Charming, competitive, intensely private, secretive about his health problems, generous and outgoing with his friends, who came from all walks of life, he was full of energy, fast on his feet, fascinated by hypnosis, and, of course, irrevocably pierced in the prime of life by an awareness of his own mortality. He became an expert pilot in his early forties, and proceeded to become an expert motorcycle rider, boatman, sportfisherman, and ham radio operator. (He was already an accomplished horseman, and raised cutting horses on the family homestead—a 700-acre farm in Little Cypress, ten miles north of Orange.) As soon as he perfected one avocation, he moved on enthusiastically to the next. He was also unpredictable, as when, out of the blue, he persuaded a dozen or so of his friends and acquaintances to invest in the successful 1960 Broadway musical *Bye Bye Birdie*.

As for his professional life, Stephenson was a resourceful and innovative attorney, who in addition to specializing in industrial-accident cases had achieved recognition among his fellow trial lawyers for

creating the so-called Pied Piper theory of liability. This he had devised several years earlier in the course of trying—and winning—a
negligence suit against an ice-cream company whose bell-ringing
truck had enticed a small girl to run into a roadway, where she was
struck by a car and seriously injured. As it happened, however, his
greatest achievement lay a dozen years down the road, for in signing
the power-of-attorney agreement with Tomplait he was taking the
first step in a pioneering legal journey whose outcome would not be
known until September 10, 1973—three days after his own death—
when an appellate court would hand down a landmark decision in a
product-liability lawsuit that he had tried against Johns-Manville and
several other leading manufacturers of asbestos insulation. It was a
journey that would consume most of Stephenson's time and energy
during the last years of his life, and it was a decision that would
trigger the greatest avalanche of toxic tort litigation in the history of
American jurisprudence.

The adverse biological effects of asbestos, a word that comes from
Greek adjective meaning inextinguishable, were observed as early as
the first century by the Greek geographer Strabo and by the Roman
naturalist Pliny the Elder, both of whom mentioned in passing a
sickness of the lungs in slaves whose task was to weave asbestos into
cloth. Strabo and Pliny were calling attention for the first time to the
disease from which Claude Tomplait would be diagnosed as suffering
nearly two thousand years later, but the ancients were much too awed
by the unique and astonishing physical properties of asbestos, which
they called "the magic mineral," to be concerned with the possibility
that it might constitute a health hazard. Indeed, their attitude toward
asbestos—a broad term embracing a number of silicate minerals,
whose delicate fibers not only can withstand the fiercest heat but are
so soft and flexible that they can be spun and woven as easily as fibers
of cotton or flax—sometimes bordered on veneration. Strabo and Plu-
tarch noted that the "perpetual" wicks used in the sacred lamps of the
vestal virgins were made of asbestos, and Pliny described asbestos
cloth, which had been used for centuries in cremations, as the rare and
costly "funeral dress of kings." The Romans were especially im-
pressed by the fact that when cloth made of asbestos was exposed to
flame it always came out whiter than before—hence the Latin word for

asbestos, *amiantus,* meaning unpolluted or undefiled—and they are said to have cleaned asbestos napkins by tossing them into the fire. During the Dark Ages, the use of asbestos in Europe appears to have diminished greatly, although it is said that the Emperor Charlemagne convinced some warrior guests from a rival kingdom that he possessed magical powers by throwing an asbestos tablecloth into the fire and then withdrawing it, unscathed, from the flames. In the latter part of the thirteenth century, when the indefatigable Venetian traveler Marco Polo was traversing a part of Siberia then known as the Great Empire of Tartary, he was shown some cloth that would not burn, and was told by his Tartar hosts that it was made from salamander's wool. Too wily to be taken in by a story like that, Polo examined the material carefully and, after making inquiries, learned that there was a mineral in the mountains of the district that contained threads like those of wool. After a long period of eclipse, the astonishing properties of asbestos were rediscovered in the Western world, with the advent of the industrial revolution in the eighteenth century, and by the late 1800s the incombustible mineral began to be used extensively to insulate boilers, steam pipes, turbines, ovens, kilns, and other high-temperature equipment. As a result, the fact that asbestos could produce lung disease, which had been forgotten since Strabo and Pliny first recorded it around the time of Christ, soon manifested itself again.

Modern knowledge of asbestosis dates from the year 1900, when Dr. H. Montague Murray, a physician in London's Charing Cross Hospital, performed a post-mortem examination on a thirty-three-year-old man who had worked for fourteen years in an asbestos-textile factory. The patient, found to have been suffering from severe pulmonary fibrosis, had been the last survivor of a group of ten men who were working in the carding room of the factory in 1886, and since Dr. Murray found spicules of asbestos in the lung tissues at autopsy he was able to establish a presumptive connection between the man's occupation and the disease that killed him.

Thirty years would go by before asbestos lung disease would be established by autopsy in the United States, but if a post mortem had been performed on Henry Ward Johns, who founded the H. W. Johns Manufacturing Company—makers of asbestos textiles, roofing, and insulation materials, and forerunner of the H. W. Johns-Manville Company—it would undoubtedly have resulted in a finding similar to that of Dr. Murray. Inspired by an encyclopedia article on asbestos, Johns had begun to experiment with the heat-resisting property of the mineral in 1858, when he was twenty-one. He subsequently invented a new roofing material by running burlap, jute, asbestos, and pitch through a clothes wringer, and set up shop in lower Manhattan, where he manufactured asbestos products. When he died in Yonkers, in 1898, his death certificate listed the cause as "dust phthisis pneumonitis"—a diagnosis that was probably a medical euphemism for asbestosis.

A few years after Murray's discovery of asbestos disease, an inspector in the Department of Labor at Caen, whose name was Auribault, reported the results of what was undoubtedly the first study of mortality among asbestos workers. According to Auribault, whose account appeared in 1906 in the *Bulletin de l'Inspection du Travail et de l'Hygiène Industrielle*, an asbestos-weaving mill had been established in 1890 at Condé-sur-Noireau, in Calvados, and during its first five years of operation, when there was no artificial ventilation and the employees were heavily exposed to dust from the looms, fifty of them died. Moreover, the director of the factory, who had previously owned a cotton mill at Gonneville, in Manche, had recruited seventeen workers from his former staff, of whom sixteen were wiped out by what Auribault, who was not a physician, mistakenly described as chalicosis —a pneumoconiosis (the general term for all dust diseases of the lungs, which comes from the Greek words for "lung" and "dust") that was common among stonecutters.

Unfortunately, Murray and Auribault never realized the importance of their findings. Testifying before a Departmental Committee on Compensation for Industrial Diseases, in 1906, Murray said, "One hears, generally speaking, that considerable trouble is now taken to prevent the inhalation of dust, and so the disease is not so likely to occur as heretofore," and the concluding recommendation of Auribault's report was simply that people under eighteen years of age should not be allowed to work in dusty conditions. Because of ignorance about the cause of the disease, and because it manifests itself slowly and insidiously over a period of ten to twenty years or more, asbestosis was probably more often than not misdiagnosed in the early part of the century as pulmonary tuberculosis, fibrosing pneumonia, or silicosis. Indeed, as in the case of Claude Tomplait, asbestosis and silicosis would continue to be confused right up to the 1960s. As a result, even though the asbestos industry was growing rapidly in most

industrialized countries—in the United States, the H. W. Johns Manufacturing Company had merged in 1901 with the Manville Covering
Company, of Milwaukee, and become the world's largest manufacturer
of high-temperature insulation for boilers and steam pipes—almost
nothing was done to control dust levels in asbestos factories, and
almost no medical information on asbestosis was gathered during the
quarter of a century that followed the disclosures of Murray and
Auribault, although many asbestos workers were undoubtedly dying
of it.

It was not until 1924 that the first clear case of death due to
asbestosis appeared in medical literature. That year, Dr. W. E. Cooke,
an English physician, who gave the disease its name, performed a
post-mortem examination on a thirty-three-year-old woman patient
who at the age of thirteen had started working in an asbestos-textile
factory that had no system to remove dust. By 1917, after thirteen
years of exposure, she had been coughing and had been in bad health,
and from then on her attendance at work had been intermittent because of shortness of breath and lassitude. The autopsy showed extensive pulmonary fibrosis and dense strands of abnormal fibrous tissue
connecting the lungs and the pleural membranes surrounding them.
Cooke's discovery, which was published in the *British Medical Journal,*
provided the point of departure for an intensive study of asbestosis in
Britain over the next seven years. The most important investigation of
this period was conducted by Dr. E. R. A. Merewether, Medical Inspector of Factories for the British Home Office. Between 1928 and 1929,
he examined 363 asbestos-textile workers out of an estimated total of
2,200 asbestos workers employed in Britain, and found that 95 of
them, or slightly more than 25 percent, showed evidence of pulmonary
fibrosis. He also demonstrated that the incidence of fibrosis increased
in direct proportion to the number of years of exposure, reaching 81
percent in the group of workers who had been employed in the industry for twenty years or more. As a result of Merewether's report,
Parliament passed legislation in 1931 that required improved methods
of exhaust ventilation and dust suppression in asbestos-textile factories, instituted periodical medical examinations for workers engaged
in particularly dusty processes in the asbestos-textile industry, and
made asbestosis a compensable disease.

Meanwhile, no investigations of the health experience of asbestos
workers were being undertaken by the United States Public Health

Service, or, for that matter, by any other American governmental health organization, and asbestosis would not become a compensable disease in most states for ten or fifteen years. However, the fact that asbestos could cause disease was no secret. As early as 1917, Dr. Henry K. Pancoast, of the University of Pennsylvania School of Medicine, who was considered to be the foremost roentgenological authority in the country, had observed lung scarring in the X-rays of fifteen asbestos-factory workers; in 1918, the United States Bureau of Labor Statistics published a report by Frederick L. Hoffman, a consulting statistician for the Prudential Insurance Company of America, in Newark, New Jersey, who not only called attention to the fact that American asbestos workers were experiencing unusually early deaths but also revealed that it had become the practice of some American and Canadian insurance companies not to issue life-insurance policies to asbestos workers because of the "assumed health-injurious conditions" that existed in the asbestos industry; in 1927, the first workmen's-compensation disability claim for asbestosis, which was filed by a foreman in the weaving department of an asbestos-textile mill in Massachusetts, was upheld by the Massachusetts Industrial Accident Board; and in 1930 the first case of asbestosis found at autopsy in this country—it occurred in a worker who had been employed at an asbestos mine in South America—was reported in a journal called *Minnesota Medicine*. During the next few years, however, the growing awareness that asbestos might constitute a serious industrial health hazard was all but buried by an avalanche of lawsuits brought by workers who were suffering from silicosis. This development took American industry by surprise, and it turned out to have consequences that would adversely affect the fate of asbestos workers—Claude Tomplait among them—for decades to come.

Silicosis is an insidious and progressive disease in which the lungs become scarred through inhalation of silica, a compound that may exist in a number of mineral forms, the most common of which is quartz. Silica is released into the air as respirable dust when various rocks, such as granite and sandstone, are drilled, crushed, or pulverized. It causes severe shortness of breath and renders the lungs highly susceptible to tuberculosis, and, depending upon the occupation of its victims, it had been known over the years as miners' consumption, miners' phthisis, stonecutters' asthma, stonemasons' disease, grinders' rot, and potters' rot. Hippocrates, who lived between 460 and 377 B.C., first described silicosis in his *Epidemics,* in which he wrote of a metal digger who "breathes with difficulty." Two thousand years later, Georg Bauer, a medieval Swiss physician who wrote under the name of Georgius Agricola, gave a graphic account of its ravages among the miners of Bohemia in his book *De Re Metallica,* saying, "When the dust is corrosive it ulcerates the lungs and produces consumption; hence it is that in the Carpathian Mountains there are women who have married seven husbands, all of whom this dreadful disease has brought to an early grave." The first pathological description of silicosis was given in 1672 by Ijsbrand van Diemerbroeck, a professor of medicine at the University of Utrecht, who performed autopsies on several stonecutters who had died of asthma and found the vesicles of their lungs so clogged with fine dust that, in running his knife through them, he thought he was cutting through sand. Measures to prevent the disease were suggested around 1700 by Bernardino Ramazzini, a professor of medicine at the University of Padua, who is said to have urged stonecutters to work with their backs to the wind. Little evidence exists to show that even such rudimentary advice was heeded, however, for by 1819 silicosis (in this case called grinders' asthma) was taking such a ghastly toll of workers who were engaged in grinding forks on dry stones in Sheffield, England, that a proposal was made to employ criminals for the task.

In the United States, silicosis appears to have escaped notice until 1887, when it was found at autopsy in the lungs of a stove-foundry worker in Poughkeepsie, New York. That same year, it was reported that twenty-three of thirty-four workers in a cutlery factory in Shelburne Falls, Massachusetts, had died of the disease during the previous decade. Around the turn of the century, one report told of thirty men who had died of silicosis after only one or two years of exposure to quartz dust in a gold-ore-crushing mill in Nevada, and between 1913 and 1915 a study of 720 lead and zinc miners in southwestern Missouri revealed that 433 of them, or 60 percent, had developed the disease. Over the next fifteen years, silicosis was found to be prevalent among granite cutters in Vermont and among subway tunnelers in New York City, and the mortality tables of a dozen life-insurance companies showed that workers exposed to silica dust in several industries were experiencing a death rate that was three times as high as expected. By

1930, more than a million workers in the nation had been exposed to harmful amounts of silica dust, and since at least one in four of them could have been expected to develop silicosis it is not hard to understand how a huge silicotic population had built up over the years. Only six states, however, had enacted laws that made silicosis a compensable disease, and since tuberculosis was often a complicating factor in diagnosis, a worker's chance of obtaining compensation even in those states was very slim. As a result, workers suffering from silicosis—especially those who had lost their jobs in the Depression—sought recourse in the only remedy that was left to them. They began to bring damage suits against their employers under the common law.

During the era of litigation that followed, it became fashionable in business circles to sneer at silicosis as "the Depression disease." In 1933, silicosis damage suits totaling more than a $100 million were pending in the United States, and by the following year the figure had risen to $300 million, creating a situation that was greeted by employers and their insurers with a mixture of astonishment, confusion, fury, righteous indignation, and predictions of bankruptcy. Ironically, the fact that many of these early lawsuits were brought by workers who were suffering not from silicosis but from asbestosis went unrecognized. The worrisome implications of the litigation did not, however, go unrecognized by the officials of the Johns-Manville Corporation, of New York City, and Raybestos-Manhattan, of Bridgeport, Connecticut —the two largest asbestos-manufacturing companies in the nation— who undertook to suppress knowledge about the health hazards of asbestos. Nor were the implications lost on officials of the nation's leading insurance companies, who, even as they settled most of the initial damage claims for silicosis and asbestosis out of court, began casting about for ways to limit their liability for pulmonary dust diseases in the future.

As it happened, a solution to their dilemma had been proposed as early as 1932 by Andrew J. Farrell, a Chicago insurance-company lawyer, who wrote an article in *Industrial Medicine* charging that many of the two hundred silicosis cases then pending in the courts of Illinois had been instigated as part of an organized racket by unscrupulous lawyers and doctors. After warning that there would probably be many more lawsuits "because of the unemployment situation and the activity of ambulance chasers," Farrell went on to say that "In those states where silicosis and kindred sicknesses are controlled by the workmen's-compensation act, there is not so much activity in stirring up claims, as the amount to be recovered is limited by the statutes." He then recommended that silicosis and other pulmonary dust diseases be taken out of the courts and covered by workmen's-compensation acts wherever possible.

Manufacturers and their insurers had good reason to believe that Farrell's solution to the silicosis-litigation problem could be implemented, for over the years they had been able to manipulate state legislators with great ease in matters relating to the workplace. A prime example was the workmen's-compensation system itself—a hodgepodge of laws that, for the most part, had been enacted with industry support in various states between 1911 and 1920. In theory, workmen's compensation was a no-fault system: it made employers liable for work-related injuries and death, regardless of whether there had been negligence, and required them to pay to employees or their families benefits that were limited by statute; in return, the employees and their families gave up the right to bring suit for full compensatory damages under the common law. However, because the lawmakers who drew up the statutes were prevailed upon by industry and its insurers to keep the cash benefits to a minimum, however, workmen's compensation proved to be a boon for employers, who were allowed to compensate for a worker's loss of life and limb at bargain prices during a time when the injury-and-death rate had soared in coal mines, steel mills, textile factories, and other corners of the nation's workplace.

Over the next few years, Farrell's proposal that pulmonary dust disease be covered by workmen's-compensation laws was echoed by a parade of prominent industrial physicians. Among them was Dr. Clarence Olds Sappington, a well-known consulting industrial hygienist from Chicago, who wrote this assessment in the April, 1935, issue of *Industrial Medicine:*

> From the manufacturer's point of view, the best possible thing that can happen to him is to be in a state where there is compensation for silicosis and to provide adequate manufacturing equipment and protective equipment for his employees; experience has proved that where this is done, the manufacturer pays less and in some cases very little for cases of silicosis. The next best thing that can happen to a manufacturer is

to be in a state where compensation is provided for silicosis, although he has not been in a position, or thinks he has not been in a position, to provide proper manufacturing equipment and proper protective equipment for his employees—for should they develop silicosis, he at least has a fee schedule to conform to and the decision depends upon a special commission. The worst possible thing that can happen to the industrial defendant is to be in a state where there is no compensation provided for silicosis and also not to provide adequate manufacturing equipment and proper protective equipment for his employees, the reasons for this being obvious.

The asbestos manufacturers, of course, were already aware that workmen's compensation would be to their benefit. In a 1935 memorandum describing a symposium on the pulmonary-disease problem and its legal implications, Vandiver Brown, the chief attorney for Johns-Manville, took special note of a speaker who stated that "the strongest bulwark against future disaster for industry is the enactment of properly drawn occupational-disease legislation," which would "eliminate the jury" as well as "eliminate the shyster lawyer and the quack doctor since fees would be strictly limited by the law." Indeed, industry lobbyists were already hard at work persuading lawmakers in states across the nation not only to amend existing compensation statutes to include silicosis and asbestosis but also to severely limit the cash and medical benefits that would be paid out for these diseases and to restrict the number of claimants who would be eligible to collect them. As things turned out, they would soon get help in this endeavor from an unexpected quarter, for within the year—as a result of public clamor that greeted the belated revelation of the Hawks Nest tunnel disaster, in West Virginia—a receptive political climate for Farrell's solution would be in the making.

Hawks Nest was a village on the New River, at the foot of Gauley Mountain, in Fayette County, about thirty miles southeast of Charleston. Between April of 1930 and September of 1932, a three-and-three-quarters-mile-long tunnel had been driven through the mountain to bring water to a hydroelectric station that was being built near the town of Gauley Bridge for the New-Kanawha Power Company, a utility corporation owned by the Union Carbide & Carbon Company, of New York. Excavation of the tunnel was undertaken by the Rinehart & Dennis Company, of Charlottesville, Virginia, and was accomplished by some two thousand laborers—of whom three-quarters were black —who had been recruited from all over the South to work for wages as low as twenty-five cents an hour. To speed the work, Rinehart & Dennis's foremen permitted compressed-air jackhammers to be operated dry, in spite of the fact that much of the tunnel was being driven through sandstone that contained 99.44 percent pure silica, and in contravention of a long-standing recommendation by the United States Bureau of Mines that wet-drilling methods be used to suppress hazardous silica dust. The dry-drilling created so much white silica dust in the tunnel that workers could scarcely see ten feet ahead, and they often looked as if they had been sprinkled with flour. Many of them soon developed acute silicosis—a vicious and rapidly developing form of the disease that often ends in suffocation—and began to die.

By the winter of 1931, rumors were circulating throughout Fayette County about the large number of deaths that were occurring among the tunnel's work force. During the spring, an inspection of the tunnel was made by the chief of the West Virginia Department of Mines, who wrote a letter to the chief engineer of the New-Kanawha Power Company warning him that the heavy concentration of silica dust in the tunnel was highly dangerous and recommending that improved ventilation equipment be installed to protect the health and lives of the workers and that respirators be issued. Neither of these recommendations was carried out, however, and by the autumn of 1931 an alarming number of the workers had fallen sick, complaining of chest pain and shortness of breath. Almost none of them had any idea that they were suffering from silicosis, for they had been told by the company doctors who examined them that they were suffering from "tunnel pneumonia" or "tunnelitis."

In the summer of 1932, after an autopsy confirmed silicosis as the cause of death of an eighteen-year-old tunnel worker, the first damage suit alleging negligence on the part of Rinehart & Dennis was brought, in the circuit court of Fayette County. Within a year, three hundred more silicosis lawsuits were filed—many of them naming the New-Kanawha Power Company as a defendant—seeking a total of more than $3 million in damages. When the first case was tried, in the spring of 1933, the chief of the state's Department of Mines testified that he had been "misinformed" about the existence of unhealthy conditions in the tunnel at the time of his 1931 inspection, and that he had verbally withdrawn his recommendations after conferring with officials of Rinehart & Dennis. The trial ended in a hung jury, and in June, just before a second trial was scheduled to begin, Rinehart & Dennis offered to settle the remaining cases for $130,000. As part of this deal, the law firm representing the plaintiff in the first lawsuit that was brought, as well as the plaintiff in the first case that was tried, was paid $20,000. By this time, hundreds of the men who had worked in the Hawks Nest tunnel had left West Virginia to find employment elsewhere, and others, having become disabled with silicosis, had gone home to rest or die. During the next two years, however, some two hundred more damage suits were brought as other workers who remained in the area fell sick with the disease. The first of these cases came to trial in the summer of 1934, and also ended in a hung jury. Almost a year later, the rest of the lawsuits were jeopardized by a ruling of the West Virginia Supreme Court that the state's one-year statute of limitations for personal-injury actions had begun to run from the date of a plaintiff's last employment with the company. At that point, Rinehart & Dennis proceeded to settle the remaining cases against it for some $70,000. As part of this deal, the attorneys representing the plaintiffs were required to turn over all of the evidence and data they had compiled to Rinehart & Dennis.

Incredibly, up until then almost nothing was known about the Hawks Nest tunnel tragedy in the nation at large. However, in December of 1935, the *People's Press*, a Chicago labor tabloid, broke the story under a banner headline that read, "476 DEAD, 1500 DOOMED, IN W. VA. TUNNEL CATASTROPHE." This revelation prompted Vito Marcantonio, a freshman Republican congressman who had won election to the seat formerly held by Fiorello La Guardia, to initiate hearings on the disaster before a subcommittee of the House Committee on Labor. The hearings, which began on January 16, 1936, and ended almost three weeks later, were filled with sad disclosures and sensational charges. The wife of a tunnel worker who had developed silicosis told how the disease had struck down her three sons, who had worked in the tunnel with their father, and who had died within a thirteen-month period at the ages of eighteen, twenty-one, and twenty-three. Philippa Allen, a social worker from New York City, who had gone to Gauley Bridge to investigate the tunnel tragedy, testified that when she had attended the annual meeting of the stockholders of Union Carbide, in April, 1935, she had unsuccessfully tried to persuade high officials of the company to admit responsibility for what had happened. "Thus a great corporation silently disowned those who made its wealth," she said. Rush Dew Holt, a United States senator from West Virginia, charged that officials of Rinehart & Dennis had known that many of the workers would die. "The company openly said that if they killed off those men there were plenty of other men to be had," he declared. An attorney for some of the tunnel workers revealed that officials of Rinehart & Dennis had paid $20,000 to other plaintiff lawyers for helping to bring about the $130,000 settlement that had enabled the company to dispose of the first three hundred lawsuits in the summer of 1933. This was too much for Marcantonio, who reminded the members of the subcommittee that the president of Rinehart & Dennis had been quoted in the press as saying the lawsuits against his firm were part of a "silicosis racket." Marcantonio then declared that "the most damnable racketeering that I have ever known is the paying of a fee to the very attorneys who represented these victims." He went on, "Not only Al Capone should be in Alcatraz, but these representatives of the Rinehart & Dennis Company, tunnel contractors, should be there with him."

On the very next day, the New York *Times* ran an editorial suggesting that some of the allegations against Rinehart & Dennis were "too harrowing" to be accepted at face value; that much of the evidence against the contractor "seems to be based on mountain gossip"; and that the company's defense deserved to be given as much publicity as the accusations. However, officials of Rinehart & Dennis declined the subcommittee's invitation to appear before it, and Congress made no further effort to investigate the charges. Nor was there any attempt by Congress to determine just how widespread the kind of practice that had provoked Marcantonio's wrath had become in an era when many corporations found themselves beset by litigation involving pulmonary dust disease. It seems probable that such practice was more prevalent than the *Times* would have liked to believe. On April 24, 1933—a few weeks before Rinehart & Dennis made its irresistible offer to settle three hundred silicosis damage suits for $130,000—members of the board of directors of the Johns-Manville Corporation directed their president to strike a deal with an attorney who represented plaintiffs in eleven asbestosis cases that had been brought against the company by former employees. Specifically, they authorized him to pay some $30,000 to settle the cases, which were pending in federal district court, in New Jersey, in return for written assurance from the attorney that he would not "directly or indirectly participate in the bringing of new actions against the Corporation." One can only speculate how Marcantonio might have reacted to this deal, because the minutes of the 1933 directors meeting did not come to light for more than forty-five years. During most of that time, Johns-Manville was extremely successful in avoiding common-law damage suits. Indeed, thirty-five years would pass before it would be forced to settle Claude Tomplait's asbestosis claim, and nearly half a century would go by before it would file for reorganization and protection under Chapter 11, claiming that it was overwhelmed by litigation it had no way of foreseeing.

As a consequence of the congressional hearings on the Gauley Bridge tunnel disaster, as it came to be known, there was a public outcry for remedial legislation, and over the next decade workmen's-compensation statutes for pulmonary dust diseases were enacted in some twenty states. Such legislation worked far more to the advantage of the employers, the insurers, and the politicians than to the advantage of the afflicted workers whom it was supposed to assist. It afforded manufacturers protection from costly common-law damage suits through the purchase of relatively low-cost premiums; it provided insurance companies with a large market in which to sell compensation policies that had a very low rate of loss payment; and it furnished the politicians with an easy way of assuaging public indignation over the silicosis scandal even as they went along with the harsh restrictions advocated by industry lobbyists, who argued that so many workers had already developed silicosis that the sheer number of claims might exhaust existing workmen's-compensation funds and make insurance rates prohibitively high.

The restrictions governing compensation for silicosis and asbestosis took many forms, and were incorporated into the various laws with considerable ingenuity. To begin with, almost all states required a worker to file his compensation claim within a certain period after his last exposure to the hazard that caused his illness or injury. Such statutes of limitations, which usually ran from one to three years, were supposed to prevent fraud and unreasonable delay, but by ignoring the fact that, once inhaled, asbestos and silica dust, which are virtually indestructible, continue to react within the lungs for a lifetime, and can thus cause disease many years after exposure has ceased, they also had the effect of drastically reducing the number of workers who were eligible to bring claims. To make compensation even more difficult, many states barred claims for pulmonary dust diseases unless workers could prove that their exposure to harmful dust had occurred over a specified period, and some states required claimants to show that they had been exposed to asbestos or silica dust for a substantial period.

In addition to imposing time limitations on exposure, a number of states refused to pay compensation for silicosis and asbestosis in the absence of total disability—a condition that was often difficult, if not impossible, for a worker to prove—and many states fixed the maximum benefits to be paid for total disability or death from these diseases at levels that were far below those paid out for other types of disease and injury. Moreover, although workmen's compensation was supposed to be a no-fault system in which negligence need not be established—the idea being to spare workers the delay and expense of prolonged court trials—claims for asbestosis and silicosis were routinely contested by many insurers, for they could benefit from the delay by collecting investment earnings on the unpaid claims or by eventually settling with sick workers and their families for far less than these financially distressed people might otherwise have been willing to accept. For thousands upon thousands of workers who became disabled by silicosis and asbestosis, the workmen's-compensation statutes that were enacted in the 1930s and 1940s amounted to a swindle, in which men and women, who had been unsuspectingly robbed of their health, were cheated out of just recompense for their loss of earning power, their suffering, and, in many cases, their early death. Moreover, these statutes helped sow the seeds of disaster for tens of thousands of other workers, who, like Claude Tomplait, were then being exposed to harmful levels of mineral dust, because workmen's compensation was almost always enacted as an exclusive remedy that deprived workers of the right to sue their employers for negligence under the common law, and thus eliminated the possibility of large court awards that might have served as an incentive for industry to remedy hazardous dust conditions in the workplace.

The extent to which the manufacturers, the insurance companies, and their allies in the state legislatures succeeded in this effort to limit compensation for pulmonary dust diseases can be gauged by the fact that by 1955 only a small fraction of the several hundred thousand workers in the United States who were estimated to be afflicted with silicosis had received any compensation whatever. It can also be measured by the fact that between 1950 and 1961—the year Claude Tomplait filed his workmen's-compensation claim in Texas—relatively few cases of asbestosis were compensated in the nation, even though tens of thousands of men and women had been employed over the years in asbestos manufacturing, and literally millions of workers had been exposed to asbestos while they were engaged in other occupations.

As for Tomplait, his experience with the Texas Industrial Accident Board proved to be typical of what happened to workers in other states who sought compensation for silicosis and asbestosis. In addition to imposing a heavy burden upon an asbestotic or silicotic worker to show that his disease was causally related to his occupation, Texas law required him to file his claim for compensation within six months after the "occurrence of the first distinct manifestation of the occupational disease." In Tomplait's case, this was deemed to have taken place on July 26, 1961, when Dr. Greco first diagnosed his complaint as pulmonary dust disease. On December 11, 1961, Ward Stephenson sent a notice of injury and claim for compensation to the Texas Industrial Accident Board, which listed Tomplait's employer at the time of the diagnosis as the Armstrong Contracting & Supply Corporation, of Houston. The notice alleged that Tomplait had developed asbestosis and silicosis, and it named Dr. Tom R. Jones as a doctor who could furnish additional information on his medical condition.

On February 24, 1962, Stephenson filed a claim for compensation for injury from occupational disease, which notified the Armstrong Contracting & Supply Corporation and its workmen's-compensation carrier—the Travelers Insurance Company, of Hartford, Connecticut —of Tomplait's action. The claim stated that Tomplait's disease had first manifested itself in July, 1961, when Tomplait was working for Armstrong Contracting & Supply at the Firestone plant, in Orange, and that he had been examined at that time by Dr. Greco. Also on February

24, Tomplait informed the Accident Board that since his incapacity began he had also worked for the Aber Company, the Johns-Manville Corporation, and Industrial Insulators. (Like Armstrong Contracting & Supply, these three companies, which had offices in Houston, were in the business of installing asbestos insulation, and they were now included in the claim as employers of last record, who might be held liable for compensating Tomplait for his injuries.) On October 19, Tomplait was examined at the Kelsey-Leary-Seybold Clinic, in Houston, by Dr. William V. Leary, a specialist in chest disease, who had been retained by the Travelers Insurance Company, and on November 13 Dr. Leary sent a report to the Industrial Accident Board. It made no mention of the fact that Tomplait had previously been found to be suffering from asbestosis, and concluded that his shortness of breath was caused by emphysema.

On December 18, 1962, a little more than a year after Tomplait had filed his claim, the Industrial Accident Board sent notice of its final award in Case W-67299 (*Claude J. Tomplait* v. *Armstrong Contracting & Supply Corporation, Industrial Insulators, the Johns-Manville Corporation, and the Aber Company*) to the parties involved, with copies to the offices of the Travelers Insurance Company, in Port Arthur; the Texas Employers' Insurance Association, in Dallas; and the Queen Insurance Company of America, in Houston. "The Board finds that the evidence submitted fails to establish that the claimant suffered occupational disease in the course of his employment for subscribing employers herein as alleged," the notice read. "Therefore, said claim is denied."

The law in most states provides that the award of a workmen's-compensation board can be appealed to an appellate court, whose jurists then decide the matter on the basis of whether the board followed correct procedures and arrived at its decision according to the evidence. In Texas, however, a plaintiff can appeal an award of the Industrial Accident Board only by filing a lawsuit against the employer's insurance company in state district court and embarking upon a trial *de novo,* in which all of the issues of the compensation claim are litigated before a jury. On December 21, a day after receiving notice of the Accident Board's decision, Stephenson filed a lawsuit on Tomplait's behalf in the 128th District Court, in Orange. The complaint alleged that Tomplait had developed silicosis and asbestosis while working for the Armstrong Contracting & Supply Corporation, and that he had become incapacitated as a result. It asked that he be reimbursed for his medical expenses and compensated for 401 weeks at $35 a week—a total of $14,035—which was the maximum amount that could be awarded for total permanent disability under the Texas Workmen's Compensation Law. It named the Travelers Insurance Company (the carrier for Armstrong), the Texas Employers' Insurance Association (the carrier for Johns-Manville), and the Queen Insurance Company of America (the carrier for Aber) as defendants. By this time, Industrial Insulators was out of the picture, because it had employed Tomplait for only a week.

As things turned out, Stephenson was mistaken in alleging that his client had developed silicosis as well as asbestosis during his employment as an insulator, for examination of Tomplait's chest X-rays in the years to come would show conclusively that he was suffering only from asbestosis. Stephenson's error stemmed from the tendency of most people, including many members of the medical profession, to confuse the two diseases, and from an impression on the part of Dr. Jones— the Houston specialist to whom Tomplait had been referred by Dr. Greco—that some of the insulation materials Tomplait had worked with contained free silica in addition to asbestos. Whatever the reason, confusion over the cause of Tomplait's chest condition, which had been further complicated by Dr. Leary's finding of emphysema, would persist for nearly three more years as physicians retained by both sides continued to disagree. Finally, in September, 1965, Stephenson sent Tomplait's X-rays to Dr. Selikoff, of the Mount Sinai School of Medicine, in New York. (Selikoff had recently conducted some pioneering studies of the health experience of asbestos-insulation workers in New York and New Jersey, and he had been brought to Stephenson's attention by officials of Houston Local 22, of the International Association of Heat and Frost Insulators and Asbestos Workers.) After reviewing seven sets of X-rays that had been taken of Tomplait's chest between 1961 and 1964, Selikoff wrote Stephenson a letter stating that Tomplait was suffering from "extensive pulmonary asbestosis." He also said that there had been a "significant progression of the condition" since 1961, and that the diagnosis was "as certain as anything can be in medicine."

In the meantime, however, the diagnostic waters had been so

muddied by the conflicting opinions of Dr. Leary and other medical consultants that Stephenson had come to believe that going to trial would be an extremely risky undertaking. Therefore, when Travelers and Texas Employers' offered to settle their part of the case, in September, 1964, for $5,000 and $1,000 respectively (the two insurance companies had been haggling between themselves for months over the extent of their liability in the matter), he had reluctantly advised Tomplait to accept. He gave the same advice for the same reason when Queen Insurance offered to settle for $1,500, in May, 1966. It was a bitter pill for Stephenson and his client to swallow, for by that time Tomplait, who had been too sick to work for almost two years, was disabled to the extent of having to carry an oxygen bottle in his car. The grand total of $7,500 that had been offered by the three insurance companies was only a little more than half of the $14,035 that could have been awarded for total permanent disability under the Texas Workmen's Compensation Law. However, Stephenson was a lawyer to be reckoned with, and he had something up his sleeve. His secretary, Mrs. Jackie Bean, remembers that after the final settlement agreement had been signed, he returned to the office, sat down in a swivel chair behind his desk, and stared grimly at the wall. Then he swung the chair around suddenly and said, "Jackie, we're not done with this case yet. We're going to sue the manufacturers."

Ordinarily, Tomplait's chances of recovering damages would have ended with his acceptance of the $7,500 settlement from his former employers' insurance carriers. But during the three and a half years that his case had been languishing in the district court in Texas, two extraordinary developments had taken place—one in law and the other in medicine—which provided the basis for Stephenson's resolve to bring suit against the manufacturers of asbestos insulation. The legal development dated from the spring of 1965, when the American Law Institute—an organization that promotes the clarification and simplification of the law—published the second edition of the *Restatement of the Law of Torts*. This was a comprehensive redefinition of tort law that had been undertaken over a period of years by a committee of eminent legal scholars, jurists, and lawyers from all over the nation, and it set forth a special new rule of strict liability that applied to the sellers of various products. The new rule, which was carefully defined in Section 402A of the *Restatement*, read, "One who sells any product in a defective condition unreasonably dangerous to the user or consumer or to his property is subject to liability for physical harm thereby caused to the ultimate user or consumer," and it made the seller of such a product liable to the user or consumer even though the seller "has exercised all possible care in the preparation and sale of his product."

As early as 1266, special criminal statutes had been enacted under the common law in England which imposed harsh penalities on victualers, vintners, brewers, butchers, and other persons who supplied corrupt or tainted food and drink. In the United States, the concept of strict liability began to be expressed during the nineteenth century in court decisions that held the seller of food and drink liable to the ultimate consumer, even though there was no evidence of negligence on the seller's part. During the first part of this century, thanks largely to Upton Sinclair's sensational novel, *The Jungle,* which exposed filthy conditions in Chicago meat-packing houses, the concept of strict liability began to be extended to third parties—ultimate consumers with whom the food seller had made no contract. During the 1950s, the doctrine of strict liability was extended beyond food and drink to cover products that were intended for intimate bodily use, such as lipstick, face powder, and other cosmetics. However, as defined in Section 402A of the *Restatement of Torts,* the new rule of strict liability was no longer limited to products that were sold for human consumption or for intimate bodily use but was extended to "any product sold in the condition, or substantially the same condition, in which it is expected to reach the ultimate user or consumer," and thus applied to such products as "an automobile, a tire, an airplane, a grinding wheel, a water heater, a gas stove, a power tool, a riveting machine, a chair, and an insecticide."

The authors of Section 402A emphasized that the new rule applied "only where the defective condition of the product makes it unreasonably dangerous to the user or consumer," and they defined the term "unreasonably dangerous" to mean that "the article sold must be dangerous to an extent beyond that which would be contemplated by the ordinary consumer who purchases it." After stipulating that such an article would not be considered unreasonably dangerous if it was accompanied by adequate directions or warning regarding its use, they went on to declare that even unavoidably unsafe products, such as rabies vaccine, would not be considered unreasonably dangerous if "properly prepared, and accompanied by proper directions and warning." Finally, they made it clear that the new rule applied even though the ultimate user or consumer might have acquired the product through one or more intermediate dealers, and they gave a broad definition to the term "user," saying that it "includes those who are passively enjoying the benefit of the product, as in the case of passengers in automobiles or airplanes, as well as those who are utilizing it for the purpose of doing work upon it, as in the case of an employee of the ultimate buyer who is making repairs upon the automobile which he has purchased." Thus, in almost every respect the special new rule of strict liability, which soon became known as 402A, could be deemed to apply to the occupational experience of Claude Tomplait, who had worked for intermediate contracting firms using asbestos-insulation products that were unreasonably dangerous because they caused asbestosis—an irreversible lung disease that Tomplait, who had never even heard of it, could not possibly have contemplated—and because they had been packaged and shipped by their various manufacturers in containers that bore no warning labels of any kind. Small wonder that when 402A came to Ward Stephenson's attention it set his legal mind to working.

As for the medical development that lay behind Stephenson's new strategy, it consisted of the epidemiological studies of the health and mortality experience of asbestos-insulation workers which had been conducted during 1962 and 1963 by Dr. Selikoff, of Mount Sinai; Dr. Jacob Churg, chief pathologist at Barnert Memorial Hospital, in Paterson, New Jersey; and Dr. E. Cuyler Hammond, vice-president for epidemiology and statistics of the American Cancer Society. Selikoff had first become interested in asbestos in 1953, when he founded a medical clinic in Paterson, New Jersey, for seventeen of his early patients were men referred by Carl Gelman, a local attorney, for chest-disease consultations. These men worked in a local factory that was owned by the Union Asbestos & Rubber Company, of Chicago— or UNARCO, as it had come to be known—which had been making amosite-asbestos insulation materials for the United States Navy since the late 1930s. (Amosite is a variety of asbestos found mainly in South Africa, and the first four letters of the word stand for "asbestos mines of South Africa.") At the time, fifteen of the men showed some evidence of pulmonary defects resulting from their inhalation of asbestos fibers, but all were working and apparently able-bodied. By 1961, however, four of them were dead. One of the men had died of asbestosis, one of lung cancer, one of cancer of the stomach, and one of malignant mesothelioma—an invariably fatal tumor of the pleura, the membrane that encases the lung, or of the peritoneum, a similar membrane that lines the abdominal cavity—which rarely occurs without some history of exposure to asbestos. At that point, Selikoff tried unsuccessfully to enlist the support of UNARCO and the United States Public Health Service for a study of workers at the Paterson plant. He then tried a different tack. Since he already knew that men who had worked in an insulation factory were dying of asbestosis and cancer at an alarming rate, he suspected that men who were installing such materials might also risk disease, and early in 1962 he made contact with officials of New York Local 12 and Newark Local 32 of the International Association of Heat and Frost Insulators and Asbestos Workers. These officials, it turned out, were extremely worried about the medical problems being encountered by their members, and were only too glad to cooperate in a study of workers' health.

During the next year, Selikoff gave X-ray examinations, pulmonary-function tests, and blood tests to 1,117 asbestos-insulation workers in the two locals and questioned them closely about the materials they used and the conditions under which they worked. He found radiological evidence of asbestosis in half of the 1,117 members of the two union locals. The extent of the fibrosis varied directly with the duration of exposure. Of 346 men whose exposure had begun less than ten years before, only 10 percent showed any abnormality, and of 379 men who had been exposed for between ten and nineteen years, more than 50 percent still had normal X-rays. On the other hand, he found that among 392 men with more than twenty years of exposure, 339 (slightly less than 87 percent) had developed asbestosis, which had by that time become moderate or extensive in more than half of the cases. Even more alarming were the results of a carefully conducted mortality study of 632 workers who were on the union rolls in the two locals as of December 31, 1942. According to the standard mortality tables, 203 deaths could have been expected among the 632 workers. Instead, there were 255, not counting 7 men who had died before incurring twenty years of exposure—an excess of 25 percent. The reason for the excess was not hard to find, because the study showed that these men had succcumbed to lung cancer at seven times the expected rate, and to gastrointestinal cancer at three times the expected rate.

The studies of Dr. Selikoff and his associates, because of their objectivity, their scope, and their thoroughness, had a great impact on the medical community when they were delivered at the international Conference on the Biological Effects of Asbestos, which was sponsored by the New York Academy of Sciences and held at the Waldorf-Astoria in October, 1964. They furnished incontrovertible evidence that industrial exposure to asbestos was extremely hazardous, and they marked a turning point in the views held by doctors and health officials around the world. In addition, they provided Ward Stephenson with ammunition for the precedent-setting product-liability lawsuit he was preparing to bring against the manufacturers of the various insulation products that had been used by Claude Tomplait.

At the outset, the biggest problem Stephenson faced was to determine just who the defendants in the case should be. Since he was starting from scratch, the only logical way to go about this was to find out what insulation products Tomplait had worked with and who had made them. During the summer of 1966, he spent long hours questioning his client about the insulating contractors he had worked for over the years, where he had worked, and what materials and substances he had used. This was something of a hit-or-miss approach, for while Tomplait could occasionally remember the trade name of a product, such as Unibestos—an asbestos pipe-covering insulation that was manufactured by the Pittsburgh Corning Corporation—he could often recollect only that he had come in contact with materials such as asbestos, calcium silicate, fiberglass, magnesium, and mineral wool. By late autumn, however, Stephenson had been able to fill in many of the gaps by interviewing men who had worked with Tomplait and by talking with officials of the Heat and Frost Insulators and Asbestos Workers. He proceeded to draw up a complaint against eleven asbestos-insulation-manufacturing companies, which he filed on December 10, 1966, in the United States District Court for the Eastern District of Texas, in Beaumont. (The lawsuit was brought in federal court because none of the defendant companies was incorporated in Texas.) The eleven were Combustion Engineering, Inc., of New York City; the R & I Refractory and Insulation Corporation, of Port Kennedy, Pennsyl-

vania; Johns-Manville Sales Corporation and Johns-Manville Products
Corporation, of New York City; Johns-Manville Fiber Glass, of Toledo,
Ohio; the Owens-Corning Fiberglas Corporation, of Toledo; the Gus-
tin-Bacon Manufacturing Company, of Kansas City, Missouri; the
Pittsburgh Plate Glass Company, of Pittsburgh; the Fibreboard Paper
Products Corporation, of San Francisco; and Eagle-Picher Industries,
Inc., of Cincinnati.

Tomplait's complaint listed twenty-six separate insulating jobs that
he had been hired to work on between 1959 and 1964—most of them
were in chemical plants, power plants, oil refineries, and shipyards in
the Golden Triangle—and it named many of the insulation products
and insulating materials with which he had come in contact during
each of these jobs. It went on to allege that although the defendants
either knew or ought to have known that their insulation products were
harmful to Tomplait's health they had not warned him of the danger
and had not placed danger warnings on the containers of the products,
and that as a result of such negligence and carelessness he had sustained "a very serious and permanent injury to his lungs and respira-
tory system." (Stephenson chose to base his allegations on the more
traditional theories of negligence and breach of warranties, rather than
on the new rule of strict liability, because 402A had not yet been
adopted in Texas.) After stating that Tomplait was suffering from an
inability to breathe that required him to carry a container of oxygen
with him at all times, the complaint alleged that he had lost his ability
to work, and that his earning capacity had been "permanently diminished and impaired." It concluded by demanding judgment against the
defendants for $500,000.

During the next two years, much of Stephenson's time was taken
up with discovery—the process by which evidence is compiled and
assessed for use in trial proceedings. To begin with, sets of written
interrogatories were drawn up and sent out to the eleven asbestos-
insulation manufacturers who had been named as defendants, as well
as to ten insulation contractors who had hired Tomplait between 1959
and 1964. Among other things, the interrogatories required the defendants to furnish names, trade names, descriptions, and contents of
all the insulation materials they had manufactured since 1940, and to
provide written answers to dozens of questions, such as whether they
had ever initiated studies to determine the effect of their products upon

the lungs and general health of the insulators who used them; whether they had knowledge of any deaths or serious diseases caused by asbestos inhalation among their own employees; and whether they had placed warnings on their asbestos-insulation products. In addition, depositions by oral or written interrogatories were taken from all the witnesses who would be called upon to testify for Tomplait, and cross-interrogatories were propounded for witnesses who were being deposed by the defendants, in order to clarify important areas of contention, such as what the defendants knew about the biological hazards of asbestos, and when they acquired this knowledge. With regard to the last question, Dr. Selikoff testified in answer to written interrogatories that during the twenty-five-year span in which Tomplait had been an asbestos insulator "literally hundreds of studies on the relation between asbestos-dust exposure and the occurrence of asbestosis were published by independent academic and scientific investigators." Selikoff also furnished a list of ten studies of the relationship between asbestos exposure and asbestosis, which had been conducted during the late 1920s and the 1930s by researchers in Britain and the United States.

This information, which was supplied by Selikoff in March, 1968, was extremely important to the case Stephenson was preparing in Tomplait's behalf, because it clearly indicated that the defendants could have known about the asbestos hazard for forty years simply by reading available medical literature. By late September, Stephenson was sufficiently confident to write to six defendants who remained in the case, offering to settle with them for a total of $100,000. (By this time, the Gustin-Bacon Manufacturing Company had been dropped from the lawsuit because of insufficient evidence that Tomplait had used any of its products; the Johns-Manville Sales Corporation and Johns-Manville Fiber Glass had been replaced as defendants by the Johns-Manville Products Corporation; Combustion Engineering and the R & I Refractory and Insulation Corporation, which Combustion had purchased in 1963, had been joined as a single defendant; and the Pittsburgh Plate Glass Company had been replaced by its subsidiary, the Pittsburgh Corning Corporation, which had been joined as a single defendant with UNARCO Industries—formerly the Union Asbestos & Rubber Company, of Chicago—from which Pittsburgh Corning had bought an asbestos-insulation factory, in Tyler, Texas, in

1962.) During the next few weeks, five of the six defendants expressed their willingness to negotiate (only the Fibreboard Paper Products Corporation refused) and at the end of November the five companies agreed to settle the case for $15,000 apiece. At that point, Judge Joe J. Fisher, the chief judge for the Eastern District of Texas, who was presiding over the case, entered an interlocutory judgment until Tomplait's complaint against Fibreboard could be litigated.

The $75,000 settlement did not mean that Tomplait was going to be $75,000 richer, however, because the Texas Workmen's Compensation Law; like the compensation laws in most states, required that he pay back any compensation award or settlement in the event he recovered damages for the same injury in a subsequent third-party lawsuit. Moreover, once the Travelers Insurance Company, the Texas Employers' Insurance Association, and the Queen Insurance Company of America had intervened to assert their claim to the $7,500 they had paid to settle his earlier workmen's-compensation lawsuit, the $67,500 that remained was further diminished when Stephenson took his 30 percent contingent fee, plus expenses. In the end, Tomplait was left with $37,500. Nearly seven and a half years had gone by since he had first walked into Stephenson's office, and he now weighed just over a hundred pounds. His medical prognosis was bleak, and his financial future depended upon the outcome of his suit against Fibreboard, which had been set for trial in the spring.

Stephenson's case against Fibreboard—or Pabco, as Fibreboard was sometimes known after being identified over the years with its subsidiary, the Pabco Industrial Insulation Company, of San Francisco—was based principally on the contention that the company knew, or should have known, that the asbestos-insulation products it manufactured were hazardous to use, and that it was negligent for not having warned Tomplait of this. (By now, the rule of strict liability had been adopted in Texas, but Stephenson still felt more comfortable with the familiar theories of negligence and breach of warranty, and for this reason he elected not to pursue the new doctrine.) Fibreboard was represented by George A. Weller, a stocky, gray-haired defense attorney from the firm of Weller, Wheelus & Green, in Beaumont, who contended that his client was not guilty of negligence, on the ground that before 1961, when Tomplait became ill with asbestosis, the company could not have reasonably foreseen that its insulation products might be harmful to use.

In order to show that Fibreboard should have foreseen that its asbestos-insulation products could cause disease, Stephenson spent considerable time at the outset of the trial—it began on May 12, 1969, in the federal courthouse in Beaumont—establishing the fact that asbestosis had been studied and written about for more than forty years, and that it had been a compensable occupational disease in many states during that period of time. Weller countered by calling Dr. W. Clark Cooper, a professor of occupational health at the University of California at Berkeley, who had been chief of the United States Public Health Service's Division of Occupational Health in 1962 and 1963. Dr. Cooper testified that the early studies of asbestosis focused primarily upon workers in English asbestos-textile mills, who were far more heavily exposed to asbestos than insulators. He went on to tell the jury that in 1938 the Public Health Service had recommended that an average dust level of five million particles per cubic foot should be considered a safe level of exposure for American asbestos workers. According to Dr. Cooper, this recommendation was based on a study of working conditions in several asbestos-textile factories in the United States and was adopted in 1946 by the American Conference of Governmental Industrial Hygienists as a threshold-limit value for asbestos dust. Dr. Cooper then described a study that had been conducted in 1945 by Professor Philip Drinker, of the Harvard School of Public Health, together with Dr. Walter Fleischer and several colleagues, of the health and working conditions of asbestos insulators in several United States Navy shipyards during the Second World War. Because they had found only a few cases of asbestosis in the shipyards, Fleischer, Drinker, and their associates had come to the conclusion that asbestos pipe covering was not a dangerous occupation, and had concluded that the five-million-particle-per-cubic-foot recommendation was a level to which asbestos workers might be exposed without adverse health effects. This set the stage for Weller to ask Dr. Cooper whether it was reasonable in his opinion to expect a manufacturer of insulation material containing 10 to 15 percent asbestos to have known in 1961 that his product was unsafe, and for Dr. Cooper to reply that it was not.

During his cross-examination of Dr. Cooper, Stephenson hammered away at Weller's foreseeability defense by getting Cooper to acknowledge that various studies of asbestosis, which had been conducted in the United States during the 1930s, were available to the manufacturers of asbestos-insulation products.

During redirect examination, Weller got Dr. Cooper to restate his opinion that as of 1961 it was not reasonably foreseeable that anyone working as an asbestos insulator would develop a serious case of asbestosis.

When it came time for recross, Stephenson countered with a single question. "Dr. Cooper," he asked, "do you know of any scientific studies made by the manufacturers of insulating products prior to the year 1961?"

"No," Cooper replied, "and that is because—"

"I don't want you to explain," Stephenson said. "I just wanted an answer. That is all."

Having dealt with Dr. Cooper, who was Weller's chief expert medical witness, Stephenson introduced the depositions of Dr. Selikoff and two other physicians who had found Tomplait to be suffering from asbestosis. He then called Dr. Greco to the witness stand. Greco told the jury that asbestosis was an incurable and irreversible disease, that scar tissue was slowly but irrevocably replacing the healthy tissue in Tomplait's lungs, and that Tomplait would gradually suffocate. For his part, Tomplait took the witness stand to testify that he was short of breath to the point of having to keep bottles of oxygen beside his bed and in his car, and that coughing made him feel as if he were being stuck with a thousand needles. He also told the jury that he had used Pabco products on many of the insulating jobs that he had worked on between 1941 and 1961, and that he could distinctly remember seeing the name "Pabco" printed on the boxes in which this insulation had been shipped. (His testimony in this regard was corroborated by that of a co-worker, Jesse J. Crawford, who also stated that he had used Pabco asbestos-insulation products on many jobs during that same period.) But Stephenson's apparently strong case crumbled when, under cross-examination by Weller, Tomplait found himself unable to remember exactly when or on precisely which jobs he had used Pabco products. In his summation to the jury, Weller emphasized this admission with telling effect, and when the trial ended, on May 19, the jury returned a verdict in favor of the defendant.

TWO

THE BOREL TRIAL

The verdict in Tomplait's case against Fibreboard ended Tomplait's chances of obtaining further damages for his disability from asbestosis. However, it marked a new beginning for Stephenson, whose success in obtaining a settlement with five of the six defendants had resulted in his acquiring as clients several of Tomplait's fellow insulators who were also suffering from asbestosis. Obsessed by the injustice of what had happened to these workers, and incensed by the apparent disregard of the insulation manufacturers for their plight, Stephenson now immersed himself in asbestos litigation. "We lawyers like to feel that by our action in bringing matters of this nature to trial, we are performing a service, and, hopefully, alerting the manufacturers to the need for an all-out effort to design preventive measures," he wrote in a letter describing the outcome of the Tomplait case to Dr. Selikoff, in July, 1969, adding, "I, too, as I know you are, am touched by these men that come into my office with this disease, who are now too old to learn a new occupation and have no choice but to continue in the trade." A few days later, speaking at a trial lawyers' seminar in Denver, he declared that victims of asbestosis "cry out for help from members of the bar," and that the legal fraternity could render "a substantial benefit to mankind" by alerting the public to the dangers of asbestos insulation. As it turned out, he could have been exhorting himself, for within a month he would take the case of a co-worker of Tomplait named Clarence Borel, and embark upon the last leg of the legal journey that had begun when Tomplait had walked into his office eight years before.

Pale, emaciated, and short of breath, Borel, who had recently turned fifty-seven, was visibly sick when he drove over to Stephenson's office, on August 20, from his home, in Groves—a town about a mile north of Port Arthur. Like Tomplait, he was a soft-spoken and slightly built man of Cajun descent—he had been born in the town of Jeanerette, Louisiana—and he was the father of six grown children. He told Stephenson that he had been an asbestos worker since 1936. He had started out at a Texaco plant in Port Arthur, had worked there for six years, and had then spent five years insulating destroyers at the Consolidated Shipyard in Orange. He went on to say that during his thirty-three years in the trade he had enjoyed relatively good health until the previous January, when he had developed pain in the right side of his chest and difficulty in breathing, while working at an oil refinery in Baytown for the Fuller-Austin Insulation Company, of Houston. At that time, his physician had hospitalized him in Port Arthur, and he had been found to be suffering from pneumonia. When his condition did not improve by the end of February, he entered Memorial Baptist Hospital in Houston, where exploratory surgery was performed on March 7, which showed that in addition to pneumonia he was afflicted with extensive pulmonary asbestosis. During the spring, he had filed a claim for workmen's compensation with the Texas Industrial Accident Board, and in June he had settled with Fuller-Austin's workmen's-compensation-insurance carrier for $8,000, plus $5,081.10 for medical and hospital expenses. He told Stephenson that he was unable to stand or walk for prolonged periods of time, and that he was incapable of lifting or carrying anything weighing more than 20 pounds. He also said that in all his years as an insulator no one had ever told him that asbestos would make him sick.

Thanks to his experience with Tomplait, Stephenson was able to get his new client's case under way without delay. Before Borel left the office that day, Jackie Bean told him to refresh his memory by looking over his prior tax returns, and to reconstruct his work record as far back as he could remember. When Borel had compiled the necessary information, Stephenson drew up a complaint seeking damages of $1 million against eleven asbestos-insulation manufacturers, and filed it in federal district court in Beaumont on October 20, 1969, under the title of *Clarence Borel* v. *Fibreboard Paper Products Corporation, et al.* (He put Fibreboard in the title of the case as a deliberate challenge to Weller, whom he had come to dislike intensely.) Of the eleven defendants, seven had been named in the complaint for Tomplait's lawsuit. In addition to Fibreboard, they were Johns-Manville Products Corporation, Pittsburgh Corning, Owens-Corning, UNARCO, Combustion Engineering, and Eagle-Picher. The four other defendants were the Philip Carey Corporation, of Cincinnati; the Armstrong Contracting & Supply Corporation, of Lancaster, Pennsylvania; the Ruberoid Company, of New York City, which was a division of the GAF Corporation, also of New York City; and the Standard Asbestos Manufacturing & Insulating Company, of Kansas City, Missouri. The complaint alleged that the manufacturers had not warned Borel of the danger of using their asbestos-insulation products, had not informed him about safe methods of handling these products, had not tested the products in order to determine the dangers involved in their use, and had not removed them from the market upon learning that they could cause asbestosis. Most important of all, however, the complaint held that the defendants should be subject to the doctrine of strict liability, alleging that their products were unreasonably dangerous because they did not carry adequate warnings of the foreseeable dangers associated with them. *Borel* v. *Fibreboard* thus became the first case in the nation to test the applicability of Section 402A to asbestos-insulation materials.

Shortly thereafter, Stephenson brought product-liability cases in behalf of Jesse J. Crawford and Samuel Potter, two co-workers of Borel, and since the same defendants were named in all three lawsuits Judge Fisher, who was presiding over them, combined them for purposes of discovery. Meanwhile, Borel's condition was growing steadily worse. In late January, 1970, he was admitted to Memorial Baptist Hospital, in Houston, complaining of sharp pains in the right side of his chest, and on February 11 he underwent surgery for the removal of his right lung. Subsequent pathology determined that he was suffering from diffuse malignant mesothelioma of the lung—an invariably fatal tumor. Several weeks after the operation, Borel left the hospital and went home to Groves. In early May, bedridden and in pain, he gave a deposition in which he testified about his career as an asbestos insulator, and on June 3 he died.

Borel's widow, Thelma, to whom he had been married for thirty-seven years, was thereupon substituted as the plaintiff, under the Texas wrongful-death statutes, and the process of discovery by means of interrogatories and depositions continued for fifteen months. During this period, Stephenson prepared himself for the coming trial with great care. To begin with, he got in touch with nearly a dozen of Borel's fellow-insulators—all of whom had worked with Borel since the early

1940s—in order to substantiate Borel's assertion that he had used and been exposed to asbestos insulation manufactured by each of the defendants. Having taken steps to make sure that he could not lose on the exposure issue as he had in Tomplait's case against Fibreboard, Stephenson then turned his attention to what he knew would be the chief defense of his opponents—the claim that asbestos manufacturers had no knowledge that asbestosis and other asbestos-related diseases could afflict asbestos insulators until 1964, when the study of Dr. Selikoff and his associates of the health experience and causes of death among the members of the New York Local 12 and Newark Local 32 furnished incontrovertible evidence that asbestos-insulation work was extremely hazardous. This defense, which became known as the state-of-the-art defense, was a variation of the foreseeability defense that had been raised by Weller in Tomplait's trial. It was devised by John Tucker, of the law firm of Orgain, Bell & Tucker, in Beaumont, who was counsel for Johns-Manville, as well as coordinator of the defense effort that was being mounted for the asbestos-insulation manufacturers by their insurance carriers. A wiry, leather-faced man, then in his middle fifties, Tucker was one of the most highly respected and capable defense lawyers in East Texas, and his state-of-the-art defense posed a potentially formidable problem for Stephenson, because Section 402A specifically limited the seller's liability by stating that he was required to give warning only about those dangers that were "reasonably foreseeable." If Tucker and his colleagues could furnish enough evidence to convince a jury that Borel's lung disease could not have been reasonably foreseen by the manufacturers of asbestos insulation until the publication of Selikoff's studies, they could jeopardize Stephenson's contention that the manufacturers were negligent because of their failure to warn, and could defeat his allegation that they were strictly liable.

At the time, Stephenson made fun of the manufacturers' claim that they had no way of knowing that it was hazardous for insulators to apply their products in the field by telling associates that it was tantamount to saying "I didn't know my pistol would kill a priest because I never shot one before, but I did know it would kill other things because I had shot game with it." During the summer and autumn of 1970, however, he prepared for Tucker's state-of-the-art defense with the utmost seriousness, sending requests to dozens of health officials and medical librarians, asking for medical and scientific literature dealing with asbestosis during the 1930s, 1940s, and 1950s. In November, he finally hit pay dirt when the assistant director of the American Medical Association's Department of Environmental, Public, and Occupational Health, in Chicago, sent him a bibliography that listed scores of articles on asbestosis that had been published during these three decades, including eighty-six articles most of which had appeared before 1938.

Early in January, 1971, Judge Fisher set May 24 as the trial date for *Borel* v. *Fibreboard,* and a few weeks later Standard Asbestos and Owens-Corning settled out of court for $3,000 apiece. Stephenson was hopeful of opening serious negotiations with the remaining defendants, but in April he discovered a lump on the left side of his face. On May 3, he underwent surgery for the removal of a small spindle-cell cancer, at the John Sealy Hospital, in Galveston, and on May 17 he asked Jackie Bean to write this letter to Judge Fisher:

Dear Judge:

Some several days ago, I talked to you about surgery that I was going to have on the left side of my face. This was done at John Sealy on May 3rd. The surgeon removed certain tissue and did not think it was malignant from looking at it. The tissue was sent to pathology for testing. The pathologist found, however, what he believed to be cancer cells. The surgeon had to stretch certain facial nerves which has caused me to have some difficulty in speaking and pronouncing words. Hopefully this will correct itself in time.

You have set down the case of Borel vs. Fibreboard et al (Civil #6449) to pick a jury on May 24th and to go to trial sometime the week of the 24th. This is a very complicated case and one which will take probably two weeks to try. I have to go back to Galveston now on a one or two trips a week schedule. The doctors are trying to decide whether to go in for more facial surgery or radium treatments, or just how to handle this situation. I do not feel up to trying the Borel case and would appreciate it if you could put it over to a later date.

I have not told anyone in legal circles, other than my secretary who is writing this letter, of this problem.

I would very much appreciate you handling this for me if you will in such a manner that it will not advise of my illness. Needless to say, it is a rather traumatic period for me anticipating each of the trips to Galveston and awaiting decisions on what course will be followed.

Sincerely,
Ward Stephenson

On May 18, Judge Fisher sent this letter to Stephenson and the twelve lawyers who were representing the defendants in *Borel* v. *Fibreboard.*

Gentlemen:

Due to the docket problems presented because of the trial now in progress, and which in all probability will continue into next week; and also because of the time-consuming nature of the above cause, I believe it advisable to pass the trial until the September Term.

You are, therefore, advised that the cause will be reset for trial for the second Monday in September 1971 and you will be advised later when it will be necessary to appear for jury selection. If any of you gentlemen have an objection to rescheduling the trial for the September Term, please advise the Court by May 24th.

Sincerely yours,
Joe J. Fisher

During the rest of May and all of June, Stephenson recuperated at home with his second wife, Marcelle (he had divorced and remarried in 1967), and by the end of August, his feeling of well-being had returned, and he was eagerly looking forward to trying *Borel* v. *Fibreboard,* which had been set down for September 21. Jackie Bean remembers that he was full of enthusiasm when, a few weeks before the trial, he returned to Orange from the Beaumont office of his old adversary, George Weller, for there he had participated in the deposing of Dr. Cooper, whom Weller was planning to call again as an expert medical witness for the defendants. "Ward was tremendously elated about how much he had got Cooper to admit on cross-examination," she recalls. "In fact, when he came through the door, the first thing he said was 'Jackie, I can't for the life of me imagine why Weller ever decided to call Cooper again, because I have just turned him into a star witness for us!' "

During the early part of September, UNARCO and Eagle-Picher settled out of court for $5,000 apiece, and at 9:00 A.M., on September 21, *Borel* v. *Fibreboard* got under way as Stephenson opened the case for the plaintiff against the remaining defendants, who, in addition to Fibreboard, were Johns-Manville, Pittsburgh Corning, Philip Carey, Ruberoid, and the Armstrong Cork Company, which had become a defendant in place of its subsidiary, Armstrong Contracting & Supply. (The trial court had instructed a verdict in favor of Combustion Engineering, because the plaintiff had failed to show that he had ever been exposed to any insulation product manufactured by that company.) In his opening statement, Stephenson told the jury that each of the defendants knew or should have known about the dangerous nature of asbestos-insulation products and their harmful effects upon the human body, but that they had not tested these products to find out if they could be safely used, and had not warned Borel of the danger to which he was exposed while handling them. He predicted that the defendants would claim that Borel's death was not their fault but that of his employers; that Borel should have worn a respirator; and that the state of medical and scientific knowledge was such that they could not have foreseen injury and death to insulation workers who used their product. By way of countering this last defense, Stephenson pointed out that a considerable amount of medical and scientific literature relating to asbestos disease had been available to each of the defendants, and that another reason they should also have known about the hazard was that workmen's-compensation laws covering the disease had been in effect in some states for more than forty years. He concluded his opening remarks by telling the jurors that Thelma Borel was claiming punitive as well as compensatory damages, because "the wrongs committed by the defendants were so gross that they should be required to pay an additional amount of money in such sum as would act as a deterrent to these defendants and others in the future from committing like offenses and wrongs."

In the opening statement for the defendants, Weller stressed the fact that Borel had never been employed by any of them, that the defendants had not had control over Borel's working conditions, and that it had been the duty of Borel's employers to furnish him with respirators and to provide him with proper working conditions. As Stephenson had predicted, Weller claimed that no medical or scientific knowledge existed before 1964 to show that asbestos insulators might be risking health problems as a result of their occupation. He then told the jurors that the workmen's-compensation laws covering asbestosis, which were on the books in Texas and other states, should have served to warn Borel that asbestos was a hazard of his trade and that Borel was guilty of contributory negligence because he had failed to wear a respirator. Weller also claimed that since 1956 Borel had received copies of a union publication, *Asbestos Worker,* that contained warnings about the harmful health effects of insulation products.

Stephenson's first witness was Harvey Legate, a forty-eight-year-old asbestos insulator from Port Arthur, who was working as a business agent for Asbestos Local 22, in Houston. Legate, whose father was an asbestos insulator and had died of asbestosis in November, 1970, told the jury that he had first met Clarence Borel in 1942, when they were both working at the Consolidated Shipyard, in Orange, and that he had subsequently worked with Borel in various chemical plants in the Golden Triangle, where they had used asbestos products made by Johns-Manville, Owens-Corning, and Pittsburgh Corning. He went on to testify that he had never been issued a respirator capable of preventing the inhalation of asbestos dust, and that no one had ever told him that it was dangerous to breathe asbestos dust until 1966, when some manufacturers placed a small warning label on boxes containing asbestos insulation. Here Stephenson offered the label in evidence. It read:

Caution, this product contains asbestos fibre.

Inhalation of asbestos in excessive quantities over long periods of time may be harmful.

If dust is created when this product is handled, avoid breathing the dust.

If adequate ventilation control is not possible, wear respirators approved by the U.S. Bureau of Mines for pneumoconiosis-producing dusts.

Legate told the jury that no one had ever informed him what was meant by excessive quantities of asbestos dust, and that in any event there was no way a worker could avoid breathing asbestos when working with asbestos insulating materials. During a long cross-examination that followed, Weller sought to establish the basis for an assumption-of-risk defense by trying to get Legate to admit that he had heard about Claude Tomplait's workmen's-compensation claim for asbestosis ten years before, and that he had known about the hazard of inhaling asbestos dust since the late 1950s. Legate was also cross-examined by John Tucker, who asked him if he had ever read the November, 1961, issue of *Asbestos Worker,* which had carried a full-page advertisement urging union members to wear their respirators.

When Legate, who would develop asbestosis in 1979, was excused from the witness stand, Stephenson called Cecil E. Gladden, a forty-four-year-old insulator from Groves, who testified that he had known Borel since 1943, and that they had worked together on jobs using asbestos products that were manufactured by Johns-Manville, Ruberoid, Philip Carey, Eagle-Picher, and Owens-Corning. When Gladden, who would develop asbestosis in 1981, had left the stand, Stephenson read portions of the oral deposition he had taken from Dr. Daniel Jenkins, a pulmonary specialist and professor of medicine at the Baylor College of Medicine, in Houston. Dr. Jenkins testified that sufficient scientific knowledge existed as early as 1940 to warn a manufacturer of asbestos insulation that his product was dangerous to human health, and he drew special attention to an article describing a case of asbestosis in an asbestos pipe coverer, which had been published in the *British Journal of Radiology* in 1934 by a chest physician, Dr. Philip Ellman. During cross-examination, however, Jenkins said that until Selikoff and his associates had performed their 1964 studies very little knowledge existed to show that the inhalation of asbestos by insulators was hazardous.

. . .

Stephenson began the second day of the trial by putting Samuel Potter, a fifty-nine-year-old insulator from Orange, on the stand. Potter, who would die of asbestosis in 1973, testified that he and Borel had worked together at the Consolidated Shipyard during the Second World War, using asbestos-insulation products manufactured by Johns-Manville, and that he had also worked with Borel in several chemical plants using insulation products manufactured by some of the other defendants. He went on to tell the jury that he himself was suffering from asbestosis, and that the disease had severely impaired his ability to breathe. During cross-examination, Weller brought out the fact that Potter was being represented by Stephenson in an asbestos lawsuit, and that until recently he had been a heavy smoker. Tucker then got Potter to admit that he had rarely used a respirator even though he had been sufficiently bothered by asbestos dust to make complaints about it.

At this point, George E. Duncan, of Beaumont, who was the attorney for Pittsburgh Corning, was allowed to present Dr. Paul Gross, a witness from out of state who could not appear at any other time. Dr. Gross, who was seventy years old, stated that he was a professor of pathology at the Medical University of South Carolina, and director of the research laboratories at the Industrial Health Foundation, in Pittsburgh. (This was a new name for the thirty-five-year-old Industrial Hygiene Foundation of America, a self-styled "association of industries for the advancement of healthful working conditions," which was almost entirely financed by industry, including Johns-Manville, and which had been retained by Pittsburgh Corning in the summer of 1963 to evaluate the dust hazard of its newly acquired asbestos factory in Tyler, Texas.) Dr. Gross then testified that he was a member of the Threshold Limit Values Committee of the American Conference of Governmental Industrial Hygienists, which had recommended to the asbestos industry in 1966 that a threshold limit of five million particles of dust per cubic foot be considered a safe level of dust to which an asbestos-factory worker could be exposed for eight hours a day, five days a week during his entire working lifetime without danger of developing disease.

During cross-examination, Stephenson launched a heavy attack upon his opponents' state-of-the-art defense. It was a tactic that took the defendants by surprise, and it enabled Stephenson to seize the initiative at a crucial point in the trial. To begin with, he established that in spite of its imposing title the American Conference of Governmental Industrial Hygienists was not an official government agency, and that it had first recommended the five-million-particle standard in 1946. He later asked, "Doctor, if five million particles per cubic foot of exposure was a danger level set by the Threshold Limit Value Committee, would there be any way to know whether a worker was being exposed to more or less than five million particles besides going into the area where the worker works and taking dust counts?"

"No," Dr. Gross replied.

"All right, sir, so if Johns-Manville or Fibreboard or any of the defendants here knew in 1947 of the five million particles per cubic foot, then would there be any way for them to tell a worker that there were dangerous exposures other than going and taking measurements as to how much dust was created by the use of their products?"

"I wouldn't think so," Gross answered.

"No, sir, I wouldn't either," said Stephenson, who had already established through interrogatories that none of the defendants had ever made such measurements when insulators were working in the field.

When Stephenson was through cross-examining Gross, Weller tried to shore up the state-of-the-art defense by getting the witness to say that the five-million-particle-per-cubic-foot level had been based on the best medical and scientific knowledge that was available at the time. In recross-examination, however, Stephenson deflated Weller's efforts by seeking Dr. Gross's opinion of the proposition that if a worker contracted asbestosis he must have been exposed to a sufficient number of asbestos fibers and particles to cause the disease, regardless of what dust levels were recommended.

"I think that is only common sense," Dr. Gross replied.

"Yes, thank you. That's all," Stephenson told him, and since there were no further questions from the defense Dr. Gross was excused from the witness stand. (What Stephenson did not know at the time, or he might have questioned Dr. Gross at greater length, was that Dr. Gross had considerable knowledge about the occurrence of asbestos disease in Johns-Manville workers. Eleven years later, at the age of eighty, Dr. Gross would testify in another asbestos case that during the late 1950s, while he was director of the Industrial Hygiene Foundation's research laboratories, he had examined lung tissue specimens from more than half a dozen dead Johns-Manville employees who had suffered from asbestosis, had found evidence of lung cancer in most of them, and had concluded that there was an association between asbestos exposure and lung cancer.)

Following Dr. Gross's testimony, Stephenson resumed the case for the plaintiff by calling four more of Borel's co-workers to the witness stand. As it happened, one of them was Claude Tomplait, who was now fifty-one years old and terribly emaciated by the ravages of asbestosis. When he took the stand, Stephenson lost little time in asking him to tell the jury how the disease was affecting him.

"Well, the way it is with me, I am sitting here right now and I am just liable to go to coughing and want to black out right quick, and when I do it is like pins and needles going through my body," Tomplait said. "As a matter of fact, I can't use my hands. If you will notice, all of my fingers are all thick and clubbed. If I could have some kind of a little old job putting things together, it would be impossible. As I say, my life is ruined from it."

As he had with other insulators, Tucker cross-examined Tomplait at length in an attempt to show that he had known about the health hazard of asbestos for many years and should have worn a respirator to protect himself. Seeking to implicate the contractors, Tucker asked Tomplait who should have supplied him with respirators.

"Well, sir, I will explain it this way," Tomplait replied. "I never knew in my life this stuff was hard on my life, no more than the air I am breathing right now, and just like for me to go out there and cut my grass and put a handkerchief over my face—"

"Your Honor, the answer is not responsive," Tucker objected.

"I didn't know it was a hazard," Tomplait insisted, "or I would have put a handkerchief over my face, but nothing was furnished to us."

Tomplait's claim that he had not known about the hazards of inhaling asbestos dust was echoed by most of the insulators who followed him to the witness stand, and by the late afternoon of the second day Weller and Tucker had by and large been frustrated in their efforts to show contributory negligence or assumption of risk on the part of Borel. At this point, seeking to keep his opponents off balance, Stephenson offered the deposition testimony of Dr. Cooper, the expert witness for the defense whom he felt he had cross-examined so effectively back in August. Reading from the cross-examination, he brought out the fact that Cooper had recently been a consultant for

Johns-Manville in an asbestos lawsuit, and had also dispensed advice to Eagle-Picher and Pittsburgh Corning. Cooper acknowledged that by 1945 more than a hundred scientific and medical articles had been published about the effects of asbestos upon human health, and that there were probably fifty such articles as early as 1930.

Soon thereafter, Judge Fisher adjourned the court for the day, and when the trial resumed the next morning Stephenson continued reading the deposition of Dr. Cooper, who stated that there was intense interest in asbestosis during the 1920s, and that during the 1920s and 1930s the literature on the disease would have made a stack about two feet high. Later in the deposition, Stephenson asked Cooper whether he knew if any manufacturer of asbestos insulating products had ever tested them, in order to determine how much asbestos dust was created when they were sawed, cut, or mixed. Cooper replied that he knew of no such tests being conducted until the past two years. Still later, Stephenson asked Cooper this question:

"Doctor, can we say that for at least fifty years it has been recognize that asbestos is a harmful—causes harm to the human body?"

By this time, Cooper had apparently become somewhat uncomfortable, for instead of answering the question directly he replied, "I want the record to show that I believe strongly that asbestos—the inhalation of asbestos—can be harmful, and that I feel it is a great responsibility for people that manufacture or sell or use asbestos to handle it with dispatch and to avoid exposures, and the record must show that I feel this very strongly." Then, after Stephenson had asked him the question for a second time, Dr. Cooper acknowledged that it had been recognized for fifty years that asbestos could cause asbestosis, and that the disease was harmful.

During the rest of the morning, Weller tried desperately to repair the damage that had been done to the state-of-the-art defense by reading other portions of Dr. Cooper's testimony, which suggested that because the vast majority of the early cases of asbestosis had been found among workers who were employed in asbestos-textile factories, where there was often heavy exposure to pure asbestos fiber, the manufacturers of asbestos-insulation products containing only 12 to 15 percent asbestos could not have been expected to know before 1964 that insulation workers who used these products were also at risk of developing asbestos disease. Weller also took considerable pains to establish that there was no possible way for anyone to tell when or where Borel might have received the exposure to asbestos that had caused him to develop his asbestosis and mesothelioma, or, for that matter, what asbestos product manufactured by which of the remaining defendants might have caused these diseases. Be that as it may, by the time Judge Fisher called a recess for lunch on the third day of the trial most observers felt that Stephenson's cross-examination of Dr. Cooper —a brilliant one, in which he had transformed a prominent expert witness for the defense into a prime witness for the plaintiff—had dealt a heavy blow to the defendants' claim that they had no way of reasonably foreseeing that exposure to their products posed a danger to human health.

During the afternoon session, Stephenson introduced in evidence a bibliography of eighty-six articles on the health effects of asbestos, most of them published before 1938. Then he read answers to written interrogatories that had been given by the defendant manufacturing companies. They enabled him to establish that none of the defendants had placed warning labels on their insulation products until 1964, and that Philip Carey and Armstrong Cork had not seen fit to provide warning labels at any time. He was also able to show that Johns-Manville, Philip Carey, and Ruberoid had known that death and serious lung disease had already occurred among their employees as a result of inhaling asbestos dust or fibers. (It would later come to light that in 1969 alone Johns-Manville had paid out $887,341 in workmen's compensation to 285 employees of its manufacturing plant in Manville, New Jersey, who had become disabled by asbestosis.) Following his reading of the interrogatories, Stephenson introduced testimony given at deposition by the chest specialist who had treated Borel in 1969 and 1970; by the surgeon who had removed Borel's lung; by the pathologists who had found Borel to be suffering from asbestosis and malignant mesothelioma; and by Borel's personal physician, who stated that his patient had suffered great pain during the last months of his life.

Stephenson began the fourth day of the trial by introducing the deposition testimony of Borel himself, who had been able to piece together an amazingly detailed work history that pinpointed exactly when and where he had used insulation products manufactured by the various defendants. Borel had testified that during his career as an insulator he had been continually exposed to heavy concentrations of asbestos dust as a result of cutting, sawing, and mixing these products. He said that in an effort to avoid inhaling the dust he had tried many different types of respirators but had found them almost impossible to breathe through. He went on to say that no one had ever told him that asbestos-insulation materials were dangerous to his health, and that he had never seen any of the defendant manufacturers testing their products in the field to see if they could devise some way of suppressing asbestos dust. He also stated that he had been bedridden since the operation to remove his lung, and that he had been in constant pain for thirteen or fourteen months.

When Stephenson had read Borel's testimony, Tucker asked permission to present a witness out of order, and when Stephenson agreed, Dr. Hans Weill, a professor of medicine at the Tulane University School of Medicine, in New Orleans, took the stand to testify in behalf of Johns-Manville. By way of establishing his credentials, Dr. Weill said that he had examined more than a hundred asbestotic workers during his career and that he was then conducting a study of asbestosis among workers in the asbestos-cement industry. (Although it was not brought out at the trial, Weill was, in fact, studying employees of a Johns-Manville asbestos-cement-products plant at Marrero, Louisiana, and his work was being financed by the Quebec Asbestos Mining Association, of which Johns-Manville had long been the dominant member.) Weill went on to tell the jury that after reviewing chest X-rays of Borel, which had been taken between 1964 and 1970, he had come to the conclusion that Borel had never suffered from asbestosis, and that his pleural mesothelioma could have developed as a result of cancer spreading from some other site.

During cross-examination, Stephenson forced Weill to acknowledge that without ever having seen Borel or examined Borel's lung, he was trying to refute the diagnosis of asbestosis which had been made at first hand by Borel's internist, by the surgeon who had removed Borel's lung, and by the pathologists who had examined tissue from Borel's lung in the laboratory of Memorial Baptist Hospital. He then proceeded to obtain an admission from Weill that Borel's mesothelioma was in all likelihood associated with his exposure to asbestos.

When Dr. Weill left the witness stand, Weller read from his cross-examination of Borel in an attempt to show that Borel had known since his early years as an insulator that breathing asbestos dust was hazardous, that he had voluntarily assumed the risk by continuing to work with the mineral, and that he was contributorily negligent for failing to wear a respirator during most of his employment. In his answers to Weller's questions Borel admitted that he had sometimes applied Mentholatum in his nostrils, or worn a wet handkerchief over his face, in an effort to avoid inhaling asbestos dust. He also acknowledged that he and his fellow-insulators had speculated about whether asbestos was hazardous, but that there was a consensus among them that the dust "dissolves as it hits your lungs."

"In other words, there was some question in your mind as to whether this was dangerous and whether it was bad for your health?" Weller asked.

"There was always a question," Borel replied. "You just never know how dangerous it was. I never did know really. If I had known, I would have gotten out of it."

"All right, then you did know it had some degree of danger but you didn't know how dangerous it was?"

"I didn't know it was dangerous like this bad," Borel said. "I really didn't."

Later in his cross-examination, Weller got Borel to admit that in 1964, during a life-insurance medical examination, he had been told that his chest X-ray was cloudy, and that this might be the result of his occupation as an insulator. Weller then asked, "Did you know at that time that you were working with asbestos and asbestos dust?"

"I knew I was working with insulation," Borel said.

"Did you know that it contained asbestos?"

"Yes, sir," Borel replied. "But I didn't know what asbestos was."

When Weller had finished reading from his cross of Borel, Stephenson called Borel's widow, Thelma, to the witness stand and asked her if her husband had ever done anything that would indicate, one way or the other, whether he thought that asbestos was harmful or not. She replied that at Christmastime he used to bring home pieces of asbestos insulation for their children to crumple up and put on the family tree as artificial snow, and she expressed certainty that if he had known that asbestos was harmful he would not have done so.

During cross-examination, Weller established that copies of *Asbestos Worker* had been delivered to the Borel home for many years. Then, in an effort to minimize the effect of Borel's death in terms of monetary damages, he got Mrs. Borel to acknowledge that she had never been given a household allowance by her husband, that she had no way of knowing what portion of his income had gone for household expenses, and that none of their six children were financially dependent upon her. At that point, Stephenson rested the case for the plaintiff, and, since it was Friday, Judge Fisher adjourned the trial for the weekend.

On Monday, Gordon R. Pate, an attorney from Beaumont who, together with Tucker, was representing Johns-Manville, opened the case for the defendants. His first witness was Joseph Ralph Shrode, an official of Houston Local 22 of the Asbestos Workers union, whose deposition testimony had been read by Stephenson on the second day of the trial, in order to show that Shrode, who had worked as an insulator at the Consolidated Shipyard during the Second World War, had never seen any of the defendants testing their products in the field or been warned that breathing asbestos dust was dangerous. It soon became apparent that Pate's strategy in calling Shrode for cross-examination was to set up an assumption-of-risk defense, for he quickly got Shrode to admit that when he was sawing asbestos-insulation products in an indoor fabrication shop during the late 1940s he had worn a respirator because he felt that it would be dangerous to inhale asbestos dust. Pate then got Shrode to acknowledge that he had not worn a respirator in the field because there "wasn't as much dust working in the field as there was working around the saw in the shop." Shrode went on to say that he had become aware of asbestosis around 1955, when he developed spots on his lungs, which his doctor told him were caused by his employment as an insulator, and that the disease had become a subject of discussion at union meetings at about that time.

During redirect examination, Stephenson got Shrode to acknowledge that when asbestos insulators worked in the field they were often working indoors in confined spaces where there was considerable asbestos dust. Nevertheless, Pate's skillful examination of Shrode, who would die of mesothelioma in 1980, had breathed new life into the defendants' contention that Borel was contributorily negligent for not having worn respirators, and it set the stage for Tucker to call Clifford L. Sheckler, manager of Johns-Manville's accident-prevention program, upon whom the defendants were relying to resurrect the state-of-the-art defense, which had been so badly damaged by Stephenson's cross-examination of Dr. Gross and Dr. Cooper. A tall, self-confident man in his middle fiies, Sheckler had first gone to work for Johns-Manville as a construction engineer in 1936—the same year in which Clarence Borel had become an insulator—and had risen steadily through the ranks. Between 1957 and 1960, he had been supervisor of safety and industrial hygiene; from 1960 to 1967, he was corporate manager of industrial health; and during 1967 and the first part of 1968 he was made manager of occupational and environmental control and given the task of starting an environmental-control department. Sheckler told the jury that during the 1960s he had become thoroughly familiar with the medical literature on asbestosis. He described it as dealing primarily with British asbestos-textile-factory employees, who were working with fiber that was 100 percent asbestos, and were far more heavily exposed than insulators using Johns-Manville insulation products, which contained only about 15 percent asbestos. He went on to say that before Dr. Selikoff's studies the only research he knew of that dealt with the health problems of asbestos insulators was an investigation of 1,074 insulators who had worked in United States Navy shipyards during the Second World War. (This was the study that had been conducted by Dr. Fleischer and Professor Drinker, and their colleagues, and it had been published, in 1946, in the *Journal of Industrial Hygiene and Toxicology* under the title "A Health Survey of Pipe Covering Operations in Constructing Naval Vessels.") According to Sheckler, Fleischer and Drinker had found only three cases of asbestosis in the entire group of 1,074 shipyard insulators—a finding that, together with the fact that dust levels in the shipyards were well within the recommended five-million-particle-per-cubic-foot range, had led them to conclude that asbestos pipe covering was not a dangerous occupation.

Sheckler told the jury that the first time he had ever heard that asbestos insulators might be at risk of developing asbestos disease was when he and Dr. Kenneth W. Smith, who was then the medical director of Johns-Manville, attended the 1964 New York Academy of Sciences' Conference on the Biological Effects of Asbestos, where they learned about Dr. Selikoff's studies of mortality and disease among asbestos insulators in New Jersey and New York. He testified that Johns-Manville began to place cautionary labels on its thermal-insulation products soon thereafter, and that during 1967 and 1968 the

company had initiated a program to make asbestos-insulation contractors across the nation aware of the potential hazards of using asbestos
materials, and to enlighten them about dust-abatement methods and
the need for supplying their employees with respirators. He went on
to draw a picture of Johns-Manville as a corporation deeply concerned
about the health and welfare of the workers who used its products,
pointing out that in 1968 the company had donated $200,000 to buy
an electron microscope for Dr. Selikoff's laboratory at Mount Sinai
Hospital.

During a grueling cross-examination that took up much of the afternoon, Stephenson forced Sheckler to admit repeatedly that at no time
during the 1930s, 1940s, and 1950s had Johns-Manville ever tried to
ascertain whether asbestos insulators were being exposed to dangerous
levels of asbestos as a result of working with the company's insulation
products. In doing so, he forced Sheckler again and again to excuse
the lack of field testing on the ground that there was nothing in the
medical literature to warn company officials that asbestos insulators
might be at risk of developing disease. Sheckler also defended Johns-
Manville's failure to test on the ground that Fleischer and Drinker had
found very few cases of asbestosis among insulators working in naval
shipyards during the Second World War. In addition, he claimed that
the company had no authority to enter a subcontractor's work area in
order to conduct such tests. Stephenson countered by pointing out that
the early medical literature clearly demonstrated the danger of inhaling asbestos fibers, and by getting Sheckler to acknowledge that for
several decades the company had installed ventilation equipment in its
factories to reduce the amount of asbestos dust that was being inhaled
by its own employees. He criticized the Fleischer-Drinker study as
misleading by pointing out that 95 percent of the insulators who had
been examined had worked in the trade for less than ten years—an
insufficient length of time for the development of asbestosis. As for the
claim that Johns-Manville had no legal right to enter a subcontractor's
job site for the purpose of conducting tests, Stephenson countered this
contention by forcing Sheckler to admit that one of Johns-Manville's
own subsidiary companies was in fact in the business of subcontracting
asbestos-insulation work. Then, after showing Sheckler some photographs of insulation workers using asbestos products in the field, he

asked whether it had ever occurred to anyone at Johns-Manville that an insulator who was engaged in sawing, cutting, and mixing asbestos-insulation products was bound to breathe asbestos dust.

Sheckler answered, "It never occurred to anyone, to the best of my knowledge, up until the time that Dr. Selikoff did his epidemiological study, that people who do not stand in fixed positions at fixed machines might have potential exposures that could possibly cause some pulmonary disease."

"I understand," Stephenson said with a mixture of incredulity and sarcasm. "Then Johns-Manville had to wait on Dr. Selikoff to show that asbestos workers were breathing the dust?"

The question placed Sheckler squarely on the defensive. "Like many other potential toxic materials—DDT and many others that we are learning of today," he replied uneasily. "I presume, if you put it that way, the answer is yes."

Sheckler, whose wife would later die of mesothelioma, was followed to the witness stand by Hugh M. Jackson, director of employee relations and management development for Johns-Manville, who had preceded Sheckler as corporate manager of industrial health. Jackson testified that Johns-Manville had been aware that asbestosis might present a problem for its factory workers as early as 1928, when it had sponsored studies by Dr. Leroy U. Gardner, of the Trudeau Foundation's Saranac Laboratory at Saranac Lake, New York, and that Gardner had been able to produce the disease in test animals by allowing them to inhale asbestos fibers. According to Jackson, Johns-Manville also sponsored research at about this same time by Dr. Anthony J. Lanza, of the Metropolitan Life Insurance Company. After conducting a survey of workers in a number of asbestos-textile-manufacturing plants, Lanza had recommended dust-control measures to prevent the occurrence of asbestosis. Jackson claimed that Johns-Manville had then undertaken to improve environmental conditions within its factories, and to give periodic medical examinations to all of its employees.

During cross-examination, Stephenson asked Jackson why Lanza's recommendations had not alerted Johns-Manville officials to the possibility that workers using their insulation products in the field might also run the risk of developing asbestosis.

Jackson replied, "We had no knowledge of the problem as we did with our own employees."

"But you didn't investigate," Stephenson declared. "I think that is clear?"

"No, I did not," Jackson admitted.

"Has Johns-Manville before 1965—let's say from 1900 to 1965 —ever employed an industrial hygienist to go out and see what effects their products were having on the worker?"

"No," Jackson replied.

"That's all," Stephenson said, turning away.

"We employed industrial hygienists to evaluate our own workers' exposures where we knew the problem was," Jackson continued.

"Yes, I understand that," Stephenson said coolly. "But you didn't employ one to go out to see what was happening to the man using your products."

With this statement, Stephenson concluded his cross-examination of the last of the five major expert witnesses who had been called to testify in behalf of the defendant manufacturers. In the opinion of most observers at the trial, each of these cross-examinations had inflicted heavy damage upon the defendants' case. To begin with, Stephenson had used Dr. Gross to counter the suggestion that the asbestos-insulation manufacturers had no reason to test the safety of their products in light of their reported observance of the five-million-particle-per-cubic-foot recommendation. Second, he had called into question the defendants' claim that they had no way of reasonably foreseeing the danger posed by their products to the health of insulation workers by getting Dr. Cooper to acknowledge that there had been a two-foot-high stack of literature on asbestosis during the 1920s and the 1930s. Third, he had thwarted the defense's effort to challenge the medical evidence by belittling Dr. Weill's belated attempt to refute the firsthand diagnosis of Borel's asbestosis, which had been made by the doctors who had attended him. And, finally, having disposed of the testimony offered by his opponents' expert medical witnesses, he had destroyed the remnants of the state-of-the-art defense by his cross-examinations of Sheckler and Jackson.

Shortly after Jackson was excused, George Duncan, the attorney for Pittsburgh Corning, put Eugene W. Holman, the company's vice-president in charge of manufacturing and technology, on the witness stand. Holman testified that when Pittsburgh Corning bought the manufacturing rights to Unibestos in 1962, it was not aware of any health problems that the product might cause the workers who used it. He said that following the publication of Dr. Selikoff's studies, his company had entered into a research program with the Industrial Hygiene Foundation in order to determine whether the amosite asbestos used in Unibestos could have harmful health effects, adding that none of the tests had so far given any indication that amosite could cause cancer or fibrosis.

Although Holman's testimony tended to place Pittsburgh Corning in the clear, it posed little threat to the plaintiff's case, and Stephenson limited his cross-examination to a few perfunctory questions. What Stephenson did not know, or he would not have allowed Holman's testimony to go unchallenged, was that Holman was then involved in what would become one of the most scandalous asbestos horror stories of the decade—the situation at the company's Unibestos-manufacturing plant in Tyler, Texas, about 160 miles northwest of the federal courthouse in Beaumont, which had begun to come to light only two months before the trial opened. In July, officials of the Department of Health, Education, and Welfare's newly formed National Institute for Occupational Safety and Health, in Cincinnati, had become convinced that a serious health hazard existed at the factory, and had communicated their concern to Holman and other Pittsburgh Corning officials. Their worry was soon justified, for within a month after Holman stepped down from the witness stand a government inspection of the Tyler plant would show that the place was grossly contaminated with asbestos dust and that nearly half of the men who had worked there ten years or longer had developed asbestosis. Eventually, this situation would lead to the closing of the plant and to a highly publicized lawsuit brought by 445 of its current and former employees or their survivors, which would eventually be settled out of court for $20 million. In the course of this lawsuit, the executive director of the British-owned asbestos-mining company that had sold amosite asbestos to Pittsburgh Corning would testify under oath that he had warned the president and other high officials of Pittsburgh Corning as early as 1961 that asbestos could cause irreversible and fatal lung disease, and that it must therefore be used with great caution.

Shortly after Holman walked out of the courthouse in Beaumont on the afternoon of September 27, George Duncan rested the case for

Pittsburgh Corning. The attorney for the Armstrong Cork Corporation thereupon proceeded to read answers to interrogatories in which his client stated that it had "no knowledge of death or lung disease among our employees attributable to the inhalation of asbestos dust or fibers." As it happened, the company should not have made this statement. It had been substituted as a defendant in the Borel case for its wholly owned subsidiary, the Armstrong Contracting & Supply Corporation, which had claimed exemption from being named as a defendant on the ground that it was an insulation contractor, not an insulation manufacturer. Armstrong Contracting & Supply could not have truthfully answered that it had no knowledge of death or disease among its employees, because it had settled workmen's-compensation lawsuits for death and disability from asbestosis as far back as the early 1950s, but officials of Armstrong Cork also knew about these claims. This, however, was something else that Stephenson did not know, so Armstrong Cork's testimony went unchallenged. In the end, it would be one of the consummate ironies of *Borel* v. *Fibreboard* that the jury would find all of the defendants guilty of negligence except for Pittsburgh Corning and Armstrong Cork.

On the final day of the trial, the attorney for Ruberoid called to the witness stand the president of an insulation-contracting company for which Borel had worked. The contractor testified that his company had recognized the existence of asbestosis as an occupational disease since 1934, when it began in business, and had carried workmen's compensation to cover it. Under cross-examination by Stephenson, however, he admitted that he had known that asbestos could cause asbestosis only for the past five or six years.

The attorney for Ruberoid then called the district manager of another insulation-contracting firm that had employed Borel. He told the jury that his company had furnished respirators to its workers for nearly twenty years.

"And do you ever have any difficulty in persuading the insulation workers in the field to take advantage of these safety devices that you make available for their use?" the Ruberoid attorney asked.

"Constantly," the district manager replied.

"Is this one of your major problems?"

"This is indeed."

On cross-examination, Stephenson got the witness to acknowledge that he had no personal experience with a respirator, but the district manager was the final witness for the defense, and his testimony was damaging because it established a basis for finding contributory negligence on the part of Borel.

At this point, Judge Fisher instructed the record to show that all of the defendants had rested their cases, and after a recess Stephenson, Weller, and Tucker made their closing statements. Stephenson went first, followed by Weller and Tucker, and then he took the podium again to give a final rebuttal. Jackie Bean, who attended the trial, remembers that he was brief and soft-spoken, making light of the contention that the manufacturers had no knowledge of the hazard and no way of foreseeing it, and reminding the jurors, some of whom had tears in their eyes, that Borel had paid for the negligence and callousness of the defendants with his life.

When Stephenson had finished his rebuttal, Judge Fisher proceeded to read his charge to the jurors. After telling them that "a corporation is entitled to the same fair trial at your hands as a private individual," he informed them that it was the burden of the plaintiff "to prove every essential element of the case by a preponderance of the evidence." He then instructed them that the defendants could not be held responsible for failure to warn Borel unless a preponderance of the evidence showed that they knew or should have known that the manner in which their products were being handled and installed by insulation workers rendered them unreasonably dangerous. Judge Fisher dwelt at length upon the doctrine of strict liability, telling the jury that "one who undertakes to manufacture an article for sale or use by others is held to the skill of an expert in that business and to an expert's knowledge of the arts, material, and processes involved." He went on to say that the manufacturer's status as an expert required him to know about possible harm that might come to people who used his product, and to communicate this knowledge to them. In this regard, Judge Fisher declared that " the manufacturer is bound to keep reasonably abreast of scientific knowledge and discoveries concerning his field, and, of course, is deemed to possess whatever knowledge is thereby imparted."

Fisher instructed the jury that contributory negligence did not constitute a valid defense in a case based upon strict liability, but that if they found contributory negligence on the part of Borel they could not find the defendants guilty of negligence. At the same time, he informed the jurors that if they found that Borel had appreciated the dangers of working with asbestos and had voluntarily assumed the risk, they could not find against the defendants on the basis of strict liability or breach of implied warranty. He said that in the event that they found for the plaintiff they would have the duty of determining the damages that Mrs. Borel was entitled to recover, but that these damages should consist only of the monetary value of services, including loss of earnings, that Borel might have provided her if had he not died, and were not to include anything for her sorrow, anguish, or grief. After telling the jurors that their verdict must be unanimous, Judge Fisher directed the court clerk to give them special interrogatories concerning the chief issues that had been raised in the case, to which they were to answer "yes" or "no." The first interrogatory asked whether they found that Borel had died as the result of negligence on the part of the defendants; the second asked if any of the defendants had committed some act of gross negligence that had caused Borel's death; the third inquired whether Borel was guilty of contributory negligence; the fourth asked whether the defendants were responsible for Borel's death through breach of warranty or strict liability; and the fifth sought to ascertain what amount of money would fairly and reasonably compensate Mrs. Borel for the damages she had sustained. At this point—it was not quite four o'clock in the afternoon—the jurors retired to deliberate. At five o'clock, they returned to the courtroom to say that they could not reach a verdict that afternoon, whereupon Judge Fisher allowed them to adjourn until nine o'clock in the morning.

By the forenoon, Jackie Bean had begun to worry. "I couldn't for the life of me imagine why that jury was taking so long," she remembers. "I was hoping that what was holding them up was how much money to award, but I couldn't help thinking that something had gone wrong. For the first couple of hours, Ward and I sat around in the corridor outside Judge Fisher's courtroom talking to Mrs. Borel and two of her daughters, who were keeping their mother company, but by lunchtime, after the jury had been out five hours, I was a nervous wreck. Ward stayed calm throughout. I don't think I ever saw him so sure about a case. Finally, at 4:00 P.M., the jury came back, and Judge Fisher directed the clerk to read the answers to the special interrogatories that constituted the verdict. There were some surprises, let me tell you. First of all, the jury found that all of the defendants had committed negligence except for Pittsburgh Corning and Armstrong Cork, and that none of them had committed gross negligence. Second—and this was the big surprise—they decided that Clarence Borel was guilty of contributory negligence. But third, and most important of all, they found that all six defendants had breached their warranties to Borel and could be held strictly liable for his death. This was the crucial part of the verdict, because Borel's contributory negligence canceled out the negligence committed by Johns-Manville, Fibreboard, Ruberoid and Philip Carey, so if the jury hadn't found for us on strict liability we would have lost the case."

As for how much money would fairly and reasonably compensate Thelma Borel, the jury fixed actual damages at $68,000, and then the judge added $9,783.30 for medical expenses, and $1,652.94 for funeral costs. This brought the total award to $79,436.24. However, it would be reduced by $8,578.85 that was recovered by the insurance company that had settled Borel's workmen's-compensation claim; by $20,902.20, which had been paid by the four defendants who had settled out of court before the trial began; and by Stephenson's 40 percent contingent fee, which came to $23,462. In the end, Mrs. Borel would receive $32,222 for the death of her husband. The long and complex appeal process had not even begun, however, and she would have to wait more than three more years to get it.

On the drive back to Orange from Beaumont, Jackie Bean recalls, Stephenson's elation over winning the case was tinged with disappointment over the amount of the monetary award, which he felt should have been much higher, and with puzzlement over the finding of contributory negligence. Later, it would come to light that the twelve members of the jury had been evenly split when they took their first vote, and had subsequently divided eleven to one in favor of the plaintiff. The lone holdout was a man who felt deeply that workers were lucky to have jobs and that no company which provided them should be judged too harshly for its actions, whatever they might be. Finally, after the other jurors had tried vainly to get him to change his mind, a face-saving deal was struck in which, in return for their finding Borel guilty of contributory negligence, he agreed to find that four of the defendants were negligent, and all six of them liable to Borel under the doctrine of strict liability. In the end, most of the jurors were unconvinced by the defense attorney's attempts to draw a distinction between inhaling asbestos dust in a factory and inhaling it in the hold of a ship, or in the confines of a chemical plant, and virtually all of them ended up believing that Claude Tomplait and the other colleagues of Borel who testified at the trial were sick men who had neither known nor understood the magnitude of the health risk of their trade.

On October 6, Stephenson filed a motion for judgment on the basis of the verdict, and during the next two weeks lawyers for the defendant manufacturers countered with motions for judgment, notwithstanding the verdict, as well as for a new trial. Judge Fisher denied all of the defense motions, and on November 30 Thelma Borel was officially notified that she had received judgment in the case. The attorneys for the six defendants were convinced that the chances for reversal were good, however, because of the finding of contributory negligence on the part of Borel, and they proceeded to appeal the verdict to the United States Court of Appeals for the Fifth Circuit, in New Orleans. On April 29, 1972, they filed a seventy-five-page defendant-appellants brief with the Fifth Circuit, requesting a reversal of the trial court's judgment, and sent a copy by certified mail to Stephenson, who had sixty days to reply.

"Ward was a lawyer who just hated to brief law, but he bit the bullet for Borel," Jackie Bean recalls. "For six solid weeks, he pored over old cases and carefully worked out his reply to each and every one of the defendants' points and arguments. Why, I must have typed and retyped his reply brief a dozen times before he was satisfied with it. Oral argument before the Fifth Circuit was held on November 14, almost fourteen months after *Borel* v. *Fibreboard* went to trial, and it lasted a couple of hours. Ward drove over to Lake Charles early in the morning, caught a plane to New Orleans, and appeared before Judge John Minor Wisdom and two other circuit judges at 10:00 A.M. When I saw him back at the office the next day, he said he thought it had gone very well. He said that he felt he had given a good answer to every question the judges had asked him, and that they had popped some really difficult ones at the defendants."

When Stephenson argued before the Fifth Circuit, he did not go up against Tucker, Weller, Pate, or any of the other defense attorneys of record in *Borel* v. *Fibreboard,* but against W. Page Keeton, who was dean and professor of law at the University of Texas School of Law, and widely regarded as one of the nation's leading scholars in the field of product liability. Indeed, Keeton had been a member of the blue-ribbon committee that had defined the special new rule of strict liability in Section 402A of the second edition of *Restatement of the Law of Torts.* The decision to retain an attorney of his stature was a joint decision by the defense counsel and may well have reflected an awareness on the part of the defendant manufacturers and their insurance carriers—in addition to Travelers, the carriers included the Aetna Casualty & Surety Company, of Hartford; the Insurance Company of North America, of Philadelphia; the Fireman's Fund American Insurance Company, of San Francisco; the Texas Pacific Indemnity Company, of Dallas; and the General Accident Insurance Company, of Philadelphia—that if *Borel* v. *Fibreboard* were lost there could be an avalanche of asbestos-disease litigation.

As it happened, no record of the oral argument in *Borel* v. *Fibreboard* was made, and whatever notes Stephenson may have jotted down have been lost. For his part, Professor Keeton remembers that in the twenty or so minutes that were allotted to him to speak he dwelled chiefly on the thesis that asbestos insulation could not be considered a dangerous product, because its usefulness and the fact that there was no good substitute for its use in high-temperature insulation far outweighed the recognized hazard it posed to human beings. Be that as it may, appellate-court judges tend to place far more weight in deciding a given case on the detailed discussion of the issues which appears in the briefs than on oral argument, and this was undoubtedly the case in *Borel* v. *Fibreboard.*

In the defendant-appellants' brief, Keeton reminded the court that Borel had admitted knowing that dust could not be good for one's health, and that Borel and his fellow-insulators had been aware of the dust problem from the time they began working in their trade. (Stephenson countered this argument in his brief for the plaintiff by stating that Borel's knowing that dust could not be good for one's health did not constitute a realization that the breathing of dust would create a serious or terminal physical illness, and he reminded the court that Borel had brought asbestos home to decorate his family's Christmas tree.) Keeton invoked the state-of-the-art defense by claiming that the defendants could not have known about the health hazard for asbestos insulators until the publication in 1964 of the study that had been conducted by Dr. Selikoff and his associates. (Stephenson responded in his brief by reminding the court of Dr. Cooper's testimony that by 1940 the medical and scientific literature concerning the adverse effects of asbestos upon human health would have made a stack two feet high.)

Keeton proceeded to argue that there should be no liability imposed on the manufacturers of asbestos products just because harm was reasonably foreseeable from their use for ordinary purposes, pointing out that harm was reasonably foreseeable from the ordinary use of almost any product—a hoe, a knife, a lawn mower, penicillin, an automobile—even when utmost care was exercised. To support this contention, he cited *Davis* v. *Wyeth Laboratories,* a 1968 case involving a plaintiff who had contracted polio after receiving a dose of Sabin oral polio vaccine, and who had been successful in claiming that its manufacturers should be regarded as having guaranteed to each and every user that the vaccine was fit and safe for his individual use, rather than that it was reasonably fit and safe for public consumption. (The plaintiff had, nonetheless, won his case because of the manufacturer's failure to warn.) As for the Borel case, Keeton said that the plaintiff was in the position of asserting that virtually all asbestos products of all manufacturers had been designed in an unreasonably dangerous manner. "This is on its face preposterous," he wrote, adding that his clients had been unable to find a single case holding an entire industry subject to liability for an occupational disease that took twenty or more years to develop.

Preposterous or not, holding the entire asbestos industry liable was precisely what Stephenson had been up to from the very beginning in *Borel* v. *Fibreboard,* and in his reply to the appellants' brief he had reiterated his position with telling irony and logic. Regarding Keeton's citing of *Davis* v. *Wyeth Laboratories,* he told the court that the defendant asbestos manufacturers were apparently suggesting that if a product was useful its maker did not have to warn the consumer of dangerous side effects. He went on to point out that the defendants had not been able to cite a single case that held this to be so. He then unleashed a wickedly effective attack upon Keeton's argument by quoting several paragraphs from an article that Keeton himself had written about product liability and failure to warn, which had appeared two years earlier in *The Texas Law Review.* In the article, Keeton had taken a position that contradicted the major assertions he had just made in behalf of his asbestos-manufacturer clients. Indeed, at one point, he wrote, "My principal thesis is and has been that theories of negligence should be avoided altogether in the products liability area in order to simplify the law, and that if the sale of a product is made under circumstances that would subject someone to an unreasonable risk in fact, liability for harm resulting from these risks should follow."

As might have been expected, the Fifth Circuit Court judges asked Keeton some telling questions about the inconsistencies between the views on product liability he had expressed as a legal scholar and those he was now espousing as an advocate for the defendant manufacturers. As for Stephenson, he had described what he felt about the defendant manufacturers' conduct in no uncertain terms in his brief. "In the case at hand, plaintiff feels that the defendants long ago discovered the danger of their products but just simply did not want to say anything about it to scare off any prospective customer," he wrote. He went on to point out that it would be a mockery of justice if a manufacturer could avoid liability on the ground that he did nothing to discover the wrong or eliminate the danger.

Following the oral argument, Stephenson caught up on office work that had been allowed to languish because of his commitment to Borel, while Weller, Tucker, and the other defense lawyers made motions for rehearing and rehearing en banc. Thanksgiving and Christmas were spent at the ranch in Little Cypress with Marcelle and the two boys, and were happy and uneventful family affairs. Then, a few weeks into the new year, Stephenson caught a bad cold that settled in his chest and developed a low-grade fever that would not go away. Finally, at Marcelle's urging, he went to Dr. Howard Williams, his physician and longtime friend, who, after listening to Ward's chest with his stethoscope, sent him to Orange Memorial Hospital for X-rays. When the chest films revealed an ominous shadow in the right lung, Stephenson drove down to Houston to see Dr. Daniel Jenkins, the pulmonary specialist at the Baylor College of Medicine, who had testified in behalf of Borel at the trial. The news was bad. Jenkins told Stephenson that he had developed a large tumor in his lung, and recommended immediate surgery to remove it. This was performed at Methodist Hospital in Houston on February 21.

After a ten-day stay in the hospital, during which he received radiation therapy, Stephenson spent the rest of the winter recuperating at home. In April, he began a second course of radiation therapy, which, initially required him to go to Houston everyday. Because the radiation made him intensely ill, he was driven there in a thirty-five-foot mobile home, which enabled him to lie down during the trip, and afforded him the privacy he needed to cope with this latest crisis to his health. Most of the time, he was driven by Marcelle or one of his sons. Occasionally, he was driven by Marlin Thompson, his law partner and close friend, who had been hired by Ward's father in September of 1953 and had become a full partner in the firm after Mr. K.W.'s death, in 1958.

On May 13, the defendants' motions for rehearing and rehearing en banc in Borel were denied. Shortly thereafter, they got in touch with Stephenson and agreed to settle the case of Samuel Potter, who would die of asbestosis in September, for $75,000. That same week, Stephenson and his wife motored to Austin, where they spent a few days in the hill country playing golf. By the end of the month, he was feeling well enough to come into the office for two or three hours a day. In June, however, he developed pain in his back and his left ankle, which was soon diagnosed as bone cancer, and which indicated that the malignancy in his lung was spreading through his body. In July, his peripheral vision deteriorated and he began to experience difficulty reading, and a brain scan taken at Methodist Hospital revealed that the cancer had spread even farther. When he returned to the ranch in Little Cypress, he was confined to a hospital bed in the master bedroom. He had his short-wave radio equipment installed, and he spent long hours during the rest of July and August calling around the world. Jackie Bean, who lived nearby, stopped at the house at the end of every day to bring him his mail and to brief him on matters of importance at the office. She remembers that he never failed to ask if anything had come down from the Fifth Circuit on Borel. "I don't guess we heard on Borel today or you would've called me, Jackie," he would say.

Early in September, Stephenson began to go downhill fast. On Tuesday, September 4, tropical storm Delia swept through the Gulf of

Mexico and struck the Gulf Coast, and Marcelle took him to Orange Memorial for the night. He was back home the next day, fiddling with his ham radio, but also slipping into and out of coma. He made his last overseas contact Thursday, and on Friday night, September 7, at 9:00 P.M., he died.

A week later a broken-hearted Jackie Bean wrote a letter to Dr. Selikoff, which began:

> Dear Dr. Selikoff:
>
> It is with great sadness that I write to tell you of the death of Mr. Stephenson. He died Friday night, September 7, 1973, of cancer. He had had his right lung removed February 21, 1973, and following surgery, he had extensive radiation treatments and was hospitalized several times.
>
> I wanted you to know about this, since he worked so very closely with you over the years on his asbestosis cases. As you can well imagine, these cases took up so very much of his time since about the year 1966, when we first filed a case against the manufacturers of asbestos insulation. He wrote to you about the trial of the Clarence Borel case in Federal Court in Beaumont and advised you that the case was on appeal to the Fifth Circuit Court of Appeals. He argued the case November 14, 1972, and we anxiously awaited the Court's decision. Ironic as it may seem, the opinion arrived on September 11th, just four days following his death. I cannot tell you how elated I was that Mr. Stephenson won the case on appeal, but how saddened I was that he never knew the outcome.

As it turned out, Jackie Bean was mistaken when she told Selikoff that Ward Stephenson never knew the outcome of Borel, for early in September, someone in the Fifth Circuit, who knew that he was dying, had telephoned him the news that the judgment of the trial court had been affirmed. Marlin Thompson, Stephenson's law partner, learned about it the last time he saw Stephenson alive. "It was in the middle of the week, just before Ward slipped into his final coma," he recalled not long ago. "I was over to the house visiting with him, and we were talking about some of the asbestos cases I would be trying, and right in the middle of this Ward paused and looked up and said very matter-of-factly, 'By the way, Marlin, we won Borel.' "

THREE

THE CASE OF THE TYLER PLANT

The Fifth Circuit Court of Appeals' decision in *Clarence Borel* v. *Fibreboard Paper Products Corporation et al.* triggered the greatest avalanche of toxic-tort litigation in the history of American jurisprudence. Some twenty-five thousand lawsuits were brought over the next decade as word spread that asbestos manufacturers could be held strictly liable under the law. The landmark opinion was written by Judge John Minor Wisdom, who pointed out that Section 402A of the *Restatement of the Law of Torts* required a manufacturer to disclose the existence and the extent of reasonably foreseeable risk involved in the use of his product, and went on to declare that "an insulation worker, no less than any other product user, has a right to decide whether to expose himself to the risk."

Judge Wisdom rejected the manufacturers' claim that it was up to insulation contractors to warn their employees about the hazards of asbestos, saying that a seller could be liable to the ultimate consumer or user for failure to give adequate warnings. As for the defendants' claim that evidence was lacking to support the jury's finding that each of them was the cause of injury to Borel, Judge Wisdom said that it was impossible to determine with absolute certainty which particular exposure to asbestos resulted in injury to Borel but that it was indisputable that Borel had contracted asbestosis from inhaling asbestos dust, and that he had been exposed to the products of all the defendants on many occasions. According to Wisdom, this was strong circumstantial evidence that each defendant was the cause of some injury to Borel. He concluded his opinion with this paragraph:

> In reaching our decision in the case at bar, we recognize that
> the question of the applicability of Section 402A of the Re-
> statement to cases involving "occupational diseases" is one of
> first impression. But though the application is novel, the under-

lying principle is ancient. Under the law of torts, a person has long been liable for the foreseeable harm caused by his own negligence. This principle applies to the manufacture of products as it does to almost every other area of human endeavor. It implies a duty to warn of foreseeable dangers associated with those products. This duty to warn extends to all users and consumers, including the common worker in the shop or in the field. Where the law has imposed a duty, courts stand ready in proper cases to enforce the rights so created. Here, there was a duty to speak, but the defendants remained silent. The district court's judgment does no more than hold the defendants liable for the foreseeable consequences of their own inaction.

As things turned out, it took several years for the implications of Borel to be fully appreciated by the trial lawyers of the nation, and for asbestos insulators, shipyard workers, and their families to learn that their health might have been seriously jeopardized by exposure to asbestos dust. If Ward Stephenson had lived, the whole process would undoubtedly have been accelerated. Stephenson had made strenuous efforts to alert his colleagues in the legal profession to the plight of asbestos workers, and he would have known how to capitalize on the Borel trial and its pleadings, which provided a detailed blueprint for uncovering the widespread coverup conspiracy that had been perpetrated by the asbestos industry and its paid consultants for nearly half a century. However, the plaintiff lawyers who now took up asbestos litigation not only were deprived of his dozen years of experience but often failed to grasp the tantalizing clues that he had uncovered in Borel, and thus lost an opportunity to shortcut the arduous years of discovery that lay ahead.

An exception was Stephenson's law partner, Marlin Thompson, who first became involved in asbestos litigation during Ward's final illness, when he tried and won a workmen's-compensation lawsuit in a Texas state court. Thompson, who was forty-six when Stephenson died, was born in the town of Lufkin, Texas, and grew up on a farm near Cleveland, about eighty miles west of Orange. He graduated from the University of Texas School of Law in 1952, and in 1953 he started work at Stephenson & Stephenson. At the time of Stephenson's death, he knew very little about asbestos litigation, and felt as if the roof had caved in on him. "There I was with a dozen product-liability asbestos lawsuits on my hands and almost no idea about how to proceed with them," he recalls. "What I did was study Borel and play catch up as best I could. In January of 1974, I settled three cases, including that of Jesse J. Crawford, who had testified for both Tomplait and Borel, and from then on, new clients came pouring in as more and more asbestos insulators from Local 22 in Houston got sick.

"The first strict-liability case I tried was for Bill Condray, a job foreman, who had also testified for Borel. Condray was sixty-seven years old. He had worked with asbestos for more than forty years, and he came to us in 1975, when he found that he had developed asbestosis. During 1976, he developed lung cancer, which spread to the bone marrow in his elbow, and by the time his case came to trial, early in March of 1977, he was dying in a Houston hospital. The thing I'll never forget about Condray is how angry he was. He had been in the hospital about six weeks, and everyone had expected him to die long before the trial got under way, but he swore that he wasn't going to die until he heard the jury verdict. Another thing that made the case memorable was that Dr. Daniel Jenkins, who had been Ward Stephenson's chief expert witness against the state-of-the-art defense in Borel, and who had diagnosed Ward's lung cancer and attended him while he was at Methodist Hospital, decided to testify for the asbestos-insulation manufacturers. In fact, under direct examination by a defense attorney, Jenkins proceeded to contradict the main points he had made in the deposition that Ward had taken of him back in August of 1971. I countered by reading him selected portions of that deposition, including his statement that by 1940 there was adequate medical and scientific knowledge to put a manufacturer of asbestos products on notice about the danger of these products. The jury went out at four P.M. on a Thursday, and when they came back, two hours later, they returned a verdict for Condray and awarded him seventy-five thousand dollars in damages. I called him right away and told him the news, and it was as if he had hung on just long enough to hear it, because he died a day and a half later. As for Jenkins, he continued to testify for the asbestos-insulation manufacturers over the next few years, but after my cross-examination got disseminated, and he got blown out a few times, they stopped using him and found someone else."

.   .   .

The Fifth Circuit Court opinion affirming the trial court's judgment in Borel was, of course, an ominous harbinger for the manufacturers of asbestos insulation, but because juries in East Texas—particularly those in the labor-union stronghold of the heavily industrialized area known as the Golden Triangle—had always tended to be sympathetic toward plaintiffs and working people. Johns-Manville, the nation's largest asbestos manufacturer, refused to accept Borel as the final word in determining its liability in other jurisdictions. A year and a half later, it appealed a second adverse jury decision in a strict-liability action involving asbestos insulation, in the hope of obtaining an appeals-court reversal that would counteract Borel. The case in question was brought by a sixty-year-old insulator from Duluth, Minnesota, named John A. Karjala, who learned in 1966 that he had developed asbestosis. Three years later, Karjala retained an attorney after reading a letter in the *Asbestos Worker* written by Ward Stephenson to the president of the Asbestos Workers union, in Washington, D.C., informing him of the out-of-court settlements in Claude Tomplait's lawsuit and asking him to alert the membership of his union about the implications of the case. Karjala's lawyer, Paul J. Louisell, wrote to Stephenson, who sent him a copy of the complaint in *Borel* v. *Fibreboard,* and in February, 1971, Karjala filed a product-liability lawsuit in the United States District Court for the District of Minnesota, against the same manufacturers who had been defendants in Borel. During 1972 and 1973, all of the defendants settled out of court except for Johns-Manville. When the case went to trial, in September, 1974, the company again claimed that it could not have foreseen the danger to insulators who used its asbestos products until the 1964 report of Dr. Selikoff and his colleagues. However, after evidence was presented to show that Johns-Manville had had early knowledge of the health hazards of asbestos, the jury returned a verdict in favor of Karjala, who would die of mesothelioma the following summer, awarding him $250,000.

In April, 1975, Johns-Manville appealed the verdict to the Eighth Circuit Court of Appeals, in St. Louis, claiming that Judge Miles W. Lord, who had presided over the trial, had misstated the law when he instructed the jury on strict liability, and also that Karjala's action should be barred by the Minnesota statute of limitations. However, in September, the Eighth Circuit upheld Lord on the matter of strict liability and affirmed the trial court's judgment on the question of the statute. Thus, in the space of three years, Johns-Manville had appealed and lost two strict-liability cases involving asbestos-insulation products in two separate federal jurisdictions. The consequences proved disastrous for the company and its colleagues in the asbestos industry, as well as for their insurance carriers, because the Borel and Karjala cases were written up in the *Federal Reporter* and circulated to law libraries and lawyers across the nation.

The most bitter and costly lesson of all, of course, was the grim reckoning that was unfolding with regard to the health experience of the eighteen thousand men who were members of the International Association of Heat and Frost Insulators and Asbestos Workers. Dr. Selikoff and his colleagues at Mount Sinai had continued to observe the causes of death among an original group of 632 asbestos insulators they were studying, and by 1976 a broad picture of the asbestos-disease toll among them had become tragically clear. Nineteen percent of them were dying of lung cancer; 9 percent were dying of gastrointestinal cancer; 8 percent were succumbing to mesothelioma; and 9 percent were being killed by asbestosis and other noninfectious lung diseases. The fact that more than one in three of them were dying of cancer led to the inescapable conclusion that there was an epidemic of malignancy among these men.

Meanwhile, Selikoff had been keeping close watch over seventeen patients who had come from a UNARCO insulation factory in Paterson, New Jersey, which had been shut in November, 1954. By 1974, only two of these men were alive. Of the fifteen who had died, seven were victims of lung cancer, two of cancer of the stomach, four of asbestosis, and one of malignant mesothelioma. (The other death was caused by heart disease.) In 1968, Selikoff and his colleagues began to trace the 933 who had worked at the factory between 1941 and 1945, and thus, if they were still alive, had passed the twenty-year mark since their initial exposure to asbestos dust. By the end of 1976, it was apparent that they had uncovered a tragedy similar to the one that had befallen the asbestos-insulation workers, for the rate of lung cancer among the former UNARCO factory workers was seven times the expected rate.

As things turned out, when UNARCO had shut the Paterson factory, it had opened a similar plant in Tyler, Texas, which was awarded a large contract by the Navy to provide amosite-asbestos pipe covering for nuclear submarines. However, in 1962, UNARCO's managers decided to quit the asbestos business altogether, and they sold the Tyler plant to the Pittsburgh Corning Corporation—a joint venture of the Pittsburgh Plate Glass Company (now called PPG Industries) and the Corning Glass Works. By the summer of 1963, the new owners were apparently entertaining some misgivings about working conditions in the factory, for at that time they asked the Industrial Hygiene Foundation of America to evaluate the asbestos-dust hazard there. However, the foundation's industrial-hygiene engineers misinterpreted the threshold limit for asbestos dust, and instead of warning Pittsburgh Corning that the high level of asbestos fibers in the airborne dust they had measured in the plant constituted an appalling health hazard, they merely made recommendations for better housekeeping and better ventilation equipment.

Three years later, conditions were even worse. By that time, the company had acquired a new medical consultant—Dr. Lee B. Grant, a retired colonel, who had been chief of aerospace medicine for the United States Air Force Logistics Command, and who had become medical director of one of Pittsburgh Corning's parent corporations, the Pittsburgh Plate Glass Company, in 1964. At Dr. Grant's request, a survey of the Tyler plant was conducted in November, 1966, but the engineer who performed it also misinterpreted the recommended standard for asbestos dust, and although he suggested that better ventilation equipment be installed, he failed to report that workers at the factory were breathing concentrations of asbestos fibers ten times as high as those which were supposed to protect them from disease.

In March, 1967, an environmental survey of the Tyler plant, which consisted of taking eighty-two samples of air in the factory, was conducted by engineers sent there by Dr. Lewis J. Cralley, who was associate program chief for field studies and epidemiology in the Public Health Service's Division of Occupational Health, in Cincinnati. More than a year passed before Cralley's people got around to informing Pittsburgh Corning that the asbestos-fiber counts were considered high in more than half of the samples, but their report did not mention that a health hazard might exist at the Tyler plant. Nor did it advise J. W. McMillan, the works manager of the factory, to improve the ventilation system or to institute better housekeeping practices. However, McMillan did not remain in the dark about the situation for very long, because on April 3, Dr. Grant wrote him a letter telling him that the dust levels measured by Cralley's group constituted "a significant health hazard," and saying, "you must anticipate that both some cases of asbestosis and an increased incidence of pulmonary carcinoma will develop in your employee population as a result of continued exposure to these levels for 15 or more years."

At this time, the Occupational Health people had no legal authority to enter and inspect factories, and they were operating under a pledge of confidentiality that precluded any possibility that the data they collected in their surveys would be made known to the workers whose health was being affected or to the unions representing them. This quiet state of affairs was fine by the asbestos industry. On the one hand, the industry could state publicly that, with its assistance, the United States Public Health Service was investigating the possible hazards of industrial exposure to asbestos. On the other hand, it could rest assured that because of the pledge of confidentiality none of the results would find their way into the hands of anyone who might seek to remedy any hazards that were found.

Meanwhile, as the health situation at the Tyler plant went from bad to worse to appalling, a parade of government inspectors continued to troop through the place without any apparent awareness of the manifest hazards there. Additional surveys were performed in 1969 and 1970, which also failed to warn of the existence of any possible health risks, even though the American Conference of Governmental Industrial Hygienists had by now proposed that the threshold-limit value for asbestos dust be lowered from five million particles per cubic foot—the standard that had been in effect for more than twenty years—to two million particles per cubic foot, which was considered to be the equivalent of twelve asbestos fibers longer than five microns per cubic centimeter of air. (Five microns is one-five-thousandth of an inch, and a cubic centimeter is an amount equal to what might be contained in a small thimble.) Thus, over a six-and-a-half-year period, five separate studies and inspections of the factory had been conducted, and more than a hundred samples of air had been gathered and transported to laboratories in various parts of the country, where they had been counted, weighed, assayed, and painstakingly analyzed by industrial hygienists who, depending on what standard they were using, had reported their findings in terms of dust particles per cubic foot or dust weight per cubic meter or fiber counts per cubic centimeter but never in terms of what the dust and fibers that the workers were inhaling might do to their health.

In December of 1970, Congress passed the Occupational Safety and Health Act, which authorized the federal government to develop and set mandatory occupational-safety-and-health standards applicable to any business that engaged in interstate commerce. The Secretary of Labor was given the authority to promulgate these standards and to enforce them by conducting inspections of factories and other work-places and by issuing citations and imposing penalties if the standards were violated. The Department of Health, Education, and Welfare was made responsible for developing criteria for the establishment of the safety and health standards, including regulations for dealing with toxic materials and harmful physical agents. So that the Department could perform these functions, the act provided for a National Institute for Occupational Safety and Health, called NIOSH, which replaced the Bureau of Occupational Safety and Health, and which was given au-thority to enter factories for inspections and investigations. As a result, the business-as-usual attitude that had characterized government pol-icy toward the asbestos industry for so long was soon to be shattered by a series of disclosures that, fittingly, would have their apotheosis in the revelation of the working conditions at the Tyler plant.

In late October, 1971—a few weeks after Eugene Holman, a vice-president of Pittsburgh Corning, testified at the Borel trial that research financed by his company had given no indication that amosite asbestos could cause cancer or fibrosis—NIOSH investigators con-ducted an inspection of the Tyler factory. In some areas of the plant, they found asbestos-dust levels to be more than twenty times as high as a recently recommended Department of Labor emergency standard for asbestos of five fibers longer than five microns per cubic centimeter of air. Since asbestos-induced cancers generally take at least twenty years to develop, and the Tyler plant had been in operation for only seventeen years, they did not expect to find neoplasms among the 63 men working there. However, they did find indications of asbestosis in seven of the 18 workers who had more than ten years of employment at the factory. And when they got around to examining Pittsburgh Corning's employment records they discovered that a total of 895 men had worked in the plant at one time or another. Considering the disastrous mortality figures of the men who had worked in the Paterson factory between 1941 and 1945, this was disturbing news, to say the least.

A preliminary report of the NIOSH survey declaring that an extremely serious occupational-health situation existed at the Tyler plant was sent on November 16 to the regional administrator for the Occupational Safety and Health Administration (OSHA), in Dallas. On November 23, two officials from the OSHA office made an inspection of the factory and found inadequate housekeeping, insufficient dust control, and improper wearing of respirators. Yet the inspectors failed to cite Pittsburgh Corning for any serious violations of the Occupational Safety and Health Act—infractions that could result in death or serious physical harm. Instead, they cited the company for some nonserious violations, including insufficient dust control, and proposed a fine of $210.

In spite of the mildness of the penalties that accompanied them, the OSHA citations caused considerable consternation to the management of Pittsburgh Corning by setting March 31, 1972, as the date for completing extensive improvements in the ventilation and dust-control systems of the Tyler plant. Consequently, Pittsburgh Corning's board of directors met in the middle of December and decided to shut the factory. Production stopped on February 3, 1972, and over the next two months the plant was subjected to a cleanup of prodigious scope and intensity. By the end of February, most of its heavy equipment had either been cut up and buried or sold for junk, and by the end of April, practically nothing remained except two dilapidated wooden buildings, which had once been warehouses at Camp Fannin, a Second World War training center and prisoner-of-war camp. At that point, the managers of Pittsburgh Corning apparently thought that they had put their troubles behind them. As for the 895 men who had worked in the Tyler plant over the years, they were out of sight and out of mind. In a sense, they, like much of the factory itself, were buried.

As things turned out, a major legal problem for Pittsburgh Corning and PPG Industries would soon be posed by a young lawyer named Frederick M. Baron, who at this point was not even a year out of law school. Baron was born in 1947, of Russian-Jewish parents, in Cedar Rapids, Iowa. His father had died when he was eight years old, and his mother had remarried and had taken her son to her new husband's home near Austin. In 1965, Baron entered the University of Texas in Austin, where he got his B.A. degree in history and government, and in the fall of 1968 he entered the University of Texas School of Law. After graduating from law school, in May, 1971, Baron went to work for the firm of Mullinax, Wells, Mauzy & Collins, in Dallas, and on September 21—the day the Borel trial began in Beaumont—he was licensed to practice law in Texas. Two years later, as Ward Stephenson lay dying, and the Fifth Circuit was preparing to hand down its decision in *Borel,* Anthony Mazzocchi, director of the legislative department of the Oil, Chemical, and Atomic Workers International Union (OCAW), who had been trying in vain for months to get someone to represent the workers at Pittsburgh Corning's Tyler plant—half a dozen firms had turned the case down—called Mullinax, Wells, Mauzy & Collins, whose senior partners accepted the case reluctantly and turned it over to Baron. Baron went to Tyler to meet with Herman Yandle, who had been chairman of the union committee at the Pittsburgh Corning factory, and learned what had gone on there. When Baron got back to Dallas, he spent the next few weeks reading decisions in old silicosis cases, and during the first week of October he got hold of the Fifth Circuit's decision in *Borel,* which had just been handed down.

"*Borel* convinced me that I should go the strict-liability route," Baron recalled ten years later. "However, the Tyler workers were factory employees who manufactured asbestos insulation, and were not allowed by law to sue their employer, and in order to bring a product-liability lawsuit in their behalf I obviously had to find a defective product. One big question was whether raw amosite asbestos was a product, and, if so, whether I could bring an action against the mining companies that supplied it. Another was whether or not I could sue Pittsburgh Corning's owners—PPG Industries and the Corning Glass Works. In October, I went ahead and signed up seven or eight prospective plaintiffs, including Herman Yandle, to power-of-attorney agreements. Then I drew up a complaint on their behalf, and on January 2, 1974, I filed a class-action lawsuit in federal district court in Tyler, asking one hundred million dollars in damages against PPG and its medical director, Dr. Lee B. Grant, Pittsburgh Corning, the Corning Glass Works, and several other defendants."

Baron explained that he was able to name Pittsburgh Corning in his complaint because one of his clients was the widow of a Tyler factory worker who had recently died of asbestosis, and under Texas law an employer could be sued if an employee's death occurred through gross negligence. "I wanted Pittsburgh Corning in the case so I could find out who had supplied raw asbestos to the Tyler plant, so once I filed my complaint, I asked the presiding judge to sign an order requiring the company to furnish me with a list of all its asbestos suppliers," he said. "As you may imagine, the fact that I was suing the defendants for one hundred million dollars made headlines in Texas and across the nation. It also made me nervous. I was twenty-six years old at the time, and I had only been practicing law for a little more than two years, and I was afraid that I was in over my head. However, within a couple of weeks a trial lawyer named Rex Houston, who comes from Henderson, a town near Tyler, and who can talk the peel off a banana, also filed product-liability lawsuits in behalf of some Tyler plant workers. And at the beginning of February I got a call from Scott Baldwin, of Jones, Jones & Baldwin, in Marshall—a town near the Louisiana border, about fifty miles east of Tyler—who told me that he had signed up some prospective plaintiffs from the Tyler plant. When Baldwin proposed that the three of us share any new clients from the factory, I was thrilled to death because he was a consummate trial lawyer, whose prowess with juries was legendary."

Baron went on to say that when Pittsburgh Corning responded to the order requiring it to furnish the names of its asbestos suppliers, he amended the complaint in *Yandle* v. *PPG Industries,* as the Tyler cases were titled, to name as additional defendants the North American Asbestos Corporation, of Chicago; Cape Industries, Ltd., of London; and EGNEP (Proprietary) Ltd., of Johannesburg, South Africa—a company that mined and sold between 90 and 95 percent of the world's supply of amosite asbestos. During the spring of 1974, some of the other defendants filed a motion to stop discovery until the issue of whether the case should proceed as a class action was resolved. In the autumn of that year, Judge William Steger, who was presiding over the case, held a trial on the issue and handed down a decision denying class action on several grounds, including the fact that the 570 Pittsburgh Corning employees who worked at the Tyler plant over a ten-year period could not possibly have had the same exposure to asbestos dust. He then instructed Baron and his associates to renew their discovery.

. . .

During the winter of 1975, Baron, Baldwin, and Houston sent interrogatories and requests for documents to the various defendants and
made arrangements to take depositions of some of their employees.
Among them was Dr. Grant, the medical director of PPG, who was
central to the theory Baron had evolved for trying the case. "We
alleged that by allowing Dr. Grant to consult for its subsidiary, Pittsburgh Corning, PPG was liable under a theory of law governing the
negligent performance of undertaking to perform services, which is
sometimes referred to as the good Samaritan doctrine," Baron explained. "Our contention was that Dr. Grant had failed to exercise
reasonable care of the workers at the Tyler plant, because he had
failed to inform them that asbestos could be harmful to their health,
and that PPG was liable because Grant was their medical director
and their agent. However, when we took Grant's deposition, we
could not get him to admit that there was any specific health hazard
at the Tyler plant before 1968, so we decided to focus our discovery
upon the English and South African companies that had supplied
Pittsburgh Corning with amosite asbestos. We felt sure we could
stick the mining companies for having failed to place warning labels
on the shipments of asbestos they had sent to the Tyler plant, and
with this in mind, we sent up to Chicago in May to depose Charles
G. Morgan, who was president of the North American Asbestos Corporation—a wholly owned subsidiary of Cape Industries, Ltd., of
London, a huge holding company. North American consisted of Morgan and four female secretaries. Its sole function was to serve as a
marketing agent, or service organization, for the selling of South
African asbestos in the United States, Canada, Mexico, and the
Caribbean. In this connection, Morgan took orders for asbestos from
Pittsburgh Corning and placed them with the Cape Asbestos Fibres
Company, of Uxbridge, near London. Cape Asbestos Fibres, another
wholly owned subsidiary of Cape Industries, Ltd., then placed the
order with EGNEP, Ltd., a South African mining company that was
also owned by Cape Industries, and whose name is a backwards
spelling of Penge, an area in South Africa where amosite asbestos is
mined. Morgan told us that sales transactions between EGNEP and
North American Asbestos took place at dockside in South Africa,
where North American was paid a 3½ percent commission on the
gross amount. As a result, EGNEP and Cape Industries could claim

that they did no business in the United States and that they were not, therefore, subject to the jurisdiction of any American court.

"Morgan also told us that during periods when EGNEP could not furnish Pittsburgh Corning with sufficient amounts of amosite, North American Asbestos had been able to purchase it from the United States government's General Services Administration, which controlled a huge supply of the stuff that had been stockpiled in Baton Rouge, Louisiana, during the Second World War. North American then resold it to Pittsburgh Corning at a profit of five dollars a ton. Morgan went on to say that a Dr. Richard Gaze, who was executive director of Cape Industries, Ltd., as well as a member of the board of directors of North American Asbestos, had furnished him with information regarding the health hazards of asbestos when he had first gone to work for North American, in 1971. According to Morgan, Dr. Gaze came to the United States once or twice a year to attend North American's board of directors' meetings. All of this was very intriguing, of course, and since Cape Industries was a very large and very solvent company it now became our prime target. The trouble was, we didn't want to sue Cape Industries in England, because there is no product-liability law in England as we know it, and since the company claimed that it did no business in the United States, it was not clear whether or not we could sue it here. When we got back from Chicago, Scotty Baldwin, Rex Houston, and I held a two-day strategy meeting out at Scotty's house on Sabine Lake, and decided to subpoena EGNEP and Cape Industries, Ltd., under an international agreement that had been signed by both Britain and South Africa. We then called Richard Bernays, of Touchstone, Bernays & Johnston, in Dallas—the law firm that represented North American Asbestos, EGNEP, and Cape Industries—and asked him to produce Dr. Gaze for deposition in London. We also asked him to produce officials of EGNEP for deposition in Johannesburg. Scotty and I then got visas for South Africa, and in the first week of June we flew to London to depose Gaze."

Scott Baldwin is a small, dark-haired man with a mischievous smile who looks a bit like Burgess Meredith. He was born in 1928, in Marshall—a town of twenty-five thousand people whose economy, like that of many other East Texas towns, is based upon petroleum and timber—and he has lived there all his life. His grandfather was a lawyer in Marshall, his father was a doctor, and after graduating from the University of Texas School of Law, in 1953, Baldwin opened an office there. Over the past thirty years, he has developed one of the most successful personal-injury practices in the United States, winning approximately $15 million for his plaintiff clients, as well as a reputation for being one of the best cross-examiners in the business, and today he is president of the sixty-thousand-member Association of Trial Lawyers of America.

"Our strategy toward Cape Industries and EGNEP was directed at piercing the corporate veil," he recalled recently. "When we deposed Charles Morgan, it became apparent that the North American Asbestos Corporation was nothing more or less than a bucket shop. That's East Texas slang for one of those fly-by-night oil-field offices staffed by some guy and a secretary who try to talk people into investing in a dry hole. In order to zero in on Cape Industries, the parent company, we knew we would have to show that it was directly responsible for selling a defective product. To avoid tipping our hand, we let the Cape people and their lawyers think that we were going after the South African mining company, EGNEP, but during the deposition of Richard Gaze we went straight for the jugular. We went after Cape Industries through him."

According to Fred Baron, Baldwin's deposition of Gaze was nothing short of masterly. "Our London solicitor's office was in Salisbury Court, in the Strand," he recalls. "It was a wonderfully musty place, at least two hundred years old, and straight out of Dickens. In fact, the reporter was using a dip-pen and an inkwell. When the deposition got under way, on the afternoon of June 4, we all sat down at a huge conference table. Richard Gaze was a tall, elegant, and immaculately tailored man of fifty-seven, who wore a Harris-tweed suit and vest. Scotty, on the other hand, had put on a loud sports jacket, slacks, and yellow-and-black checked socks, and right off the bat he crooked his leg over the edge of the table and announced in a deep East Texas drawl that he had a bit of trouble understanding English accents and would Dr. Gaze please be sure to speak slowly and distinctly. Scotty was deliberately acting like a hay-seed in order to get Gaze riled up, which is a tactic we lawyers sometimes use when we know we have a reluctant witness on our hands, because it is usually easier to get information out of someone who is angry or on the verge of losing his composure.

"In any case, he quickly got Gaze to admit that he had known about the health hazards of asbestos from the very first day he had gone to work for Cape Industries in 1943, and that he had felt a sense of responsibility to make sure that Cape's subsidiary companies were advised of these hazards. A bit later, Scotty lowered the boom by asking Gaze point blank if he had ever advised any purchaser of asbestos that the stuff might be harmful to the workers who used it. At first, Gaze pleaded a faulty memory, but then he gave an answer that brought my heart to my throat. He said that he had warned the directors of Pittsburgh Corning that asbestos could pose a very serious danger to their workers way back in 1961, even before Pittsburgh Corning had bought the Tyler plant from UNARCO. He went on to say that he had discussed the problem at length with Russell Brittingham, who was then president of Pittsburgh Corning, and with Robert Buckley, who was a vice-president of the company."

At this point in the deposition, Baldwin asked Gaze how long these discussions had continued.

"For as long as I was visiting Pittsburgh," Gaze replied.

"Was that until the time they quit buying from you?" Baldwin asked.

"Yes," Gaze said. "My last visit to Pittsburgh would be in 1970 or 1971. I am not sure."

"Would it be fair, then, to say, Dr. Gaze, that you discussed this asbestos and the potential hazards of it with Pittsburgh from 1961 down to about 1971?"

"Yes," Gaze answered.

Later, Baldwin asked Gaze if, as executive director and chief scientist of Cape Industries, he could have caused a warning label to be placed on the bags of asbestos that were shipped to the Tyler plant from South Africa between 1961 and 1971.

"I could have recommended it," Gaze replied.

"And you could have seen that it had been done had you seen fit to do so?"

"Yes."

On the following day, just before the deposition ended, Baldwin again asked Gaze if he had realized that asbestos was dangerous to work with back in the 1950s.

"Yes, but I want to make my position quite clear on this, Mr. Baldwin," Gaze replied. "I realized that precautions needed to be taken in the handling of this material. What I realize now I was in error about was the extent of the precautions which needed to be taken."

"What precautions do you feel should have been taken that were not when you look back?" Baldwin asked.

"With hindsight, I believe that our siting of dust exhaust machinery was not sufficient to reduce the concentration of asbestos dust in the atmosphere to a sufficiently low level."

"But what I am asking you is you don't intend to imply that you have just recently come upon the knowledge that asbestos can cause the condition of asbestosis."

"No," said Gaze, who would die of mesothelioma in 1982, at the age of sixty-five. "I knew that asbestos, improperly handled, could cause asbestosis, or breathing asbestos dust at too high quantities for too long a time could cause asbestosis. I have known this since the first day I was employed."

A few days after Gaze was deposed, Baldwin and Baron were notified that their visas to South Africa had been canceled because of a South African law that prohibits disclosure of information about its strategically important industries. However, Gaze's testimony had contradicted PPG's claim that it didn't know about the hazards of asbestos, and it had also contradicted the contention of Cape Industries that it did no business in the United States. Moreover, Gaze had testified that Cape Industries exercised control over its South African operations. For these reasons, Baldwin and Baron came back from England feeling a lot better about their case. Soon after returning to Dallas, Baron left Mullinax, Wells, when the firm wouldn't permit him to try an asbestos case in Florida, and was forced to relinquish *Yandle* v. *PPG Industries.* However he was able to stay in the litigation because Rex Kirby, a lawyer in Tyler who had signed up some fifty clients from the Pittsburgh Corning plant, offered to associate him in his cases and to split the attorney's fees with him. As a result, he eventually came to represent almost ninety plaintiffs from the Tyler factory.

During the rest of 1975 and in 1976, Baron, Baldwin, and Houston focused their attention on the involvement of the United States government in the case. "We knew that the General Services Administration had shipped amosite asbestos to the Tyler plant in the same burlap sacks—without warning labels of any kind—in which EGNEP had originally shipped it to the States, so we figured that at the very least we could nail the government for failure to warn," Baron said. "Then, in 1976, a Department of Labor inspector admitted in a deposition that he had not worn a respirator in the Tyler plant for fear of alarming the workers and causing them to ask questions about their health. The minute he said that we knew we had a second heavy rap to hang around the government's neck, but it wasn't until the winter of 1977, when we deposed Dr. Lewis J. Cralley of the Public Health Service that we found our 'smoking gun.' Cralley admitted that when the division was preparing to study asbestos factories across the nation, back in the 1960s, he had entered into a confidentiality agreement with industry that prohibited him from giving out details concerning the exposure of the men who worked in them. He also admitted that, as a result, the Public Health Service never made any recommendations either to workers or to their unions about how they might protect themselves from the hazard of toiling in the excessive dust levels that existed in the Tyler factory and other asbestos plants."

Six months later Baron and two other plaintiff attorneys deposed Charles E. van Horne, who had been assistant manager and safety director of the Tyler plant from 1964 to 1968, and manager of the factory from then until 1972, when it was shut. A gray-haired, self-assured man in his early fifties, van Horne had been hired by J. W. McMillan, the former manager of Tyler plant, who had died of meso-thelioma in 1970. During his deposition, which took place in Tyler in August of 1977, van Horne was questioned about the letter Dr. Grant had written to McMillan on April 3, 1968, informing him that the dust levels measured in the Tyler plant by Cralley's group posed a significant health hazard, and that some employees would develop asbestosis and lung cancer as a result. According to van Horne, McMillan did not appear to take Grant's warning seriously, saying, "I have lived, eaten and breathed asbestos for years, and I smoke, and I don't think they know what they're talking about."

Judge Steger had set trial for *Yandle* v. *PPG Industries* at the end of the month, and he now began to put pressure on the attorneys involved in the case to reach a settlement. "We knew that he meant business when he ordered that all thirty-five of us report to the United States marshal at 9:00 A.M. one morning, and that we be locked inside his conference room at the rear of the courthouse every day from then on, with an hour out for lunch, until we had explored and exhausted all of the possibilities for settlement," Baron said. "So there we sat, staring across a table at each other, scared to death of going to trial. We plaintiffs' attorneys were nervous about the sheer complexity of the case we would have to present—for example, having to explain the enormous disparity in exposure to asbestos among the various workers at the Tyler plant—and we were afraid of losing the jury because of it. As for the defendants' lawyers, they were worried about the damaging depositions we had taken. The question was how and on what basis to settle.

"Back in July, Scotty, Rex Houston, and I had reviewed the medical records of our clients in order to figure out what the case was worth. About four hundred and fifty men had worked at the Tyler plant between 1962 and 1972—the ten-year period in which Pittsburgh Corning had owned it. The trouble was, some of these men had been there for the entire decade; others had worked for a few years; still others had been employed for a matter of months; and many had worked in the factory only a week or two. One of our biggest problems was to try to determine what value we should place on the cases of men who had minimal exposure and no sign of disease, because there was a large possibility that such cases might be dismissed. In the end, we established a baseline of fifteen thousand dollars for these cases, which we considered adequate compensation for worry and emotional strain. Then we assessed the serious cases—men who had developed asbestosis or cancer—and we came up with values ranging from a hundred and fifty thousand dollars for partially disabling asbestosis to four hundred thousand dollars for cases of asbestosis or asbestos-related cancer that had ended in death. Eventually, we came to the conclusion that the whole thing could be settled for twenty million dollars."

Though somewhat Draconian, Judge Steger's tactic of locking the attorneys for both sides in his conference room proved to be an effective way of achieving a settlement. "We spent sixteen hours a day, five days a week, for three hellish weeks in that room," Baron recalls. "During that time, I came to know why Scotty Baldwin is considered to be one of the most brilliant legal tacticians in the country. From the very beginning, he insisted that the key to a good settlement lay in convincing PPG that its liability was deepest. PPG and its primary insurance carrier, Travelers, had hired David Armstrong, an attorney in Pittsburgh, to handle their case, so once we got locked up in Judge Steger's conference room Scotty began working Armstrong over to convince him that PPG could wind up paying the whole ticket. The idea was to get Armstrong to apply the screws to the other major defendants—Cape Industries and the United States government. However, the two lawyers from the Department of Justice who had been assigned to the case dug in their heels and refused to talk settlement of any kind. At that point, Armstrong told them that unless the government admitted its responsibility in the Tyler affair and agreed to kick in to a fair settlement, the other defendants would team up with the plaintiffs and lay the entire blame at the government's doorstep. He had already tried to convince them that he meant business by filing a third-party complaint against the United States. The two government lawyers then did just what we hoped they would do. They pressured their superiors in the Justice Department to come up with some money.

"Meanwhile, Armstrong had dragged UNARCO into the case, claiming that UNARCO had sold Pittsburgh Corning a defective plant in 1962. Armstrong had pegged UNARCO for a half-million-dollar contribution to the settlement, but Scotty took UNARCO's attorney aside and told him that he could get his client out of the case for a cool million, and the UNARCO people agreed to this offer even though they had a motion of dismissal pending before Judge Steger. PPG had also brought the Oil, Chemical, and Atomic Workers International Union into the case, claiming that the union had failed to protect the health of the Tyler workers by not providing them with respirators. Let me tell you, there was a lot of arm-twisting going on. The defendants' first settlement offer was nine million dollars. We turned it down flat, and after two more weeks in Steger's pressure cooker they agreed to settle for the twenty million dollars we were asking. The OCAW contributed one hundred and fifty thousand dollars. UNARCO kicked in the million. PPG and Pittsburgh Corning forked out eight million and fifty thousand. Cape Industries and EGNEP got nailed for five million two hundred thousand. And the United States government, after much screaming and protesting, finally agreed to ante up five million seven hundred and fifty thousand dollars of taxpayers' money. No one, of course, admitted any liability."

The settlement agreement in *Yandle* v. *PPG Industries* was reached in secret on September 28, 1977, but because of subsequent recalcitrance on the part of the government, the plaintiffs received no money until the spring of 1978. "The government people dragged their feet shamefully, and it took tremendous pressure from Judge Steger and the rest of us to get them to live up to their part of the bargain," Baron said. "In the end, I feel we did about as well as we could for our clients in terms of money, though I have mixed feelings about some of the other aspects of the settlement. For example, Armstrong insisted that we plaintiff attorneys agree not to take on any new clients from the Tyler factory work force. We were also asked to agree that whatever evidence we had obtained in the course of our discovery in the case would not be handed over to subsequent plaintiffs. At the time, I went along with these demands, but I have since come to realize that it was a serious mistake to do so, and I'm convinced that if we had said no to Armstrong he would have backed down. In any event, in keeping with the terms of the agreement, Judge Steger issued a gag order forbidding all parties from discussing the case. At the same time, he sealed all of the papers in the case. As a result, the deposition of Richard Gaze, which provided powerful evidence of what the Pittsburgh Corning people really knew about asbestos disease and when they knew it, remained under wraps for the next five and a half years."

This turned out to have serious consequences for hundreds of asbestos-disease plaintiffs, who would bring product-liability lawsuits against Pittsburgh Corning during the next five years, because the company was already claiming in answers to interrogatories that it had no knowledge of the asbestos hazard until the middle of the 1960s—a contention that plaintiff lawyers had no way of effectively countering. In January of 1978, four months before Judge Steger issued his seal order, Robert E. Buckley, the Pittsburgh Corning vice-president whom Gaze said he had warned about the asbestos hazard back in 1961, testified in a deposition he gave in connection with some asbestos-disease lawsuits brought by shipyard workers and their survivors in Virginia that Gaze had never told him about the hazard, and that he had not become aware of it until 1965 or 1966, when he read some newspaper articles about it. After Judge Steger's order, Pittsburgh Corning not only continued to claim that it was ignorant of asbestos disease until the publication of Dr. Selikoff's studies in 1964—thus implying that it had entered into the business of manufacturing and selling asbestos products back in 1962 without knowing of the asbestos hazard—but made such claims without being seriously contradicted. This state of affairs went on until 1983, when H. Seward Lawlor, an enterprising attorney with Glasser & Glasser, a law firm in Norfolk, Virginia, learned about the Gaze deposition. After prevailing upon Judge Steger to release it, Lawlor and some colleagues succeeded in having it admitted in evidence in future asbestos-disease cases in which Pittsburgh Corning was a defendant, and went on to turn up evidence that company officials had been sent articles about the asbestos hazard as early as May of 1962.

As for the Tyler-plant settlement, it got a tremendous amount of publicity all across the nation in the winter of 1978. It brought Baron, Scott Baldwin, and Rex Houston a lot of new business, and it made them a lot wealthier. In fact, after paying referral fees to more than a dozen other lawyers who had signed up plaintiffs from the Tyler factory and associated their cases with Baron, Baldwin, and Houston, each of the three made more than a million dollars for his five years of work. As for their former clients and the other Tyler-factory workers, researchers from the University of Texas have determined that they are dying of lung cancer at a rate that is four or five times the national average. But the majority of these workers are just now approaching twenty years since onset of their exposure to asbestos, and epidemiologists such as Dr. Selikoff expect that fully one-third of the nearly nine hundred men who worked in the factory during the seventeen years and three months it was in operation will die of asbestosis or asbestos-related cancer. It is not known how many of their wives, children, and other relatives will develop asbestos disease as a result of household exposure. It is known, however, that the mother of Herman Yandle—he received $130,000 in the settlement—died of mesothelioma in February of 1983, at the age of sixty-nine. Her only exposure to asbestos occurred during the 1960s, when she washed the work clothes worn by Herman and his brother, who were living at home while they worked at the factory.

FOUR

DISCOVERY

In the years to come, actions similar to *Yandle* v. *PPG Industries* would be initiated in other parts of the country by asbestos-factory workers who sought to get around the shield of workmen's compensation, either by suing the mining companies that supplied raw asbestos to their employers or by suing their employers for fraudulent suppression of information regarding the danger of asbestos. Most of the early lawsuits, however, were brought by individual insulators who, like Clarence Borel, sued the manufacturers of the asbestos insulation they had used in their work for failure to warn them that the stuff was hazardous to their health. As discovery was undertaken in these cases a vast amount of incriminating evidence began to come to light, and when it was pieced together it told a story of corporate misconduct going back fifty years.

One of the most important early finds was made by Thomas W. Henderson, a thirty-six-year-old lawyer from Pittsburgh. Henderson is a lanky, dark-haired, and bespectacled man, who was born in Washington, Pennsylvania, a small manufacturing town about twenty-five miles southwest of Pittsburgh. His father was a steelworker at a local sheet-mill plant, and as a boy Henderson worked in the plant's pickling area, where steel sheets were cleaned with acid before being shipped. After graduating from Washington High School, he went to Brown University where he received a degree in sociology in 1962, and then to law school at Duquesne University, in Pittsburgh. Upon graduating from Duquesne, he joined a law firm in Pittsburgh and soon met a man named George Cope, who was chairman of a United Steelworkers of America safety-and-compensation committee at a Jones & Laughlin Steel Corporation mill. During 1967 and 1968, Cope sent Henderson a number of coke-oven workers who were suffering from lung cancer as a result of their exposure to coal-tar-pitch volatiles. At that time, the Pennsylvania workmen's-compensation law for occupational disease contained a two-year statute of limitations and provided only $60 a week for total disability.

In 1971, Henderson brought a second-party lawsuit against the Allied Chemical Corporation, alleging that it had designed a defective coke oven whose door had crushed a steelworker to death, and when the case was settled out of court in 1973 for $50,000, he became interested in the possibility that product-liability law might provide the best legal route to obtain justice for the cancer-stricken workers he represented, who by then numbered thirty-five. Meanwhile, in 1972, he had acquired two steelworker clients—Andrew Carollo and Roy DeRocco—who worked as pipe coverers at the Wheeling-Pittsburgh Steel Corporation's Monessen plant and had been found to have developed early signs of asbestosis. Henderson filed workmen's-compensation claims for both men in the spring of 1973, and in the autumn he read a notice about the Borel case in the monthly newsletter of the Association of American Trial Lawyers, and set about to obtain a full copy of the Fifth Circuit's decision.

Later in 1973, Henderson met Dr. Thomas F. Mancuso, a research professor of occupational health at the University of Pittsburgh's Graduate School of Public Health. After hearing about Henderson's asbestos cases, Mancuso advised him to get in touch with Dr. Harriet L. Hardy, a well-known public-health scientist, who was assistant medical director in charge of the environmental medical services at the Massachusetts Institute of Technology. Henderson followed Mancuso's advice, and in the spring of 1974 he and Dr. Hardy had lunch at the MIT Faculty Club in Cambridge. It was a meeting that led to some astonishing disclosures.

Dr. Hardy told Henderson that during the late 1940s she had attended a symposium on occupational disease at the Trudeau Foundation's Saranac Laboratory, in Saranac Lake, New York, where animal experiments involving asbestos had been conducted since the early 1930s. At the meeting, she encountered Dr. Kenneth W. Smith, the medical director of Canadian Johns-Manville, who told her that he was concerned about a recent study showing that lung cancer was present in a high percentage of deaths caused by asbestosis among asbestos factory workers in England. Dr. Hardy said that she advised Smith to have a study of the association between lung cancer and asbestosis performed at the Harvard School of Public Health, but that Smith later told her he couldn't get permission from his superiors at Johns-Manville to do this.

In June, 1974, Henderson filed a product-liability lawsuit in behalf of Carollo and DeRocco in the Court of Common Pleas of Allegheny County against a number of leading asbestos-insulation manufacturers. Among them were Johns-Manville; Owens-Corning; Pittsburgh Corning; Eagle-Picher; and Forty-Eight Insulations, Inc., of Aurora, Illinois. During the next year, he amended the complaint to include UNARCO Industries; the Philip Carey Manufacturing Company; and the Celotex Corporation. Meanwhile, he sent out the usual interrogatories, and during the course of the discovery process he learned that Dr. Smith had retired as medical director of Johns-Manville in 1966, and was living in Windsor, Ontario.

"I called Dr. Smith at his office in Windsor late in the afternoon of November 4, 1975," Henderson recalls. "I told him that I was an attorney involved in asbestos litigation, that I was suing his former employer, and that I had talked with Harriet Hardy. Imagine my surprise when he not only proceeded to talk very cordially to me but seemed eager to answer my questions. A week later, I flew to Windsor and met with him for nearly four hours. Dr. Smith was a portly, partly bald, and cherubic-faced man of sixty-one with an easy smile and a gentle manner, and he was then engaged in rehabilitating alcoholics and in giving psychiatric counseling to students at a local university. He himself had taken early retirement from Johns-Manville because of an alcohol problem, but he told me that he had not had a drink in six years.

"He then proceeded to tell me some astonishing things that had happened during his career at Johns-Manville, which had begun in 1944. For example, he told me that in 1949 he knew that asbestosis was developing among the workers in the asbestos mines and mills Johns-Manville operated in Quebec Province. Even more important, he said that he soon became convinced that employees of Johns-Manville's insulation-purchasing customers, who worked as insulators and pipe coverers, were also at risk of developing disease. In fact, Smith said that during the early nineteen-fifties he and Hugh Jackson, Johns-Manville's corporate safety manager, had discussed whether to place warning labels on asbestos-insulation products. Smith's disclosures about what J.-M. officials knew and when they knew it were, of course, sticks of legal dynamite, and to make sure I had all the ammunition he could provide I met with him twice again, in November and December. He then agreed to come to the States and give a deposition in the case of *Carollo and DeRocco* v. *Forty-Eight Insulations Inc., et al.*, as it was called. He also furnished me with copies of letters, memos, and other documents, which clearly showed that he and other high-ranking officials of Johns-Manville had early knowledge about the hazards of asbestos and that they should have taken steps to protect the health of workers such as Carollo and DeRocco, and who had no idea that using asbestos could be harmful to them. As for Dr. Smith's motive in revealing all of this incriminating evidence, I can only tell you what I surmise. I think that his conscience was bothering him and that he wanted to set the record straight."

Up to that point, Johns-Manville and its primary product-liability-insurance carrier, the Travelers Insurance Company, had no idea that Smith had been talking to Henderson, who was careful to tell no one except his closest associates about his three trips to Windsor. In the meantime, he arranged to depose Hugh Jackson in order to pin him down under oath about just when he and Smith had first discussed placing warning labels on Johns-Manville asbestos-insulation products.

Jackson was deposed in Pittsburgh on December 17, 1975. A little more than four years earlier, he had testified under oath in *Borel* v. *Fibreboard* that until Dr. Selikoff's 1964 study he and other Johns-Manville officials had no idea that asbestos insulators might be encountering health problems as a result of their occupation. Nevertheless, when Henderson asked him if there had ever been any discussions about placing warning labels on asbestos-containing products between 1947 and 1960, he gave this reply: "If there were, it would have been toward the—and I don't know of a clear recollection, that is why I am stating it this way—if there were, it would have been toward the 1960 date rather than earlier."

"Do you recall there being these discussions?" Henderson asked.

"I can answer that with the exception of the timing of it," Jackson said cautiously. "Yes, Dr. Smith—and again I am going to put it in the time area approaching the 1960 period—had discussions."

Henderson then asked Jackson if his answer "was that sometime in the fifties approaching the 1960 year there were discussions at least between you and Dr. Smith with respect to the placement of certain warnings on packaging containing asbestos products?"

"Yes," Jackson replied.

After gaining these admissions from Jackson, Henderson announced that he would call Dr. Smith. This not only took Manville's attorneys by surprise but made them extremely nervous. In fact, one of them telephoned Henderson to say that Smith was no longer an employee of the company and probably would not consent to testify. Still, at 10:00 A.M. on January 13, 1976, Dr. Smith presented himself at the offices of Johns-Manville's attorneys, Stein & Winters, which were in the Frick Building, in downtown Pittsburgh, and the deposition got under way. To begin with, Smith testified that he had graduated from McGill University medical school, in Montreal, in 1941, and that in 1944 he became a medical officer for the Canadian Johns-Manville Company at its Jeffrey Mine—the world's largest chrysotile-asbestos mine—in the town of Asbestos, Quebec. (Chrysotile asbestos is a variety of the mineral that accounts for about 95 percent of the world's production of asbestos.) For the next two years, he worked under the direction of Dr. R. H. Stevenson, the medical director of Canadian Johns-Manville, whom he succeeded in 1946. Smith went on to say that he saw workers who were afflicted with asbestosis from almost the first day he came to work for Canadian Johns-Manville. When Henderson asked him if there had been any incidents revealing that people other than Johns-Manville employees were exposed to the hazards of asbestos, he gave an interesting reply.

"You take me back a few years, but early in my career with C.J.-M. —in say, '44 to '47—Metropolitan Life was conducting personnel studies of employees and nonemployees in Thetford and, to a lesser degree, in our town," Smith said. "And, walking through the town of Asbestos on a dry August day, you could see little rolls of asbestos fiber rolling along the street like tumbleweed, and you just assumed that anybody walking the streets—the storekeepers or policeman walking his beat, or anybody in the house—would be exposed to that airborne dust. And I can remember rather vividly Dr. Stevenson, as our senior citizen, standing at the edge of our open pit one day—"

"Your open pit being—" Henderson interrupted.

"The asbestos mine," Smith said. "We were standing on the edge of the open pit on the eastern side. The whole town of Asbestos was behind us, and, of course, the winds are constantly from the west, blowing across the mine, across the mill, and into the town. And Stevenson said, 'What a shame that the town wasn't built on that hill over there on the western side of the pit. There would have been no dust in the town.' "

"Who else was present during that statement by Dr. Stevenson?" Henderson asked.

"I believe A. R. Fisher was, as I recall it," Smith answered.

"Who was A. R. Fisher?"

"A. R. Fisher at that time was vice-president, production, for the corporation in New York," Smith said.

"This specific incident occurred, as best you can remember, about when?"

"Oh, sometime between '45 and '49. I remember that rather vividly because I picked up a piece of asbestos fiber from the rock there and was crushing it, and chrysotile fiber—you can take the fiber and crush it with your fingers like this and make a ball of wool out of it, and in so doing I had a spicule enter my finger and later developed a small tumor there."

Following the deposition, Smith furnished Henderson with the report of an industrial-hygiene survey he had conducted of 708 men who worked in dusty areas of the milling operation at Asbestos, where asbestos ore was crushed, dried, separated, packed, and shipped. Smith made the survey in 1948 and sent his report to Johns-Manville's New York headquarters early in 1949. The report said that out of the 708 workers only 4 men—all of whom had four years of exposure or less—had X-rays that showed normal, healthy lungs. On page 3, Smith described his policy toward seven workers who showed signs of early asbestosis. "It must be remembered that although these men have the X-ray evidence of asbestosis, they are working today and definitely are not disabled from asbestosis," he wrote. "They have not been told of this diagnosis for it is felt that as long as the man feels well, is happy at home and at work, and his physical condition remains good, nothing should be said. When he becomes disabled and sick, then the diagosis should be made and the claim submitted *by* the Company. The fibrosis of this disease is irreversible and permanent so that eventually compensation will be paid to each of these men. But as long as the man is not disabled it is felt that he should not be told of his condition so that he can live and work in peace and the Company can benefit by his many years of experience. Should the man be told of his condition today there is a very definite possibility that he would become mentally and physically ill, simply through the knowledge that he has asbestosis."

Smith sent this report to A. R. Fisher, who marked it for the attention of Vandiver Brown, the corporate attorney, and J. P. Woodard, who was the director of industrial relations. Six and a half years later, Fisher, who had by then become president of Johns-Manville, delivered a talk entitled "The Economics of Industrial Health," at the twentieth annual meeting of the Industrial Hygiene Foundation of America, which was held at the Mellon Institute, in Pittsburgh. "We in industry realize that as good citizens it is part of our obligation to society to help improve the health of the nation as well as the community," he told his audience. He went on to declare that during the thirty-two years he had been with Johns-Manville he had observed "the increasing interest in and the progress made by our company in the field of occupation health."

As for Dr. Smith, his conscience had apparently not yet begun to bother him. A few days after Fisher's speech, he informed a meeting of industrial-relations managers at Hot Springs, Virginia, of the ethics that should guide company doctors who diagnose disease in employees, as if he had never heard of, let alone written, the memo in which he recommended against telling the Canadian workers who had developed asbestosis of their condition. "Our plant doctors are required by the American Medical Association code of ethics, and also in many areas by civil law, to discuss the results of physical examinations with each employee as if the employee were a private patient," Smith told his listeners. "Should any physical or mental defects be noted, which if left without attention might cause disease or injury, these defects and recommended corrective procedures should be discussed with the employee so that he can take proper precautions to maintain and protect his health."

As might be expected, Dr. Smith's deposition of January 13, 1976, posed serious problems for Johns-Manville's state-of-the-art defense, which was predicated on the assertion that no one at the company could possibly have foreseen that asbestos-insulation products might pose a health hazard until Dr. Selikoff and his associates published their 1964 study of the mortality rate among insulation workers. For this reason, Henderson planned to make extensive use of the deposition and the documents in *Carollo and DeRocco* v. *Forty-Eight Insulations,* which was slated to go to trial in March. However, the proceedings were postponed when DeRocco fell ill with pneumonia and had to be hospitalized, and the case was ultimately settled out of court for $150,000. Meanwhile, Henderson had begun to hear of other lawyers who were handling asbestos lawsuits. One of them was an attorney from Knoxville, Tennessee, named Paul T. Gillenwater, of Gillenwater, Whelchel, & Roberts, who had been involved in asbestos litigation for nearly a year. Another was Robert E. Sweeney, of Sweeney, Mahon, & Vlad, in Cleveland, a former congressman-at-large from Ohio, and general counsel for the Cleveland Building and Construction Trades Council, who had filed an asbestos-product-liability lawsuit in the summer of 1973.

During 1975, Sweeney had arranged several informal discussions between fellow-lawyers who were involved in asbestos litigation, and in the spring of 1976 Gillenwater organized a formal meeting of sixteen attorneys in the field in order to share ideas and discuss tactics. The meeting was held in Atlanta, and among those attending were Gillenwater, Henderson, Sweeney, and Jon L. Gelman, then with Gelman & Gelman, of Paterson, New Jersey. Gelman & Gelman specialized in workmen's compensation, and was then representing nearly two hundred former workers from a large asbestos-products plant that had been operated by Raybestos-Manhattan, in nearby Passaic, between 1929 and 1973. This meeting and subsequent ones proved so beneficial to the participants that in 1978, they founded an organization called the Asbestos Litigation Group, which would play a tremendously influential role in directing asbestos litigation in the years to come. At the time of the Atlanta gathering, however, they were groping through unfamiliar territory and pooling their discovery resources. One of the participants was Allen Schmitt, a lawyer from Louisville, Kentucky, who represented the Louisville Trust Company, administrator of the estate of William Virgil Sampson, who had died of mesothelioma in 1972, after spending ten years working for a small fabricating company engaged in making asbestos wallboard and laboratory tabletops. As it happened, *Louisville Trust Company* v. *Johns-Manville Products Corporation* was slated to go to trial in Jefferson Circuit Court, in Louisville, within a few weeks, and since Schmitt was going up against Lively Wilson, a leading defense attorney with Stites, McElwain & Fowler, of Louisville, as well as against Dennis Markusson, who was corporate counsel for Johns-Manville, he brought Henderson into the case as co-counsel.

Since state-court rules of evidence in Kentucky, as in most other states, stipulated that a deposition could not be introduced in evidence unless all the defendants in the case were present at its taking, Henderson traveled to Windsor on April 21 to depose Dr. Smith for a second time. One of the high points came when he asked Smith whether he had ever formed an opinion that asbestos dust could pose a health hazard to people in the general population. Smith observed that "the good Lord gave us all the same breathing apparatus," and went on to say that "wherever there is dust and people are breathing dust, they are going to have a potential hazard."

Since Lively Wilson's defense in *Louisville Trust* v. *Johns-Manville* was based largely upon the state-of-the-art claim, Smith's testimony that inhaling asbestos was hazardous to anyone, not just asbestos-factory workers, played an extremely important role in the trial, which began late in April, 1976; it enabled Henderson to emphasize Johns-Manville's strict liability in his closing argument to the jury, which awarded a verdict of $90,000 to Sampson's estate. This was a major triumph for Henderson, who had not only plunged into the case on short notice but had beaten Lively Wilson, one of the best defense lawyers in the country, in Wilson's home town. The next few months were a heady time for Henderson as offers to associate himself in new cases came pouring in. During the summer and fall of 1976, he participated as co-counsel in several product-liability cases, all of which were settled out of court by the defendant manufacturers, and by the end of the year it looked as if he and the other plaintiff attorneys had Johns-Manville and the rest of the asbestos industry on the run. Their euphoria was short-lived, however, because in the autumn of 1976 Dr. Smith declined to give any further depositions, claiming that he needed more time for his private practice. Then, in August, 1977, he died, and a major weapon against the state-of-the-art defense died with him.

Lively Wilson, meanwhile, was improving this defense by placing new and effective emphasis upon a 1946 study of asbestos-insulation workers in military shipyards that had been conducted by Dr. Walter Fleischer and Professor Philip Drinker of the Harvard School of

Public Health; it concluded that asbestos pipe covering was not a hazarous occupation, and two of the defense attorneys had usd it in *Borel*. Moreover, since the whole burden of proof in strict-liability cases rested upon the plaintiff, Henderson and other plaintiff lawyers were faced with the difficult task not only of persuading jurors that the defendant companies had known of the asbestos hazard decades earlier but also of presenting complex medical evidence in a manner that would convince jurors by a preponderance of the evidence that the plaintiffs' illnesses had been caused by their exposure to asbestos. As a result, defense attorneys were able to persuade juries in several cases that came to trial after *Louisville Trust* v. *Johns-Manville* that defendant asbestos manufacturers could not have known about the health hazard to insulators before 1964. In some instances, especially in lung-cancer cases where cigarette smoking was involved, they were also able to cast doubt upon whether a plaintiff's disease had developed as a result of his exposure to asbestos. Thus, after the plaintiff lawyers had run up a string of half a dozen victories, the defense won three in the early part of 1977, and two more before the end of the year, and by the middle of 1978 the score in asbestos-product-liability lawsuits that had gone to trial stood even, at 8–8. It was now clear to Henderson and other attorneys representing sick asbestos workers that if they were going to persuade juries on a regular basis that Johns-Manville and other leading asbestos companies had early knowledge of asbestos disease, and should be held strictly liable for their failure to warn they were going to have to go in search of more ammunition.

As it happened, some important digging had already begun. Back in April, 1975, an attorney named Karl Asch had been sitting in the living room of his home, in Springfield, New Jersey, reading the 1974 annual report of Raybestos-Manhattan, of Trumbull, Connecticut—a leading manufacturer of asbestos products—when he came across a passage that startled him. A tall, bespectacled, and partly bald man in his middle forties, Asch had recently returned to private practice after a five-year stint as prosecutor of Union County. He had graduated from Columbia University in 1951, and, after time in the Army, from the law school there in 1956, and, after joining Asch & Asch, his father's firm, had become a specialist in accident and personal-injury cases, as well as in negligence suits involving industrial explosions, tire failures, food poisoning, defective escalators, and the like. However, he had never handled a case involving occupational disease until a week or so after resigning as county prosecutor, when Jerome Gelman, Jon Gelman's uncle, who was representing former employees from Raybestos-Manhattan's Passaic plant in workmen's-compensation actions, asked him if he would be interested in bringing a product-liability lawsuit in their behalf.

During the next few weeks, Asch prepared himself by studying the Borel case. He also made inquiries about Raybestos-Manhattan, and learned that it had been formed in 1929 by an industrial entrepreneur named Sumner Simpson, of Bridgeport, Connecticut. At that time, Simpson had merged his own company, the Raybestos Company, of Bridgeport, makers of asbestos brake linings and woven clutch facings, with two other companies—the Manhattan Rubber Manufacturing Company, of Passaic, makers of brake linings and friction products, and the United States Asbestos Company, of Manheim, Pennsylvania, manufacturers of asbestos-textile products. As for the Passaic plant, Asch learned that it had employed up to three thousand men during the Second World War, that a thousand men were working there when it was shut down, in June, 1973, and that very dusty conditions had prevailed during much of the forty-four years it had been operated by Raybestos-Manhattan. He was reading through the company's 1974 annual report in the hope of finding out more about its operations when he came across these paragraphs:

For many years it has been known that prolonged inhalation of asbestos dust by factory workers could lead to disease. As early as 1930, Raybestos-Manhattan commissioned the Metropolitan Life Insurance Company to survey all its factories and to make recommendations for the elimination of conditions which might present health hazards. Following presentation of the reports and recommendations, extensive long-range engineering programs were instituted at all plants to develop effective dust control systems.

In addition to pioneering in the design of engineering controls, Raybestos-Manhattan joined with other asbestos products manufacturers in the mid-1930's in funding long-range research programs on the biological effects of asbestos. Because of the long latent period of asbestos-related disease, the disease being found today among some industry employees is a result of conditions existing decades ago when little was known about the health effects of asbestos or proper means of control.

Asch could scarcely believe this self-congratulatory passage. On the one hand, he represented more than two hundred clients, many of them sick and dying, who had never once seen a warning label on any of the bags of raw asbestos they had used in the Passaic plant. On the other hand, here was the owner and operator of that very plant admitting in print that it had not only known for nearly fifty years that inhalation of asbestos dust could make these workers sick but had even commissioned studies of the problem and undertaken preventive measures. It struck Asch immediately that the health surveys, recommendations, and research programs that were mentioned in the annual report could be of immense value in the product-liability lawsuit that he was preparing in behalf of the Passaic workers.

Under New Jersey law, there was a two-year statute of limitations for filing a product-liability lawsuit, and in order to preserve the rights of a number of workers who had instituted workmen's-compensation claims in the late spring of 1973, Asch worked furiously during the latter part of April to draft a complaint. On May 6, 1975, he filed it in Federal District Court for the District of New Jersey in behalf of 286 former workers, together with the wives of those workers who were married. Among the defendants were the Johns-Manville Products Corporation; Bell Asbestos Mines, Ltd., of Thetford Mines, Quebec; Asbestos Corporation, Ltd., which was owned by General Dynamics, of St. Louis; Cassiar Asbestos Corporation, Ltd., of Vancouver, British Columbia; the Asbestos Corporation of America; and the Metropolitan Life Insurance Company. The complaint, which was entitled *Charles Lee Austin and Edna Austin* [his wife] *et al.* v. *Johns-Manville Products Corporation et al.*, charged the mining companies, all of which had sold raw asbestos to Raybestos-Manhattan, with failing to warn workers at the Passaic plant that asbestos could be harmful to their health. It also charged that Metropolitan Life had assumed a duty to provide Raybestos-Manhattan with information and instruction on how to protect the health of these employees but had negligently failed to do so.

Over the next four years, Asch filed additional complaints as more and more of the Passaic workers developed disease, and these were consolidated for purposes of discovery, until by November, 1979, there were 668 plaintiffs in the lawsuit. During the rest of 1975, he drew up and sent out the usual interrogatories, and in December, he mailed a request for production of documents to Stryker, Tams & Dill, a Newark law firm that represented Metropolitan Life, asking the carrier to produce copies of all documents and correspondence relating to the surveys of the health conditions in Raybestos-Manhattan's various plants and facilities, which it had performed during the early 1930s. In its initial response, Metropolitan Life claimed that it couldn't find the papers in question. Asch then brought a motion to compel further production in specific areas, and toward the end of 1976 the insurance company finally released a report of some surveys that had been performed for Raybestos-Manhattan during the early 1930s by Dr. Anthony J. Lanza, who had been the assistant director of its medical department. Asch was still not satisfied, however, because Metropolitan Life had not included any correspondence between it and Raybestos, so he decided to go at the problem from another angle. In February, 1977, he obtained a subpoena duces tecum, ordering William S. Simpson, who was a son of Sumner Simpson, and the chief executive officer of Raybestos-Manhattan, to give testimony at a deposition, and to bring with him all documents pertaining to working conditions at the Passaic plant, health histories and insurance records of all the workers who had been employed there since 1920, and medical records concerning any workmen's-compensation claims for occupational-health problems.

During the year and a half that had passed since his initial request for document production, Asch had come to suspect that there had been a cover-up concerning early knowledge of asbestos disease. However, he did not anticipate finding hard proof of it. "When I arrived at Raybestos-Manhattan's headquarters in Trumbull, Connecticut, on the morning of April twelfth, I didn't expect to get a lot of incriminating evidence," he recalled recently. "It was a beautiful spring day, full of sunshine and soft breezes. The headquarters building sat on a grassy knoll surrounded by tall trees, and Simpson's office was sumptuous. In addition to myself, a number of prom-inent defense lawyers were on hand. As for William Simpson, he was a silver-haired, well-tailored man of sixty, who had been president of Raybestos-Manhattan since 1967, and chief executive officer as well as chairman of the board, since 1974. The deposition started out routinely. Simpson testified that after graduating from Williams Col-lege, in 1939, he went to work as a trainee in the advertising depart-ment of Raybestos-Manhattan's Stratford plant, and that in 1953, the year his father died, he became general manager of the factory. He said that he had first visited the Passaic plant in the early nine-teen-forties, that he had made many subsequent visits over the next thirty years, and that he had never noticed any unusually dusty con-ditions there."

After lunch, which was served in the corporate cafeteria, Asch asked Simpson whether Raybestos had ever retained any independent consultants to assist it with regard to plant safety and health, and whether it had ever obtained information on asbestos disease from its insurance company. This was a key question, of course, and after conferring with his attorneys Simpson acknowledged that Dr. Leroy U. Gardner, the director of the Trudeau Foundation's Saranac Laboratory for the Study of Tuberculosis, had been retained to perform animal studies, and that studies of plant safety and health had been performed by the Metropolitan Life Insurance Company. When Asch asked where the records of these studies were kept, he was told by attorneys for Raybestos-Manhattan that a carton containing the personal papers of Sumner Simpson was in a nearby room, and that these papers included reports of the studies that Metropolitan Life had performed for Raybe-stos. Asch then resumed his questioning of William Simpson, who admitted that he had examined the file and read the Metropolitan Life reports during the early 1940s. Simpson said that after his father's death the carton had been stored in the vault at the company's head-quarters in Stratford. According to Simpson, it contained "personal documents, as I understand them, relating to my father's early work with asbestos."

Five years earlier, Johns-Manville had moved its corporate head-quarters from New York City to Denver, and during the process had apparently discarded or misplaced the correspondence that had passed between its officials and Sumner Simpson. One can only imagine how the news was greeted in Denver that this correspondence was intact at Raybestos-Manhattan and had been placed in the hands of a plaintiff attorney. As for Asch, who spent the next several days reviewing Simpson's papers, he was elated.

"I realized that I had hit pay dirt," he recalls. "Even a quick run-through of the papers told me that neither Johns-Manville nor Raybestos-Manhattan—two of the largest asbestos companies in the United States—would ever again be able to claim with any validity that they had not known about the hazards of asbestos. I was also struck by the stark contrast between what high officials of these two giant companies had known about asbestos disease more than forty years ago and the ignorance of those facts on the part of the men who had worked for them and who were now my clients. As for the defense lawyers, who were sifting through the same papers, they were all capable counsel who could not have helped realizing the profound legal significance of what they were reading. At the time, they made no comment. Later, however, some of them would refer to Sumner Simpson as an old pack rat for having tucked away all those incriminating documents. My guess is that Simpson was an ambitious and intelligent man, who realized early on that the growing knowledge of asbestos disease posed a serious threat to his corporate empire, and who set out to neutralize that threat. As for his son William, my impression of him was that he respected his father deeply, and wouldn't have dreamed of destroying any of his records, which have become universally known among asbestos litigators as the Sumner Simpson papers. Whatever you want to call them, they are collectively a smoking gun."

Among the earliest of the documents in the Sumner Simpson file are the minutes of a meeting that was held on November 28, 1933, in the office of W. R. Seigle, chairman of the board of Johns-Manville, at the company's headquarters at 22 East Fortieth Street, in Manhattan. The meeting had been called to discuss Simpson's suggestion that joint action be taken to standardize methods of dust control in asbestos factories, and among those attending it were Seigle; E. M. Voorhees, secretary of Johns-Manville; Vandiver Brown, head of the company's legal department; and Dr. Anthony Lanza, who had undertaken a health survey of the asbestos industry several years earlier, and who wanted to reexamine certain workers to whom he had given chest

X-rays at that time. Some idea of what the Johns-Manville people had in mind came in the final paragraph of the minutes of the meeting. It read, in part:

> Mr. Voorhees asked Dr. Lanza if he thought the Metropolitan Life Insurance Company would be willing to make dust counts at the various plants once or twice a year at such places and under such conditions as they might see fit for the purpose of determining progress made in improving dust conditions, Mr. Voorhees' idea being that unbiased reports of this character would be helpful to us, if favorable, in the event we should ever be involved in litigation.

On December 29, 1933, another meeting was held in Seigle's office. It was attended by Seigle, Voorhees, and Brown, and also by Sumner Simpson, and the four agreed to allow Metropolitan Life to bring its survey up to date. The minutes of the meeting said, "While it may be desirable because of changing conditions to publish the first report of the Metropolitan Life Insurance Co., our past policy of keeping this matter confidential is to be pursued and the question of publicity deferred until such time as the second report is available for our analysis."

Metropolitan Life's first report, written in 1931, was entitled "Effects of the Inhalation of Asbestos Dust Upon the Lungs of Asbestos Workers." Its authors—Dr. Lanza and two colleagues—declared in their introduction, "In 1929, the Metropolitan Life Insurance Company was approached by firms representing the asbestos industry in the United States with the request that a hygienic study be made of that industry." They went on to say that "officials representing these firms were desirous of ascertaining if asbestos dust was an occupational hazard in their establishments and, if so, what was the nature of this hazard and what should be done to prevent or control it." Lanza and his associates observed that while one or two isolated cases of asbestosis had been reported in American journals "the industry itself appeared to be quite uninformed of the existence of any such occupational disease."

Whatever their ignorance in 1929, officials of Johns-Manville and Raybestos-Manhattan did not long remain uninformed about the hazard of asbestos. Between October, 1929, and January, 1931, Dr. Lanza and his colleagues not only measured high dust levels in several of their textile plants but also took chest X-rays of 126 workers who had more than three years of employment in the industry, and found that no less than 67 of them had already developed asbestosis, and that another 39 showed some signs of it. Lanza and his colleagues concluded that "prolonged exposure to asbestos dust causes a pulmonary fibrosis of a definite type distinct from silicosis demonstrable on X-ray films," and that "clinically, it is of a type milder than silicosis." They warned that while the cases of asbestosis they had observed had not resulted in marked disability "it is possible for uncomplicated asbestosis to result fatally." And they ended their report by recommending that Johns-Manville and Raybestos-Manhattan "seriously face the problem of dust control in asbestos plants," and that employees of these factories be given periodic physical examinations and chest X-rays.

Johns-Manville and Raybestos-Manhattan had been in possession of this report for more than two years when Vandiver Brown wrote Lanza a letter acknowledging receipt of galley-proof sheets that Lanza had submitted for publication in a United States Public Health Service Report. In his letter, which was dated December 10, 1934, Brown asked Lanza to reinstate two observations that had been deleted from the original version of the report—one was the suggestion that asbestosis appeared to be a milder lung disease than silicosis—saying that both observations "presented an aspect of your survey that was favorable to the industry and we should like to see them retained." Brown also informed Lanza that he was planning to transmit the galley proofs to George S. Hobart, of the law firm of Hobart & Minard, of Newark, and would send Hobart's editorial comments to Lanza.

As it happened, twenty months earlier Hobart had helped advise Johns-Manville on how to get out of a ticklish situation involving negligence suits that had been brought by employees who had developed asbestosis while working at the company's factory in Manville, New Jersey. His advice concurred with that of attorneys at Davis, Polk, Wardwell, Gardiner & Reed, a New York City firm which handles Manville's legal affairs to this very day. The minutes of a Johns-Manville board of directors meeting held on April 24, 1933, spelled out the details:

The President advised the meeting that Messrs. Hobart & Minard of Newark had been approached by the attorney for the plaintiffs in the eleven pending "asbestosis" cases with an offer to settle all the cases upon a much lower basis than had ever been previously discussed. He further stated that our general counsel, Messrs. Davis Polk Wardwell Gardiner & Reed, as well as Messrs. Hobart & Minard, had recommended that we settle for approximately $30,000 provided written assurance were obtained from the attorney for the various plaintiffs that he would not directly or indirectly participate in the bringing of new actions against the Corporation.

Hobart sent his editorial comments on Lanza's article to Brown by letter on December 15, 1934. After telling him that he had compared Lanza's proof with Metropolitan Life's original report, Hobart said that he did not want Lanza's report to "suggest that asbestosis might be assumed to be 'similar' to silicosis," and that "it would be very helpful to have an official report to show that there is a substantial difference between asbestosis and silicosis." He also described a version of the state-of-the-art defense similar to the one that Johns-Manville would pursue when Ward Stephenson finally cornered it, some forty years later, in the federal district court in Beaumont, Texas, saying that "it is only within a comparatively recent time that asbestosis has been recognized by the medical and scientific professions as a disease" and that "one of our principal defenses in actions against the company on the common law theory of negligence has been that the scientific and medical knowledge has been insufficient until a very recent period to place upon the owners of plants or factories the burden or duty of taking special precautions against the possible onset of the disease to their employees."

On December 21, 1934, Brown sent Hobart's editorial suggestions to Lanza with a plea for consideration. "I am sure that you understand fully that no one in our organization is suggesting for a moment that you alter by one jot or tittle any scientific facts or inevitable conclusions revealed or justified by your preliminary survey," he wrote. "All we ask is that all of the favorable aspects of the survey be included and that none of the unfavorable be unintentionally pictured in darker tones than the circumstances justify. I feel confident we can depend upon you . . . to give us this 'break' and mine and Mr. Hobart's suggestions are presented in this spirit."

When the United States Public Health Service published the Metropolitan Life study, on January 4, 1935, it was apparent that Dr. Lanza had accepted many of Hobart's editorial suggestions. By that time, Lanza had become a leading figure in the field of occupational medicine. Born in New York City, he had received his medical degree from George Washington University in 1906 and had then joined the United States Public Health Service. In 1914 and 1915, he helped to direct a study of silicosis among the lead and zinc miners of Missouri, and in 1926 he went to work for Metropolitan Life. In 1935, he discussed his survey of asbestos mines and asbestos-textile mills before the eighty-sixth Annual Session of the American Medical Association in Atlantic City, and took pains to point out that "the clinical picture of asbestosis was milder than that of silicosis." He also predicted that "asbestos plants are being cleaned up and the dust is being controlled."

Lanza later wrote a revealing chapter on pulmonary dust disease for a book entitled *Silicosis and Asbestosis,* which was published in 1938 by Oxford University Press. "Silicosis and asbestosis burst upon the amazed consciousness of American industry during the period 1929–1930," he stated at the outset. He went on, "Arising out of the period of economic depression, the situation with respect to silicosis and asbestosis became manifest as a medicolegal phenomenon of a scope and intensity that was at once preposterous and almost unbelievable," adding that "Damage suits, under the common law, were instituted against employers by employees, alleging pulmonary dust diseases, in industrial centers all over the United States, to an amount in excess of 100,000,000 dollars." After describing how this situation led to the modification of existing compensation laws to include pulmonary dust diseases, Lanza declared that the harsh restrictions that were built into them—for example, a limit of $3,000 for permanent disability or death in New York State and a limit of $3,600 in Pennsylvania—did not reflect "a desire to deprive working men of their just dues but a feeling that it was necessary to place a drastic check on the expected avalanche of silicotic claims." He went on to explain that the damage suits "confused and terrified industrialists and insurance officials," and inspired "dread" among them. Lanza was undoubtedly speaking with authority, because during this same period he was helping Johns-Manville and Raybestos-Manhattan defend against claims for damages that were being brought against them by employees who were afflicted with asbestosis. After World War II, he left Metropolitan Life to become professor of industrial medicine at New York University Medical Center, and shortly before his death at the age of eighty, in 1964, the university renamed its laboratories at Sterling Forest the Anthony J. Lanza Research Laboratories for Environmental Medicine.

On September 25, 1935, Miss A. S. Rossiter, the editor of an industry trade magazine called *Asbestos,* which was published in Philadelphia, wrote a letter to Sumner Simpson. It began:

> Dear Sir:
> You may recall that we have written you on several occasions concerning the publishing of information, or discussion of, asbestosis and the work which has been, and is being done, to eliminate or at least reduce it.
> Always, you have requested that for certain obvious reasons we publish nothing, and, naturally, your wishes have been respected.
> Possibly by this time, however, the reasons for your objection to publicity on this subject have been eliminated, and if so, we would like very much to review the whole matter in *Asbestos.*

On October 1, Simpson sent a copy of Miss Rossiter's letter to Vandiver Brown along with some thoughts of his own on the matter. "As I see it personally, we would be just as well off to say nothing about it until our survey is complete," Simpson wrote. "I think the less said about asbestos, the better off we are, but at the same time, we cannot lose track of the fact that there have been a number of articles on asbestos dust control and asbestosis in the British trade magazines. The magazine *Asbestos* is in business to publish articles affecting the trade and they have been very decent about not re-printing the English articles."

Two days later, Brown wrote in reply to Simpson's suggestions, "I quite agree with you that our interests are best served by having asbestosis receive the minimum of publicity." It is obvious that Miss Rossiter was persuaded to continue to be "decent" about the matter, because in the early spring of 1939 she wrote Simpson that she understood that all information on asbestosis was to be kept confidential and that "nothing should be published about asbestosis in *Asbestos* at present." Apparently she continued to be troubled by the subject, however, for in June, 1943, she sent Simpson a copy of a letter that had been written by a man named Elliot DeForest, who was secretary of an insulation-industry trade organization in Seattle, to the supervisor of safety for the Washington State Department of Labor and Industries. DeForest was protesting the promulgation of a new safety standard for asbestos-containing products, which had occurred because of reports from England that asbestos could cause asbestosis. "We feel that if such a so-called disease were advertised to the general public, and our workmen in particular, that it would give them an excuse upon which to place claims for all sorts of allied ailments and our particular industry would be unduly burdened by such parasites," DeForest wrote. He went on to say that "this foreign disease . . . should be left in Europe where it belongs and not brought to our local communities and create hysteria and fear amongst the families of our contented workmen who are now enjoying good health and living to a ripe old age."

In her covering letter to Simpson, Miss Rossiter suggested that "perhaps you might like to contact Mr. DeForest on the subject." Simpson forwarded the letters to Brown, who wrote back within a few days to let Simpson know what he thought about the matter. "I am inclined to let Mr. DeForest learn the facts of life and asbestosis from the State of Washington Department of Labor and Industries," he said.

It was one thing, of course, for the two giants of the asbestos industry to censor the contents of an industry trade journal and quite another for them to deal with the growing number of negligence lawsuits that were being brought in the mid-1930s as more and more American workers began to develop asbestosis. Some idea of how worrisome this litigation was can be seen in a letter that Simpson wrote on October 19, 1935, to Dr. William J. McConnell, who had become director of Metropolitan Life's industrial health section. In the letter Simpson complained bitterly about a recent decision by Metropolitan Life not to allow one of its officials to testify for Raybestos in some asbestosis lawsuits that had been brought by workers at the company's textile plant in North Charleston, South Carolina. He told McConnell that he had been led to believe that "we would have your assistance in trying these unfair suits, which would eventually be a benefit to you, and also have considerable bearing on the Dust racket, about which so much has been published lately," and he threatened to take the matter up with the president of Metropolitan Life.

McConnell wrote back a few days later to assure Simpson that "arrangements had been made to assist your company in the present litigation," but the public furor over the Gauley Bridge disaster, which erupted during the winter of 1936, encouraged the bringing of more lawsuits, and by the autumn of that year Simpson was writing letter after letter in a desperate attempt to control a situation that he obviously feared was getting out of hand. Some idea of his mood can be gained from a letter he wrote to E. H. Jeffords, general manager of Raybestos-Manhattan's plant in North Charleston, South Carolina, on November 5, 1936, concerning a request by Dr. Lanza that the United States Public Health Service be allowed to take chest X-rays of employees at the plant in connection with a health survey of asbestos-textile factories. Simpson told Jeffords that "you may advise the Public Health Service that they may take the pictures, with the understanding that they are not available for any purpose whatever except public health information, and you want to stress the fact that we do not want them given to shyster lawyers and doctors so as to be the subject of suits, for, as you know, we have had enough adjustments for any one company."

On November 20, 1936, Vandiver Brown wrote to Dr. Leroy Gardner, director of the Saranac Laboratory, informing him that he and Simpson had interested eight or ten asbestos-products manufacturers in financing his animal experiments on asbestosis for a three-year period at a cost of $5,000 a year. Brown told Gardner that "the results obtained will be considered the property of those who are advancing the required funds, who will determine whether, to what extent and in what manner they shall be made public," and added, "In the event it is deemed desirable that the results be made public, the manuscript of your study will be submitted to us for approval prior to publication." On November 23, Gardner sent Brown a letter saying, "The Saranac Laboratory agrees that the results of these studies shall become the property of the contributors and that the manuscripts of any reports shall be submitted for approval of the contributors before publication." Over the next decade, Dr. Gardner honored the bargain of silence he had entered into, but apparently with some misgivings, for not long before he died in October, 1946, he sorrowfully told Dr. Harriet Hardy that because of an agreement he had signed with Johns-Manville he was unable to publish the findings of his experiments, even though many of the test animals that he was exposing to asbestos dust were suffering from pulmonary dust disease.

Back in the tense autumn of 1936, two weeks after Gardner had made his pact with Brown, Simpson received a letter from George S. Fabel, president of the Southern Asbestos Company, of Charlotte, North Carolina, telling him about a number of asbestosis lawsuits that had been brought against his company. Fabel's reaction to publicity about asbestosis was even stronger than Simpson's, as can be seen in a letter he had written to the editor of the Philadelphia *Record,* about what he thought of an article that had appeared in the newspaper in August, 1935; the article, which was written by John L. Spivak, who had described the suffering of workers in asbestos mills in the South. Fabel declared that Spivak's piece was "unconfirmed dramatized tommyrot," and that its "tear-jerking" style made him furious. He went on to say that competent doctors testifying in court trials and insurance examinations had not substantiated Spivak's claim that people working in textile mills had been known to contract asbestosis within eighteen months.

Spivak replied to Fabel's charges in a letter to the editor which was published in an adjacent column. "Obviously, if such testimony was given at court trials, then persons suffering from asbestosis were seeking compensation which had been denied them, for injuries they claimed resulted from their work," he wrote. "It is to be regretted that Mr. Fabel did not see fit to tell for which side the competent doctors he mentions gave their testimony. Were they not doctors paid by the asbestos mill to defend the claims against it?" Spivak pointed out that insurance companies had known about the asbestos hazard for many years. As evidence of this, he cited a paper on working conditions in asbestos-textile mills that had been delivered by officials of the Penn Mutual Life Insurance Company, of Philadelphia, at an intercompany occupational rating conference that was held at the home office of the John Hancock Mutual Life Insurance Company, in Boston, in May of

1928. After quoting from three reports on pulmonary asbestosis among asbestos-textile workers that had appeared in the *British Medical Journal*, the Penn Mutual officials advised their colleagues that "until we have the benefit of our experience with this class of workers, we should continue to look upon those who may be exposed to large quantities of dust . . . as risks to be selected with great care and only at an extra premium that will provide for an estimated extra mortality of 50 per cent, disability not to be granted."

Thus did the officials of leading life-insurance companies consider, in 1928, how to protect their profit on the estimated early death of asbestos-textile workers. A year later, the Metropolitan Life Insurance Company, the nation's largest life-insurance carrier, undertook a survey of health conditions in asbestos-textile mills, which showed that a serious health hazard existed in these factories—a finding that did not deter Metropolitan Life from allowing Johns-Manville attorneys to edit and partially water down the report of this survey prior to its belated publication, in 1935. By then, of course, the Depression was in full swing, and the attention of most Americans was on the need for jobs, not on job health. Within a few years, the nation's attention would be almost totally absorbed by the war effort, and the economic boom that accompanied it. By 1942, owing largely to these circumstances and to the efforts of Simpson and Brown to keep knowledge of the asbestos hazard from being made public—efforts that were not hindered by any of the insurance companies in the United States—the first asbestos litigation crisis had disappeared. Many states had already amended their workmen's-compensation statutes to take away the right of workers afflicted with asbestosis to bring suit against their employers under the common law. As a result, during the late 1930s and early 1940s, Raybestos-Manhattan and its workmen's-compensation insurance carriers were able to settle dozens of asbestosis claims at an average of only a few thousand dollars apiece. Meanwhile, public concern over the plight of asbestos-factory workers had dwindled, and in spite of warnings from a few pioneer scientists, the vast majority of the members of the medical profession chose, through apathy, to look the other way. Millions of unsuspecting American workers—four and a half million men and women in the wartime shipyards alone—were left to undergo exposure to dangerously high levels of asbestos dust as they applied insulation products made by Johns-Manville, Raybestos-Manhattan, and other asbestos manufacturers to high-temperature pipes in the holds of vessels, and to pipes and boilers in power plants, oil refineries, and other installations, or as they worked at trades in close proximity to such operations. Because of the long latent period for the development of asbestos disease, and the laborious turning of the wheels of justice, the whole ghastly story now began all over again, as if it were the replay of a disaster film whose reel had been rewound and started up in slow motion. Twenty years would pass before Claude Tomplait would seek the help of Ward Stephenson. Thirty years would pass before Stephenson would win the landmark decision in *Borel*. And not for forty years would the Johns-Manville Corporation—by then it was called Manville Corporation—feel compelled to file for protection under Chapter 11 of the federal Bankruptcy Code in order to stay the 16,500 claims that had been brought against it by workers who had needlessly sickened or died as a result of exposure to its products, and to avoid standing trial in the tens upon tens of thousands of similar lawsuits that could be expected in the future.

As things turned out, Karl Asch never got the chance to introduce Sumner Simpson's papers in evidence in *Austin* v. *Johns-Manville*, because the case was settled out of court early in 1981 for $15.5 million. By then, Metropolitan Life had been dismissed as a defendant in 268 of the cases, on the ground that the plaintiffs had failed to provide responsive answers to its interrogatories, and the presiding judge had ordered the cases to be tried four at a time. At that point, Stanley Levy, a trial specialist experienced in handling multiplaintiff litigation, who was with the New York firm of Kreindler & Kreindler and was handling some two hundred lawsuits that had been brought against Johns-Manville and other asbestos manufacturers by workers engaged in building nuclear submarines at the Electric Boat Division of the General Dynamics Corporation, in Groton, Connecticut, had been brought into the case as co-counsel. Under the terms of the agreement, the $15.5 million was placed in an interest-bearing account, and two retired state court judges, who were appointed as special masters by Judge Harold A. Ackerman, who was presiding over *Austin* v. *Johns-Manville* in federal district court, spent the next six months reviewing the cases of the 683 plaintiffs who had by then brought suit, and evaluating what each of them would be worth if it came to trial. This was an immensely complicated undertaking, requiring the special masters to assess each plaintiff's medical record, as well as his or her financial and family history, and it is to their great credit that when they finished their task only 3 out of the 683 plaintiffs objected to the share they had been allotted. By that time, because of the accrued interest, the pot amounted to some $18 million. After Gelman, Asch, and Levy received their one-third contingent fees, this sum was reduced to about $12 million, which was allotted among the 683 plaintiffs in payments that ranged from $1,250 to over $200,000.

In addition, most of the Passaic workers were awarded compensation for asbestosis by the New Jersey Department of Labor's Division of Worker's Compensation, but Raybestos-Manhattan proceeded to enforce a provision of a "sweetheart" contract that had previously been negotiated by the workers' union representatives, which provided for reducing a retiree's pension benefits by an amount equal to any workmen's-compensation award he was eligible for. At that point, one of the employees brought suit in New Jersey state court challenging the validity of this pension-offset provision, and when the suit was removed to federal district court the judge held that it was invalid. The Court of Appeals for the Third Circuit reversed this decision, however, and in May, 1981 the United States Supreme Court unanimously upheld the appeals court ruling, declaring that the state law could not supersede federal law, which permits offsets of pension benefits based upon workmen's-compensation awards. As a result, Raybestos-Manhattan, which was self-insured at the time, was able to pay very little workmen's compensation for the irreversible lung disease afflicting workers who had toiled in the company's Passaic factory. Moreover, Raybestos went into court and filed a lien on the $15.5-million settlement in *Austin* v. *Johns-Manville,* claiming that it was entitled to additional reimbursement under a provision of the New Jersey Workers' Compensation Act, which stated that in the event that an injured employee received from a third party or his insurance carrier an amount equivalent to or greater than the liability of the employer or his carrier, the employer or his insurance carrier shall be released from liability and reimbursed. At this point, some of the beleaguered Passaic workers, represented by Jon Gelman, challenged Raybestos-Manhattan's position before Judge Ackerman. In September, 1982, a magistrate appointed by Ackerman recommended that the company be reimbursed only once—either as a pension-benefit offset or as a lien

—and referred the matter to the New Jersey Division of Workers' Compensation. Before the issue could be litigated, however, Raybestos settled out of court to the advantage of the plaintiffs.

Thus ended the legal saga of the Passaic asbestos workers. Their plight and their bleak future have probably been forgotten by most of their fellow-citizens in Passaic and the surrounding communities. Yet they and other factory workers were engaged in manufacturing products, such as brake linings, insulation, and acoustical-ceiling tiles, that, because they were sold and used throughout the land—acoustical-ceiling tiles have found their way into thousands of school buildings—have become a source of continuing exposure to asbestos for the general population. It is ironic but not surprising, therefore, that in January, 1983, Gelman's seven-year-old son, Michael, brought home a snowman that he had fashioned in his first-grade class at the Lafayette elementary school, in Wayne, from a product called Fibro-Clay —a modeling compound manufactured by the Milton Bradley Company between 1967 and 1975—which consisted of a white powder that made a claylike substance when it was mixed with water. Suspicious because the snowman kept flaking into fibers, Gelman sent a sample of the substance to Dr. Selikoff at Mount Sinai, who, after having it tested, informed Gelman that it contained approximately 50 percent asbestos in a highly respirable form. A subsequent check determined that Fibro-Clay had been used in the Lafayette school for seven years, and that it had also been used in schools in Passaic, Passaic Valley, Prospect Park, East Rutherford, Oakland, New Milford, and Paramus. No one knows the extent of the potential health hazard that has been encountered by the hundreds of children who used the compound in classrooms in this one area alone, but Dr. Selikoff believes that it could carry a significant risk, because, as he puts it, "asbestos fibers, once inhaled, remain in the lungs for life, and even relatively brief exposure to the mineral can cause lung disease twenty to thirty years down the road." As for exposures to asbestos in schools nationwide, the Environmental Protection Agency has estimated that as many as 15 million students may be attending schools with asbestos-containing ceiling panels and other exposed asbestos surfaces, and that 1.2 million teachers and other school employees may also be undergoing daily exposure to the mineral.

. . .

While Karl Asch was unearthing the Sumner Simpson papers, in the spring of 1977, Gene Locks, of Greitzer & Locks, in Philadelphia, who represented about a hundred asbestos insulators from the Norfolk Naval Shipyard, the Newport News Shipbuilding & Dry Dock Company, and the Philadelphia Naval Shipyard, was also working hard to pry loose evidence of early knowledge on the part of asbestos manufacturers that their products were harmful. A heavyset, aggressive lawyer of forty, Locks had received his law degree from Columbia University School of Law in 1962 and had started a personal-injury and workmen's-compensation practice in Philadelphia. In 1976, he was engaged in pretrial discovery in an asbestos case, when he learned that several of the leading manufacturers of asbestos insulation had been members of the Asbestos Textile Institute—a trade association that had been formed in 1944. Upon subpoenaing the records of the institute's meetings, which were stored at its headquarters in nearby Willow Grove, Locks came into possession of some papers that have come to be known as the ATI minutes. They furnished compelling evidence of early knowledge of the asbestos disease hazard on the part of the institute's members, which in 1946 included Johns-Manville; Raybestos-Manhattan; the Union Asbestos & Rubber Company; the Carolina Asbestos Company, of Davidson, North Carolina; the Philadelphia Asbestos Company, of Philadelphia; the Keasbey & Mattison Company, of Ambler, Pennsylvania; and the Southern Asbestos Company, which was regularly represented at the meetings by its president, George S. Fabel.

Early ATI minutes describe a September, 1946, meeting at which members of the institute's dust control committee agreed that arrangements should be made for the Industrial Hygiene Foundation of America to conduct a survey of dust conditions in asbestos-textile plants. In June, 1947, W. C. L. Hemeon, the foundation's chief engineer, presented the findings of a preliminary survey he had conducted in these factories, and recommended that a program for dust control and medical surveillance be inaugurated. However, by June, 1948, the members of the institute's air hygiene committee—a new name for the dust control committee—were entertaining second thoughts about the wisdom of implementing Hemeon's recommendations, and the program he had urged upon them was put permanently on the shelf. The actual report of Hemeon's survey would not turn up until the summer of

1978, and would be regarded by many attorneys as one of the most incriminating documents ever found in the asbestos litigation.

In April, 1949, ATI members who met in Chicago discussed an article that had been published in *Scientific American,* which they felt "unjustifiably incriminated asbestos as a carcinogenic material." By October, 1952, the members of the air hygiene committee were warning that "the suspect relation of asbestos to cancer is a matter receiving the attention of Compensation Commissions and is of great importance to Institute members." Two years later, physicians employed by the member companies—among them Dr. Smith, the medical director of Johns-Manville—were told by Dr. Gerrit W. H. Schepers, the medical director of the Saranac Laboratory, that the West German government had recognized asbestos as a cause of lung cancer and that a recent British study had shown that the incidence of lung cancer in workers with asbestosis was ten times that of lung cancer in workers who had developed silicosis. According to the minutes of this meeting, Schepers "suggested that particles of asbestos be inserted in animal lungs in order that research be done on this problem [cancer and asbestosis] so that facts may be determined to combat unjust compensation claims."

At a meeting held in March, 1955, members of the air hygiene committee decided to delay a decision on Schepers's proposed study until an additional proposal could be obtained from another research agency. Six months later, Ivan Sabourin, general counsel for the Quebec Asbestos Mining Association, of which Johns-Manville was a leading member, warned them that the relationship of cancer to asbestos exposure posed a major health problem for the asbestos industry. In March, 1956, the members of the air hygiene committee were addressed by Dr. Smith, who was disturbed by the fact that a referee of the Pennsylvania State Compensation Board had just issued a finding of "Asbestosis-Cancer" in a workmen's-compensation case. In doing so, the referee had quoted from a report written by Dr. Wilhelm C. Hueper, chief of the environmental-cancer section at the National Cancer Institute, who had declared not only that all workers in the asbestos industry were susceptible to developing asbestosis-cancer but also that the disease might be discovered in people who merely lived in the vicinity of asbestos factories. Smith strongly recommended that the ATI engage the Industrial Hygiene Foundation to study the relationship between the two diseases in order to "combat current derogatory literature now being circulated throughout the United States and Canada."

The next day, ATI's board of governors announced the appropriation of sufficient funds to initiate a preliminary survey that was designed to "investigate the possibility of more concerted action designed to refute the work of Dr. Hueper." A year later, however, six of the eight members of the institute's new air hygiene and manufacturing committee voted against going ahead with the study, pointing out that the Quebec Asbestos Mining Association was financing a similar investigation, and that "There is a feeling among certain members that such an investigation would stir up a hornet's nest and put the whole industry under suspicion."

As for the study being financed by the Quebec Asbestos Mining Association, it was entitled "An Epidemiological Study of Lung Cancer in Asbestos Miners," and was conducted during 1956 and 1957 by Dr. Daniel C. Braun, the medical director of the Industrial Hygiene Foundation, and T. David Truan, one of the foundation's statistical consultants. It was then carefully reviewed by Dr. Smith, who told Sabourin that he had "noted deletion of all references to the association of asbestosis and lung cancer," and that "Dr. Braun and his staff are to be congratulated heartily for this very valuable contribution to our medical knowledge." An expurgated version of the Braun-Truan study appeared in June, 1958, in the American Medical Association's *Archives of Industrial Health.* Among the deletions was an entire section entitled "Asbestosis and Lung Cancer."

Over the next few years, Dr. Smith continued to advocate the suppression of reports about the health hazards of asbestos. At a meeting of the air hygiene and manufacturing committee held in September, 1961, he urged that "irresponsible reporting" in the medical literature "be eliminated to avoid the high cost of compensation and product-liability litigation." As for the officials of the asbestos industry who listened to this kind of talk, they appeared to believe that they would be able to continue the thirty-year-old coverup of the asbestos hazard indefinitely. On October 8, 1964, at a meeting at the Barbizon-Plaza Hotel in New York City, the ATI's board of governors held a long discussion about how to combat unfavorable publicity concerning asbestos exposure and cancer which had been created by Dr. Selikoff prior to the international Conference on the Biological

Effects of Asbestos, which was to be held later that month under the auspices of the New York Academy of Sciences. A few weeks later, Cadwalader, Wickersham & Taft, the institute's law firm, sent a letter urging caution in the public disclosure of information about the connection between asbestos and mesothelioma to the executive director of the academy, Mrs. Eunice Thomas Miner. She rejected it out of hand.

In the summer of 1977, Locks was able to use the newly discovered ATI minutes to good advantage in settling a number of cases involving shipyard workers who had been exposed to insulation products manufactured by Johns-Manville and other members of the institute. He also sent the documents to a number of his colleagues. Among them was Paul T. Gillenwater, of Knoxville, who was happy to get his hands on the ATI minutes because he had lost the first asbestos case he had ever tried, a few months earlier, when the presiding judge refused to allow him to introduce the Smith deposition as evidence, on the ground that one of the defendants had not been present when it was taken. The son of a poultry wholesaler, Gillenwater was born in Knoxville in 1932, and graduated from high school there in 1950. After spending two years with an advertising agency, he joined the Navy, and upon his discharge, in 1954, he got married and went to the University of Tennessee, in Knoxville, where he studied business administration. He then entered the University of Tennessee College of Law and obtained his law degree in 1958. In 1961, he opened a law office in Knoxville and began to specialize in personal-injury and automobile-accident cases. Over the next ten years, he tried a number of product-liability lawsuits involving defectively constructed cars, transformers, and the like, but he had never been involved in a product-liability case involving occupational disease until the spring of 1975, when an asbestos insulator in his early thirties named Thomas Daniels, who had spent much of his ten years in the trade working in power plants that were being built for the Tennessee Valley Authority, walked into his office complaining of lung problems. After listening to Daniels, Gillenwater, who had never heard of asbestosis, turned him over to a young lawyer named Arthur Roberts, Jr., who handled the firm's workmen's-compensation cases.

"I gave Daniels to Roberts because I detest the whole compensation system," Gillenwater said recently as he sat in his unprepossessing office, in a one-story brick building in West Knoxville. "Here in Tennessee, as in most states, the manufacturers and the insurance companies have always controlled how the compensation statutes were written, and for this reason the deck has always been stacked against the worker. So when Tommy Daniels came into my office with what seemed like a clear-cut workmen's-comp complaint, I turned him over to young Roberts, who, as a matter of course, thumbed through the *American Law Reporter*—a digest of court cases—to see if there might be a third-party lawsuit in the making. And, lo and behold, Roberts came across the *Borel* decision and got all excited, and came back to me with the idea of suing the manufacturer of the insulation materials that Daniels had used. After reading *Borel* myself, I called down to Ward Stephenson's office, in Orange, Texas, found out he had died, and talked to Marlin Thompson, who told me which insulation companies to sue, and in June of 1975 I filed a product-liability lawsuit in Daniels's behalf in federal district court against Johns-Manville and some other manufacturers. The newspapers picked up on the story and gave it a lot of publicity, and before I knew it I had ten insulator clients who were suffering from asbestosis. Like Daniels, all of them were union men who had worked for the Brooks-Fisher insulation company, an Atlanta-based firm that sold insulation products for Johns-Manville. Brooks-Fisher had come up here in the late nineteen-forties, when the government was building the atomic-bomb-manufacturing facility out at Oak Ridge, and by crazy coincidence my wife, Dorothy, had worked as a secretary for the company back in the fifties, not long after we got married. In fact, I remember that her little green Volkswagen used to be covered with white asbestos dust when I would go over there to pick her up."

In the autumn of 1975, Gillenwater took on a client named Jakie Starnes, an insulator who had developed early signs of asbestosis, and whose father had died of asbestosis and lung cancer. "Jakie Starnes was then in his early thirties and, like his father and Tommy Daniels and most of the other insulators in East Tennessee, he had been exposed to asbestos while insulating thousands upon thousands of feet of high-temperature pipe in steam plants and power dams of the Tennessee Valley Authority," Gillenwater said. "In the winter of 1976, I filed a lawsuit for him in federal district court, in Greeneville —about seventy miles east of here—against Johns-Manville, Owens-

Corning, Owens-Illinois, Fibreboard, Celotex, and the Rock Wool Manufacturing Company, of Leeds, Alabama, a company that made asbestos-cement products. In the spring, I got my hands on the Smith and Jackson depositions that had been taken by Tom Henderson, and over the next few months, all of the defendants in the Starnes case except Rock Wool offered to settle. However, Starnes refused to settle with Johns-Manville, because he blamed the company for his father's death, so the case against Johns-Manville and Rock Wool Manufacturing went forward. In September, the presiding judge ruled that we couldn't introduce Henderson's Smith or Jackson depositions into the case because Rock Wool had not been present when they were taken. At that point, I went out to Denver and deposed Jackson, who was equivocal about whether he and Dr. Smith had held discussions about placing warnings on asbestos-insulation products. I then made arrangements to take Dr. Smith's deposition on October twentieth at a Holiday Inn, in Detroit. On October eighteenth, however, Smith telephoned me to say that he would not be coming. He told me he had received a telephone call 'from out West,' as he put it, warning him not to cross the Canadian border. On November second, he wrote me a letter saying that he couldn't testify anymore because he needed to devote more time to his private practice. Whatever the case, with Smith unwilling to testify, my ammunition was seriously depleted."

When Starnes came to trial, in February, 1977, the defense lawyer, Dennis Markusson, the Johns-Manville corporate counsel, erected the familiar state-of-the-art defense, claiming that while the company knew that asbestos was harmful to factory workers as far back as the 1930s, it did not know that asbestos was a hazard for insulators until the pioneering epidemiology of Dr. Selikoff and his colleagues was published in 1964. His chief witness was Dr. Paul Kotin, who was Johns-Manville's medical director and senior vice-president for health, safety, and environment. Before joining the company, in 1974, Kotin had been dean of the Medical School at Temple University, in Philadelphia, and before that he had held high government posts as scientific director of the National Cancer Institute and founding director of the National Institute of Environmental Health Sciences at Research Triangle Park, North Carolina. A gray-haired, soft-spoken, and loquacious man of sixty, he testified with the authority of a physician and trained pathologist who had been in positions of considerable responsibility, and he made an effective case for Johns-Manville by pointing out that the 1946 Fleischer-Drinker study of shipyard workers, which had concluded that asbestos pipe covering was not a hazardous occupation, had been universally accepted by the medical community. Kotin went on to declare that judging the validity of their conclusion in retrospect was tantamount to Monday-morning quarterbacking.

During cross-examination, Gillenwater asked Kotin whether Johns-Manville should have known that inhalation of dust from its asbestos products would pose a health hazard for insulators and issued warnings to that effect. Kotin responded by saying that the company had no more responsibility for doing so "than the Bayer corporation has for going into my home when I take an aspirin." He declared that just because the liquor industry made liquor available it could not be held culpable for the fact that people will drive while drunk, and he went on to suggest that the same analogy should apply to Johns-Manville as a supplier of asbestos products in the workplace.

The Starnes trial ended with the jury's acquitting Johns-Manville and Rock Wool of any liability, and in November, 1977, the Daniels trial, which involved only Johns-Manville, ended in similar fashion. In assessing these verdicts, Gillenwater points out that both plaintiffs were men in their thirties who were still working and earning a living, and maintains that the jurors simply did not believe that they were sick. "Let me tell you, those two trials were an eyeopener for me," he says. "They made me realize that we were going to be in big trouble if we continued trying cases of early asbestosis on the basis of the evidence we had. As things stood, we had little or no choice about going to trial in such cases, because health-surveillance programs being undertaken for the Asbestos Workers union by Dr. Selikoff and other physicians were turning up X-ray evidence of early fibrosis, which automatically triggered the running of the statute of limitations in most states. The only solution was to go out and dig up more evidence that insulation manufacturers had early knowledge of the asbestos hazard—especially the hazard for insulators—and to present it in a way that would be convincing to juries. This was a tall order, of course. It meant that we plaintiff lawyers were going to have to spend a lot more time and money investigating what the asbestos companies had done in the past. It also meant that we were going to have to get lucky."

As things turned out, Gillenwater would contribute greatly to this effort by looking into the contract-unit companies that had been set up in the 1930s and '40s by Johns-Manville, Armstrong Cork, Fibre-board, Owens-Corning, Philip Carey, and other asbestos-insulation manufacturers in order to bid on large insulation jobs in shipyards, power plants, and oil refineries. "In 1976, I learned that the Brooks-Fisher insulation company—the firm for which my wife had worked back in the nineteen-fifties—had been bought by Johns-Manville," he said. "Then I found out that Johns-Manville and other insulation manufacturers had had contract units for years. At first, I didn't realize their significance. Then, after I lost the Daniels case, it occurred to me that some of the insulators who had worked for these contract units must have developed asbestosis and filed workmen's-compensation claims for disability. If that was so, Johns-Manville and the other insulation manufacturers who owned the contract units must have known for many years that their products were making insulators sick. And if *that* was so it would deal a heavy blow to the state-of-the-art defense, which was built upon the claim that they knew no such thing until 1964. Of course, everything hinged on whether we could actually locate some contract-unit disease claims. And that's where we got lucky, because in January of 1978 a young lawyer we knew in South Carolina dug one up by searching through the *Decennial Digest*—a listing that is compiled every ten years of all cases that have been appealed. It was the workmen's-compensation claim of an asbestos insulator who had developed asbestosis in the late nineteen-forties as a result of working for a contract unit of the Armstrong Cork Company, and it was our first really big break."

FIVE

A TURN
IN THE TIDE

In the spring of 1976, Gillenwater and his law partner, Ward Whelchel, had found themselves representing plaintiffs in three asbestosis cases they could not file in Tennessee, because of the state's one-year statute of limitations. Since their clients had once worked at a nuclear-power plant near Aiken, South Carolina, Gillenwater and Whelchel referred the cases to a thirty-one-year-old trial lawyer named Ronald Motley, who had made a reputation specializing in product-liability actions in South Carolina, where there was a six-year statute of limitations. The son of a service-station owner, Motley had been born and brought up in a blue-collar section of North Charleston. He went to college at the University of South Carolina, in Columbia, and in 1971 he received his law degree from the law school there. He then spent two years as a clerk for the United States District Judge Solomon Blatt, Jr., in Charleston, and later practiced part time with a plaintiff lawyer who specialized in personal-injury cases. In 1975, he joined Blatt & Fales, a small but highly regarded law firm in Barnwell—a town of about five thousand inhabitants in the farming region just south of Aiken—whose founder and senior partner, Solomon Blatt, was Judge Blatt's father, the Speaker of the South Carolina House of Representatives and a legendary plaintiff lawyer in a state that had been famous for plaintiff lawyers since the days of John C. Calhoun.

Ambitious, assertive, and self-confident, Motley is a lanky, black-haired man who bears a resemblance to the French actor Jean-Paul Belmondo and speaks with a deep drawl. He soon made a name for himself at Blatt & Fales by bringing in several sizable settlements in product-liability cases—the largest was a settlement for a case involving a defective heater that killed some children—and by 1976, when Gillenwater and Whelchel referred their asbestos cases to him, he was lecturing on product-liability law around the state, and would soon be elected president (the youngest ever) of the South Carolina Trial Law-yers Association.

"I filed my first asbestos case in June of 1976 in federal court in Charleston, and settled it for more than a hundred thousand dollars a year and a half later," Motley remembers. "That got a lot of publicity in the press, and I started getting calls from union lawyers in other parts of the state, as well as in Georgia and North Carolina. Before the summer was over, Terry Richardson—a partner of mine at Blatt & Fales—and I had been referred into seventeen cases, which we later settled for sums ranging from about fifty thousand to about two hundred and fifty thousand dollars. Then, in November of 1977, I tried my first case and came a cropper. The plaintiff was a nonunion asbestos insulator named William Baumgardner, who had developed asbestosis, and the trial was held in federal district court in Aiken. Among the defendants were Johns-Manville, Raybestos-Manhattan, and Owens-Corning. By that time, I had not only the Smith deposition but also the minutes of the Asbestos Textile Institute, which had been unearthed by Gene Locks, and I was pretty cocksure.

"As things turned out, however, Lively Wilson blew me out of the water with a brilliant three-pronged medical state-of-the-art defense, which he orchestrated with the aid of a videotaped deposition from Dr. Kotin, Johns-Manville's medical director. First, Kotin made effective use of the Fleischer-Drinker study, just as he had in the Starnes and Daniels cases, to advance the claim that Johns-Manville and other insulation manufacturers had no reason to suppose that asbestos in-sulators were at risk of developing asbestosis. Second, he pointed out that the threshold-limit value of five million particles per cubic foot, which was in effect until 1968, was based on a study of textile factories in which workers were exposed to one-hundred-percent asbestos fiber, whereas the insulators were working with materials that contained only about fifteen percent asbestos. And, finally, he dismissed individ-ual case reports showing disease among asbestos insulators by claim-ing that they were isolated anecdotes plucked from the garbage heap of medical literature. To buttress Kotin's testimony, Wilson brought in Dr. Forde McIver, a well-known sixty-year-old pathologist from the Medical College of South Carolina, in Charleston, who was then in private practice. Both Kotin and McIver were older, experienced-looking men, who spoke persuasively and told the jury in effect that they, veteran medical doctors, had had no idea that asbestos insulators were in jeopardy until 1964, when Dr. Selikoff descended from Mount Sinai with his tablets of epidemiological truth. For my part, I not only got nowhere with them in cross-examination but made the mistake of trying to counter them with younger doctors, including a pathologist who had been a student of McIver's. This gave Wilson the opportunity to point out that my expert witness had not even started medical school when Selikoff performed his studies of the insulation workers. As for our big ammunition—the Smith deposition—it went down the tubes when the presiding judge decreed that it be read by his law clerk, who managed to do so in a monotone so flat that it's a wonder the jurors didn't fall asleep. I made use of the ATI minutes, of course, but they turned out to be not as significant as we had hoped when presented in isolation. In the end, the judge instructed the jury to decide the medical state-of-the-art question first, and the jury stayed out less than an hour before finding that the defendants could not have known that asbestos insulators were at risk of developing disease, and, therefore, had incurred no duty to warn Baumgardner that their products could be harmful to his health."

After losing the Baumgardner case, Motley concluded that he needed more discovery and better expert witnesses if he was going to prevail over Lively Wilson's improved state-of-the-art defense. With this in mind, he traveled to Chicago in December, 1977, and persuaded Dr. Bertram Carnow, of the University of Illinois's School of Public Health, to be an expert witness for the plaintiffs. He then went to New York City, where he conferred at length with Dr. Selikoff, in order to acquire the benefit of his expertise in asbestos disease. Afterward, he spent a week at the National Library of Medicine, in Bethesda, Maryland, combing through the medical literature for additional reports of asbestosis among insulators. Far and away the most important discovery he would make during this period, however, would take place in the library of the University of South Carolina School of Law in early January, 1978.

"Around the time I lost Baumgardner, Gillenwater told me about his brainstorm that some of the contract-unit employees must have filed for workmen's compensation for asbestosis disability in years past," Motley continued. "Hoping to find evidence of this, I went to the law library and spent a week poring over digests that listed state and federal appellate-court decisions going back to the nineteen-thirties. The digests didn't break the cases down by topic but listed them by plaintiff and defendant, so I picked Armstrong Cork, which came first alphabetically, and read until my eyes blurred over. It was like trying to find a needle in a haystack, of course, but I finally came across *Hyatt* v. *Armstrong Cork Company*—a workmen's-compensation claim brought in 1953 by an insulator named Floyd Hyatt, who had developed asbestosis a few years earlier. During the next few months, we located dozens of other contract-unit disease claims that had been brought during the nineteen-fifties against Armstrong Cork, Johns-Manville, Owens-Corning, and Philip Carey. They dealt a serious blow to the medical state-of-the-art defense, which depends heavily upon the judgment of doctors such as Kotin and McIver as to what the consensus among the medical profession about asbestos disease might have been at a given time, but is extremely vulnerable to documents showing what a company actually knew or should have known about asbestos disease, as opposed to what expert witnesses say that it might have known. *Hyatt* v. *Armstrong Cork* and the other contract-unit disease claims furnished convincing proof that a number of leading manufacturers knew about the hazard to insulators long before 1964, and once we got our hands on these claims the medical state-of-the-art defense was never the same again."

At the time Motley dug up *Hyatt* v. *Armstrong Cork*, he was in the middle of conducting discovery for a case involving an asbestos insulator named Gordon Luther Barnett, who had died in his sixties of mesothelioma, and for whose estate he had filed a lawsuit in the Court of Common Pleas of Greenville, South Carolina, against Johns-Manville, Raybestos-Manhattan, Owens-Corning Fiberglas, Celotex, Keene, Armstrong Cork, Eagle-Picher, Forty-Eight Insulations, Pittsburgh Corning, Nicolet, and Covil, a local distributor of asbestos-insulation products. After finding *Hyatt* v. *Armstrong Cork*, Motley subpoenaed Armstrong Cork's workmen's-compensation records for contract-unit employees, and the company responded by producing a list of the names and addresses of a hundred insulators who had filed occupational-disease claims between 1953 and 1976. Thirty-seven of the claims were brought during the eleven-year period between September, 1953, when Floyd Hyatt filed his claim, and October, 1964, when Dr. Selikoff and his colleagues announced the results of their study of disease among asbestos insulators in New Jersey and New

York—an event that Armstrong Cork and other defendant manufacturers had always contended was the first time they had any inkling whatsoever that their asbestos-insulation products could be harmful to the health of those who used them. Upon examining the list, Motley was struck by the fact that eighteen of the thirty-seven claims had been filed in California. As a result, he and Gillenwater hired a thirty-two-year-old environmental activist named Barry Castleman, from Washington, D.C., to go to California and look up the hearing records of these claims at the California Industrial Accident Commission.

Meanwhile, on March 27, 1978, Motley went to trial in the Barnett case before Circuit Court Judge James Price, and once again found himself up against the redoubtable Lively Wilson, who once again called upon Dr. Kotin and Dr. McIver to testify that until 1964 Johns-Manville and the other defendants had no way of knowing that insulators such as Barnett were at risk of developing illness. To counter Wilson's defense, Motley introduced the deposition of Dr. Smith, the former medical director of Johns-Manville, and the list of insulators who had filed occupational-disease claims against Armstrong Cork. Wilson contested both pieces of evidence, claiming that Smith was a disgruntled employee who could not be believed, and pointing out that the contract-unit disease claims against Armstrong Cork did not involve Johns-Manville and were statistically insignificant. The trial ended on April 6, and after six hours of deliberation the jury returned a verdict in favor of the defendants. Astonished and disappointed, Motley made a motion for a new trial on the ground that the verdict went against the weight of the evidence. Such motions are rarely granted unless there are highly unusual extenuating circumstances, and Judge Price denied Motley's even though he would later declare that he personally had been persuaded by the plaintiff's case. The loss in *Barnett* was Motley's second in a row, and was particularly galling in light of the fact that he was now zero for two against Lively Wilson. Within a few weeks, however, some stunning developments in the Barnett case would vault Motley into the front rank of asbestos litigators and profoundly alter the course of asbestos litigation.

The new turn in the tide of events began when Gillenwater subpoenaed Armstrong Cork's compensation records for its contract-unit employees, just as Motley had done a few months before. But this time, instead of responding with a list of the names and addresses of workers who had brought claims, Armstrong Cork produced dozens of actual claim files for Gillenwater, including a number of compensation hearings that had been held before the California Industrial Accident Commission during the 1950s. These hearing records showed that asbestos insulators employed by contract units had brought claims for disability from asbestosis not only against Armstrong Cork but against Johns-Manville, Owens-Corning, Philip Carey (a firm that was later purchased by Celotex), and the Mundet Cork Corporation, of North Bergen, New Jersey. The records also indicated that these companies had notified their insurance carriers of the claims and had hired lawyers to defend themselves. Thus, contrary to their assertions in court, it was clear that five of the defendants in *Barnett*—Johns-Manville, Armstrong Cork, Celotex, Owens-Corning and Keene—had known long before 1964 of the hazard to asbestos insulators, or could be held legally responsible because they owned companies that had known of it. When Motley heard about the California claims from Gillenwater, he decided to file another motion for a new trial in *Barnett*, on the ground that substantial and important evidence that should have been produced for the first trial had not come to light until after it was over.

As luck would have it, Motley was about to acquire even more ammunition from Gillenwater. Just before the Barnett case went to trial, Gillenwater had gone to Hartford, Connecticut, to look for contract-unit disease cases in the records of the Travelers Insurance Company, the holder of workmen's-compensation coverage for some of the contract units owned by Johns-Manville, and in those of the Aetna Casualty & Surety Company, which carried insurance for Owens-Corning and Philip Carey, by then owned by Celotex. In Hartford, he was joined by Karl Asch, who told him about the Sumner Simpson file, which had been in his possession for nearly a year. It was the first Gillenwater had heard of the Simpson papers, and when Johns-Manville and Raybestos-Manhattan were acquitted at the conclusion of the Barnett trial, a few days later, he told Motley about them.

On April 26, 1978, the asbestos hazard received some belated national attention when, nearly fourteen years after the New York Academy of Sciences' international Conference on the Biological Effects of Asbestos had clearly indicted the mineral as a potent carcinogen and lung-disease-producing agent, Secretary of Health, Education, and Welfare Joseph A. Califano, Jr., issued a statement that this was indeed the case. Califano went on to say that the total number of workers exposed to asbestos since the beginning of the Second World War was estimated at between 8 million and 11 million, including 4.5 million men and women who had undergone significant exposure while working in wartime shipyards. He then announced that he had ordered the surgeon general of the United States to send an advisory letter to all 400,000 physicians in the nation describing the health risks posed by asbestos. At the same time, he urged that workers who had been exposed to asbestos to stop smoking cigarettes, citing Dr. Selikoff's 1968 finding that cigarette smokers exposed to asbestos were likely to incur lung cancer at a rate up to ninety times as great as that of people who neither smoked nor worked with asbestos.

Secretary Califano's announcement was soon followed by a second New York Academy conference on asbestos disease—this one was entitled Health Hazards of Asbestos Exposure and was held at the New York Hilton in late June. Among those in attendance was Karl Asch, who had been invited to deliver a paper on the legal and political ramifications of asbestos disease. Asch proceeded to level some scathing criticism at a bill known as the Asbestos Health Hazards Compensation Act, which had been introduced in the House by Representative Millicent Fenwick, of New Jersey. Among other things, Fenwick's measure, which had been drafted by lawyers connected with the asbestos industry, proposed to eliminate any further product-liability actions against the industry and to use the federal treasury to pay off existing claims, before an industry fund was set up to pay compensation to workers who developed asbestos disease in the future. According to Fenwick, whose congressional district included the town of Manville, where Johns-Manville had operated a complex of asbestos factories since 1912, one reason for relieving the asbestos manufacturers of financial liability was that "the full scope of the diseases causally related to asbestos and/or cigarette tobacco smoke was unknown to industry, labor, government, or medicine until recent times." This contention was bitterly assailed by Asch, who described some of the correspondence that had passed between Sumner Simpson, of Raybestos-Manhattan, and high officials of Johns-Manville, and asked "why the American taxpayer should pick up the costs for those who sowed the seeds of asbestos death and disease."

Also attending the conference were Ronald Motley, who wanted desperately to get his hands on the Sumner Simpson papers, and Henry Weinstein, a staff writer for the Los Angeles *Times*, who was interested in them as well. Upon hearing that the papers might be found at the federal district courthouse in Newark, where *Austin* v. *Johns-Manville* had been filed, Motley, Weinstein, and Barry Castleman, who was also at the conference, took a cab out there, only to learn that under New Jersey procedure the documents were being held by Johns-Manville's attorneys. At that point, Weinstein called the company's outside counsel, David Gross, at the Newark firm of Budd, Larner, Kent, Gross, Picillo & Rosenbaum, and asked to see them, but Gross refused. In the end, Motley got the Simpson papers through court order, and submitted them in his motion for a new trial in the Barnett case, which he made on June 30.

On August 24, following a hearing on July 17, Judge Price issued an order granting a new trial in the case against Johns-Manville, Raybestos-Manhattan, Owens-Corning, Celotex, Keene, and Armstrong Cork. Judge Price ruled that the correspondence between Raybestos-Manhattan and Johns-Manville "reflects a conscious effort by the industry in the 1930's to downplay, or arguably suppress, the dissemination of information to employees and the public for fear of the promotion of law suits," and that contrary to the defendants' state-of-the-art defense the "voluminous evidence of contract-unit disease claims constitute compelling proof of actual notice to certain manufacturers that asbestos-containing thermal products indeed caused disease in insulators."

Judge Price's unusual order eventually led to an out-of-court settlement of the Barnett case. In the meantime, the Sumner Simpson file and the contract-unit disease claims enabled Motley to have the videotaped 1977 deposition of Dr. Paul Kotin—a deposition that had been used with telling effect in winning jury verdicts for the defendant manufacturers in several trials—thrown out, on the ground that the evidence that had been withheld had rendered previous cross-examinations ineffective. The new evidence made it possible for Motley and other plaintiff lawyers to cross-examine Dr. Kotin with such effectiveness in future depositions that Johns-Manville eventually ceased to use him as an expert witness for the state-of-the-art defense. Most important of all, it encouraged Motley and his colleagues to dig out more of what Johns-Manville and the other giants of the asbestos industry had known about asbestos disease, and when they had learned it. As a result, the next year saw a virtual landslide of discovery of incriminating documents from the asbestos manufacturers.

One of the most important discoveries occurred when Motley made a motion for Raybestos-Manhattan to produce additional documents that were being stored at the offices of its attorneys, in Morristown, New Jersey, and so came into possession of the report of the dust surveys and medical studies that had been conducted during the spring of 1947 in ten asbestos-textile plants belonging to Raybestos-Manhattan, Johns-Manville, and other member companies of the Asbestos Textile Institute by W. C. L. Hemeon, the head engineer of the Industrial Hygiene Foundation of America, and Dr. C. Richard Walmer, who was the foundation's medical director. The existence of the Hemeon report, which was never published, had been known to the plaintiff attorneys since 1977, when Gene Locks had found mention of it in the minutes of the Asbestos Textile Institute's 1947 meetings, but none of them had the slightest idea of how incriminating it would prove to be. Hemeon started out by telling the members of the institute that there was a serious lack of information about the incidence of asbestosis among their employees, because programs for taking chest X-rays existed in only five of the ten factories he had surveyed. He then informed them that in two facilities where such programs were in operation—the Raybestos-Manhattan factory in Manheim, Pennsylvania, and the Johns-Manville plant in Manville, New Jersey—he had found that about 20 percent of the work force had developed the disease. Having alerted the member companies to the fact that asbestosis was occurring among their workers, Hemeon warned them that adherence to the threshold limit of five million particles of dust per cubic foot provided no assurance that asbestosis would not develop in workers who were employed over long periods of time, and he recommended that studies be initiated to develop a better standard.

As might be expected, Hemeon's findings and recommendations further weakened the state-of-the-art defense by contradicting the contention of the asbestos manufacturers that they had every reason to believe that the five-million-particle standard was safe—a claim they had been advancing in every trial since *Borel*. Accordingly, the Hemeon report soon became a major weapon in the arsenal of disclosure that was being amassed by the plaintiff lawyers. "From a legal standpoint, Hemeon conducted far and away the most significant study of asbestos disease that was ever done in the United States," Motley has declared. "It's not just a smoking gun; it's a stick of dynamite with a burning fuse."

Gillenwater agrees with Motley's assessment of the importance of the Hemeon report, and goes on to explain how he and other plaintiff lawyers have used it in court. "You take the expert medical witnesses whom Johns-Manville and the other defendant manufacturers keep putting on the stand," he says. "Up until the time we got our hands on Hemeon, they had been testifying in trial after trial that during the nineteen-forties, fifties, and early sixties everybody in the medical profession thought that five million particles was a perfectly safe level of exposure for workers. But then we started asking them on cross-examination if they had ever heard of the 1947 Hemeon report, which strongly suggested that the five-million-particle standard might not be safe. And, of course, since the Hemeon report was never published, they had to answer that they had not heard of it, which gave us the chance to show the jury that the defendants' medical experts were not so expert after all, and that their opinion of what the medical profession may or may not have known back in the nineteen-forties was, in fact, irrelevant. In short, Hemeon afforded us a perfect opportunity to remind the jury that it is the asbestos industry which is on trial. The way I like to do this is to ask the expert witness the following question: 'Was it responsible, Doctor, for the asbestos industry not to tell you and your colleagues in the medical profession that in fact a medical survey of the lungs of asbestos workers showed that they were developing asbestosis in large numbers way back in the nineteen-forties in conditions where the five-million-particle standard was being met?' I do the same thing with the contract-unit disease claims. I say, 'Dr. So-and-So, you're here testifying in behalf of industry about what you think doctors and medical scientists could have known about asbestos disease among insulators back in the nineteen-forties and fifties. But here in black and white are workmen's-compensation claims that show exactly what the asbestos manufacturers knew and when they knew it. Why didn't the defendant manufacturers inform you about these claims, Doctor?' Let me tell you, questions like these rarely draw much of an answer from the expert witnesses, and they have a devastating effect upon the state-of-the-art defense."

At about the same time that Motley was digging up the Hemeon report, Gillenwater got a telephone call from a man who said that he was a former employee of Johns-Manville and that he had some interesting documents he felt Gillenwater should see. The caller suggested that Gillenwater catch a plane to Washington, D.C., the next day and take a room at the Hyatt-Regency Washington hotel. He then told Gillenwater that he would meet him in the lobby, come to the room, leave the documents on a table, and go into the bathroom to wash his hands, and that he would not be surprised if the documents were gone when he returned. In this rather bizarre fashion, Gillenwater came into possession of the notes of several lengthy meetings of the Manville health review committee, which were held at the Johns-Manville manufacturing complex in Manville, New Jersey, between July, 1957, and April, 1958, in order to evaluate the health status of employees who were afflicted with pulmonary disease. The members of the health review committee included Dr. Smith, the company's medical director; Dr. David T. DuBow and Dr. Edwin D. Merrill, both of whom were Manville plant physicians; and Clifford L. Sheckler, who was then supervisor of safety and health at the Manville complex. A medical secretary made notes of what was said at the various meetings, and some of the dialogue she recorded was incriminating, to say the least, because it clearly indicated that Johns-Manville had developed a corporate policy of not informing sick employees of the precise nature of their health problems for fear of workmen's-compensation claims and lawsuits.

A typical case involved whether to give a medical examination to a forty-nine-year-old woman who had developed first-stage asbestosis after working as a spinner in the textile plant for seventeen years, and was thought to be ready to institute a compensation claim. Dr. DuBow advised against calling her in for examination on the ground that "we may aggravate this into something decisive." He gave similar advice in the case of a woman who had developed moderately advanced asbestosis after working for sixteen years as a weaver and spooler in the textile plant, and was being considered for transfer to a non-dusty area. "If she is called in, she will get hysterical, and I am sure you will have a claim on your hands," he declared.

At a subsequent meeting, Sheckler, who later acknowledged that he had handled several hundred workmen's-compensation claims for asbestosis at the Manville plant between 1957 and 1959, discussed the problem of how to deal with a fifty-two-year-old worker with twenty-eight years of employment, who was upset because the company had not informed him of changes in his chest X-rays, and was thought to be ready to file a formal claim. "I foresee one-hundred-percent total disability," Sheckler said. "They have us over a barrel. There is a new case law. You must make a bona-fide offer prior to the filing of the formal. If not made before, the offer has no meaning. That means we do or we do not do it. We have to outguess these people at this point. We do not know when or if they will file."

No guesswork was necessary, however, in dealing with the case of a fifty-two-year-old shift foreman, who had developed asbestosis after working for twenty-three years in the Transite pipe department, where asbestos water pipe was fabricated.

"Advanced pneumoconiosis," Dr. Smith declared after looking at the patient's medical file.

"Should we change him?" inquired Sheckler, who wanted to know if a transfer to a non-dusty area was in order.

"Won't make any difference," Smith replied.

"If he hits sixty-five, I will be surprised," Dr. DuBow said.

On the basis of such advice, Sheckler decided to take no action other than to watch the patient carefully and retire him on disability, if, as he put it, it became "necessary."

Because Sheckler was one of Johns-Manville's leading expert witnesses for the state-of-the-art defense, the discovery of his role on the Manville health surveillance committee—a discovery that came almost seven years after he had testified in the Borel case that Johns-Manville had always been deeply concerned about the health and welfare of its employees—did little to enhance his credibility, and the plaintiff lawyers were able to use the new disclosures to challenge his testimony far more effectively that they had in the past.

During that summer, Motley sent copies of key documents from the Sumner Simpson file to Dr. Selikoff in order to keep him abreast of the latest disclosures of culpability on the part of the asbestos industry. Selikoff, for his part, advised Motley to get in touch with Dr. Schepers, the former director of the Saranac Laboratory, who was then working for the Veterans Administration in Washington, D.C., saying that Schepers might have some interesting stories to tell. At the 1964 Conference on the Biological Effects of Asbestos, Schepers had said that when he had gone into the northeastern Transvaal in 1949 to make a clinical survey of the asbestos industry in South Africa for the South African government, he had found barefoot Bantu children spending their days inside large jute shipping bags, where they were forced by overseers armed with whips to trample down fluffy amosite asbestos as it came cascading over their heads into the bags. According to Schepers, a number of these children had developed asbestosis with cor pulmonale—right-sided heart failure, which often accompanies the disease—before the age of twelve, and he had told his listeners at the conference that he would be very surprised if any of them had lived long enough to develop either lung cancer or mesothelioma.

In July, shortly after filing his motion for a new trial in the Barnett case, Motley followed Selikoff's advice and telephoned Schepers at his home, in Great Falls, Virginia. "I told Dr. Schepers who I was and what I was up to and asked to meet with him," Motley recalls. "On August seventeenth, Paul Gillenwater, Gene Locks, and I talked with Schepers for seven hours at the Hyatt Regency, on Capitol Hill. Schepers told us that the South African government had sent him to the United States in 1949 to study the pneumoconiosis problem under Dr. Anthony J. Lanza, who had retired from the Metropolitan Life Insurance Company, and was then at the New York University Medical Center. He acknowledged that Lanza, who became his mentor, had been overinfluenced by the asbestos industry in dealing with the problem of asbestos disease, but he defended Lanza by pointing out that he would not have been able to conduct his research if he had not gone along with the industry's dictates. During this visit, Schepers spent three months at the Saranac Laboratory with its director, Dr. Arthur Vorwald, who was a longtime consultant for the asbestos industry. He also met Vandiver Brown, the corporate counsel for Johns-Manville, who wanted him to delete material that was embarrassing to Johns-Manville from a report he was preparing for his superiors in South Africa. In 1954, Schepers returned to the United States and replaced Vorwald as the director of the Saranac Laboratory. Soon thereafter, he was asked to review the chest X-rays, autopsy material, and health records of some of Johns-Manville's dead workers, and to write reports about them. Schepers later allowed us to examine copies of these reports, which he had stored in the basement of his house. Each of them was entitled Medico-Legal Opinion in Respect of Occupational Chest Disease, and he had sent the originals to Johns-Manville's Manhattan headquarters, on Fortieth Street. Some of the employees had worked at the Johns-Manville plant in Manville, New Jersey; others had worked at the factory in Waukegan, Illinois; and a few had worked at the company's plants in Nashua, New Hampshire, and in Billerica, Massachusetts. Schepers had found that many of them had died of right-sided heart failure provoked by asbestosis.

The most important document in Schepers's basement proved to be an article he and two associates had written about the biological effects of a thermal-insulation material called Kaylo, which had been published in the September, 1955, issue of the American Medical Association's *Archives of Industrial Health*. The Owens-Illinois Glass Company, of Toledo, Ohio, had developed Kaylo during the late 1930s, and had begun manufacturing it in the early 1940s. The trade name was derived from the so-called K factor—an engineering term for the rate at which heat passes through an inch of insulation. The better the insulation, the lower the heat loss, or K factor; hence the name "Kaylo." In the text of his article, Schepers made no mention of Kaylo by name, referring instead to hydrous calcium silicate, a commercial product made from calcium hydroxide and silica with a chrysotile-asbestos content of about 15 percent. However, in the opening paragraph he revealed that the biological effects of this product upon test animals had been studied in inhalation experiments at the Saranac Laboratory starting in 1943, and in the concluding section he said that its dust had caused fibrosis and lesions in the lungs of the test animals that "closely resembled those found in experimental asbestosis," and that this harmful effect was probably caused by the chrysotile asbestos it contained.

Starting in 1930, Dr. Leroy U. Gardner, the director of the Saranac Laboratory, had conducted inhalation experiments with asbestos dust. He had used pure asbestos in his early animal experiments, however, so the industry had always been able to claim that his results could apply only to the exposures undergone by asbestos-factory workers, who used 100 percent asbestos fiber. Thus, Schepers's mention of the fact that an asbestos-insulation product containing only 15 percent asbestos had been shown to cause disease had tremendous implications for the state-of-the-art defense. Small wonder that when he found this tantalizing clue in Schepers's basement Motley and his colleagues embarked on an intensive search to determine exactly what was known about the harmful effects of Kaylo and how early this knowledge had been imparted to its maker, Owens-Illinois. Their efforts ultimately led to the discovery of what have come to be called the Kaylo documents —some thirty thousand pages that revealed prior knowledge of asbestos disease not only on the part of Owens-Illinois but on the part of the Owens-Corning Fiberglas Corporation, also of Toledo, which had begun to distribute Kaylo in 1953 and had bought the entire Kaylo line from Owens-Illinois in 1958.

The search for the Kaylo documents began in the spring of 1979, when Tom Henderson served a subpoena duces tecum upon the director of the Saranac Laboratory in connection with two asbestos lawsuits that he had filed in nearby Albany. In May, he and Barry Castleman spent a day and a half sifting through several thousand pages of documents that had been retrieved from an old shed on the laboratory grounds, and found records of early experiments with Kaylo, as well as correspondence between Dr. Gardner and high officials of Owens-Illinois. During the summer, the quest for other Kaylo documents led to the Armed Forces Institute of Pathology, in Washington, D.C., to which the widow of Dr. Vorwald, who succeeded Gardner as director of the Saranac Laboratory, had deeded his medical papers following his death, in 1974. (Among these papers was a letter that had been written to Vorwald in 1951 by Dr. Samuel L. Keller, the physician at Johns-Manville's plant in Waukegan, Illinois, who lightheartedly invited Vorwald to visit the plant so that he could "see the manufacture of asbestosis and silicosis as produced in Waukegan.") The rest of the Kaylo documents were produced by Owens-Corning from the summer of 1979 through the winter of 1980, as a result of litigation involving sick workers at a Kaylo-manufacturing plant in Berlin, New Jersey, which Owens-Corning had bought from Owens-Illinois in 1958. Since these workers were prevented by the state's workmen's-compensation statute from suing their employer, they had brought a product-liability action against a number of asbestos-mining companies, claiming that the companies had failed to warn them about the health hazards of asbestos. The mining companies, in turn, erected a sophisticated-user defense, claiming that they had no reason to warn the Owens-Corning workers, because Owens-Corning knew more about the health hazards of asbestos than they did. In order to prove this contention, the defendants subpoenaed Owens-Corning to produce its records and documents dealing with Kaylo, and when Owens-Corning was forced by law to accede to the request the plaintiff lawyers simply gathered them in like trout gobbling up a hatch of mayflies on a stream.

On February 12, 1943, U. E. Bowes, Owens-Illinois's director of research, wrote Dr. Gardner that he was sending him samples of a newly developed thermal-insulating material, which turned out to be Kaylo. Bowes asked Gardner to conduct tests to determine if the product was hazardous from "the standpoint of the employees working in the plant where the material is made or where it may be sawed to desired dimensions," and also "from the standpoint of applicators or erectors at the point of use." By May, 1944, Gardner reported that he had produced a condition similar to asbestosis by injecting Kaylo into the lungs of test animals. In November, Bowes told him to "proceed with whatever investigations are necessary to establish the degree to which the material we are manufacturing at Berlin, New Jersey, constitutes a hazard, either to employees engaged in the manufacture of it or to others in the use or installation of it," and Gardner wrote back that he would expose test animals to high concentrations of Kaylo dust in order to determine whether it could be inhaled into the lungs and cause pulmonary disease.

Dr. Gardner died in October, 1946, and a year later his successor, Dr. Vorwald, who had served as a pathologist at the Saranac Laboratory from 1934 to 1942, sent an interim report on the Kaylo experiments to Owens-Illinois, saying that it had been "tentatively concluded that Kaylo alone fails to produce significant pulmonary damage when inhaled into the lung." In the autumn of 1948, however, Vorwald informed Bowes that "in all animals sacrificed after more than 30 months of exposure to Kaylo dust unmistakable evidence of asbestosis has developed, showing that Kaylo on inhalation is capable of producing asbestosis and must be regarded as potentially-hazardous material." In the final paragraph of his letter, Vorwald warned Bowes and Owens-Illinois that Kaylo might pose a grave danger to the company's employees. "I realize that our findings regarding Kaylo are less favorable than anticipated," he wrote. "However, since Kaylo is capable of producing asbestosis, it is better to discover it now in animals rather than later in industrial workers. Thus the company, being forewarned, will be in a better position to institute adequate control measures for safeguarding exposed employees and protecting its own interests."

On February 7, 1952, Vorwald sent the final report of the study of the biological effects of Kaylo to Willis G. Hazard, an industrial-hygiene specialist in Owens-Illinois's industrial relations division. The report was entitled "Investigation Concerning the Capacity of Inhaled Kaylo Dust to Injure the Lung," and it was marked "CONFIDENTIAL." It informed Owens-Illinois that 450 animals had been exposed to Kaylo in a special chamber over a five-year period, and that when Kaylo dust was inhaled for a prolonged period it was capable of producing fibrosis typical of asbestosis in the lungs of such animals. In an accompanying letter, Vorwald warned Hazard that "the results of the study indicate that every precaution should be taken to protect workers against inhaling the dust." At the same time, he took pains to assure Hazard that Owens-Illinois would be spared any embarrassment by these findings. "We hope to publish this study either separately or in combination with similar studies pertaining to other dust," he wrote. "In doing so, however, reference will be made only to hydrous calcium silicate and not to 'Kaylo'; thus the interest of your company will be safeguarded. Of course, the final manuscript will be forwarded to you for review before being released to the publisher."

Presumably encouraged by Vorwald's guarantee of anonymity, the managers of Owens-Illinois went ahead with the production of Kaylo at factories in Berlin and Sayreville, New Jersey, and instituted a program of giving pre-employment and annual X-rays to the 505 people who worked in these plants. As for the publication of the Saranac Laboratory's findings, this did not occur until September, 1955, more than three and a half years after Vorwald had submitted his final report. By that time, Dr. Schepers had replaced Vorwald as director of the laboratory, and he was asked to evaluate the results of the experiments that had previously been performed on Kaylo. Schepers's article based on this evaluation, though it triggered the search for the other Kaylo documents twenty-four years later, caused little consternation at the time among the managers of Owens-Illinois. In fact, they appeared to be delighted with Schepers's final paragraph, which blamed the chrysotile-asbestos component of Kaylo, rather than its hydrous-calcium-silicate content, for the fibrosis it produced in the lungs of test animals. "This means that Kaylo is no more harmful than the universally used heat insulation—asbestos—in fact less so, since

Kaylo contains a very small percentage of asbestos," Hazard observed
in an intracompany memo that was sent on October 5, 1955, to Milton
M. Olander, the industrial-relations director of Owens-Illinois. He
went on to assure Olander that there was no mention whatsoever of
either Kaylo or Owens-Illinois in Schepers's article.

While Schepers's article on the disease potential of Kaylo was regarded with relative equanimity by the managers of Owens-Illinois, in
downtown Toledo, two other articles written by him in the same issue
of the *Archives of Industrial Health,* warning that glass fibers should
be regarded as potentially harmful, caused repercussions of almost
seismic proportions in the general offices of the Owens-Corning Fiberglas Corporation, also in downtown Toledo. In a memorandum sent on
December 6, 1955, to Harold Boeschenstein, the president of Owens-
Corning, a company official analyzed the legal implications of Schepers's articles, warning that they "can be cited effectively in damage
suits against us." A few months later, another Owens-Corning official
recommended to Boeschenstein that an investigation be undertaken to
determine "whether Saranac's business is slipping and whether he
[Schepers] resorts to alarmist tactics to sell the Laboratory's services."
The information, he assured Boeschenstein, could be gathered "on a
confidential basis" and used "as a weapon in reserve."
  Examination of other Kaylo documents show that such procedures
were old hat at Owens-Corning. Back in the spring of 1941, company
officials had learned that the Asbestos Workers union might try to
claim that Fiberglas constituted a health hazard, in order to win
increased wages in upcoming labor negotiations with insulation contractors. In a memo sent to Boeschenstein in January, 1942, Edward
C. Ames, Owens-Corning's public-relations manager, outlined a strategy for dealing with this threat. He proposed to "gather as a weapon
in reserve an impressive file of photostats of medical literature on
asbestosis," which he said could be used to split the union rank and
file, and to "play all the stops on asbestosis" if the leadership persisted
in its plan regarding Fiberglas. In the end, officials of the Asbestos
Workers union accepted an alternative proposal, and Owens-Corning
was spared the necessity of warning the nation's insulators about the
health hazards of the asbestos materials they were using. Ten years
later, the company's managers no doubt considered this outcome fortu-

nate when they reached an agreement with their counterparts at Owens-Illinois to act as the nationwide marketing distributor for Kaylo, an asbestos-containing insulation product. And in 1958, Owens-Corning purchased the entire Kaylo line, including the Kaylo-producing plant in Berlin, New Jersey, which made it the sole manufacturer of the stuff. As part of the deal, Owens-Illinois shipped the Saranac Laboratory file on Kaylo to its new owner; this meant that Owens-Corning knew or should have known when it bought Kaylo that the product was hazardous to health. Meanwhile, as early as 1956, insulator employees of Owens-Corning's contract units had begun to file workmen's-compensation claims for disability caused by asbestosis. But none of this appeared to bother the new makers of Kaylo, who did not get around to warning that Kaylo was dangerous to inhale until December of 1966.

In the summer of 1969, Owens-Corning finally came to the realization that big legal trouble might lie ahead. In August, John Vyverberg, an executive in its New York offices, sent a memo to the company's leading officials informing them that the firm had settled the Claude J. Tomplait case out of court earlier in the year, and had been named as a defendant in two new lawsuits. Vyverberg went on to point out that although Aetna was handling the company's defense in these cases, "any settlements are indirectly paid by us." He then wrote a pair of sentences that, coming two months before Stephenson filed *Borel*, were prophetic, to say the least. "This is just the beginning, in my opinion," he told his colleagues. "Unfortunately, the trend is toward litigation instead of claim settlement through workmen's compensation."

As it happened, the beginning was not terribly serious for Owens-Corning, which, like other asbestos manufacturers, erected the familiar state-of-the-art defense and dug in its heels. The company had settled the Tomplait case for $15,000 and it would get out of the Borel case for a mere $4,225. Over the next decade, Owens-Corning and Aetna would settle over a hundred cases for relatively small amounts largely because plaintiff lawyers had no way of proving that Owens-Corning officials had prior knowledge of the risk of asbestos disease for insulators. All that changed in 1979, of course, when the trail of discovery led to an abandoned shed on the grounds of the Trudeau Foundation's laboratory at Saranac Lake, and to some long-forgotten files at the Armed Forces Institute of Pathology, in Washington, and when officials of Owens-Corning were forced by subpoena to produce the rest of the incriminating record which the company had possessed for nearly forty years. From then on, Owens-Corning became a prime target for higher damage awards and, together with Owens-Illinois, was subjected to intense pressure by other defendant manufacturers to contribute more heavily to out-of-court settlements in product-liability cases brought by asbestos insulators who had used Kaylo.

SIX

THE CALIFORNIA CONNECTION

eanwhile, some stunning disclosures about the past conduct of Johns-Manville were coming out of California, where the company had operated manufacturing plants for many years in Long Beach, Lompoc, Carson, Redwood City, Stockton, and Pittsburg—the last being an industrial town in Contra Costa County, about thirty-five miles northeast of San Francisco. The California discovery got its start in 1968, when a Mexican-born shingle-cutting-machine operator named Marcos Antonio Vela, who had developed asbestosis after working for thirty-two years at the Pittsburg plant, where asbestos shingles, roofing, and insulation products had been manufactured since 1926, retained a workmen's-compensation attorney named Maurice S. Marcus, from nearby Pleasant Hill. Upon learning that Vela had been examined by a physician under contract to Johns-Manville, who had failed to inform him that he had developed lung disease, Marcus referred his new client to a medical-malpractice lawyer in San Francisco. Vela then filed suit against the physician, Dr. Kent Wise, who in 1963 had succeeded his father, Dr. David Wise, as the doctor for some 375 employees at the Pittsburg plant. (The elder Wise had served there under contract to Johns-Manville since 1926.) In 1973, after a three-week trial in Contra Costa Superior Court, during which medical records containing Kent Wise's handwritten notation that Vela was suffering from asbestosis were introduced in evidence, a jury awarded Vela $351,000 in damages. It was an unprecedented verdict against an industry physician, and, as might be expected, it provoked considerable uneasiness within the industrial-medical community.

During 1973 and 1974, Marcus referred five similar asbestosis cases from the Pittsburg plant to a fifty-year-old lawyer named George W. Kilbourne, who had been associated with him a few years earlier. Kilbourne filed them as medical-malpractice suits, but knowing that many other workers at the Pittsburg plant had developed asbestosis, and that Dr. Wise's malpractice insurance would be exhausted long before their cases could be tried, he realized that it would soon be necessary to find a defendant with large financial resources. (In the lexicon of plaintiff lawyers, such defendants are often referred to as "deep pockets.") As it turned out, the Pittsburg plant workers were prevented from suing Johns-Manville by the California Labor Code, which stipulated that workmen's compensation was an exclusive remedy, but the more Kilbourne thought about this, the more he became convinced that he should mount a legal challenge to the exclusivity of workmen's compensation, on the ground that Johns-Manville had engaged in conspiracy and fraud by failing to inform his clients that they had developed lung disease as a result of their exposure to asbestos. For this reason, he decided not to rely on third-party lawsuits against the mining companies that had supplied raw asbestos to the Pittsburg plant, as Karl Asch had done in the case of the workers at Raybestos-Manhattan's Passaic plant, and as Fred Baron had done in the case of the employees at Pittsburgh Corning's Tyler plant. "I came to the conclusion that if my clients couldn't sue Johns-Manville for what that company had done to them, then workmen's compensation was nothing more than a license for manufacturers to kill," he has said. It was a conclusion that marked the start of a long journey of discovery for Kilbourne, who would turn out to be one of the most innovative asbestos litigators since Ward Stephenson, and an excruciating thorn in Johns-Manville's corporate hide.

Born in Berea, Kentucky, in 1923, Kilbourne was the son of a coal miner and part-time farmer, who eventually developed and died of black-lung disease. After graduating from high school, he attended college for a year, and then joined the Marines. He spent the Second World War in the Pacific theater, and upon being discharged he entered the University of Michigan, graduating in 1946 with a degree in engineering, and then went to law school at the University of California at Berkeley, from which he graduated in 1951. After five years in general practice in Berkeley, he moved to Sullivan, Indiana —a coal-mining town south of Terre Haute—where he spent the next six years handling personal-injury and workmen's-compensation cases, many of them for District 11 of the United Mine Workers. In 1963, he moved back to Berkeley, and in 1975 he opened his own law office in Pleasant Hill and soon began to acquire clients from the nearby Pittsburg plant. The first of these was a man named Reba

Rudkin, who had developed asbestosis after working at the factory for twenty-nine years. The second was a fifty-seven-year-old worker named Harold Browner, who walked into Kilbourne's office off the street one day in the summer of 1975 seeking a lawyer to represent him on a drunk-driving charge—a case complicated by the fact that after working at the Pittsburg plant for twelve years Browner had developed asbestosis and had undergone surgery for the removal of parts of both lungs, and had been unable to blow hard enough to activate the breath-analysis test that had been administered by the police officers who arrested him.

Late in 1975, Kilbourne and Steven Kazan, a malpractice attorney who had been with the firm that handled the Vela case, filed lawsuits in behalf of Rudkin and Browner in Contra Costa Superior Court against Dr. Kent Wise, who by then had been named as a defendant in at least eight lawsuits seeking damages of more than $50 million, and against Dr. David Wise, who in the 1950s had pronounced Browner fit only a few months before he was found to have developed disabling asbestosis. Browner's suit was later dismissed when the judge in the case ruled that under California's statute of limitations he should have brought his action in the 1950s, when he had undergone lung surgery and learned that he had developed asbestosis. A third defendant was Johns-Manville Corporation, which was accused of negligence for imposing an inadequate medical-surveillance program on the plaintiffs, and for allowing them to be exposed to asbestos in spite of knowing that asbestos exposure could lead to serious lung disease. As for Dr. Kent Wise, he countersued Johns-Manville—the company had refused to defend either him or his father—for $10 million in each case, claiming that he had been deceived by company officials, who had hired him only for the purpose of performing pre-employment and annual physicals, and had assured him that he would not be responsible for reading X-rays of workers who developed pulmonary disease.

By the late summer of 1977, Kilbourne and Kazan had filed similar lawsuits in behalf of nearly thirty other workers from the Pittsburg plant—some of whom had died—who had developed asbestosis or other lung disease. In October of that year, on the basis of newly discovered evidence, a Superior Court judge ruled that the two attorneys could amend the lawsuits to accuse Johns-Manville of conspiracy and fraud. By that time, Kilbourne and Kazan had also filed suit against Johns-Manville in behalf of forty-one workers who had either developed asbestosis or lung cancer or a form of silicosis after working at the company's plant in Lompoc, a town near the Pacific Coast forty-five miles northwest of Santa Barbara, where large deposits of diatomaceous earth—a substance formed by the accumulation over millions of years of the siliceous shells of small aquatic plants called diatoms—had been mined, milled, and used in insulation products since 1928. Johns-Manville's lawyers appealed the judge's ruling in the Pittsburg cases, on the ground that the company could not be held liable for conspiracy and fraud under the California Labor Code provision that workmen's compensation was an exclusive remedy, and this marked the beginning of a series of appeals and decisions that would delay any of the cases from going to trial for the next three years. During this time, both Browner and Rudkin died of lung cancer, and Kilbourne embarked upon his ambitious and imaginative program of discovery which enabled him to make disclosures about Johns-Manville's corporate policy regarding asbestos disease that surprised and shocked even the most hardened plaintiff attorneys.

The new evidence that persuaded the Superior Court judge to allow Kilbourne and Kazan to charge Johns-Manville with conspiracy and fraud had been dug up in 1976 by a San Francisco journalist named Paul Shinoff, who had obtained copies of minutes of some meetings of Johns-Manville industrial-relations managers that were held in the 1960s. At one of these meetings, the ubiquitous Dr. Smith urged the managers to support the company's industrial-health program, citing a scandalous health situation that had existed at the Lompoc facility during the early 1950s. Smith told the managers that dusty and unhealthy conditions had caused the workers at Lompoc to go out on strike and that the California State Department of Public Health had threatened to close the plant unless Johns-Manville cleaned it up and operated it according to state health regulations. He also told them about an article in the January, 1952, issue of *Search*, the monthly journal of the California Tuberculosis Association, whose cover showed a picture of the Lompoc plant beneath a stamp that read "Death by Dust."

Smith claimed that *Search*'s assessment of working conditions at the Lompoc plant was exaggerated, but the hearing records of some twenty death or disability claims that were brought before the California Industrial Accident Commission during the 1930s, 1940s, and 1950s bear stark witness to the devastating human suffering and tragedy that occurred there. A particularly grim episode is described in the record of a death claim that was brought on January 4, 1932, by a woman named María Martínez, who filed it against the Celite Company—a Johns-Manville subsidiary that operated the Lompoc plant—and several insurance firms, including Travelers, Standard Accident, and the Pacific Indemnity Company. María Martínez's husband, Macedonio, had died in August, 1930, at the age of thirty-three, after working for only two and a half years at the Lompoc plant as a janitor, bag loader, and ore crusherman. The report of Dr. Milton V. Duncan, of Lompoc, who signed a death certificate listing the case of Martínez's death as "acute edema of the lungs" reads like a horror story. "I saw Macedonio Martínez on the morning of August 23, 1930, at about 6:00 A.M.," Dr. Duncan wrote. "I was called to his house by a friend and found him sitting on a bed gasping for breath—blood fleck foam coming from his mouth and nose—a half pint of similar fluid in a can beside the bed had been expectorated previously. His expression was that of extreme terror—his face was pale and his skin clammy with cold perspiration; pulse about 150 thready; heart sounds indistinct; chest full of bubbling, piping rales. He was talking loudly in Spanish, repeating the word 'morir.' In a few seconds he began to gasp harder and with a rush of fluid from his nose and mouth he expired."

At a claims hearing that was held in April, 1932, Dr. Duncan testified that he believed Martínez might have been suffering from silicosis, but the assistant medical director of the California Industrial Accident Commission disagreed, ascribing Martínez's death to a cardiovascular lesion, and in July of that year the workmen's-compensation referee in the case denied María Martínez's claim. According to the hearing report, she was pregnant when he died, and for six months thereafter, she suffered from "a mental state which precluded her giving any thought to business affairs." It is not known what became of her. It is known, however, that seven months before Macedonio Martínez died, he was given a physical examination and a chest X-ray during a health survey of the Lompoc plant, which was conducted by two physicians from the University of California Medical School, in San Francisco, and that they found him to be suffering from pulmonary dust disease.

Many of the other early Lompoc compensation claims reveal similarly dismal stories of sick and dying men who were suffering from silicosis but whose ailment was often misdiagnosed by medical doctors retained by insurance companies, whereupon the men were denied benefits for disability by referees of the Industrial Accident Commission. This state of affairs would probably have continued if the California State Department of Public Health had not threatened to shut down the Lompoc mill and quarry in 1952, forcing Johns-Manville to institute dust-control measures and employee-health programs at its Lompoc facility, and to place warning labels on insulation products containing diatomaceous earth. By that time, Macedonio Martínez had been dead for more than two decades.

As for Dr. Smith, who claimed that the conditions at Lompoc had been exaggerated, he continued to reveal the true nature of Johns-Manville's corporate policy regarding occupational disease at subsequent industrial-relations managers' meetings. In January, 1966, he declared that one of the company's chief "external health problems" was "the widespread adverse publicity given to the use of asbestos fiber and its connection with cancer." Smith, who was about to retire from Johns-Manville, ended his talk by saying, "In closing, let me reassure you concerning the alleged association of cancer and asbestos. Nowhere in Johns-Manville have I seen any concrete evidence that this association does exist."

Not surprisingly, the minutes of the industrial-relations managers' meetings made Kilbourne wonder just how early high-ranking officials of Johns-Manville had known that company employees were developing lung disease because of their exposure to asbestos, and he began to study the early literature about asbestos disease. One night during the late autumn of 1977, while he was reading *Silicosis and Asbestosis*, which had been published back in 1938, he came across the chapter that Dr. Lanza had written about the health and economic aspects of pulmonary dust disease, and read the passage that seemed to answer his question. "Silicosis and asbestosis burst upon the amazed consciousness of American industry during the period 1929–1930," Lanza had written, and he had gone on to say, "Among the first claims for damages were those for asbestosis, a hitherto unheard of disease in the United States."

The more Kilbourne thought about these sentences, the more he wondered if there might be some reference to the early claims for damages in Johns-Manville's corporate records. Investigating further, he learned that in 1927 J. P. Morgan & Company, of New York City, had bought a controlling interest in Johns-Manville, and that since that year at least one Morgan officer had sat on its board of directors. Assuming that the records of board of directors' meetings had been maintained through the years, he made a motion in the Rudkin case to compel Johns-Manville to produce the minutes of any meeting at which the subject of compensation claims for asbestosis had been discussed. At first, company officials claimed that the board members had held no such discussions until 1968, but when Kilbourne made subsequent motions for production, someone in Johns-Manville's legal department rooted through some old records that had been stored in the basement of the company's headquarters, in Denver, and found the minutes of board of directors' meetings that had been convened between 1928 and 1935. These documents were sent to Arthur J. Moore, of Moore, Clifford, Wolfe, Larson & Trutner—an Oakland law firm that had been retained by Travelers to defend Johns-Manville in the Pittsburg plant cases—and Moore sent them along to Kilbourne in the autumn of 1978. Among them were the minutes of the April 24, 1933, board meeting at which the directors present had authorized the president of the company to settle eleven pending asbestosis cases for $35,000 if he could get the attorney for the plaintiffs to agree not to bring any more lawsuits.

Kilbourne was, of course, tremendously excited by the discovery of these early asbestosis claims, and a few days later he called the clerk of the federal district court in Newark to find out if they were still on file. The clerk informed him that the cases were in some archives that had been stored in Bayonne, and that an attorney for Johns-Manville had come by and requested copies of them a week earlier. The clerk went on to say that he had spent a lot of time preparing a cross-indexed list that would enable the company attorney to find the claims in the archives, and that he was not about to do the whole thing all over again. Kilbourne then proceeded to notice production of the list from Johns-Manville, but company officials denied that it existed. Assuming that the Johns-Manville people had obtained copies of the claims from the Bayonne archives, he noticed production of the records themselves. During the next year and a half, company officials claimed first that they had no idea what he was talking about, then that the records he was seeking did not exist, and, finally, that they had no way of retrieving them. As a result, Kilbourne was forced to file three separate motions to compel their production, and did not come into possession of them until September of 1980.

The records of the early New Jersey asbestosis claims included the eleven lawsuits that had been settled in 1933 and nine other cases which were disposed of between 1930 and 1962. (The earliest case had been filed on May 8, 1929, by Anna Pirskowski, who had quit work at the Manville plant back in 1922, because, according to her complaint, her inhalation of asbestos used in Johns-Manville's manufacturing process caused her "to suffer permanently with a malignant disease.") Sixteen of the twenty cases—the eleven that were settled in 1933 and five that were dismissed on April 14, 1930—were brought by Samuel Greenstone, an attorney from Newark, who approached Johns-Manville's outside legal counsel Hobart & Minard sometime in early 1933 with an offer to settle the eleven remaining cases at what was apparently considered a bargain rate. Greenstone may well have been anxious to settle because each of his clients in the five cases that were dismissed in 1930 had signed a statement in the late autumn of 1929 declaring that he or she had no desire to pursue a lawsuit against Johns-Manville, and would not have initiated it had Greenstone not put him or her up to it.

In view of the sudden and almost simultaneous reluctance of these five people to sue Johns-Manville, Greenstone's offer to settle the other eleven cases cheaply appears to have been the strategy of a man who was simply hoping to prevent history from repeating itself. In any event, the covenant he was forced to sign to the effect that he would neither directly nor indirectly participate in the bringing of any new lawsuits against the company was undoubtedly worth the $35,000 settlement price, for it effectively neutralized him as a legal threat. Indeed, more than ten years would pass before another lawsuit alleging negligence for asbestos disease would be brought against Johns-Manville by one of its New Jersey employees.

.   .   .

Although Kilbourne's various motions to produce had simply asked for the factory workers' asbestosis claims that were referred to in the 1933 board of directors' meeting, someone at Johns-Manville had inadvertently sent him a list that included the cases of Frederick Le Grand and Fred C. Wenham, two asbestos insulators from New Jersey who had brought and settled third-party lawsuits for negligence and breach of warranty—the first ever filed against the company by insulators—in 1957 and 1961. (The breach-of-warranty complaint was subsequently dismissed in Le Grand's case.) This was a major blunder, for it furnished incontrovertible proof that Johns-Manville had known for more than seven years before Dr. Selikoff had announced his findings, and more than a dozen years before *Borel*, that insulators were developing serious lung disease as a result of using its asbestos-insulation products.

"You won't believe what I've found," Kilbourne said when he called Gillenwater to tell him about his discovery of the Le Grand and Wenham cases. "They've even listed the plaintiff's attorneys!" Gillenwater immediately called both lawyers—William L. Brach, of East Orange, who had represented Le Grand, and Franklin Swersky, of Springfield, who had represented Wenham—and arranged to depose them. Then he sent one of his associates to Newark to obtain the records in the two cases, which had been filed in the United States District Court for the District of New Jersey. The record of the Le Grand case was particularly revealing, because it showed that Johns-Manville's responses to Brach's interrogatories had been something less than accurate.

In 1926, Le Grand had joined Newark Local 32 of the Asbestos Workers union—this was one of the two locals whose ghastly mortality experience from asbestos disease would later be documented by the epidemiological study of Dr. Selikoff and his colleagues—and over the next twenty-eight years he applied asbestos insulation, most of which was manufactured by Johns-Manville, to high-temperature pipes and other equipment in oil refineries, factories, schools, hospitals, and other facilities in New Jersey and New York. His physician, Dr. Samuel Einhorn, of Newark, testified that Le Grand had been found to have asbestosis following a heart attack in February, 1956, when he underwent hospitalization and extensive testing. In April, 1957, Le Grand received a 75 percent permanent-disability award from the

Workmen's Compensation Division of the New Jersey Department of Labor, and in July of that year he filed a third-party lawsuit for negligence and breach of warranty against the Johns-Manville Products Corporation. His complaint alleged that he had developed asbestosis as a result of handling Johns-Manville asbestos-insulation products, that the company knew or should have known that these products were unsafe, and that it was negligent in having failed to warn him about the hazards associated with their use. The interrogatories that Brach propounded and sent to Johns-Manville asked whether the company had been aware that asbestosis was developing in workers who had been exposed to its asbestos-insulation products; whether it had issued any warnings about the risk of handling these products to anyone other than its employees; and when it had first "learned that any of its own employees had contracted the disease commonly called asbestosis." In April, 1958, Herbert Morton Ball, who was secretary of the Johns-Manville Products Corporation, replied to these questions under oath, saying that the company had no knowledge of any case of asbestosis ever being contracted by an applicator of its asbestos-insulation products, and that since it had "never received notice of any claim of asbestosis resulting to any persons other than our employees who were engaged in the manufacture of the products, we had no reason to issue any warnings, instructions or preventions to any other persons." Ball also said that asbestosis "was first contracted by an employee of this defendant at one of its plants in 1946."

If these answers were, as Ball swore, "true to the best of my information and belief," he must have been one of the most poorly informed secretaries in all of corporate history, for dozens of cases of asbestosis had occurred in contract-unit insulators, and disease claims had been filed by these employees all during the early 1950s. Moreover, high officials of Johns-Manville had known since the early 1930s —thanks to the report of Dr. Lanza, of the Metropolitan Life Insurance Company, and to the eleven lawsuits that were settled in New Jersey —that workers in the company's asbestos factories were developing pulmonary asbestosis. Ball's denials notwithstanding, Brach proceeded to negotiate an out-of-court settlement with John J. Monigan, Jr., of Stryker, Tams & Horner, of Newark—the law firm that later represented Metropolitan Life in the Passaic workers' lawsuit—and Le Grand agreed to drop his complaint against Johns-Manville for $35,000. An order dismissing the case was signed on April 6, 1959, and the court hearing that was held at the time is particularly note-worthy because of an unusual agreement that Brach and Monigan made with the Travelers Insurance Company, which not only carried Johns-Manville's general liability insurance, but held workmen's-com-pensation coverage for the insulation company that had employed Le Grand. The agreement stipulated that there would be no attempt by the workmen's-compensation department of Travelers to assert a lien against the $35,000 settlement paid out in behalf of Johns-Manville. Among other things, this furnished clear proof that Travelers—a firm that sold Johns-Manville $16 million worth of primary product-liabil-ity insurance between 1947 and 1975—had been placed on notice at least a dozen years before *Borel* as to what its potential liabilities might be with respect to asbestos disease.

In January of 1978, there had been a surprising development in the lawsuits that Kilbourne and Kazan had filed against Dr. Kent Wise in behalf of Rudkin and other workers from the company's Pittsburg plant. This occurred when Wilbur L. Ruff, of Treasure Island, Florida, who had worked for Johns-Manville for forty-four years and had been manager of the Pittsburg plant between 1963 and 1966, gave a sworn statement to Wise's lawyer, Marrs A. Craddick, of Walnut Creek. Ruff said that when Wise was hired to replace his father as part-time physician at the Pittsburg plant, in 1962, it was with the understand-ing that he would be responsible only for conducting pre-employment and periodic physical examinations of employees, and would not be responsible for taking or evaluating their chest X-rays. Ruff went on to say that Dr. Smith and Clifford Sheckler, who had become corporate manager of industrial health, came out to Pittsburg once or twice a year to review the chest films that were taken in connection with periodic physicals, and that Dr. Wise was under instructions not to discuss either the films or any other chest findings with the workers he exam-ined.

"Do you know whether, in fact, abnormal chest findings ever were discussed with any employee of the Johns-Manville plant by Mr. Sheckler, Dr. Smith, or the industrial-relations manager while you were plant manager there?" Craddick asked.

"Not while I was plant manager," Ruff replied.

Craddick then asked if there had been "a policy in the company at that time not to talk to the employee about chest findings, findings that suggested asbestosis, pneumoconiosis, or mesothelioma."

"Yes, it was policy," said Ruff, who repeated his testimony in a deposition that was taken a few weeks later.

The policy described by Ruff soon became known as Johns-Manville's hush-hush policy, and it proved to be damaging to the company's defense in the Pittsburg plant cases. Within a few months, Judge Martin Rothenberg, of the Contra Costa Superior Court, rejected Johns-Manville's claim that the only recourse of Pittsburg plant employees who had developed asbestos disease was to collect damages through workmen's compensation. In his decision, Rothenberg declared that Johns-Manville had "chosen to conceal the danger from its employees rather than invest funds into finding a safe way of handling the product," and that the company had undoubtedly done so because it was less expensive to pay workmen's-compensation benefits than to provide a healthy workplace. The ruling made headlines in Contra Costa County, for by this time some eighty former workers at the Pittsburg plant or their survivors had filed $10 million punitive-damage lawsuits against the Johns-Manville Corporation on charges of fraudulent concealment and negligence. In August, 1979, however, an appellate court reversed Rothenberg's decision. Kilbourne then appealed the matter to the California Supreme Court, and after nearly a year the Supreme Court reversed the appellate court's decision with a five-to-two ruling which enabled the Pittsburg plant workers to proceed with their cases.

In September, 1980, Judge Rothenberg instructed Kilbourne and Kazan to select a sample case for a trial whose outcome would determine the issue of liability in the other eighty cases. As a result, the lawsuit of a worker named Bob Alan Speake was severed from the rest. A frail sixty-six-year-old man who was suffering from asbestosis, Speake had worked for thirty-three years at the Pittsburg plant before retiring in 1975. His complaint, like the complaints of his colleagues, accused Johns-Manville of negligence for having exposed him to harmful amounts of asbestos dust and for having failed to inform him that he had developed asbestos disease. However, like many of his fellow-workers, he had been a pack-a-day cigarette smoker, and the prospect of trying his suit as a precedent was not without risk for Kilbourne and Kazan.

As for the Johns-Manville people, the dismal prospect of having to explain away Wilbur Ruff's testimony about the company's hush-hush policy regarding asbestos disease was compounded by their knowledge that Travelers, which had defended Johns-Manville in the vast majority of asbestos lawsuits since *Borel*, would soon announce that its $16 million in primary comprehensive and general-liability insurance was exhausted, and that it would no longer assume the company's defense. Because of this impending development, Johns-Manville had brought a declaratory judgment action in San Francisco Superior Court against the Home Insurance Company, of New York City—the holder of its first layer of excess insurance between 1963 and 1976—and against twenty-five other insurance companies, which carried the rest of Johns-Manville's estimated $600 million worth of primary and excess coverage. In the suit, which was filed in March, 1980, Johns-Manville claimed that Home and the other defendants owed it indemnification because they were insurers of record during the period in which victims of asbestos disease had been exposed to its insulation products. For their part, many of the defendant carriers —there would ultimately be twenty-seven of them—asserted that they were required only to indemnify Johns-Manville when asbestos disease was diagnosed or became otherwise manifest during the insurance-policy period. In addition, Home alleged that Johns-Manville had fraudulently concealed the asbestos health hazard from Home's under-writers, who would not have issued excess coverage if they had known about the problem. There was supreme irony in this. Not only was Home's complaint against Johns-Manville similar to that of thousands of sick and dying workers who were suing the company but its action might well force Johns-Manville to disclose additional evidence of fraudulent concealment, and, no matter which of them won or lost the lawsuit, both might have to defend against that evidence. To avoid the prospect of such legal gridlock, the presiding judge in the various suits and countersuits, granting a motion by Johns-Manville, issued a pro-tective order that allowed all the parties in the cases to restrict the information or materials they disclosed.

During the early winter of 1981, the impending announcement by Travelers served to intensify a siege mentality that had been develop-ing among high officials of Johns-Manville, who had realized for nearly a year that they would sooner or later face the dismal prospect of going to trial on their own in cases that Travelers would normally have defended or settled out of court. (The fact that Johns-Manville was running out of primary insurance, together with a tremendous increase in the number of asbestos claims that were filed during 1980, had already caused the company's independent accountants to issue a qualified statement regarding its financial position for that year.) All things considered, therefore, Speake's lawsuit could scarcely have been severed for trial at a worse time as far as Johns-Manville was concerned. It was the first lawsuit to come to trial of approximately a thousand such lawsuits that had been brought in other parts of the country by Johns-Manville factory employees who had succeeded in penetrating the exclusive-remedy shield of workmen's compensation by suing for fraud. Thus, *Speake* held the potential of making Johns-Manville vulnerable to lawsuits that could conceivably be brought by tens of thousands of workers whom it had employed over the years in its asbestos mills and manufacturing plants. Indeed, it challenged the very underpinnings of workmen's compensation itself—a system that had been erected largely for the purpose of protecting American manufacturers and their insurers from common-law actions brought by injured workers. *Speake* was also important for the basic ethical reason that had preoccupied Kilbourne from the beginning: ten years after *Borel*, Johns-Manville was finally and for the first time on trial for essential wrongdoing committed by its officials for half a century in covering up the asbestos health hazard.

With so much at stake, it was not surprising that the process of discovery in *Speake* would provide some fascinating new disclosures. The first of these came about as a result of Kilbourne's desire to use the Sumner Simpson letters as proof that Johns-Manville had suppressed information about asbestos disease as early as the 1930s. Under the ancient-documents rules that exist in most states, documents more than thirty years old are presumed to be authentic. California had never adopted such a rule, however, so under the California evidence code the signature of Vandiver Brown, as well as the contents of the letters he wrote and received, would have to be independently verified before they could be introduced as evidence. Since Brown, Simpson, and most of the other people who figured in the correspondence were presumed to be dead, and since Raybestos-Manhattan was not a defendant in the case, this promised to be a difficult task. In February, 1981, Kilbourne telephoned Karl Asch, who had unearthed the

Sumner Simpson papers, to talk with him about the problem. During their discussion, Kilbourne recalled that several of Brown's letters had referred to payment of the salary and expenses of an industrial hygienist named Otto L. Binder, whom Johns-Manville had listed as dead in its reply to one of Kilbourne's interrogatories. Since Binder would have been an ideal person to verify Brown's correspondence, Kilbourne said in passing to Asch that it was too bad he had died, to which Asch replied that Binder was not dead at all but living in retirement in Indiana, and that he had been deposed a year or so earlier in some cases that had been brought in the Eastern District of Pennsylvania.

The fact that Binder was alive—indeed, Johns-Manville was paying him a pension—was soon overshadowed by the disclosure that still another figure from the 1930s who the company had claimed was dead had been found to be alive. This was none other than Vandiver Brown himself—a chief architect of the asbestos coverup—who had retired suddenly from Johns-Manville, in 1951, at the age of fifty. In April, 1981, Aaron H. Simon, an attorney with the Los Angeles firm of Greene, O'Reilly, Agnew & Broillet, was having difficulty in persuading the presiding judge in some asbestos cases he was handling to admit the Sumner Simpson correspondence in evidence, largely because he lacked independent authentication of Vandiver Brown's signature. For this reason, Simon hired an investigator to go to the Appellate Division of the New York State Supreme Court to get a copy of Brown's signature on the oath of office he had taken upon being admitted to practice in New York, and to find out where he had died in order to get a copy of his will. In the course of carrying out this mission, the investigator discovered that Brown was not dead, as Johns-Manville had been repeatedly claiming in its answers to interrogatories, but was still on the New York State Bar Association's list of member attorneys, and receiving its monthly journal at his home in Waco, Texas, where he was born and had grown up.

When Simon called Brown in Waco, the telephone was answered by a maid. She said that Brown was in Scotland, where he spent a good part of the year, and she gave Simon the telephone number of a man named Tom M. Oliver, Jr., who turned out to have been appointed Brown's legal guardian by the court of McLennan County, Texas, in 1975, when Brown, then seventy-four, was found to be a person of unsound mind. Oliver later told members of the plaintiff's bar that Brown, the son of a well-to-do cotton broker, was a chronic alcoholic, who had become senile as a result of an arteriosclerotic condition of the brain. Before any of this became known, however, Kilbourne, who had learned from Kazan by way of Simon that Brown was alive, made a motion in *Speake* v. *Manville* for the issuance of a subpoena to depose Brown in Scotland. The news of Kilbourne's motion caused consternation among lawyers at Moore, Clifford, Wolfe, Larson & Trutner—the Oakland law firm that was defending Johns-Manville in the Speake case—and an attorney was immediately dispatched to Edinburgh, where he hired counsel to resist the taking of Brown's deposition. Other Johns-Manville attorneys were sent to Waco, where they obtained evidence of Brown's incompetence, which they presented to the judge in the Speake case. While in Waco, they also made an agreement with the First National Bank of Waco, the guardian of Brown's estate, under which they would defend Brown and the bank against any lawsuits that might be brought against them.

Early in May, Fred Baron, the Dallas litigator who had gained prominence in the Tyler case, called a meeting of the innermost counsel of the Asbestos Litigation Group to decide how to deal with the matter, and a compromise was worked out between the asbestos litigators and David Britt, a lawyer for the First National Bank of Waco: Baron would be permitted to interview Brown in Edinburgh and determine for himself whether or not Brown was competent to give a deposition, and if Baron came away convinced that Brown was competent, Britt would litigate the issue in the United States, rather than in Scotland.

In July, Baron flew from Dallas to Edinburgh with his wife, Lisa Blue, a psychologist and lawyer, who was then a prosecutor in the district attorney's office of Dallas County. When they arrived for the meeting with Brown at the office of Johns-Manville's solicitor, Baron was ushered into an inner office and handed a lengthy psychiatrist's report, which stated that Vandiver Brown was incompetent and not capable of giving a deposition. When he returned to the anteroom, where his wife was waiting, he sat down beside her and began to read the report and at that point two men walked in from the street. "There were only three chairs in the anteroom, and when the younger of the two men sat down, Lisa immediately got up and gave her seat to the older man," Baron recalls. "He was a remarkably handsome and distinguished-looking man, with soft, clear skin and thick white hair that was immaculately combed. He wore a starched striped shirt, with a red bow tie, a green tweed sports coat, and a perfectly pressed pair of tan slacks, and when he sat down in Lisa's chair he asked her if she would like to sit on his lap. At that point, Lisa smiled at him and asked if he were by any chance from Waco, and he started to sing 'Deep in the Heart of Texas.' It was Vandiver Brown, of course, and he was singing 'The stars at night are big and bright' for the second time when the solicitor came out to take him and his companion into the inner office. About five minutes later, the attorney representing Johns-Manville ushered me into the office, where I sat across from Brown at a large conference table. I had been told that I could not ask him any questions about the asbestos litigation, so I started out be asking him how he was doing today, and he said 'Fine.' I then asked him if he had ever worked in New York City, and he told me he didn't remember. When I inquired if he had ever worked for Johns-Manville, he gave me the same answer. He did, however, remember that he had gone to school in Waco. When I asked him if he was an attorney, he said, 'I think I was, a long time ago.' I then asked him about his home outside Edinburgh, and he turned to his companion and asked if anything had happened to the house. By that time, it appeared obvious to me that Brown was either totally out of it or not willing to respond to my questions. Since I saw the futility of going on with the interview, I soon ended it. When I got back to my hotel, I wrote out a long and detailed report about what had taken place, which was later circulated among members of the Asbestos Litigation Group. After returning to Texas, I requested David Britt to produce any documents relating to Johns-Manville which might be in Brown's house in Waco, but after making a thorough search Britt reported that none could be found."

Subsequent investigation by asbestos litigators revealed that Brown was believed to have retired suddenly from Johns-Manville when it was discovered that he was a homosexual, for that precluded him from further advancement within the company. At that time, it is said, he severed all ties with the company, and left all his papers and memorandums behind. Whether the whole truth of the matter will ever be known is doubtful, because he died in Waco on September 2, 1983, at the age of eighty-two.

In addition to claiming that key officials such as Otto Binder and Vandiver Brown were dead, Johns-Manville had consistently frustrated orderly discovery in the California lawsuits by ignoring notices to produce documents, denying the existence of requested documents, and refusing to admit their authenticity and the authenticity of the signatures that had been affixed to them. To speed things up, Judge Coleman Fannin, who had replaced Judge Rothenberg as the presiding judge in the Speake case, appointed a retired jurist to hold separate evidentiary hearings to authenticate hundreds of documents that Kilbourne and Kazan had assembled for the upcoming trial. These hearings began in the spring of 1981 and continued through the summer and early autumn. Johns-Manville's attorneys argued against the admission of almost every piece of evidence—particularly the letters of Vandiver Brown—claiming that company officials had no idea where the letters had come from and no way of authenticating Brown's signature. However, Johns-Manville finally admitted the authenticity of Brown's signature on some thirty letters and memorandums when it learned that a handwriting expert retained by Kilbourne would testify that the signatures were identical to a duly acknowledged signature that Brown had affixed to a 1943 deed in his father's probate.

The trial of *Bob Alan Speake* v. *Johns-Manville Corp. et al.* got under way on November 30, 1981, and was litigated over the next nine weeks. In their opening statements, Kilbourne and Kazan told the jury that Manville had known about the health hazards of asbestos since the early 1930s and had deliberately and fraudulently concealed this knowledge from Speake. On Manville's behalf, Weyman Lundquist, the senior trial attorney for the other law firm representing Manville in *Speake*—the San Francisco firm of Heller, Ehrman, White & McAuliffe, of which Secretary of Defense Caspar Weinberger had been a member for many years—denied the allegation of fraudulent concealment, claiming that the company had been in the forefront of research into asbestos disease. Lundquist also claimed that Speake's health problem stemmed chiefly from his forty years of cigarette smoking, and that he had voluntarily assumed health risks when he had gone to work at the Pittsburg plant.

During the trial, Kazan brought out the fact that although chest X-rays of Speake taken in 1961 and 1964 showed signs of lung scarring Speake was never informed of this finding. Kazan then introduced in evidence Dr. Smith's 1949 memorandum in which he acknowledged that employees suffering from asbestosis "have not been told of this diagnosis, for it is felt that as long as the man feels well, is happy at home and at work and his physical condition remains good, nothing should be said." Kazan followed this up by introducing a letter that Smith had written in 1959, after reviewing the chest X-rays of longtime employees at the Pittsburg plant. "Of the thirty films reviewed, twenty-one showed positive evidence of pulmonary disease," Smith wrote. "Five films were doubtful and four showed no evidence of disease. I know that you understand the very serious financial exposure to the company should these cases progress to the point of disability." Additionally damaging information about Johns-Manville's corporate medical policy was presented when Dr. Wise testified that he had first met Dr. Smith in 1963, when Smith came to the Pittsburg plant to review chest X-rays, and that Smith had informed him then that he was not to counsel any workers who might develop occupational lung disease. (Kilbourne and Kazan later agreed to dismiss their complaint against Wise, explaining that the chief reason he had been kept as a defendant in the case was that they suspected that some Manville executives might try to blame him for the hush-hush policy.)

Damaging as Smith's letters and Wise's testimony appeared to be, Kilbourne and Kazan were disappointed by the limits of the evidence they were allowed to present at the trial. Judge Fannin, who was said to be opposed to the assessment of punitive damages, refused to let them introduce the Sumner Simpson letters, on the ground that since Johns-Manville had already admitted that asbestosis lawsuits were brought against it in the 1930s the letters were cumulative. For the same reason, the judge also refused to allow them to introduce the minutes of the 1933 directors' meetings concerning the eleven asbestosis claims that were settled in that year, as well as evidence about forty-two lawsuits that were brought in 1934 and 1935 by workers who had developed asbestosis at Johns-Manville's plant in Waukegan, Illinois.

When it came time for the defense attorneys to present Johns-Manville's case, they called two radiologists, who testified that Speake's pulmonary problems were caused by his cigarette smoking. They later called Dr. Paul Kotin, who had retired as Johns-Manville's senior vice-president for health, safety, and environment upon reaching the age of sixty-five, five months earlier. Kotin, who had rarely been called as a witness by Johns-Manville since Ronald Motley had used the Sumner Simpson letters and the contract-unit disease claims to rebut his previous testimony, proceeded to tell the jury that he had gone to work for Johns-Manville because "It was a company that had demonstrated through the years a great responsibility, a commitment —a leading-edge commitment, if you will—to the principles of occupational medicine." During cross-examination, Kotin was asked by Kazan whether an asbestos manufacturer had a duty to educate its customers in the safe and proper use of its products, and he responded with the same analogy that he had used when Gillenwater had cross-examined him in the Starnes trial, almost five years earlier. "Well, you know, it can no more insure responsible use than the Bayer aspirin company can guarantee that I don't take a hundred aspirin tablets to commit suicide," he said.

One of the highlights of the Speake trial occurred when Lundquist called John A. McKinney, Manville's chairman and chief executive officer, to the witness stand to testify to the character and integrity of the company he directed. A distinguished-looking silver-haired man of fifty-eight, who was earning $436,000 a year, McKinney was a native of Texas and had gone to work for Johns-Manville as a patent attorney in 1951, shortly after graduating from Georgetown University School of Law. He had become the firm's chief executive officer in 1977, and had since spent at least half his time on the company's asbestos-litigation problems, devising and directing legal strategy with a staff of in-house attorneys, and meeting with legislators on Capitol Hill in an effort to enlist their support for the enactment of a federal compensation system that would relieve Johns-Manville of some of its legal and financial burdens. McKinney, who had never before appeared in court to testify in an asbestos trial, told the jury that there was "a sense of family and a sense of mutual concern" at Johns-Manville, which he had always found very satisfying. He went on to extol Lewis H. Brown, who had been president of Johns-Manville between 1929 and 1946, and chairman of the board and chief executive officer from 1946 until his death in 1951, for inspiring "reverence" among his employees during the early 1930s by directing the adoption of such progressive policies as the forty-hour work week, periodic physical examinations for all workers, and safety programs designed to create a healthy workplace. Thanks to Judge Fannin's refusal to allow Kilbourne and Kazan to introduce into evidence the minutes of the early directors' meetings, McKinney was not required to answer questions about any of Brown's less reverential achievements, such as advising the company's directors in 1933 that eleven pending asbestosis lawsuits could be settled out of court provided that the attorney for the plaintiffs could be persuaded not to bring any more cases against the company.

In his closing argument to a jury of nine women and three men, Kilbourne said that Johns-Manville had exhibited a "conscious disregard" for Speake's right to know that if he worked long enough at the Pittsburg plant he would get sick. Kazan, in his, said that Johns-Manville should be made an example of "so that other companies will know what they did for the past fifty years was unacceptable and they can't get away with it." As for Lundquist, he told the jury that Speake was one of fourteen thousand plaintiffs who had lawsuits pending against Manville, and that if a huge award were made to him it might set a precedent that could ruin the company.

The *Speake* jury deliberated for twenty-six hours before returning a general verdict against Johns-Manville. Its members awarded Speake $150,000 in compensatory damages but refused to give him punitive damages. As might be expected, Kilbourne and Kazan were elated to win a landmark case demonstrating that Manville could no longer expect to be protected by the exclusive remedy of workmen's compensation, but they were disappointed by the amount of the compensatory award, which they felt should have been much higher, and by the jury's refusal to grant punitive damages. Kilbourne reacted to the verdict with special bitterness, calling it a victory for Johns-Manville. Now a white-haired man of sixty, with a mustache and a goatee, he had been working on *Speake* and his other asbestos cases for six and a half years. During that time, he had seen forty-nine of his asbestos clients die while their lawsuits were pending, and he had developed a profound contempt for Johns-Manville's tactics of obfuscation and delay. His contention that the case for fraudulent concealment had been severely handicapped by Judge Fannin's refusal to admit in evidence the Sumner Simpson letters and the minutes of the 1933 directors' meetings was powerfully reinforced when two of the jurors declared that they felt they had not been shown sufficient proof of deliberate intent on the part of Johns-Manville to conceal the asbestos hazard from Speake.

In spite of Kilbourne's disappointment, the Speake case marked a threshold in asbestos litigation, for as the information he had unearthed between 1978 and 1982 was added to the crushing weight of incriminating material that had already been amassed as proof of the company's past misconduct, juries across the nation began to award punitive damages against Johns-Manville. Indeed, as a direct result of all this discovery, punitive damages totaling more than $6 million were awarded against the company in ten of some sixty-five asbestos cases that were tried in 1981 and during the first half of 1982. What seems ironic is that what had come to light was undoubtedly just a small part of the history of neglect and deceit on the part of the nation's asbestos manufacturers. Thousands of documents had either disappeared or been discarded years before. Among the records that had disappeared were those of some thirteen hundred experimental studies of asbestos and other hazards that had been conducted at the Saranac Laboratory over three decades, along with virtually all the papers that had been presented at the Seventh Saranac Symposium— a week-long meeting on pulmonary dust disease that was held in late September, 1952. Unlike the proceedings of six previous meetings, those of the Seventh Symposium were never published, supposedly for budgetary reasons. Some observers believe, however, that they were suppressed because of pressure from asbestos manufacturers and the insurance industry. If they had not been, the meeting might well have gone down in history as the first major conference ever held on the biological effects of asbestos—an honor that went to the New York Academy of Sciences' conference that was organized twelve years later by Dr. Selikoff. Still, it is known that the Seventh Saranac Symposium was attended by more than two hundred medical doctors, research scientists, state and federal public-health officials, insurance-company executives, and manufacturers, who came from far and wide, and that they heard startling disclosures concerning asbestos disease from some of the leading participants in a drama that had then been unfolding for more than twenty years. From England came Dr. E. R. A. Merewether, Medical Inspector of Factories in Great Britain, who had conducted the first epidemiological study of asbestosis, back in 1928, and who now presented data that strongly linked asbestosis and lung cancer. From the Medical College of the University of South Carolina came the celebrated pathologist Kenneth M. Lynch, who, back in 1935, had been the first to suggest such a link. And from the National Cancer Institute came Wilhelm C. Hueper, who had warned for nearly a decade that asbestos was a potent carcinogen. (Hueper, who would later be among the first to warn of the dangers of DDT, was a scientist of remarkable foresight, as can be seen from a stunningly accurate appraisal of the coverup of occupational cancer that he had published in a 1943 bulletin of the American Cancer Society. "Industrial concerns are in general not particularly anxious to have the occurrence of occupational cancers among their employees or of environmental cancers among the consumers of their products made a matter of public records," Hueper wrote. "Such publicity might reflect unfavorably upon their business activities, and oblige them to undertake extensive and expensive technical and sanitary changes in their production methods and in the types of products manufactured. There is, moreover, the distinct possibility of becoming involved in compensation suits with extravagant financial claims by the injured parties. It is, therefore, not an uncommon practice that some pressure is exerted by the parties financially interested in such matters to keep information on the occurrence of industrial cancer well under cover.")

Other participants in the 1952 symposium who had played or would play major roles in the asbestos saga were Dr. Vorwald, director of the Saranac Laboratory, who had organized the meeting; Dr. Lanza, formerly of the Metropolitan Life Insurance Company; Dr. Smith and Hugh M. Jackson, of Johns-Manville; Professor Philip Drinker, of Harvard University's School of Public Health; Dr. W. Clark Cooper, of the United States Public Health Service; Ivan Sabourin, counsel for the Quebec Asbestos Mining Association; Dr. Paul Cartier, director of that association's clinic at Thetford Mines; Dr. Daniel C. Braun, medical director of the Industrial Hygiene Foundation, Inc.; Dr. Harriet L. Hardy, of the Massachusetts General Hospital; and Willis G. Hazard, the industrial-hygiene specialist of Owens-Illinois. Also present, and thus privy to early knowledge of the carcinogenic hazard posed by asbestos, were representatives of such major insurance companies as Travelers; the Employers Mutual Liability Insurance Company, of Wausau, Wisconsin; the American Mutual Liability Insurance Company and the Liberty Mutual Casualty Company, both of Boston; the Lumbermen's Mutual Casualty Company, of Chicago; the New Jersey Self Insurers Association; and the State of New York Insurance Fund.

If a significant number of the fifty-odd medical doctors who attended the Seventh Symposium had spoken out or had insisted that its papers and discussions be made public, they might well have blown the lid off the asbestos coverup and saved thousands of lives, untold pain and suffering, and millions of dollars. Instead, with the exception of the wonderfully outspoken Hueper, too many of them remained silent, and the conference simply marked the nadir of a year in which the asbestos industry, with the tacit approval of its insurers, successfully suppressed information about the most important industrial carcinogen the world has ever known. Furthermore, in the years to come a number of these physicians—among them Dr. Cooper, who testified for the defendants in the Tomplait and Borel trials—would see fit to take active roles in support of the asbestos industry. As for those who chose silence, it might be said that they were acting in the time-honored tradition of the American medical profession, whose members, by and large, continue to avoid speaking out on important matters of occupational and environmental health, out of élitist deference to an old-boy network that precludes them from voicing criticism either of one another or of a private-enterprise system that, by contaminating homes, hospitals, schools, and other buildings with asbestos, and befouling drinking-water supplies with toxic chemicals, has created public-health problems of staggering magnitude for the entire nation. In any event, because of timidity on the part of doctors, obtuseness on the part of public-health officials, and complacency on the part of Congress, the asbestos industry not only was allowed to conduct a highly successful coverup of medical and scientific knowledge about asbestos disease all during the 1950s, 1960s, and early 1970s but also, because of the Bankruptcy Code, has been allowed to continue doing business as usual to this very day. Indeed, only the uncompromising commitment of Dr. Selikoff, who has worked tirelessly for more than twenty years to make his findings known, and the dedication of Ward Stephenson and the plaintiff lawyers who, following his lead, carried on after *Borel*, have brought to light the truth about the suffering wrought by the asbestos industry upon tens of thousands of unsuspecting workers in the United States—a truth that, like the truth Émile Zola wrote about in "J'Accuse," had for years been buried underground, where, growing and gathering force, it had been waiting to burst forth.

SEVEN

GETTING OFF THE RISK

In the early 1980s, it was recognized in financial circles that asbestos litigation was going to cause a hemorrhage of serious, if not catastrophic, proportions in the assets of asbestos-insulation manufacturers and their insurers. Thanks largely to growing awareness of the asbestos hazard on the part of millions of wartime shipyard workers, there had been a large increase in the number of product-liability lawsuits. In 1976, 159 cases were filed against Johns-Manville alone; in 1978, 792 claims were filed against the company; and by 1982 lawsuits for asbestos disease were being brought against it at the rate of 6,000 a year. At the same time, the expense of asbestos litigation was also mounting. In 1979, Manville's average cost of settling a claim was about $21,000, but by the beginning of 1982 it had doubled.

By the end of 1982, the defendant insulation manufacturers and their insurers had paid out some $600 million in compensation to plaintiffs and in legal fees, in order to close out some 3,800 product-liability lawsuits, and to reach settlements with some of the 20,000 or so plaintiffs whose asbestos product-liability suits were still pending. Beyond these liabilities, what had been causing growing uneasiness in financial circles for several years—especially in the insurance industry, which was being forced to pick up two-thirds of the $600-million tab—was the fact that no one could accurately estimate how much the asbestos litigation was ultimately going to cost, for the simple reason that no one knew how many people had been exposed to harmful levels of asbestos dust, how many of them would eventually develop asbestos disease, or how many of the victims would file product-liability lawsuits. One insurance-company executive estimated that loss and loss-adjustment expenses for asbestos claims filed as of February, 1981, would be close to $1.35 billion compared with premiums of $6.3 billion that had been collected in 1980 for all

liability coverage except medical malpractice. Another study estimated that total compensation payments for asbestos-related
disabilities and deaths over the next twenty to thirty years might run
between $8 billion and $87 billion, with the most likely total about
$40 billion. A third study estimated that before the year 2010 be-
tween 83,000 and 178,000 new claims would be filed, and set the
total liability of the insurance industry at between $4 billion and $10
billion. Since insurance companies operate by balancing investment
earnings from premiums against anticipated losses and expenses,
these wildly fluctuating estimates clearly showed that the open-ended
asbestos litigation was creating imbalance and fiscal uncertainty
within the insurance system. Indeed, the asbestos lawsuits were pos-
ing the threat of incalculable loss—the nightmare of all insurers,
whose sleep was also troubled by the fact that they had sold billions
of dollars' worth of comprehensive general-liability coverage, including pollution-liability insurance, to chemical companies and other
manufacturing firms that might prove as vulnerable to product-liability lawsuits as the makers of asbestos insulation. Their peace of
mind has scarcely been restored by the avalanche of lawsuits resulting from the deadly chemical leak at Union Carbide's plant in Bhopal, India, or the prospect that tens of thousands of people whose
drinking water has been contaminated by toxic chemicals seeping
from hazardous-waste dumps may also sue, or the possibility that
class-action lawsuits may be brought against them by disgruntled
shareholders who are unhappy because of a serious downturn in the
property and casualty industry which has taken place in recent years.

Leading insurers had begun to worry about the implications of
asbestos litigation as early as 1977, when they held a meeting in New
York City to discuss the growing number of asbestos lawsuits they
were being called upon to defend and settle. However, they found
themselves deeply split on how to interpret the standard language of
their comprehensive general-liability insurance policies. Since 1966,
these policies had provided for indemnification should a claim be
presented for "bodily injury"—a phrase that had been legally defined
to include sickness or disease—caused by an "occurrence," which
meant an accident including exposure to conditions that resulted in
bodily injury during the policy period. At issue was the question of
whether insurance coverage should be triggered during the time of a
claimant's exposure to asbestos or at the time his asbestos disease had

been discovered or diagnosed. This question was complicated by the fact that during the latency period usually necessary for the development of asbestos disease—ten to forty years—each of the defendant asbestos-insulation manufacturers had invariably had a number of different insurers, and may also have been self-insured for certain periods of time. Advocates of the exposure theory—up until then, it had provided the basis for most claims settlement—argued that each exposure to asbestos dust was an occurrence causing bodily injury to the claimant, with physical damage repeated on each subsequent inhalation, until the cumulative effect of all of these exposures resulted in disability or death from asbestos disease. The exposure theorists reasoned that asbestos inhalation was a continuing tort, and that all of the insurers who were on the risk for issuing policies during the time of a diseased worker's exposure were required to defend and indemnify the insured insulation manufacturer. By contrast, advocates of the manifestation theory argued that inhalation of asbestos caused bodily injury only when asbestos-related disease manifested itself through medical diagnosis, or when the claimant knew, or should have known, that he was suffering from asbestos disease. For this reason, they held that only the insurer who was on the risk at the time of manifestation should be required to defend and indemnify the insulation manufacturer who was being sued.

Traditionally secretive, insurance companies have always preferred to resolve ambiguities of contract interpretation through compromise and settlement—there is an old saying in the industry that the best file is a closed file—and for this reason carriers have been notably reluctant to involve the judiciary in such matters, fearing not only that juries and judges might be sympathetic to those on the other side, whether claimants or insured parties, but also that court-ordered discovery procedures might result in the disclosure of insurance practices that could engender legislative scrutiny and produce unwanted regulation. In this instance, however, the disagreement was so profound and the amount of money at issue so substantial that the dispute soon found its way into the courts, where insurance companies began to wage an uncharacteristically bitter struggle among themselves and with their clients—the asbestos-insulation manufacturers they had insured—over who should be responsible for compensating the victims of asbestos disease.

The first major crack in the insurance industry's façade occurred on June 27, 1977, when the Insurance Company of North America (INA), which had its headquarters in Philadelphia, informed Forty-Eight Insulations—a small asbestos-manufacturing company in Aurora, Illinois, which was owned by the giant Foster-Wheeler Corporation, of Livingston, New Jersey—that INA would no longer defend or indemnify Forty-Eight Insulations in any lawsuits alleging that asbestos disease had manifested itself after October 31, 1972. This was the expiration date of the last of a series of insurance policies that INA had sold Forty-Eight since 1955. Nine days later, INA filed an action in federal district court in Detroit, seeking a declaratory judgment that would affirm the manifestation theory against Forty-Eight and four carriers that had insured Forty-Eight after 1972. Among these carriers were Travelers Indemnity, of Rhode Island, and the Liberty Mutual Insurance Company, of Boston. Forty-Eight had manufactured asbestos-insulation products between 1934 and 1970, and at the time of the filing it had been named as a defendant in 99 asbestos product-liability lawsuits. However, in seeking a ruling in favor of the manifestation theory, the managers of INA were looking nervously to the future, knowing that their company had held primary insurance coverage for two other insulation manufacturers that had become major targets of asbestos lawsuits—the Keene Corporation, of New York City, and Nicolet Industries, of Ambler, Pennsylvania—and that under the exposure theory this coverage would surely be triggered. INA had also sold a considerable amount of excess-insurance coverage to Keene, Nicolet, Johns-Manville, Armstrong Cork, and Owens-Corning, which could be called into account if and when payments for asbestos-disease claims exceeded the dollar limits of primary policies. As things turned out, the concern of INA's managers was well founded, for by 1982 Forty-Eight, Keene, and Nicolet were faced with a total of more than fifteen thousand lawsuits, and INA's potential liability in asbestos litigation would be estimated to be $20 billion. (In the same year, INA was merged with another insurance giant—the Connecticut General Life Insurance Company, of Bloomfield, Connecticut—to form the CIGNA Corporation, the nation's second largest shareholder-owned, multi-line carrier, whose headquarters are in Philadelphia.)

After a lengthy and complex trial, which took place in the spring of 1978, United States District Judge John Feikens ruled against INA in favor of the exposure theory, declaring that INA's manifestation argument was a departure from the traditional approach of the insurance industry. In his opinion, Judge Feikens pointed out that none of INA's policies "contains language that makes manifestation a factor in determining whether or not there is a duty to defend." He also pointed out that INA had defended Forty-Eight in most of the hundred and fifty-odd asbestos cases that had been brought against it between 1974 and 1977, without ever raising the point that "manifestation of the disease must occur during the coverage period as a requirement for coverage."

INA immediately appealed Judge Feikens's ruling to the United States Court of Appeals for the Sixth Circuit, in Cincinnati. The appeal was supported by Liberty Mutual and two of the other insurance companies that had been named as defendants in the original action. Liberty Mutual's reasons for advocating the manifestation theory were not hard to see. In addition to holding primary product-liability coverage for Forty-Eight for part of 1976 and all of 1977, it had sold primary coverage to Armstrong Cork from 1973 to 1980, to Keene in 1967–68 and again from 1974 to 1980, and to Eagle-Picher from 1968 to 1979—three manufacturers that were being named as defendants in thousands of asbestos-disease lawsuits.

The appeal of the district court decision in *INA* v. *Forty-Eight* was strenuously opposed by Forty-Eight and Travelers. Forty-Eight, of course, had everything to gain from the exposure theory, which maximized its insurance coverage. As for Travelers, which held Forty-Eight's primary coverage for 1976, it supported the exposure theory and suggested that the court might want to consider a pro-rata version of it under which those insurers who were on the risk from the time of a claimant's first exposure to asbestos until he filed his claim were responsible to pay in proportion to the time their several policies were in effect. Although Travelers itself had much to lose through the exposure approach, as a result of having sold primary product-liability insurance over the years to such major defendants as Johns-Manville, Armstrong Cork, and Pittsburgh Corning, it was in a stronger position than many insurers, because it had sold relatively little excess insurance to the asbestos industry. Among the carriers with significant liability for excess coverage were INA; Lloyd's of London; the Commercial Union Insurance Company, also of London; Aetna Life & Casualty, of Hartford; CNA Insurance Companies, of Chicago; the Home Insurance Company of New York City's and the American International Group, also of New York City.

Travelers was operating on the assumption that once its primary policies were exhausted, liability for indemnification and defense costs would automatically be transferred to the excess carriers, and that any gaps in coverage would be the responsibility of the insulation manufacturers; in May 1981, in fact, Travelers announced that it supported the exposure theory as the fairest way to resolve the growing problem of asbestos litigation, declaring that it provided a workable basis for multiple carriers to pro-rate their obligations to a single policyholder, and was the best method of giving the policyholder a broad base of insurance coverage.

During oral argument, which was heard by the Sixth Circuit in October, 1979, lawyers for the appellants warned that Judge Feikens's ruling for the exposure theory could "plague the nation's trial courts and appellate courts, together with insurers and insureds alike, for many years to come." Nevertheless, a year later, the Sixth Circuit affirmed the lower court's adoption of the exposure theory by a two-to-one margin. Noting that beginning in 1976, Forty-Eight's insurance coverage contained such a high deductible that "as a practical matter, Forty-Eight is uninsured for asbestosis occurring after" that year, the majority judges supported the exposure theory on the ground that "insurance policies must be strictly construed in favor of the injured and to promote coverage." As for the plague of cases they had been warned about, the jurists were not about to assume any responsibility for that. "We think that the 'plague' will come regardless of how we decide this case," they wrote. "The cause of the plague, however, is an insurance industry which adopted a standard policy which is inadequate to deal with the problems of asbestosis."

By this time, as might be expected, a number of other declaratory-judgment actions had been filed in other jurisdictions by insurers or defendant manufacturers who, depending on the particular circumstances—and, of course, on the extent of their financial liability—were either for or against the exposure theory. In June, 1978, faced with more than five hundred asbestos-disease claims, the Keene Corporation filed suit for declaratory judgment and damages against INA, Liberty Mutual, Aetna Casualty & Surety, and the Hartford Accident & Indemnity Company, of Hartford—four companies that had issued comprehensive general-liability policies to Keene or its predecessors since 1961—alleging that the insurers had failed to defend and indemnify it. The Keene Corporation was formed in 1967. In 1968, it bought Baldwin-Ehret-Hill, Inc., of Trenton, New Jersey, which was a maker of asbestos insulation until 1972. Keene was acquired by the Bairnco Corporation, of New York City, in 1981.

Keene v. *INA*, which was brought in federal district court for the District of Columbia, proved to be another novel and complex case in insurance law. It was decided on appeal in October, 1981, when the Court of Appeals for the District of Columbia Circuit not only overturned the lower-court decision to adopt a pro-rata exposure theory but ruled that Keene could utilize the limits of any single liability policy, and carried the exposure theory a step further by embracing what came to be known as the triple-trigger approach. Under this theory, insurance coverage could be triggered by the initial inhalation of asbestos fibers, by exposure-in-residence to the fibers—meaning the continuing damage inflicted upon lung tissue by asbestos fibers that had already been inhaled—and by the manifestation of asbestos disease. Declaring that asbestos disease was "unknown and unknowable" to Keene at the time it had bought its insurance, in 1961, the court ruled that the company should be "free of all liability for asbestos-related disease." Needless to say, with Keene having by then been named as a defendant in more than six thousand asbestos lawsuits, the appellate decision was a blow to insurers across the nation. They protested bitterly that the courts had undertaken to rewrite insurance policies in order to give Keene the best of all possible worlds, and predicted dire consequences for the insurance industry.

By the late autumn of 1981, no fewer than nineteen declaratory-judgment actions concerning insurance liability for asbestos-related disease were pending in federal and state courts, and pressure was mounting for the United States Supreme Court to involve itself in the controversy. In December, however, the Supreme Court declined to hear an appeal of *INA* v. *Forty-Eight,* and in March, 1982, it declined to hear *Keene* v. *INA.* In its petition for a hearing in *Keene* v. *INA,* Hartford Accident & Indemnity told the justices that the asbestos cases presented potentially the most costly product-liability claims "ever to confront American industry" and constituted "perhaps the most important insurance-law issue ever to be litigated in our judicial system." Hartford went on to complain that under the appellate-court ruling in *Keene* v. *INA* "an insurance company which has issued a standard comprehensive liability policy for a period of one year—or even one month—is potentially liable for forty years of losses." A majority of the Supreme Court justices were unmoved by these arguments, however, and by a five-to-three vote they let stand the appeals-court ruling that had greatly expanded an insurer's obligation to pay for asbestos-related disease by embracing the triple-trigger approach.

At the time, some observers felt that the Supreme Court's refusal to hear appeals of the declaratory judgments involving insurance coverage might increase pressure on Congress to devise a legislative solution to the problem of how to compensate the victims of asbestos disease. Asbestos-insulation manufacturers, led by Johns-Manville, had been trying since 1975 to persuade the lawmakers to pass legislation embodying various federally financed compensation schemes that were designed to bail them out of their financial and legal difficulties. As for the insurance industry, once the appeals court had decided in favor of the exposure theory in *INA* v. *Forty-Eight,* it also began casting about for alternative solutions to the problems posed by asbestos litigation. Speaking before a conference of special-risk underwriters in New York City in January, 1981, Anthony M. Lanzone, a specialist in insurance law and defense litigation, recommended that the industry establish an asbestos compensation trust that would be financed by all potentially liable insurers, whether they subscribed to the exposure or the manifestation theory, and administered by an arbitration panel, whose members would review relevant medical reports and insurance-coverage history before determining the percentage of an insurer's payment, and whose decisions would be binding. He went on to warn that asbestosis and other industry-related diseases would "plague the insurance industry well into the future" unless their scope and magnitude were recognized.

Lanzone's warning was reiterated at the end of April, 1981, by Victor B. Levit, managing partner of the law firm of Long & Levit, of San Francisco and Los Angeles, in a talk he gave at Lloyd's of London at the invitation of that venerable institution's non-marine claims committee. Levit and his firm were representing Travelers in the year-old declaratory-judgment action that Johns-Manville had brought in San Francisco Superior Court against the Home Insurance Company and more than a score of other carriers, both primary and excess, including Lloyd's, in an effort to apply the exposure theory to its insurance coverage. As for Lloyd's—syndicates of underwriters who have long been considered to be the boldest in the world—it had incurred tremendous potential liability as a result of having sold huge amounts of excess coverage since the 1930s, to leading American asbestos-insulation manufacturers, including Johns-Manville.

At the outset of his talk, Levit cited an insurance industry estimate that asbestos-disease lawsuits would cost the insurance industry $1.35 billion a year, but he went on to say that this situation might reflect only the tip of an iceberg and to warn that toxic-latent-disease claims could eventually threaten the solvency of some insurance companies. By way of example, Levit talked about the thousand-odd lawsuits brought against some of the manufacturers of diethylstilbestrol, or DES—the synthetic female hormone that had been designed to prevent the loss of fetuses by miscarriage but had later been found to produce cancer in some of the daughters of women who had taken the drug. He also mentioned mass litigation involving Agent Orange, the dioxin-containing herbicide that had been widely used as a defoliant in Vietnam; the Love Canal and other hazardous-waste dumps, of which there may be, according to the Environmental Protection Agency as many as fifty thousand in the United States; the Three Mile Island nuclear power plant, where a partial meltdown of the reactor in 1979 had already resulted in a $25 million settlement for persons living within twenty-five miles of the facility; radiation-induced injuries that were alleged to have resulted from the government's testing of nuclear weapons in Nevada and the Marshall Islands; and tampons and toxic-shock syndrome.

In outlining the seriousness of the mounting latent-disease litigation, Levit placed strong emphasis on a 1980 decision of the California Supreme Court, which reversed a lower-court ruling in *Sindell* v. *Abbott Laboratories*. This was a DES case in which the Supreme Court had shifted the burden of proof from the plaintiffs, who had traditionally been required to show that they had been harmed by the product of a particular defendant, to the defendant manufacturers, who, if they were to escape liability would thenceforth be required to prove that their products had not been used by the plaintiffs. The California Supreme Court did so because there were some two hundred manufacturers of DES and almost no way for a plaintiff to prove whose DES her mother had taken.

The decision in *Sindell* v. *Abbott* was of particular concern to Levit's client, Travelers, and to other insurance carriers who provided asbestos manufacturers with coverage, because, soon after it was handed down, Robert E. Sweeney, an experienced litigator from Cleveland, had amended the complaints of forty-two asbestos insulators to include allegations of market-share liability, and had then proceeded to negotiate settlements totaling nearly $1.5 million with fifteen asbestos manufacturers. In the largest settlement—a $477,000 payment in the wrongful-death case of a forty-six-year-old pipe coverer who had died of the invariably fatal, asbestos-induced tumor called malignant mesothelioma—Johns-Manville agreed to contribute $135,000, and Pittsburgh Corning agreed to pay $25,000. In the end, however, Travelers, which held primary coverage for both firms, paid most of those sums.

By extension, of course, the *Sindell* decision had serious implications for Levit's audience at Lloyd's, because of the huge amount of excess insurance that Lloyd's had sold over the years to Johns-Manville, which was fast running out of primary insurance with Travelers. Levit became the bearer of additional bad tidings when he predicted that the Supreme Court would deny a hearing in *INA* v. *Forty-Eight,* and that an asbestos-health-hazards-compensation bill that had been introduced into the Ninety-Sixth Congress in 1980 by Senator Gary Hart, Democrat of Colorado, to set up a pool financed by government and industry to compensate the victims of asbestos disease, had little chance of being enacted by Congress because "it has been labeled as a Johns-Manville bailout bill." Levit closed his talk with a gloomy look at the future, predicting that "there will be many more claims than we can possibly anticipate from toxic substances, that such claims will often take many years to manifest themselves, and that the pounds and dollars involved will be far greater than we can possibly imagine."

Levit's lugubrious view was soon followed by a drumbeat of dire predictions that appeared to be designed to create the proper climate for a federal solution to the problem of asbestos disease. Some of the direst were to be found in a position paper entitled "Asbestos: A Social Problem," which was issued on May 12, 1981, by the Boston headquarters office of Commercial Union, a subsidiary of the British-owned Commercial Union Assurance Company that had incurred potentially overwhelming liability as a result of carrying what was widely estimated to be $1.5 billion worth of primary and excess coverage for various asbestos-insulation manufacturers. Commercial Union not only held primary coverage for Johns-Manville between 1934 and 1948, and for Raybestos-Manhattan between 1967 and 1969, but had provided first-layer excess coverage for Pittsburgh Corning between 1960 and 1970, and for UNR Industries between 1964 and 1970; in addition, it had sold excess-insurance policies over the years to Johns-Manville, Armstrong Cork, Owens-Corning, and some forty other asbestos-insulation manufacturers. Since most of Commercial Union's coverage was for the period in which most of the disease-producing exposure to asbestos had taken place, the company had become a fierce advocate of the manifestation theory, and now that the manifestation theory had encountered rough sledding in the courts Commercial Union was trying to paint asbestos litigation as a calamity requiring federal intervention.

In their position paper, the Commercial Union people enumerated the inadequacies of litigation as a compensation remedy, pointing out that costly pretrial discovery could consume years of time, and that after legal fees, workmen's-compensation reimbursement, and medical expenses a plaintiff who received a hundred-thousand-dollar jury award might take home less than half that amount. (The fact is, however, that pretrial costs were significantly increased by the refusal of most defendant manufacturers to permit the use of pretrial discovery that had been taken in other cases, thus forcing plaintiff attorneys to conduct the same discovery over and over again. Moreover, it was through pretrial discovery that the culpability of the asbestos industry had been established to the extent that juries were by now routinely making awards far in excess of $100,000 in asbestos-disease cases.) The Commercial Union people went on to say that proliferating asbestos claims were jeopardizing the financial stability of many insurance companies. Indeed, they pointed out that it was not inconceivable that several million claims for asbestos disease might eventually be filed, and that "the damages that will be ultimately awarded will exceed the combined assets of the insurance and asbestos industries." They then warned that this could result in a situation in which "private individuals will hold homeowners', health, and automobile insurance contracts that are worthless because there will no longer be sufficient assets to provide the protection purchased."

In the concluding section of their paper, Commercial Union's authors cited the need for a federal solution to the "pervasive social problem" of asbestos disease, claiming that citizens have "traditionally looked to the federal government to protect them from threats to public health," and arguing that many people suffering from asbestos disease had been first exposed to asbestos while working in shipyards during the Second World War, when the government required the use of vast amounts of asbestos in ship construction. In a curiously insensitive assessment of who was enduring the consequences for this, they wrote, "In effect, we are still paying for the war effort, only now it is private industry, rather than the government, that is doing so."

In calling for federal legislation to solve the problems created by asbestos litigation, Commercial Union was ignoring the fact that two bills had already been floated in Congress to accomplish this goal and had been shot down in committee. The first of these measures had been introduced in August, 1977, by Representative Millicent Fenwick, a Republican of New Jersey, whose district included the town of Manville—home of Johns-Manville's giant asbestos-manufacturing complex. Fenwick's bill, which was called the Asbestos Health Hazards Compensation Act, and which was said to have been written with the assistance of Johns-Manville's legal staff, sought to bar victims of asbestos disease from bringing product-liability or other common-law tort actions against the asbestos industry, the tobacco industry, or the federal government, and instead to compensate them from a federally administered central fund. It proposed that claims accruing before January 1, 1980, be paid by the United States Treasury, and subsequent claims out of a fund financed by mandatory contributions from the asbestos and tobacco industries together with equal contributions from the federal treasury. In 1979, the minimum base compensation for an asbestos worker who could prove that he was totally disabled by asbestos disease came to about $500 a month, while the maximum benefit for a man with a dependent wife and two or more children came to about $1,000 a month.

As might be expected, the legislation proposed by Representative Fenwick was the target of much bitter criticism. None, however, was more bitter than that leveled by her colleague, Representative George Miller, a Democrat of California, who had chaired hearings into the asbestos coverup in 1978, and whose district included Johns-Manville's Pittsburg plant. Testifying before the Subcommittee on Labor Standards on May 2, 1979, Miller declared that Fenwick's bill had been "drafted and supported by the asbestos industry itself," and he pointed out that "under the terms of this legislation, the obligation of paying for decades of neglect, negligence, cover-up and lies would be foisted upon the American taxpayer." Miller told his colleagues that to consider enacting such legislation would send "a clear message to every industry in this nation which produces hazardous or toxic substances" that "the federal government is willing to pay for your recklessness."

The second bill to compensate the victims of asbestos disease, which was also entitled the Asbestos Health Hazards Compensation Act, was the one that Senator Gary Hart introduced in 1980, after consultation with Johns-Manville, which in 1972 had moved its world headquarters from New York to the Denver area. Hart, it would turn out, had ties to Johns-Manville, and his bill was, if anything, even more favorable to the asbestos industry than Fenwick's. It not only proposed to bar the victims of asbestos disease from filing suits under the tort system but left the administration of asbestos-compensation claims with the states. Since the provisions of many state workmen's-compensation statutes had been heavily influenced by employers and their insurers, the statutes tended to be grossly biased against claimants. Moreover, all of them required diseased workers, or the survivors of workers who had died, to prove their claims in adversarial proceedings that could be contested by manufacturers and their insurance carriers. It is true that Hart's bill, which the *Syracuse Law Review* later described as being "of questionable constitutionality," called for the establishment of federal minimum standards for compensating asbestos workers, providing that compensation for total disability or death could not be less than two-thirds of a claimant's average gross weekly wage during the highest three of the five years preceding his disability or death. But it proposed that adherence to the minimum standards would be voluntary on the part of the states, and that workers who failed to receive adequate payments would have to file petitions for supplemental compensation with a federal benefits-review board.

With such profound shortcomings, neither the Fenwick nor the Hart measures—each of them appeared to reflect a desire on the part of its author to accommodate a powerful corporate constituent, and both had been bitterly attacked as Johns-Manville bailout bills—had a prayer of being enacted by Congress when they were reintroduced in 1981.

What, then, had prompted Commercial Union to issue its desperate call for a federal legislative solution in May of that year? According to some observers, the answer is that Travelers, shortly after making its announcement, in April, that it would no longer indemnify or defend Johns-Manville in asbestos-disease lawsuits, had sent a similar announcement to Pittsburgh Corning, to which it had sold $10 million worth of primary comprehensive general-liability insurance between 1961 and 1970. At that point, Pittsburgh Corning sent a written demand for indemnification in pending litigation to the Employer's Liability Assurance Corporation, Ltd., of London—a firm that had covered Pittsburgh Corning with more than $20 million worth of first-layer excess insurance during the same period and had become part of Commercial Union in 1968. By way of reply, Commercial Union brought a declaratory-judgment action on May 21 in the United States District Court for the Eastern District of Pennsylvania, in Philadelphia, against Pittsburgh Corning and its owners—PPG Industries and the Corning Glass Works—as well as against Travelers, INA, and the American Motorists Insurance Company, of Long Grove, Illinois. INA had provided Pittsburgh Corning with primary insurance between 1970 and 1973, and American Motorists, a subsidiary of the Kemper Corporation, also of Long Grove, had provided it with primary coverage between 1973 and 1975. In a ten-count complaint, Commercial Union accused Pittsburgh Corning, PPG, and Corning Glass of misrepresenting and concealing the dangers of asbestos from Commercial Union in order to buy more coverage. It accused Travelers of failing to properly defend asbestos-disease lawsuits that had been brought against Pittsburgh Corning, PPG, and Corning Glass, and of wrongfully paying settlements under the exposure theory, with the result that Travelers exhausted its primary-policy limits and thus coerced Commercial Union into defending and indemnifying Pittsburgh Corning and its owners. In addition, Commercial Union accused INA and American Motorists of entering into an agreement with Travelers to allow it to settle improperly under the exposure theory, and, not surprisingly, went on to maintain that the manifestation theory should apply in the case. Application of the manifestation theory would, of course, have got Commercial Union off the risk, for the simple reason that Pittsburgh Corning had been making asbestos-insulation products only since 1962, and asbestos disease, which usually takes at least ten years to develop, had not manifested itself to any great extent among

Pittsburgh Corning's employees before 1970, when Commercial Union ceased carrying Pittsburgh's first-layer excess coverage.

As might be expected, Commercial Union's declaratory-judgment action provoked a number of summary-judgment motions, cross-claims, and counterclaims on the part of the defendants. Chief among them was a motion by PPG, the purchaser of Pittsburgh Corning's insurance, asking Judge James T. Giles, Jr., who was presiding over the case, to declare that the policies issued by Travelers and Commercial Union were exposure policies, and to direct Commercial Union to assume PPG's defense and to pay judgments and settlements in future asbestos lawsuits, on the ground that Travelers had exhausted its coverage. Early in November, Judge Giles ruled in favor of PPG on the exposure-versus-manifestation issue, declaring that cumulative damage from asbestos inhalation occurs prior to manifestation of disease, and that the exposure theory governed the triggering of Commercial Union's coverage. Commercial Union then announced that, pending an appeal of Giles's ruling, it would assume Pittsburgh Corning's defense in some 7,600 asbestos lawsuits that were pending against the company. For the next eight months or so, litigation of the nine remaining counts in *Commercial Union* v. *Pittsburgh Corning* dragged on in Judge Giles's court in Philadelphia. It attracted little public notice, but, because Judge Giles refused the entreaties of both Commercial Union and Pittsburgh Corning to close any of the hearings he held or to permanently seal any of the records they produced, the case provided some rare and enlightening glimpses into the intricate world of insurance underwriting.

Most enlightening of all was a widely circulated chart that had been drawn up to show the bewildering assortment of comprehensive general-liability insurance policies that PPG Industries had bought to cover itself and its subsidiary, Pittsburgh Corning, against product-liability lawsuits between 1961, the year before Pittsburgh Corning purchased UNARCO's asbestos-insulation business, and 1975. During each of the first nine years of that period, PPG (which was known as Pittsburgh Plate Glass until 1968) had bought a million-dollar primary-insurance policy from Travelers, and for each of the last five years it had bought a million-dollar primary policy from either INA or American Motorists. Starting in 1960, PPG also bought increasing amounts of excess insurance at three-year intervals, in order to protect itself and Pittsburgh Corning in the event that the limits of its primary coverage were reached. As a result, Pittsburgh Corning soon became one of the most heavily insured asbestos-insulation manufacturers in the business. Some observers believe that PPG did this knowing full well, because of Dr. Gaze's 1961 warning about the health hazards of asbestos, that by buying into the asbestos-insulation business, Pittsburgh Corning was embarking upon a hazardous enterprise vulnerable to the possibility of product-liability litigation. In any event, over the first three-year period PPG bought $2 million worth of first-layer excess coverage from Employer's Liability (the English firm that later merged with Commercial Union) and $18 million worth of additional excess coverage from a number of other insurers—among them the American Re-Insurance Company, of New York; the General Reinsurance Company, of Greenwich, Connecticut; and Travelers. Its total insurance coverage for the three years, including primary coverage, amounted to $21 million. During the second three-year period, PPG increased its first-layer excess coverage with Employer's to $10 million, and then proceeded to buy $20 million worth of excess on top of that, bringing its total insurance coverage for that period to $31 million. During the third three-year interval, it bought additional layers of excess insurance, which brought its total coverage to $51 million.

From then on, PPG continued to increase its excess insurance until, during the three-year period beginning in 1972, it had a total coverage of about $150 million. (The first $40 million of excess coverage was held by the Home Insurance Company, Lloyd's, and various British insurers, and the remainder was held by more than a dozen other carriers.) Even more surprising was the fact that if all the layers of primary and excess insurance that had been bought by PPG over the fourteen-year period were stacked on top of one another, and then triggered—a not impossible eventuality under the triple-trigger theory of insurance coverage embraced by the appellate court's decision in *Keene* v. *INA*—Pittsburgh Corning's product-liability coverage amounted to $997 million, for which, because excess insurance had been sold at bargain rates during much of that time, PPG had only spent an estimated half a million dollars in premiums. Most important of all, however, was the fact that, in keeping with traditional insurance practice, the carriers of PPG's excess policies had laid off much of their risk by selling between 50 and 75 percent of it to various reinsurance companies in the United States, and these, in turn, had ceded portions of their risk to reinsurance investors in the London market—the largest reinsurance industry in the world—which then ceded to reinsurance companies in Germany, Switzerland, Japan, Bermuda and various islands in the Caribbean. What could well prove troublesome about this practice was that some of the reinsurers might not possess sufficient capital to cover their losses if the asbestos claims against Pittsburgh Corning, which in 1981 had penetrated the first layers of excess coverage, reached into the reinsurance layers and began to test their financial security.

As might be expected, other asbestos manufacturers had also bought large amounts of cheap excess coverage from insurance carriers that also reduced their exposure by purchasing reinsurance from syndicates backed by investors who had little reason to expect that they would ever be called on to make good on the risk. (Over the years, for example, the return for reinsurance investors associated with Lloyd's has rarely fallen below 100 percent.) And it was for this reason that by 1981 asbestos product-liability litigation was seen as threatening to undermine the whole insurance enterprise—a rickety edifice at best, whose structural integrity, like the schemes of Ponzi and the periodic chain letters that have been his legacy, apparently depended on the maintenance of unlimited confidence that, if worse came to worst, the risk could be passed on and on, until money would somehow be found to pay for the losses. Accordingly, strenuous efforts were undertaken during that year to shore things up before the situation got out of hand. A representative of one of the nation's leading multiple-line insurance carriers made a special trip to England to assure the people at Lloyd's, as well as other investors in the London Market, that asbestos claims would not be allowed to cause a major collapse within the insurance system. On the home front, insurance-company representatives and their lawyers held meetings with other insurance companies to explore ways of coordinating defense efforts in order to reduce the rapidly increasing legal costs of asbestos litigation. And Aetna Life & Casualty, the nation's largest investor-owned insurance company, acquired the American Re-Insurance Company—a firm that was believed to be especially vulnerable to asbestos claims—in a move that some observers felt was a rescue operation designed to prevent the loss of a key card in a house that might be built of cards. Meanwhile, out of public sight and mind, in courts around the country, insurers were trying to get off the risk by accusing one another of improperly settling asbestos claims, and by continuing to do battle with their insureds over the exposure-versus-manifestation issue. In several cases—most notably in *Commercial Union* v. *Pittsburgh Corning*—they were even asking for a recision of the insurance policies they had issued, on the ground that asbestos manufacturers had misrepresented and concealed the hazards of asbestos from insurance underwriters, and so had bought product-liability coverage through fraud.

In reality, many of the nation's insurers had known for decades that asbestos workers were dying early, but had kept silent while their underwriters wrote policies for workmen's compensation and comprehensive general liability as fast as they could put pen to paper, and as the premiums from those policies were invested with the full expectation that few, if any, claims for asbestos disease would ever be made. It was the life-insurance companies that first became aware of the excessive mortality rate among asbestos workers—a simple matter of studying their actuarial tables and discovering that the workers were experiencing premature deaths. As early as 1918, an official of the Prudential Life Insurance Company, of Newark, New Jersey—in 1984, with amost $80 billion in assets, it was the nation's wealthiest life-insurance company—acknowledged that it had become the practice of many carriers not to issue life-insurance policies to asbestos workers. In 1928, officials of the Penn Mutual Life Insurance Company, of Philadelphia, and the John Hancock Mutual Life Insurance Company, of Boston, and other leading life-insurance carriers assessed asbestos workers as risks who were to be selected with great care, and who were to be issued policies bearing extra premiums that provided for an extra mortality rate of 50 percent. A year later, the Metropolitan Life Insurance Company, of New York—it was then the largest life-insurance company in the United States, and was the carrier of group life insurance for Johns-Manville's employees—undertook a health survey of the asbestos-textile industry for Johns-Manville and Raybestos-Manhattan and found that large numbers of asbestos-textile workers were developing incurable and potentially fatal pulmonary disease.

In 1935, the United States Public Health Service published a version of Metropolitan's original report of this survey, which contained changes favorable to the asbestos industry that had been suggested by Johns-Manville lawyers, and forty years later Metropolitan

Life was named as one of several defendants in lawsuits brought by 286 former workers and their wives at Raybestos-Manhattan's Passaic plant, who alleged that the insurance company had conspired to withhold and suppress information that was vitally important to their health and well-being. Although Metropolitan Life was subsequently dismissed as a defendant in the vast majority of these cases, the company saw fit to contribute to a $15.5 million settlement that was reached early in 1981 and all 683 plaintiffs who had by then brought suit. Moreover, in the spring of 1984, Judge Harold Ackerman, who had presided over the Passaic cases, refused to dismiss a complaint alleging conspiracy to withhold and suppress information that had been brought against Metropolitan Life by a former worker at Johns-Manville's plant in Manville, New Jersey, who was being represented by Karl Asch, the lawyer responsible for unearthing the Sumner Simpson letters. The case is one of eighty or so similar cases from the Manville plant that were consolidated by Judge Ackerman, who later ruled that Metropolitan Life could be held as a defendant in claims of negligence, fraudulent concealment, and conspiracy in all of them, and it is not expected to go to trial until 1986. When it does, it may finally settle the question of whether Metropolitan Life—with assets in 1984 of almost $70 billion, it was the nation's second-wealthiest life-insurance carrier—can be held legally accountable for altering passages in its 1935 report of asbestos disease to suit the asbestos industry and for allegedly withholding vital information from asbestos workers.

As for the property and casualty insurers, they also had early knowledge of the health hazards of asbestos. For example, the Aetna Life & Casualty Company—with assets of more than $50 billion it is the nation's largest publicly held multiple-line carrier—has carried workmen's-compensation insurance over the past fifty years for a number of asbestos-insulation manufacturers and has carried primary product-liability insurance for Owens-Illinois, Owens-Corning, Armstrong Cork, Keene, Celotex, and AMATEX (formerly the American Asbestos Textile Corporation), of Norristown, Pennsylvania. In addition, Aetna has incurred tremendous potential exposure to asbestos claims as a result of providing excess product-liability coverage for some of these same companies, and for Johns-Manville as well. Aetna is today an ardent supporter of the manifestation theory. As early as 1934, however, Dr. Roscoe N. Gray, surgical director of the Aetna Life Insurance Company, wrote a book entitled *Attorneys' Textbook of Medi-*

cine, with a section on asbestosis that in effect demolished the validity of the manifestation theory. After declaring that asbestos fibers, once inhaled, "continue their slow, insidious tissue destruction through the years, even though exposure may long have terminated," and that asbestosis is obviously caused by all the asbestos that has been inhaled, Gray advised that "disability should be charged pro-rata to all carriers during the entire time of asbestos exposure."

By the time Gray's book appeared, Aetna was undoubtedly learning about the ravages of asbestos as a result of paying claims, and by 1941 the company's underwriters had obviously drawn some conclusions from that experience, for on May 19 of that year, at a meeting of the American Industrial Health Association in St. Louis, Aetna's safety director gave a talk in which he stressed that workers engaged in the manufacture of fiber glass were not subject to special risk and "don't require as high a rate as for asbestos." In his audience was a representative of the Hartford Accident & Indemnity Company, which is one of the larger casualty insurers in the nation. (It is part of a cluster of insurance companies known as the Hartford Group, which is heavily exposed to asbestos claims as a result of having underwritten product-liability insurance for Keene and American Optical during the early 1970s.) However, the Hartford people probably learned little about the asbestos hazard that they didn't already know, for they had settled a workmen's-compensation claim for asbestosis brought by a Raybestos-Manhattan worker as early as 1932.

During the 1950s, Travelers settled many workmen's-compensation claims for asbestosis that were brought against Johns-Manville and Armstrong Cork by asbestos insulators who had developed the disease as a result of working for insulation contract firms that were wholly owned by the two manufacturing companies. These settlements show that Travelers either was or should have been aware of the asbestos health hazard for insulation workers for nearly a decade before the risk was documented by Dr. Selikoff and his colleagues. At the same time, Travelers was selling millions of dollars' worth of product-liability coverage to Johns-Manville, and was thus presumably obliged to contribute to the 1959 settlement of *Le Grand* v. *Johns-Manville*—the first third-party product-liability lawsuit ever filed by an asbestos insulator against Johns-Manville. This, of course, indicates that Travelers and Johns-Manville should have known that insulators were at risk of developing asbestos disease. Yet, starting in the early

1970s, Travelers and Johns-Manville defended asbestos lawsuits brought by insulators for at least ten years with the claim that they had no such knowledge until 1964.

As evidence that Travelers should have known early about the carcinogenicity of asbestos, it is worth noting that the company sent a representative to the Seventh Saranac Symposium, in 1952, a meeting at which the subject of asbestos-related lung cancer was thoroughly discussed. The 1952 symposium was also attended by an official of Liberty Mutual—a Boston-based carrier whose attorney complained nearly thirty years afterward that "we're finding so many things to be carcinogenic, you never know what you're insuring that might turn up as a carcinogen later." Still another participant in the 1952 symposium was the American Mutual Liability Insurance Company, of Boston (it later moved to the nearby town of Wakefield), which sent two delegates to the conference. American Mutual Liability had been incorporated in 1887, and had long been considered to be a leader in the field of workmen's-compensation insurance, which, by 1952, accounted for fully two-thirds of its almost $70-million annual business. The company had carried workmen's compensation for several shipyards during the Second World War, including the Bath Iron Works Yard, in Bath, Maine, and the Ingalls Shipbuilding Corporation's facility at Pascagoula, Mississippi. It also insured a number of asbestos manufacturers; in fact, in 1956, four years after the Seventh Saranac Symposium it was carrying workmen's-compensation coverage for asbestos plants owned by the Carolina Asbestos Company, the Union Asbestos & Rubber Company, the Asten-Hill Manufacturing Company, and the Keasbey & Mattison Company, of Ambler, Pennsylvania.

American Mutual Liability had apparently encountered few problems with its asbestos-manufacturing clients until the late 1950s, when it received six claims for asbestosis filed by workers employed at Keasbey & Mattison's factories in Ambler. (One of the Ambler plants was engaged in the manufacture of asbestos pipe covering; another made asbestos cement board; and the third turned out asbestos-textile products. In addition, Keasbey & Mattison owned an asbestos-cement factory in St. Louis, and an asbestos-textile mill, in Meredith, New Hampshire.) Keasbey & Mattison had been founded in 1873, and it had made milk of magnesia exclusively until Dr. Royal Mattison, one of its founders, accidentally spilled some milk of magnesia on a hot pipe and, finding that it adhered, got the idea of using it to make insulation. In the late nineteenth century, Keasbey & Mattison began adding asbestos to its magnesia insulation products, and in 1934 it became a wholly owned subsidiary of Turner & Newall, of Rochdale, England, owner of the Turner Brothers Asbestos Company, also of Rochdale, which is one of the largest asbestos manufacturers in Great Britain. No one knows just when officials of Keasbey & Mattison first learned that asbestos could cause disease, but they surely knew it by 1936, when Sumner Simpson, the president of Raybestos-Manhattan, wrote to Augustus S. Blagden, their president, proposing that the company join with Raybestos-Manhattan and Johns-Manville in financing animal studies that would help the asbestos industry defend against workmen's-compensation claims for asbestosis. Eight years later, Keasbey & Mattison became a charter member of the Asbestos Textile Institute, and over the next decade it sent representatives to numerous meetings at which the problem of asbestosis was urgently discussed. Thus, the Keasbey & Mattison people could hardly have been surprised when, in the late 1950s, workmen's-compensation claims for asbestosis were filed by their employees in Ambler. What happened after that provides still another example of the disregard for human life that has characterized the actions of asbestos manufacturers from one end of the nation to the other. It also provides reinforcement for the conclusion that insurance companies in the United States had early knowledge of the asbestos health hazard.

In June, 1956, an engineer from American Mutual Liability's Atlantic Division surveyed Keasbey & Mattison's Ambler factories, found that asbestos-dust concentrations were within permissible limits in all of them, and described his findings to superiors in a report labeled "Special Risk." In September, John B. Skinner, an industrial hygienist for American Mutual Liability, who had attended the 1952 Saranac Symposium, and Joseph E. Leahy, an engineer for the insurance company, inspected Keasbey & Mattison's asbestos-textile factory in Meredith, New Hampshire, and measured high concentrations of asbestos dust in the carding room, where twenty-eight workers were employed. In a report that was sent to his superiors, as well as to officials of Keasbey & Mattison, Skinner predicted that if the conditions in the carding room at the Meredith plant were not corrected, nearly 20 percent of the workers would develop asbestosis within five to ten years, and that half of them would develop the disease if they were exposed for more than fifteen years.

In spite of Skinner's predictions, the Keasbey & Mattison people did little or nothing to improve the ventilation system in their Meredith plant, for when Joseph Leahy, who was now an industrial hygienist at American Mutual Liability, reinspected the factory, in May, 1958, he found asbestos dust in the same high concentrations as before. At the time, the managers of the insurance company made inquiries to ascertain their liability, and learned that under the New Hampshire Workmen's Compensation Statute asbestosis was subject to claim only in the event of total disability. By the summer of 1959, when six claims for asbestosis had been filed by workers at Keasbey & Mattison's Ambler plants, where asbestos-dust levels had been found to be within permissible limits, and the chest X-rays of fourteen other employees showed signs of disease, the American Mutual Liability people began to worry about being confronted by a flood of additional asbestosis claims if Pennsylvania began to pay for partial disability. Still, as one of them put it, the existing situation was such that "a claimant has to be a stretcher case in Pennsylvania before he can file a claim which will be considered."

In September, 1961, officials of American Mutual Liability were highly critical of an attempt by Robert R. Porter, then the president of Keasbey & Mattison, to enlist their support in trying to prevent the United States Public Health Service from undertaking a long-overdue study of the relationship between asbestos exposure and lung cancer. At that time, Porter's motives were analyzed in a memo by William E. Shoemaker, assistant manager of the engineering department at American Mutual Liability's Atlantic Division. He observed that if Porter would see fit to do something about controlling asbestos-dust levels he might not have to worry so much about the proposed study of asbestos and cancer. "It appears that their chickens are a little closer to coming home to roost," Shoemaker wrote, referring to asbestosis that was developing among Keasbey & Mattison's employees. "We must be very careful that they stay where they belong and don't roost on us."

Five months later, Shoemaker sent Keasbey & Mattison an excerpt from an article that had appeared in the July, 1955, issue of the American Medical Association's *Archives of Industrial Health*, which described an investigation of asbestos disease that had been conducted by the Factory Department in Great Britain. Among other things, the article stated that the connection between asbestosis and cancer of the lung was becoming clearer; that cases of asbestosis were being found in workers who applied asbestos insulation to pipes and boilers; and that protective measures were difficult in insulation operations, "particularly if asbestos is being sprayed." Since Shoemaker knew that Keasbey & Mattison was selling a sprayed asbestos-insulation product called Limpet—it had been licensed to do so by Turner Brothers, the makers of Limpet—he implied that the company might encounter liability as a result. Indeed, he counseled that "even though your company does not spray-apply the Limpet they sell, your legal advisers would appear wise in being sure that you are properly protected."

As things turned out, Keasbey & Mattison sold its assets within a few months and got out of the asbestos-manufacturing business. The asbestos-textile plant in Meredith, New Hampshire, was shut down, and the asbestos plants in Ambler were purchased by Nicolet, AMA-TEX, and the Certain-Teed Products Corporation, of nearby Ardmore, which also bought the asbestos-cement plant in St. Louis. The franchise to sell and apply Limpet was given to the Armstrong Contracting & Supply Corporation, a subsidiary of Armstrong Cork, and was later transferred to the Atlas Asbestos Company, of Montreal, a subsidiary of Turner & Newall. As for the American Mutual Liability Insurance Company, it issued new guidelines in 1965 for underwriting, stipulating that any asbestos manufacturer it insured thereafter would be required to institute a medical program for its employees and to install adequate dust-control systems in its factories.

The Keasbey & Mattison affair might have remained buried forever if it had not been for Ronald Motley, the indefatigable litigator from Charleston, South Carolina. He uncovered documents detailing the relationship between Keasbey & Mattison and American Mutual Liability in 1979, during the discovery proceedings in a case involving the Ingalls Shipbuilding Corporation. In the spring of 1981, nearly twenty years after Keasbey & Mattison had got out of the asbestos business, Motley used the evidence of this relationship to good advantage in settling *Dana Bond* v. *Atlas Asbestos Company and Turner & Newall, Ltd.* for a record $1.4 million. The case involved a high-school teacher in Missouri who had worked for three weeks one summer with his father spraying Limpet on the steel girders of high-rise buildings, and had died of mesothelioma at the age of thirty-three. Turner &

Newall and J. W. Roberts, Ltd.—a Turner & Newall subsidiary that had developed the spray gun and process by which Limpet was applied —paid $650,000 toward the settlement; Armstrong Contracting & Supply paid another $650,000; and Armstrong Cork paid the rest.

Also in the spring of 1981, Paul Gillenwater had attempted to name the American Mutual Liability Insurance Company as a defendant in a series of lawsuits that had been brought by asbestos insulators in the circuit court for Knox County, Tennessee. Gillenwater's complaint alleged that the carrier had actively conspired to alter, misrepresent, and suppress knowledge of the hazards of exposure to Keasbey & Mattison's asbestos-insulation products. The presiding judge in the cases dismissed Gillenwater's complaint, however, on the ground that the carrier could not be held liable for the allegations under Tennessee law; Gillenwater decided that an appeal would probably be to little avail, so the question of whether American Mutual Liability can be held legally responsible for its past conduct has yet to be tested.

A few weeks before Motley settled the Bond case, Commercial Union brought its declaratory-judgment action accusing Travelers of failing to properly defend asbestos-disease lawsuits that had been brought against Pittsburgh Corning, PPG Industries, and Corning Glass Works, and accusing Pittsburgh Corning and its owners of concealing the dangers of asbestos from Commercial Union's casualty underwriters. Commercial Union's lawsuit crowned a series of moves that had branded it as a maverick in the insurance world. In addition to leveling bitter criticism at the fellow-insurers who advocated the exposure theory, the company opposed block settlements—a time-honored practice in which insurance companies settle multiple claims against them by paying the same amount of money to a substantial number of claimants. Commercial Union had also been calling upon its fellow-insurers to file cross-complaints against the United States, on the ground that the government had been responsible for asbestos exposure in the shipyards during the Second World War, and to file cross-complaints against the tobacco industry on the ground of scientific evidence showing that asbestos workers who smoked cigarettes ran a far greater risk of developing lung cancer than those who did not smoke.

Naturally, none of this sat very well with Commercial Union's colleagues in the highly conservative insurance community, who feared that because of the government's claim to immunity from asbestos lawsuits they might merely multiply their legal costs with little chance of success. They also worried that if they sued the tobacco companies, for which some of them provided insurance coverage, they not only would be suing themselves but also would be antagonizing an immensely wealthy industry which could afford to wage brutally expensive warfare in the courts. As a result, most insurers refused to follow Commercial Union's call, and pursued the so-called empty-chair theory in the hope of getting jurors to assume that the government and the tobacco industry bore some of the responsibility for asbestos disease even though neither was seated at the defense table.

Meanwhile, during 1981 and 1982, Commercial Union continued to send out a barrage of protest against the exposure theory and continued to make dire predictions about the adverse effects of asbestos litigation on the insurance industry. These predictions were perhaps voiced most strongly in January, 1982, when Paul W. MacAvoy, who was then Frederick William Beinecke Professor of Economics at Yale, and who had formerly been a member of President Ford's Council of Economic Advisers—he is now dean of the Graduate School of Management at the University of Rochester—released the results of a study entitled *The Economic Consequences of Asbestos-Related Disease*, which he had undertaken with two associates and which had been financed by Commercial Union.

To begin with, Professor MacAvoy and his colleagues estimated that over the next twenty to thirty years total asbestos-disease damage awards could amount to as much as $90 billion, though $30 billion was more likely, and that the bulk of the money would probably come from the casualty and property carriers that had insured the asbestos manufacturers. They went on to predict that if some insurance carriers went bankrupt, "policyholders with seemingly no stake in asbestos suits will be forced to bear, though inadvertently so, part of the costs of the underestimation of the size of eventual asbestos claims." As for whether the insurance companies had any responsibility for underestimating the asbestos-disease hazard, Professor MacAvoy and his associates managed to conclude that although asbestos manufacturers had had knowledge of the hazard for decades, it was "only barely perceived" by the insurance industry, which, as a result, failed to charge sufficient premiums for the liability policies it issued to asbestos manufacturers.

In February, 1982, Professor MacAvoy, who was then a regular contributor to the *Times* Sunday Business section, published an article in the section entitled "You, Too, Will Pay for Asbestosis," which was based upon the findings of his study. In his article, Professor MacAvoy did not repeat his contention that the insurance industry had failed to be aware of the health hazards associated with asbestos exposure. Instead, after informing his readers that when he had been a teenager looking for a summer job, some thirty years earlier, his parents had warned him against going to work in an asbestos-insulation factory, he appeared to suggest that asbestos workers were to blame for the tragedy that had fallen them, because they did not have parents as prescient as his own. "Faced with such dangerous operations, workers should have demanded higher wages or insurance against those hazards," he wrote. "Even without strong union support, in an expanding economy merely following advice such as that of my parents should have created relative scarcity and consequently higher wages in the insulation industry." As for who would finally pay for the costs of asbestos litigation, Professor MacAvoy suggested that insurers might raise the money by doubling the premiums on automobile and product-liability policies. He concluded his article by warning his readers that "another social disease has struck, and the bell tolls for thee at the insurance office, as premiums go up to pay for it."

In a letter of reply that was published in the *Times* a week later, Robert Sweeney, the Cleveland litigator, took MacAvoy to task for his analysis of the asbestos problem. "It is most unfair to call the asbestos problem a social disease and to pass on the cost of retiring it by raising premiums on all types of insurance," Sweeney wrote. "The asbestos industry has engaged in practices that are indefensible. The insurance industry has written the coverage and perhaps has done so incompetently."

Within a few months, Professor MacAvoy's pronouncement that the asbestos hazard had been "only barely perceived" by the insurance carriers who wrote product-liability coverage for the asbestos industry received a jolt when Commercial Union found itself back in federal district court before Judge James T. Giles, who had decided to hear arguments on whether he should summarily rescind the product-liability-insurance policies sold by Commercial Union to PPG Industries and Pittsburgh Corning, on the ground that the two companies had deceived Commercial Union about the asbestos hazard. Appearing before Judge Giles on June 24, 1982, a lawyer for Pittsburgh Corning argued against recision by quoting from Commercial Union's own 1937 engineering manual, which stated that "a potential asbestos hazard is to be looked for wherever asbestos dust is created," and that "industries which have this exposure to asbestos dust include insulation." After saying that "someone cannot be deceived with regard to what he already knows," the attorney for Pittsburgh Corning went on to cite testimony given by Commercial Union's own underwriters which indicated that they had written product-liability insurance for the asbestos industry on the assumption that the primary insurance carrier had adequately investigated the risk.

In arguing for recision of the insurance policies, Commercial Union's lawyer attempted to revive the all but moribund state-of-the-art defense by asserting that his client could not have known that asbestos insulation was hazardous for the workers who installed it until 1964, when Dr. Selikoff and his associates announced the results of their study of mortality among asbestos insulators. He explained that Commercial Union's 1937 engineering manual referred only to the writing of workmen's-compensation insurance for asbestos-factory workers, and he suggested that because PPG and Pittsburgh Corning had prior knowledge of the hazard for insulators their purchase of product-liability insurance in the early 1960s was fraudulent.

Judge Giles did not appear to buy this argument. "Commercial Union is not a giant-come-lately to the insurance business, and they had information going back to 1937 pointing a finger at asbestos," he declared. "What is it that Commercial Union could not have discovered using its own resources with respect to asbestos? What research could it not have done? What intelligence did it not have?"

As things turned out, Commercial Union withdrew the allegation that it had been deceived about the asbestos hazard before Judge Giles could rule on it—no doubt because his impatient questions clearly indicated how he felt about the matter. Of course, Judge Giles could have asked the very same questions of any of the thirty or so other carriers that had insured the asbestos industry for product liability over the years, since even a cursory assessment of their actuarial tables, rating schedules, physicians' reports, workmen's-compensation claims, underwriting guidelines, and safety-and-engineering manuals would probably show that, far from barely knowing of the asbestos hazard, virtually all these companies had not only known for decades that inhalation of asbestos could cause incurable lung disease but also had good reason to suspect that lung disease was taking a heavy toll of the nation's asbestos workers. If at some point along the way Aetna, Travelers, Commercial Union, Liberty Mutual, INA, Hartford, Home, Lloyd's, or any of the other major insurers of the asbestos industry had gone public with their inside knowledge, they might well have been able to save tens of thousands of lives and untold suffering and pain. Such disclosure, however, would have encouraged claims and damage suits, and run counter to basic insurance-company practice, which is to write as much coverage as possible, and as cheaply as possible, in order to reap a rich harvest of policy premiums that, when invested, will return enough money to pay for future claims and make a profit for the company. So the insurers of the asbestos industry decided to say nothing, look the other way, and, when necessary, pay asbestos claims quickly and quietly out of court. This strategy, which they pursued for many years, enabled them to take in millions of dollars in premiums by selling billions of dollars' worth of product-liability insurance, and to remain confident as they did so that asbestos claims and, therefore, underwriting losses could be kept to a minimum. At the same time, it helped to conceal behind a dam of silence a vast and ever-increasing reservoir of disease, disability, and death. Only after Ward Stephenson won *Borel* did the dam slowly give way and the deluge of litigation for which the carriers and the manufacturers whom they insured now seek public remedy come cascading down upon their heads.

EIGHT

TRIAL AND JUDGMENT

While the asbestos manufacturers and their insurance companies were suing one another in a mad scramble to avoid liability, attorneys for the plaintiffs' bar were chalking up some impressive victories in asbestos lawsuits around the country. Their success had been hard earned over more than a decade. In the fall of 1971, Ward Stephenson had won a verdict of $68,000 in *Borel* v. *Fibreboard*. After Stephenson died, in 1973, his partner, Marlin Thompson, continued to settle asbestos claims in East Texas for between $60,000 and $120,000 over the next two years. In the autumn of 1974, Paul J. Louisell, an attorney in Duluth, obtained a damage award of $250,000 in *Karjala* v. *Johns-Manville*. And in the spring of 1976, Tom Henderson, a lawyer in Pittsburgh, used his deposition of Dr. Kenneth W. Smith, Johns-Manville's former medical director, to win a $90,000 verdict against Johns-Manville for the estate of an asbestos worker named William J. Sampson, who, like Borel and Karjala, had died of mesothelioma. During the next two years, however, plaintiff attorneys encountered great difficulty in getting the Smith deposition admitted in evidence in other jurisdictions, and they lost a number of important cases to defense attorneys like Lively Wilson, of Louisville, Kentucky, who had fashioned a highly effective state-of-the-art defense for Johns-Manville.

Things began to look brighter for the plaintiff lawyers in the winter of 1978, when it was announced that three Texas attorneys—Fred Baron, Scott Baldwin, and Rex Houston—had negotiated a settlement of $20 million for 445 former workers or their survivors at Pittsburgh Corning's asbestos-insulation factory in Tyler, Texas. In June, in a suit against Johns-Manville and four other asbestos manufacturers, Richard Glasser, Gene Locks, and Robert Hatten won a verdict of $750,000 for the family of an asbestos insulator named Ira Dishner, of Yorktown, Virginia, who had died of mesothelioma. Partly because of a highly restrictive Virginia statute of limitations, these damages were subsequently negotiated down to $275,000, but *Dishner* v. *Johns-Manville* encouraged plaintiff attorneys across the country, for the government had just announced that as many as eleven and a half million American men and women who had been exposed to asbestos on the job, including about four and a half million who had worked in the nation's shipyards during the Second World War, were at serious risk of developing asbestos disease, and the surgeon general had sent a letter about the problem to nearly four hundred thousand physicians.

Above all, however, 1978 would be remembered by the asbestos litigators as the year of great discovery, thanks to the dissemination of such incriminating documents as the Sumner Simpson correspondence, which had been unearthed by Karl Asch a year earlier; the minutes of early Johns-Manville board of directors' meetings that were uncovered by George Kilbourne; and the asbestosis claims brought by insulators working for contract units owned by Johns-Manville and other leading manufacturers, which had been painstakingly excavated from old workmen's-compensation files by Paul Gillenwater, Ronald Motley, and Barry Castleman.

As might be expected, these dramatic disclosures of early knowledge of the asbestos hazard on the part of defendant manufacturers seriously weakened their state-of-the-art defense in the eyes of jurors across the nation, and by 1979 the tide in asbestos litigation was turning. Johns-Manville's primary insurer, Travelers, began settling cases out of court "like a broken slot machine," in the words of one plaintiff attorney, rather than risk the possibility of incurring large damage awards as a result of going to trial. Aetna did the same for Owens-Corning, especially after the plaintiff attorneys got their hands on the Kaylo documents in the spring of 1979. Aetna also began settling regularly on behalf of the Celotex Corporation, the owner of Philip Carey, after Gillenwater and Glasser discovered that Dr. Thomas Mancuso of the University of Pittsburgh's Graduate School of Public Health, had warned officials of Philip Carey about the health hazards at their asbestos-insulation plants as early as 1963. As for lesser defendants, their hopes of escaping unscathed received a devastating blow in May, when Fred Baron, one of the lead attorneys for the worker plaintiffs from Pittsburgh Corning's asbestos factory in Tyler, Texas, and Louis Robles, an attorney in Miami, won a jury verdict of $450,000 from Keene Corporation for an asbestos insulator named Evelio Lopez. Keene, a relatively small insulation manufacturer, had elected to go to trial in this case after fourteen other defendants, among them Johns-Manville, had settled out of court for $170,000. In July, Glasser, Locks, and Hatten negotiated a $227,500 settlement with Johns-Manville and six other asbestos manufacturers in behalf of a shipyard welder in Virginia, and in a case involving a former shipyard worker in California a $300,000 settlement was reached toward the end of the year.

The upward spiral in asbestos verdicts and settlements continued during the early part of 1980, when a federal jury in Beaumont, Texas, took only eight minutes to deliberate before awarding $3 million in compensatory damages to Alberta Migues, the widow of Russell Migues, an asbestos insulator from nearby Groves, who was represented by Marlin Thompson and Walter Umphrey, an attorney from Port Arthur. (Groves was the town where Clarence Borel had lived, and, like Borel, Migues had died of mesothelioma, after suffering greatly.) The award was far and away the largest ever made to a single plaintiff in an asbestos lawsuit, and was all the more remarkable for the fact that, as in the Lopez case against Keene, it was made against a lesser defendant—in this instance, Nicolet Industries, which had refused to settle out of court even though thirteen other defendant manufacturers had done so, for a total of $400,000. Although the amount was subsequently reduced to $1.5 million by Judge Robert M. Parker, who had refused to allow the jury to consider punitive damages, the Migues award sent a shiver down the spines of insurers across the nation.

As things turned out, the decision in the Migues case against Nicolet was later reversed by the Fifth Circuit Court of Appeals, in New Orleans, which found that Judge Parker had been in error when he had granted a motion by the plaintiff to prevent Nicolet from litigating the issue of whether asbestos was unreasonably dangerous. (Parker had ruled that the unreasonably dangerous nature of the mineral had been established in Borel and was thus a matter of law.) In finding against Parker, however, the Fifth Circuit justices noted that there were more than three thousand asbestos plaintiffs in the Eastern District of Texas alone, and sympathized with his attempt to deal with the problem. "It is understandable that the district courts will seek ways of eliminating the need to continuously reinvent the asbestos liability wheel in every one of these cases," they declared. "Considerations of judicial economy demand a more streamlined mechanism for compensating asbestos victims and apportioning liability among those responsible for causing injury." Judge Parker proceeded to take the justices of the Fifth Circuit at their word, and when the Migues case against Nicolet was retried, in July, 1982, it was part of an unusual proceeding in which five separate lawsuits were tried simultaneously on the issue of liability before five six-member juries that were seated in the same courtroom. On this occasion, a jury once again returned a verdict for Alberta Migues, but before the issue of damages could be litigated the case was settled for $150,000.

In May, 1980, three months after the first Migues trial had ended, a jury in Los Angeles Superior Court returned a $1.2 million verdict against Johns-Manville and Raybestos-Manhattan in a case that had been brought by a forty-year-old insulator named Richard J. Hogard, who had developed asbestosis after working for ten years at the nearby Long Beach Naval Shipyard. According to reports at the time, the jurors became skeptical of the defendants' claims that they could not have been aware before 1964 of the health risk to asbestos insulators when Hogard's attorney, Robert B. Steinberg, who was not allowed by presiding Judge Earl F. Riley to introduce the Sumner Simpson letters, showed the jurors early reports in the medical literature stating that exposure to asbestos was harmful. Although the amount of the award was later reduced to $250,000, *Hogard* v. *Johns-Manville* was important because it was expected to set a precedent for more than a thousand similar lawsuits that had been brought in Los Angeles County by former shipyard insulators. It was also noteworthy because, like Judge Parker in *Migues,* Judge Riley refused to allow the jurors to consider assessing punitive damages against Johns-Manville and Raybestos-Manhattan. Basing his decision on California case law, Judge Riley ruled that the Simpson-Brown letters were not admissable because they had been written long before Hogard went to work as an asbestos insulator. He also decided that punitive damages would be unfair because the defendants had sold asbestos to the shipyard to meet United States Navy shipbuilding specifications.

Punitive damages, which are meted out as punishment for outrageous and reckless misconduct, and as a deterrent to future misdeeds, had been sought in virtually every asbestos-product-liability lawsuit that had been brought since 1966, when Ward Stephenson filed a complaint on behalf of Claude Tomplait against Fibreboard Paper Products Corporation, the first asbestos-insulation-product-liability lawsuit. They had never been awarded, however, chiefly because the judges who presided over asbestos trials, like most of their colleagues, were loath to approve of them—a traditional reluctance that was all the stronger because of judicial concern that if punitive damages became commonplace in asbestos cases, defendant manufacturers might go bankrupt and thus deprive future plaintiffs of the chance of obtaining compensation. The fact that punitive damages had never been awarded had, of course, not gone unnoticed. Indeed, in testimony given before the Senate Committee on Labor and Human Resources, in August, 1980, John A. McKinney, Johns-Manville's chairman and chief executive officer, underscored his denial that Johns-Manville had knowingly exposed workers to the hazards of asbestos dust by emphasizing that in all the litigation to date there had not been a single instance in which a jury or trial judge had awarded punitive damages against any asbestos company. "I can think of no greater demonstration that the coverup charge is a complete fabrication," McKinney told the committee.

McKinney's assertion notwithstanding, the prospect of punitive damages was hanging over Johns-Manville's corporate head, for the amounts in jury verdicts had been rising in direct proportion to the dramatic disclosures of misconduct on the part of Johns-Manville, and it was not hard to predict that once jurors and judges became persuaded of the company's essential culpability punitive damages would follow. Moreover, by this time Johns-Manville knew that its primary insurance with Travelers was fast running out and that Home and other excess insurers were not going to take up its indemnification and defense without a protracted court battle. This meant that until the dispute over insurance coverage was resolved Johns-Manville was either going to have to go to trial in more and more asbestos cases—a course of action that might well provoke the awarding of punitive damages—or drastically deplete its cash reserves by settling out of court. Given the circumstances, Johns-Manville had little choice but to run the risk of going to trial. Thus, in the spring of 1980 punitive damages had come to be regarded by many insiders in the company as the wild card in the deck, and McKinney's confident pronouncement before the Senate committee seems to have been a matter of mere wishful thinking. Whatever it was, juries from one end of the nation to the other soon began to play the wild card against Johns-Manville.

As things turned out, the first punitive damages were meted out not against Johns-Manville but against the North American Asbestos Corporation, of Chicago—a small company that had been set up by Cape Industries, of London, to act as an agent for the selling of South African asbestos in the United States. The case was unusual because the plaintiff, Charlotte Hammond, was the wife of a fifty-four-year-old former worker of an old UNARCO insulation factory in Bloomington, Illinois, who, though suffering from asbestosis—he subsequently died of mesothelioma—had been unable to bring a claim against North American because the two-year Illinois statute of limitations had expired. Since the statute of limitations for loss of consortium in Illinois was then five years, Mrs. Hammond brought suit on that basis. During a ten-day trial, which was held in February, 1981, in McLean County Circuit Court, in Bloomington, Tom Henderson, of Pittsburgh, and James Walker, an attorney from Bloomington, who were representing Mrs. Hammond, introduced evidence to show that a former president of North American, Robert E. Cryor (who had died of mesothelioma in 1970), had learned about the health hazards of asbestos while working for UNARCO back in the 1940s. After deliberating for a day, the jury awarded Mrs. Hammond compensatory damages of $125,000 and punitive damages of $375,000.

Subsequent events in the legal efforts of the Bloomington factory workers to obtain compensation provide an example of the vagaries that can attend asbestos litigation. To begin with, Mrs. Hammond's punitive-damage award was taken away when an appeals court ruled that, under Illinois law, punitive damages could not be awarded in a derivative lawsuit such as hers. Then, in January, 1982, another McLean County jury awarded $35 million in punitive damages and almost $22 million in compensatory damages to a group of fifty-four former employees of the Bloomington factory, or their survivors, who had brought lawsuits against Cape Industries and two of its wholly owned subsidiaries, Cape Asbestos Fibres Ltd., and EGNEP, a South African mining company, on the grounds of strict liability in tort and willful and wanton misconduct. However, in spite of having previously contributed $5.2 million toward the settlement in 1978 of the Tyler factory lawsuit, Cape Industries and its two subsidiaries refused to pay the Illinois award, claiming that they were no longer doing business in the United States, and Henderson and Walker, who also represent these plaintiffs, have been unsuccessful so far in having the judgment enforced under international law.

Meanwhile, punitive damages had been assessed during 1981 in a number of other asbestos cases. In a trial that began in February and concluded in May, a federal-court jury in Philadelphia awarded punitive damages totaling nearly $450,000 against Johns-Manville and Celotex after a nearly four-month-long trial involving fourteen former workers at the old Philip Carey insulation plant, in Plymouth Meeting, Pennsylvania, or their survivors, who were represented by the Philadelphia firm of Greitzer & Locks. At about the same time, Robert Sweeney won a jury award of $500,000 in punitive damages, together with $350,000 in compensatory damages, in a case that had been brought against Johns-Manville by the widow of an asbestos insulator named Edward Moran, who had died of lung cancer. Considerable attention was paid by the *Wall Street Journal* and other leading newspapers to the *Moran* verdict, which was subsequently upheld by the Sixth Circuit Court of Appeals, and from then on punitive damages began to be awarded with increasing regularity. In early July, Gene Locks won a $600,000 jury verdict, including $50,000 in punitive damages for a former asbestos-factory worker and his wife in a case that went to trial against Johns-Manville after Owens-Corning and Celotex had settled out of court. And at the end of July, following another trial in which Johns-Manville was the sole defendant, a county circuit-court jury in Jacksonville, Florida, awarded the record-breaking sum of $1,857,600 to a former Navy boiler attendant named Edward Janssens and his wife, Patsy. This amount included $750,000 in punitive damages and $400,000 for loss of consortium—the highest awards that had ever been made in either category in an asbestos lawsuit. In September, 1984, a Florida District Court of Appeals affirmed the lower court verdict in *Janssens*, saying that Johns-Manville's conduct amounted to "wanton disregard for the health and safety of persons using its asbestos products, and in November, the Appeals Court turned down the company's request for rehearing, saying that it had shown "reckless disregard for human life or the safety of persons." In April of

1985, the Florida Supreme Court turned down Manville's request for a hearing.

The Janssens case was unusual not only because of the size of the award but because Janssens, who had not developed pulmonary problems until 1973, had been exposed to asbestos from 1943 to 1951, when he had applied asbestos insulation to the boilers of ships while serving in the Navy. As for Johns-Manville, it had been named as the sole defendant because Janssens could not recall using asbestos products that were made by any other company, and it had gone to trial confident of a victory because it did not believe that it could be held liable for Janssens's asbestosis, and because Janssens had not become seriously disabled. Among Janssens's attorneys, however, was Ronald Motley, whose argument for punitive damages was powerfully buttressed by the Sumner Simpson letters and the deposition of Dr. Smith. It was the first trial win in an asbestos case for Motley, who had recently settled the Bond case in Missouri for a record-breaking $1.4 million and it gained him national recognition.

The growing trend toward punitive damages continued in the autumn of 1981, when Karl Asch won a $300,000 punitive award, together with $110,000 in compensatory damages, for an insulator in New Jersey, in a case that went to trial against Bell Asbestos Mines, of Canada, and Johns-Manville. Elsewhere, plaintiff attorneys were using the threat of punitive damages to drive up the price of out-of-court settlements, and by the winter of 1982 asbestos manufacturers were desperately arguing for the elimination of punitive damages in various jurisdictions throughout the nation. In January, an attorney for Raybestos-Manhattan told a judge in Hawaii, who was about to schedule the first of 141 lawsuits that had been filed on behalf of former workers at the Pearl Harbor Naval Shipyard, or their survivors, that punitive damages could "turn punishment into annihilation." At the same hearing, a Johns-Manville attorney warned that punitive damages constituted "overkill" that would destroy companies and prevent future plaintiffs from getting any kind of compensation. As things turned out, the judge ruled that the issue was for the jury to decide, and some months later, at the conclusion of the first trial, the jury declined to assess punitive damages but awarded compensatory damages of more than half a million dollars to the family of Tristan Nobriga, an electrician at the naval base, who had died of mesothelioma.

Meanwhile, at the end of March, a federal-court jury in Galveston,

Texas, had returned another huge verdict against Johns-Manville, awarding a million dollars in punitive damages and $1,060,000 in compensatory damages to the widow and the estate of a shipyard pipefitter who had died of mesothelioma. (The Fifth Circuit Court of Appeals later reduced the punitive damages to $300,000 and the compensatory damages to $290,000.) A week later, a federal jury in Knoxville, Tennessee, also found against Johns-Manville, awarding $220,000 in punitive damages and $280,000 in compensatory damages to a retired insulator who had become disabled by asbestosis as well as $140,000 to his wife for loss of consortium. In May, after finding Johns-Manville strictly liable and negligent, a jury in Philadelphia awarded $1 million in punitive damages, together with $100,000 in compensatory damages, to a former shipyard worker and his wife. (The man had developed thickening of the pleura—the membranes that encase the lungs—after working for seven years at the New York Shipyard, in Camden, New Jersey.) And early in June, Ronald Motley, Scott Baldwin, and several other attorneys won a $1,016,500 federal jury verdict against Johns-Manville and Raybestos-Manhattan for James L. Jackson, a former sheet-metal worker at the Ingalls Shipbuilding Corporation, in Pascagoula, Mississippi, in the first asbestos case to come to trial out of more than five hundred cases that were pending in that state. Jackson, who had developed asbestosis, received $391,500 in compensatory damages from the two companies, together with $500,000 in punitive damages from Johns-Manville, and $125,000 in punitive damages from Raybestos-Manhattan—the first punitive judgment that had ever been made against Raybestos in an asbestos lawsuit. On June 23, in a federal-court trial in which Johns-Manville was the sole defendant, Paul Gillenwater and an associate, Douglas Nichol won a record-breaking jury award of $2.3 million, including $1.5 million in punitive damages, for James Ovett Cavett, a retired boilermaker suffering from asbestosis and lung cancer, who had spent forty years working in power plants owned by the Tennessee Valley Authority. In September of 1982, Johns-Manville appealed the decision in the Sixth Circuit, claiming that the award of punitive damages violated its constitutional guarantee of due process, and that it was being "punished over and over for the same course of action."

In voting to award punitive damages against Johns-Manville and other defendants, juries were, of course, responding to evidence showing that asbestos manufacturers had engaged in a coverup of the asbestos hazard for nearly half a century, but they were also reacting to the skill with which this evidence was presented by plaintiff attorneys and to the manner in which it was received and dealt with by lawyers for the defendants. Their reaction was often anger, for as time went on and the disclosures of misconduct mounted, plaintiff attorneys were able to use evidence of the coverup not only to attack the state-of-the-art defense but also to rouse feelings of outrage in jurors. Defense lawyers could only try to mitigate this by calling in experts to dispute the medical diagnosis of diseases, or, when appropriate, by pointing out that a plaintiff had contributed to his injury by smoking cigarettes.

The legendary importance of evoking sympathy from jurors had been demonstrated in the Borel trial, when Ward Stephenson had succeeded in bringing tears to the eyes of several members of the jury during his closing argument. However, jury anger did not become a major factor in the outcome of an asbestos trial until 1978, in Norfolk, Virginia, when Glasser, Hatten, and Locks won compensatory damages of $750,000 from Johns-Manville for the family of Ira Dishner, who, like Borel, had died of mesothelioma. At the outset, *Dishner* v. *Johns-Manville* posed thorny problems for the three plaintiff lawyers. For one thing, they were up against the redoubtable Lively Wilson, who had won a string of victories with his state-of-the-art defense. Even worse, they had to contend with an archaic Virginia statute of limitations, which required that the only exposures to asbestos they could ask the jury to consider were those that had occurred within two years prior to the filing of the lawsuit. Since *Dishner* v. *Johns-Manville* had been filed on March 17, 1977, and Dishner had quit working with asbestos at the end of October, 1975, this meant that Glasser, Hatten, and Locks had to figure out some way of convincing the jury that his mesothelioma—a tumor that generally takes between twenty and forty years to develop—had been caused by his exposure to Johns-Manville products during the seven-and-a-half-month period between March 17, 1975, and October 31, 1975, when he had been employed at an Amoco refinery near Yorktown.

In an effort to surmount this hurdle, the three attorneys conducted months of exhaustive discovery that enabled them to reconstruct the building of the refinery from its blueprint stage, and to learn precisely what insulation materials had been used there during the twenty years it had been in operation. As a result, they were able to find witnesses who testified that Johns-Manville Thermobestos insulation had been used to cover 80 to 90 percent of the fifty thousand feet of pipe that was estimated to be in the refinery; that Thermobestos had been typically used to replace worn-out insulation; and that during 1975 Johns-Manville Transite pipe had been cut to size on the very table where Dishner and his fellow-workers ate their lunch. At the end of the trial, Glasser, an energetic and articulate thirty-six-year-old lawyer, who had received his law degree from the University of Virginia Law School in 1965 and, along with two brothers, become a partner in his father's Norfolk firm, delivered a brilliant closing argument. First, he reminded the members of the jury that Johns-Manville had failed to warn Dishner and his fellow-insulators of the risk of cancer from using Thermobestos and other Johns-Manville asbestos products. Then he reminded them that Johns-Manville had admitted that exposure to asbestos caused mesothelioma, and that Dishner had died of the disease. And then he administered the coup de grâce. "So it helps boil down the issue," he declared. "Did the last exposures hurt him, or has Johns-Manville pulled off the perfect crime?"

In the face of this kind of challenge, defense counsel had little choice other than to remind the members of the jury that under Virginia law they were not to consider any exposures that Dishner might have incurred before March 17, 1975, and to point out that seven and a half months was nowhere near long enough a period of time for the development of mesothelioma. For their part, the jurors were so infuriated by the logic of that argument that they quickly returned a verdict of $750,000—an amount more than three times as large as any judgment that had ever been made in an asbestos case. Antiquated or not, however, the law is the law, and when Johns-Manville moved to appeal the verdict on the ground that the jury had not followed the Virginia statute of limitations in arriving at its decision, Glasser, Hatten, and Locks were forced to negotiate the award down to $275,000.

By this time, Johns-Manville and other defendants were relying heavily on the testimony of expert medical witnesses about the hazards of cigarette smoking—a habit that appears to have been indulged in by a great majority of asbestos workers—in an effort to challenge the diagnosis of asbestos disease in plaintiffs. Sometimes the testimony of these experts succeeded in influencing juries, and sometimes it did not. In any event, there was no shortage of medical doctors who were willing to put themselves at the service of the asbestos industry. One of them was Hans Weill, the Tulane professor of medicine who had testified in behalf of Johns-Manville at the Borel trial. Weill later became president of the American Thoracic Society, and a paid consultant to the Asbestos Information Association (AIA)—an industry-sponsored organization that was formed to promote the safe use of asbestos-containing products and that also did its best to soften the indictment of asbestos as a health hazard—and although he testified on occasion for plaintiffs in asbestos cases, he continued to testify for defendant asbestos manufacturers, and he recommended other pulmonary physicians who might do so. Another expert witness was Dr. Paul Kotin, the medical director of Johns-Manville, who testified for the company in a number of the early asbestos trials. Still another was Dr. William Weiss, a professor of medicine at the School of Medicine of Hahnemann University, in Philadelphia, who was also a paid consultant of the AIA and several asbestos manufacturers. Weiss, who testified for Johns-Manville in the Dishner trial and on many other occasions, had written papers in which he claimed that mild fibrosis of the lungs caused by cigarette smoking was virtually indistinguishable from the fibrosis caused by asbestos. One of the most outspoken expert witnesses for the asbestos industry was Professor Harry B. Demopoulos, a pathologist at New York University's School of Medicine, who claimed that asbestos was not a lung-cancer-producing agent and blamed cigarettes for most of the pulmonary ills of asbestos workers. Among the best-known was Dr. Oscar Auerbach, a distinguished pathologist from the New Jersey Medical School, in Newark, who had been instrumental in persuading Congress to mandate a warning label on cigarette packages, and in the 1970s had testified against Johns-Manville in workmen's-compensation cases brought by employees of the company who were suffering from asbestosis or other asbestos-related diseases. Another well-known expert witness was Dr. Horton Corwin Hinshaw, a retired clinical professor of medicine at the University of California School of Medicine, in San Francisco. A former president of the American Thoracic Society, Hinshaw had been co-author, in 1956, of a highly regarded textbook entitled *Diseases of the Chest,* and he had testified, in 1982, in the trial of *Speake* v. *Johns-Manville* that Speake was suffering not from disabling asbestosis but from emphysema and bronchitis associated with cigarette smoking. In addition to proclaiming the ills of cigarette smoking and challenging the diagnosis of asbestos disease in some plaintiffs, most of these witnesses usually supported the state-of-the-art defense by testifying that the medical and scientific community had no way of knowing until the time of Dr. Selikoff's 1964 study that asbestos disease could strike insulators.

As for the plaintiff attorneys, they also had a roster of expert medical witnesses. Among them were Dr. Bertram Carnow, professor of occupational medicine and director of the Great Lakes Center for Occupational Safety and Health at the University of Illinois Medical Center, in Chicago; Dr. Edwin Holstein, an internist and member of the staff of Dr. Selikoff's Environmental Sciences Laboratory at the Mt. Sinai School of Medicine, in New York City, who also practices occupational medicine in Edison, New Jersey; Dr. Kaye H. Kilburn, a former member of Dr. Selikoff's group, who is now a professor of internal medicine at the University of Southern California's School of Medicine, in Los Angeles; Dr. Susan Daum, another former member of Selikoff's group, who practices occupational medicine in River Edge, New Jersey; and Dr. Gerritt W.H. Schepers, the former director of the Saranac Laboratory, who had diagnosed asbestosis and lung cancer in the tissue specimens of many Johns-Manville employees who had died back in the 1950s. These physicians gave testimony about the ability of asbestos to cause asbestosis, lung cancer, and mesothelioma, and also about what the members of the medical and scientific community knew, or should have known, about asbestos disease in the 1930s, 1940s, and 1950s, and were thus used by the plaintiff lawyers to challenge the state-of-the-art defense erected by the medical witnesses who testified for the asbestos-insulation manufacturers.

Conflicting testimony between expert medical witnesses had, of course, been characteristic of asbestos trials since *Borel* v. *Fibreboard*, when Ward Stephenson cross-examined Dr. Hans Weill and countered his statements by reading excerpts from the depositions of physicians who had actually treated Borel. During 1977 and 1978, Lively Wilson had fashioned his highly effective state-of-the-art defense around the testimony of Dr. Kotin and Dr. Forde McIver, an eminent professor of pathology at the Medical University of South Carolina, in Charleston, and had used it to defeat plaintiff attorneys in a number of important cases. By 1982, however, the plaintiff lawyers had gathered so much evidence of prior knowledge of the asbestos hazard on the part of both the asbestos industry and the medical and scientific community that giving state-of-the-art testimony for Johns-Manville had become a rather uncomfortable ordeal for expert witnesses, who were then receiving as much as $1,800 a day for their services. A typical example of just how uncomfortable occurred in *Cavett* v. *Johns-Manville*—the case in which the jury awarded a record $2,300,000 in damages—when Gillenwater launched into cross-examination of Dr. Hinshaw, who had testified earlier under direct examination that before 1964 members of the medical profession were not convinced that asbestos exposure could be harmful to insulators. Gillenwater forced Hinshaw to admit that he had seen cases of asbestosis in insulation workers before 1964; required Hinshaw to acknowledge that there were dozens of case studies of asbestos disease in insulators and other nonfactory workers that had been published in leading medical journals during the 1930s and 1940s, and quoted Hinshaw a passage from his own 1956 book *Diseases of the Chest,* which stated that asbestosis included the finding of asbestos bodies (coated asbestos fibers) in the sputum or in lung tissue. Since the chief of pathology services of the East Tennessee Baptist Hospital, in Knoxville, had pointed out asbestos bodies to the jury in several large-scale colored photographs of tissue and sputum samples from Cavett's lungs—including a lung that had been removed because it had become cancerous—Hinshaw's testimony in behalf of Johns-Manville proved to be something less than convincing. Its effectiveness was also diminished by the fact that Gillenwater had been able to introduce into evidence such examples of Johns-Manville's early knowledge of the asbestos hazard as the Sumner Simpson correspondence, the contract-unit disease claims, the deposition of Dr. Kenneth Smith, and the depositions of lawyers for Frederick Le Grand and Fred C. Wenham, the two asbestos insulators who had settled third-party lawsuits with Johns-Manville back in the late 1950s and early 1960s. Most of all, however, Dr. Hinshaw's testimony had been diminished by the appearance of Cavett himself. He had once been a strapping man but he weighed only a hundred and forty pounds, and he had only a few months to live, when he was brought into the courtroom in a wheelchair early in the trial. At that time, he testified that most of the products he had used during his forty years as a boilermaker had borne the logo of Johns-Manville—an allegation that was corroborated by the testimony of co-workers—and that after using them he had looked "like somebody dumped a barrel of flour" on him.

. . .

Two months earlier, in April, 1982, Dr. Hinshaw had been the target of a similar cross-examination at the hands of Ronald Motley in the trial of *Carol Louise Tuten* v. *Johns-Manville*—a case brought by the widow of a pipe fitter who had developed asbestosis and died of pneumonia—which was held in the Duval County Courthouse, in Jacksonville, Florida. During a lengthy direct examination conducted by Albert H. Parnell, an Atlanta attorney who had become one of the lead counsels for Johns-Manville in the southeastern part of the country, Hinshaw had laid a foundation for the state-of-the-art defense by declaring that, in his opinion, the medical community was not convinced of the disease hazard for asbestos insulators until after 1964. He went on to say that cigarette smoking could produce scarring of lung tissue that was virtually indistinguishable from the scarring caused by asbestos, and that cigarettes were the leading cause of chronic bronchitis in the world today. Finally, in response to a series of hypothetical questions posed by Parnell, who obviously intended to remind the jury that Tuten had smoked, Hinshaw testified that the immune system of someone suffering from chronic bronchitis could be sufficiently weakened to render that person highly susceptible to pneumonia.

When it came time for Motley to cross-examine, he wasted little time in dealing with the cigarette issue. "I bought one of your books," he told Hinshaw.

"Thank you," Hinshaw said.

"How are you doing today, sir?"

"Fine."

"Doctor, I'll try to be as brief as possible. Let me turn to an area of asbestos disease if I might for a second. Do you agree that the only thing that causes asbestosis is asbestos?"

"Yes," Hinshaw replied.

"We're in agreement," Motley said. "OK. Cigarettes don't cause asbestosis, do they?"

"Right."

"They do not?"

"It does not," Hinshaw replied.

Later in the cross-examination, Motley asked Hinshaw to read aloud from the section on asbestosis in his 1956 book.

" 'Exposure occurs in industrial plants where asbestos products are fabricated and among those who install insulating materials,' " Hinshaw read. " 'The spinning and weaving of asbestos in combination with other textiles also results in exposure.' "

"All right, sir," Motley said when Hinshaw had finished. "Now, you cited—you reviewed the medical literature before you wrote that, didn't you."

"Yes," Hinshaw replied.

"And you [read] articles in the literature which you cite in that textbook, which included cases of asbestosis in insulation workers, didn't you?"

"I'm not entirely sure of that," said Hinshaw, who added that the information in the sentence he had quoted might have come from a book written by another medical doctor.

"All right, sir," Motley said. "Well, let me try to refresh your recollection."

"But it's not unlike that," Hinshaw continued quickly. "Insulation workers have been reported to have developed asbestosis prior to this date. I, indeed, may have seen some myself."

"And you knew, yourself, before 1956 that insulators were getting sick with asbestosis," Motley declared. "Isn't that correct?"

"I think I've actually seen one or two," Hinshaw replied. "Yes."

Having obtained this admission, Motley asked Hinshaw if it was true that back in 1961 he had told a lawyer for an asbestos company about the hazards of asbestosis and lung cancer for insulation workers.

"You'll have to show me," Hinshaw replied.

"All right, sir," said Motley, handing Hinshaw a letter. "Let me ask you if this is—if this is your signature, sir?"

"It is, yes," Hinshaw replied.

"All right, sir. Do you remember writing a report to a lawyer representing an asbestos-insulation company in 1961 where you reviewed a case of asbestosis in an insulation worker?"

"This is a letter to an attorney in Oakland, California, concerning a patient whom I had been called upon to evaluate," Hinshaw replied. "And as I recall it, he did have asbestosis, did he not?"

"Yes, sir," Motley said. "And he was an insulation worker."

"And he may have well been an insulation worker," Hinshaw agreed. "I mentioned to you a minute ago, I felt I probably have seen this. This is 1961. I may have seen it specifically sometime earlier than that. It can happen, of course, and I knew it at that time."

After this admission, which came toward the end of the cross-examination, Motley asked Hinshaw some questions that may well have given additional pause to the jurors, who later awarded Mrs. Tuten $228,633. (Because of contributory negligence on Tuten's part, this was reduced to $169,188, with Johns-Manville paying just over $41,000 of it, plus $20,000 in exchange for Mrs. Tuten's agreement not to go forward on the remainder of the trial for punitive damages.)

"All right, sir," Motley said. "Now, Doctor, let me—and I'll be through in maybe five minutes, I believe—let's talk a second about Mr. Tuten."

"Who?" Hinshaw inquired.

"Mr. Tuten," Motley said. "Do you know who that is?"

"No," Hinshaw replied.

"Mr. Tuten's widow is the plaintiff in this case," Motley told him.

"Oh," Dr. Hinshaw said.

In addition to a talent for cross-examination, Motley has an irreverent sense of humor and an undisguised contempt for Johns-Manville, which, long before it filed for reorganization under Chapter 11, he said he hoped to help bankrupt, and which he has called "the greatest corporate mass murderer in history." Following his victory over Johns-Manville in the Janssens case, in the summer of 1981—his first trial win after four losses—Motley prevailed in seven straight lawsuits that went to trial during the next year against Manville and other asbestos manufacturers, winning or helping to win jury verdicts of more than $5 million, of which $1.4 million was punitive damages. Since 1976, when he got into asbestos litigation, he has either taken on or become associated in, on a referral basis, more than three thousand asbestos lawsuits in jurisdictions ranging from Hawaii to Florida and from Maine to Missouri. He has participated in negotiations leading to settlements of about $75 million in some 650 of them; has brought in at least $10 million in fees to Blatt & Fales, the law firm he works for, in Barnwell, South Carolina; has earned some $2 million for himself; and has spent much of his life in the cabins of airplanes. During this eight-and-a-half-year period, he has acquired the respect of most of his colleagues in the plaintiff bar, the envy of some, and the disapproval of a few, who regard his courtroom style as too abrasive and his client-seeking tactics as too aggressive, and who worry that he may bring the much-feared epithet of "ambulance chaser" down upon their heads. Needless to say, he is looked upon by asbestos manufacturers and their insurance carriers with a mixture of awe, hatred, and dread.

Some measure of the asbestos industry's trepidation concerning Motley was revealed in the summer of 1980, when Raybestos-Manhattan filed motions in Mississippi and Hawaii seeking to have him barred from participation in more than four hundred pending cases because of his appearance on a CBS telecast entitled "See You in Court," in which he displayed two letters from the Sumner Simpson correspondence as proof that Raybestos-Manhattan and Johns-Manville had engaged in a coverup of the asbestos hazard more than forty years before, and claimed that "now we're seeing thousands and thousands of people dying as a result." The judges in both states refused to grant Raybestos's motion, however, and Motley later helped win jury verdicts totaling more than $1.5 million, including the first punitive damages ever awarded against Raybestos, in the first cases that went to trial in each of those jurisdictions.

As it happened, Motley had earned the enmity of Raybestos-Manhattan even before the CBS telecast, since he and the company had been engaged for many months in a battle over the admissibility of the Sumner Simpson letters, which Raybestos was trying to have excluded in several jurisdictions on the grounds that they might have been forged and that they were irrelevant. Other asbestos companies argued that they should be excluded because they were highly prejudicial to defendants other than Raybestos and Johns-Manville. Motley had proved that the first possibility was preposterous by getting William Simpson, the chairman of Raybestos-Manhattan (and the son of Sumner Simpson), to admit that his office, where the documents were stored from 1969 to 1974, was always locked when he was not in it; that it had never been broken into; and that he had no reason to believe that anyone had altered the documents between 1974, when they were turned over to John H. Marsh, Raybestos's director of environmental affairs, and 1977, when they were given into the custody of Raybestos's attorneys. As for the relevance of the letters, Motley claimed that they were of the highest probative value, because they showed not only that Simpson had known back in the 1930s that asbestos could kill but also that he had tried to suppress this information. As to whether the prejudicial effect of the letters outweighed their relevance, Motley made an analogy with the Watergate tapes, which he would use again and again in courtroom summations. "The prejudicial effect is that I have the opportunity to prove through the lips of the president of their company that he knew and covered it up," he told a judge who was holding a hearing on their admission. "Darn well right it's prejudicial. So were the Watergate tapes. Nixon would have been delighted in not having to have those things presented."

In addition to fighting for the admission of the Sumner Simpson documents—a struggle in which he was successful in most jurisdictions—Motley would soon begin to inflict heavy damage upon Raybestos-Manhattan with several new pieces of evidence. Particularly embarrassing were revelations contained in the minutes of a 1971 Asbestos Textile Institute meeting at which Dr. Joseph Goodman, a physician at Raybestos-Manhattan's North Charleston plant, characterized Dr. Selikoff as a dangerous man and discussed various ways of bringing him under control. Also embarrassing was a 1977 speech in which the company's medical director, Dr. Hilton C. Lewinsohn, had revealed that fully 50 to 60 percent of the workers who had developed asbestosis would also develop lung cancer. Even more lacerating, especially to the company's contention that it had a fine employee-health record, was a memorandum that had been handwritten in 1974 by John Marsh, who described Raybestos-Manhattan's health record as "indefensible." In closing arguments, Motley, after complimenting his opponents on their appearance, their articulateness, and their legal ability, would read Marsh's memo to the jury and then observe that it was no wonder Raybestos had run out and hired such fine attorneys.

The Sumner Simpson letters had marked a pivotal point in Motley's career, for, upon coming into possession of them in the early summer of 1978, he had used them, together with the contract-unit disease claims he had helped to uncover, to win a highly unusual order for a retrial of the Barnett case, on the ground that Raybestos-Manhattan and Johns-Manville had not disclosed information that was vital to the plaintiff's cause. These documents convinced Motley, who was smarting from two trial losses in a row to Lively Wilson, that there must be a wealth of additionally incriminating evidence about the asbestos coverup hidden away in moldering files and in the memories of witnesses who had yet to be deposed. Consequently, he spent much of the next two years seeking out witnesses who had firsthand knowledge of the asbestos coverup. One of them was Dr. Nicholas Demy, a former radiologist at the Somerset Hospital, in Somerville, New Jersey, who had diagnosed dozens of cases of asbestosis and lung cancer among Johns-Manville employees back in the 1950s but had been denied access to their occupational histories by company officials. Another was Dr. Schepers, former director of the Saranac Laboratory, who led Motley and his colleagues to the incriminating Kaylo file, which, insofar as it related to the culpability of Owens-Corning and Owens-Illinois, Motley liked to describe as "the smoking pistol, the spent cartridge, and the body all rolled into one."

During this period, Motley became so enthralled by the details of the coverup and by his growing medical expertise that he began to lose sight of the fact that he was eventually going to have to use what he had learned to make a convincing case before juries made up of ordinary men and women, who did not have his encyclopedic knowledge of asbestos disease. As a result, his presentation of the medical evidence was sometimes so laced with complex technical jargon and references to obscure sources that jurors, simply could not take it in. Informed of this by Terry Richardson, his colleague at Blatt & Fales, and by other colleagues who came to audit his trials, Motley worked hard to focus his arguments and to simplify his presentations. He also began to relax and to allow the sardonic, quick-tongued side of his personality to emerge. In the end, he came to realize that the way to convince juries of the rightness of his cause was not to bombard them with facts about the coverup or to overwhelm them with complex medical terms but to concentrate on ridiculing the contention of his opponents that no coverup existed, and to mock their efforts to place the blame for what had happened to asbestos workers on everything except asbestos.

Nowhere were these new tactics more effective than in dealing with the cigarette issue, which Motley considers to be far and away the most difficult defense to overcome. "Cigarette smoking is not only injurious to health by itself but, in combination with asbestos exposure, it is an almost surefire way to develop lung cancer," he points out. "I always tell my clients to stop smoking, and if they're foolish enough to want to continue I remind them about the jurors down South who returned a verdict in favor of the defendants when they caught sight of an asbestos plaintiff outside the courtroom sneaking a puff after he claimed he'd stopped smoking. My strategy for dealing with the cigarette-smoking issue is to get to it early and keep it out in front. For example, before beginning my opening statement I place a carton of cigarettes in an empty chair and proceed to inform the jury that I am going to tell them a story about a culprit called asbestos, but that my opponent is going to try his case against cigarettes. Later, during cross-examination, I get the defendants' expert medical witnesses to admit that the only thing that can cause asbestosis is asbestos. I also talk a lot about a guard dog at an asbestos-textile factory in Great Britain that died of asbestosis. You heard about the case? It was written up by Dr. Philip Ellman, a prominent pulmonary physician, who was in charge of the Tuberculosis and Chest Clinic in London. In an article that appeared in the July, 1933, issue of *The Journal of Industrial Hygiene*, Ellman described six cases of asbestosis. Five of the cases involved workers in asbestos factories who had developed the disease, and two of these patients had died of it. The sixth was that of the dog—a male rat terrier that had spent most of his life in the factory, and finally got so out of breath and emaciated that he had to be put out of his misery. When they autopsied the poor thing, they found his lungs to be riddled with scar tissue caused by his inhalation of asbestos fibers. That was way back in 1933. But I get a lot of mileage out of it with juries for the simple reason that the dog didn't smoke —now did he?"

In addition to the rat terrier, Motley, like all asbestos litigators, has favorite pieces of evidence that he introduces at key moments in trials to persuade jurors to return a verdict for his clients. One that he employed constantly against Johns-Manville was the letter that George S. Hobart, the Newark attorney who represented the company in asbestosis lawsuits brought during 1929 and 1930, wrote to Vandiver Brown in 1934, suggesting that Brown urge Dr. Anthony Lanza, the assistant medical director of the Metropolitan Life Insurance Company, to soften his description of asbestosis as a disease similar to silicosis in a report he was preparing for the United States Public Health Service. In his letter, Hobart indicated that his reason for wanting the change was that he he had been defending asbestosis lawsuits by claiming that "scientific and medical knowledge has been insufficient until a very recent period to place on the owners of plants or factories the burden or duty of taking special precautions against the possible onset of the disease." Motley's reason for using Hobart's letter nearly half a century later was, of course, to pound yet another nail into the coffin of the state-of-the-art defense. The way he went about this in some of his closing arguments was wickedly effective. First, he would thank the members of the jury for being so attentive to him during the course of the trial, and to his opponent as well, especially during his opponent's articulate presentation of the state-of-the-art defense. Then, shaking his head in wonderment, he would inform them that his opponent was not the first Johns-Manville lawyer to propose such an argument. And after a dramatic pause, he would proceed to read the letter that Hobart had written more than forty years before.

Another piece of evidence that Motley used again and again against Johns-Manville was the case of Frederick Le Grand, an asbestos insulator who, in 1957, had brought an unprecedented product-liability lawsuit against the company. With the possible exception of the 1947 Hemeon Report—an unpublished report of a 1947 survey conducted by the Industrial Hygiene Foundation, of Pittsburgh, which informed Johns-Manville that about 20 percent of the workers in one of its asbestos-textile factories had developed asbestosis—Motley considers *Le Grand v. Johns-Manville* to be the most devasting weapon against the company in product-user cases in the entire arsenal of evidence that has been assembled by the asbestos litigators. "*Le Grand* not only destroys Johns-Manville's state-of-the-art defense but pierces the heart of its assumption-of-risk defense," he says. "It also shows that the company engaged in a deliberate and repeated pattern of lying. Le Grand sued Johns-Manville back in 1957 because he had developed asbestosis from using their insulation products, which were obviously harmful to him. 'Why didn't you warn me?' he asked. Johns-Manville replied, in effect, 'We had no reason to warn you because you are the very first insulator we know of who got sick.' That, as it turned out, was an outright lie. In 1956, Johns-Manville had been notified by Dr. Daniel Braun, medical director of the Industrial Hygiene Foundation, that reports had appeared in the medical literature that insulators were at risk of developing asbestosis and bronchial cancer. Later, LeGrand's lawyer sent interrogatories asking Johns-Manville when it had first become aware that asbestosis was developing in factory workers. 'In 1946,' Johns-Manville replied. Another deliberate falsehood, as the minutes of the 1933 board of directors' meeting clearly show. Then, for the next twenty years—in fact, right up until the time Paul Gillen-water realized how important it was—Johns-Manville pretended that the Le Grand case had never happened. In interrogatory after inter-rogatory, the company said that the first time it had ever been sued by an asbestos insulator was in the Tomplait case, which was filed by Ward Stephenson in 1966. Lies upon lies. Do you know what I used to do with Le Grand? I used to do a regular rain dance with it. I used to ask every single witness Johns-Manville called to the witness stand about it. Why, I never let it out of the jury's mind!"

In the end, Motley has won most of his cases against Johns-Manville just as Ward Stephenson won *Borel*—through diligent inves-tigation. A typical example was the case of Dr. Harvey J. Hewett, a professor of marketing at East Carolina University, in Greenville, North Carolina, who died of mesothelioma in 1979, at the age of thirty-nine. Hewett's father, an asbestos insulator in Texas, had brought asbestos dust home on his work clothes, and the younger Hewett, who later served in the Navy, had remembered seeing pro-ducts made by Johns-Manville, Owens-Corning, and Philip Carey on board his ship. In gathering evidence for the case, an investigator from Motley's firm spent a week in Texas interviewing former co-workers of Hewett's father to find out what products they had used on specific jobs. Tom Taft, who was Hewett's local counsel in Greenville, tracked down and interviewed a number of Hewett's shipmates. In the end, they collected a detailed profile of his exposure to asbestos, which enabled Motley to settle the lawsuit for $777,500 in the summer of 1982.

In a case that was settled in May, 1981, in which Motley was associated with Richard A. Cappalli, an attorney from Cranston, Rhode Island, the client was a fifty-year-old Rhode Island man named Joseph A. Ruggieri, who had been diagnosed as having developed mesothelioma. Ruggieri's chief exposure to asbestos had occurred during a two-and-a-half-month period between November, 1949, and January, 1950, when he was serving in the Navy and was put to work repairing asbestos-covered bulkheads aboard the U.S.S. *Sabine*, a converted oil tanker, which was then being refurbished at the Brook-lyn Navy Yard, in New York. Once again, it was necessary to deter-mine whose asbestos products Ruggieri had been exposed to so Motley and Terry Richardson found and interviewed some shipmates whom Ruggieri remembered, and placed ads in the *Navy Times* asking other former crew members of the *Sabine* to get in touch with the firm. An investigator for Motley's firm also visited the Naval Historical Center, in Washington, D.C., where he learned that the *Sabine* had been built at the Sparrows Point Shipyard, near Baltimore, for the Standard Oil Company, and that when it was launched, in April, 1940, it had been called the *Esso Albany*. With the help of plaintiff attorneys in Baltimore, Motley learned from insulators who had worked at Sparrows Point in the 1940s what asbestos-containing products they had used. Finally, he and Cappalli filed suit against Johns-Manville and seven other manufacturers, and in December, 1980, they settled the case out of court for $325,000.

It was seven months later that Motley won the largest verdict of his career, for Edward Janssens, the former Navy man whose only exposure to asbestos had occurred on shipboard between 1943 and 1951. (Unlike the unfortunate Ruggieri, who died a month before his case was settled, Janssens had moderate asbestosis and no marked disability.) By this time—the summer of 1981—Motley had honed his courtroom strategy to a fine edge. He began his opening statement by telling the jury that Janssens had joined the Navy in 1942, at the age of eighteen. He said that, like all sailors and soldiers, Janssens realized that he might be killed or wounded but he had been fortunate, and had survived the war. "But there was also a silent killer stalking the ships that he served on," Motley continued. "It's a killer who had no motive, an invisible killer, a killer without smell, without taste. A killer that wounded cells, human cells, very slowly. Unlike a bullet, which is a searing and sudden pain, this killer injures very slowly, and the person who's being injured doesn't even know that this killer is wounding him. It takes twenty or thirty years before this killer finally shows his head."

Motley went on to tell the jury that in 1924, the year Janssens was born, Dr. W. E. Cooke, an English physician, had diagnosed a case of asbestosis in a factory worker and three years later, in a follow-up paper, had given the disease its name. He said that in 1942, the year Janssens joined the Navy, Dr. Alfred Angrist, who later became professor and chairman of the department of pathology at the Albert Einstein College of Medicine, in the Bronx, and who would come to testify before them, had found asbestosis and lung cancer in shipyard workers in New York. After warning the jurors that the scientific and medical evidence in the case would be difficult to understand, he predicted that no witness would come before them to dispute the fact that asbestosis was caused only by asbestos. "There is nothing else that causes it," he declared. "Cigarettes don't cause it. Silica doesn't cause it. Flour doesn't cause it. Open air doesn't cause it. It's only caused by asbestos. Look at the name. Asbestosis."

Motley informed the jurors that all medical doctors agreed that asbestosis was incurable and that nothing could be done to reverse Janssens's condition. He also told them that his client had quit smoking cigarettes a long time ago. He then brought up the state-of-the-art defense that Johns-Manville would try to erect. "It's our position, ladies and gentlemen of the jury, that asbestos dust and fibers injure anybody who breathes it," he said. "There is no such thing as an asbestos worker. There are such things as asbestos breathers. And our proof will show that by the time that Edward Janssens began work with Johns-Manville products in 1943, that asbestos had already killed office managers, boiler riveters, shipyard workers, insulators and guard dogs." As for Johns-Manville's attempt to blame the government for Janssens's health problems—the company was doing so on the ground that the Navy had specified that asbestos insulation be used in its ships—Motley argued that the government also specified the use of rat poison, but did not tell the manufacturers of rat poison not to put warning labels on it. Finally, in announcing that Janssens was seeking punitive damages because of Johns-Manville's reckless disregard for his safety, Motley said, "We will hope to prove to you, ladies and gentlemen of the jury, that Johns-Manville engaged in a coverup greater than anything Richard Nixon or anybody associated with Watergate ever could have dreamed of." In his closing statement, Motley told the jurors that with respect to the possible development of cancer, "Edward Janssens is a walking time bomb whose fuse has been lit." As evidence of Johns-Manville's reckless disregard for Janssens' safety, he cited Hobart's 1934 letter to Vandiver Brown asking for changes helpful to industry in the report of Metropolitan Life's health survey of asbestos workers; Brown's 1935 letter to Simpson, declaring that asbestosis should receive a minimum of publicity; Dr. Smith's 1949 memo about why diseased workers were not informed of their condition; and Wilbur Ruff's deposition about Johns-Manville's hush-hush policy of not informing sick workers that they were suffering from asbestos disease. In conclusion, he again recited some key dates in Janssens's life, juxtaposing them with key dates in the discovery and coverup of asbestos disease, and told the jurors that it was now 1981 and that "you and only you must decide the fate of Edward Janssens and Johns-Manville."

Almost a year later, Motley would come up against his old nemesis Lively Wilson, in *James L. Jackson* v. *Johns-Manville*—the trial involving the sheet-metal worker who had developed asbestosis while working at the Ingalls Shipbuilding Corporation, in Pascagoula, Mississippi, and was suing Johns-Manville and Raybestos-Manhattan. By this time, Motley's closing arguments were even more powerful and biting than they had been in the Janssens case. "Now, we believe, ladies and gentlemen, that there is no dispute in this case about certain things," he said. "Number One, each of these companies is in the asbestos business. They don't dispute that. Number Two, each of these companies sold asbestos to the Ingalls Shipyard. They don't deny that. Number Three, the only thing on earth known to cause asbestosis is asbestos. They don't dispute that. Asbestosis is incurable. Nobody disputed that. Asbestosis is irreversible. No one disputed that. Asbestosis is a serious disease. No one disputed that. And all but one doctor said, 'This man has asbestosis.' This one doctor, Dr. Auerbach, said, 'I am the final word.' But he is not. You, ladies and gentlemen of the jury, are the final word."

After pointing out that Auerbach was the only physician—out of nine doctors who had testified in the case for both sides—to say that Jackson was suffering not from asbestosis but from silicosis, Motley reviewed the evidence that had been presented to show that Johns-Manville and Raybestos-Manhattan had engaged in a coverup of the asbestos hazard. He then addressed himself to the overall legal strategy of the two defendant manufacturers. "Now, ladies and gentlemen of the jury, I need to spend a moment on the defenses raised by these asbestos companies," he said. "I call it the four-dog defense, and let me tell you why. There was a case one time that I was told about that happened in Alabama. This little four-year-old girl was out in the street in front of her house and a neighbor's Doberman pinscher jumped over the fence and bit her. It caused her some serious injuries, and the father had to go to court because his little girl was hurt. They got up in the closing argument and the lawyer who represented the dog owner said, 'Here are our defenses. Our first defense is, my client doesn't own a dog.' In this case, the asbestos companies are saying, 'James Jackson wasn't exposed to our product.' The second defense of the dog owner was, 'Well, we own a dog, but another dog bit her.' Asbestos companies want to shift responsibility to anyone they can—Ingalls, the Navy, the union, other defendants, smoking, silicosis. The third defense of the dog owner was, 'I own a dog, the dog bit the child, but the child knew the dog was dangerous, or the child shouldn't have been in the street.' In this case, they are going to stand up here and have the gall to tell you, 'We didn't know asbestos would kill you but James Jackson should have known.' Contributory negligence. They say it was James's fault. He shouldn't have been in the street. The fourth defense is, 'While we own a dog, and we admit our dog bit the child, the child is not hurt because of the bite. The gangrene that is in her leg came from something other than the dog bite.' "

Having riddled the defenses of his opponents with ridicule, Motley got down to the subject of the compensatory damages that should be awarded to Jackson for his medical bills, loss of wages, his pain and mental suffering, and his diminished life expectancy. "James Jackson will never be better off than you see him here," he declared. "His future is all downhill. As one doctor told you, he is close to being a pulmonary cripple. He has an incurable disease. He has indestructible fibers in his lungs. He has the agony of wondering as he sits here today, and for the rest of his life, which one of these asbestos fibers will explode and cause him cancer. And you will have in the jury room the statement of the medical director of Raybestos-Manhattan, where he said fifty or sixty percent of the people in Mr. Jackson's shoes die of lung cancer." Motley went on to justify punitive damages for reckless disregard, on the ground of Johns-Manville's hush-hush policy regarding its sick workers, and because Raybestos-Manhattan's health record in its textile plants had been, in the words of one of its own officials, "indefensible." In conclusion, he reminded the jurors that Johns-Manville was a $2 billion corporation, and told them that nearly forty years earlier the company had taken out a loan on the health and safety of its workers, and the time had come to repay it.

Incisive as Motley's performance proved to be, it was subsequently equaled by that of one of his co-counsels, Scott Baldwin—the litigator from Marshall, Texas, who had played a leading role in settling the Tyler factory case. Indeed, Baldwin's closing argument in *Jackson* v. *Johns-Manville* is considered by many plaintiff attorneys to have been one of the most dramatic summations ever given in an asbestos trial. After pointing out that there was overwhelming evidence to show that insulation products made by Johns-Manville and Raybestos-Manhattan had been widely used in the Ingalls Shipyard, Baldwin reminded the jury that neither company had placed warning labels on any of those products. At that point, he placed a large crayon-drawn chart upon a viewing board, and told the jury that it listed sixteen acts of gross indifference on the part of Johns-Manville—five of which had been joined in by Raybestos-Manhattan. He then proceeded to run through some of the highlights of these acts, and, in doing so, delivered a comprehensive summation of wrongdoing by the two companies.

"You know that by 1933 they began to have lawsuits," Baldwin said, referring to the first asbestosis lawsuits against Johns-Manville, which had actually been brought in 1929 and 1930. "They settled eleven in the year 1933, but, more important, when they settled those eleven lawsuits in 1933, they bought the lawyer. They made him agree not to bring any more lawsuits against Johns-Manville. To me that was a signal of things to come. It is like finding a dog's tooth in a bowl of chili. It suggests something to you."

Baldwin went on to remind the jury that in 1934 Vandiver Brown, the corporate attorney for Johns-Manville, persuaded Dr. Lanza, of Metropolitan Life, to delete some unfavorable references to the disease-producing potential of asbestos in a study that was published by the United States Public Health Service; that in 1935 Brown and Sumner Simpson, the president of Raybestos-Manhattan, exchanged letters in which they agreed that it would be beneficial if no articles about asbestosis would appear in the asbestos industry's trade journal; that in 1947 the Industrial Hygiene Foundation, an organization financed in part by the two companies, failed to publish a study showing that 20 percent of the workers in two of their asbestos-textile factories had developed asbestosis; that in 1949 the medical director of Johns-Manville's Canadian Subsidiary advocated a policy of not informing workers of X-ray changes showing that they were developing this incurable lung disease; and that during the 1950s, Johns-Manville and Raybestos-Manhattan made efforts to suppress public knowledge of the link between asbestos exposure and the development of cancer.

Following his dissection of the asbestos coverup, Baldwin went on to justify the $3 million in damages that he and his colleagues were seeking for Jackson. "Now let's see why these sums are reasonable," he told the jury. "You know, a famous jurist many years ago said—I think it was Learned Hand—'A corporation has no mind; it has no conscience; it has no heart; and it has no soul.' You can't strike its heart. It has none. The only way you can get the attention of a corporation and talk to it is through its pocketbook. I believe the English—this [concept of] punitive damages is not any new concept of the law; it is as old as the law itself—the English refer to it as the 'sting of the shilling.' Ladies and gentlemen, let me tell you something. You have got an opportunity. You can do something that I haven't been able to do in the last five years of this litigation. You can talk to the president of Johns-Manville. He is not too busy to talk to you, and you can send him a message. But when you do, it is going to have to be loud enough for him to hear it. And you can say to him that, at least in southern Mississippi, 'We are not going to condone this kind of action. And when you act like the record in this case has shown you acted, and inflict upon a man an incurable disease, you are going to have to respond and face the music.' And you can set the standards of your community, and you can set the standards [for] the conduct of the companies that come into this community, by sending a message to the presidents of Johns-Manville and Raybestos-Manhattan that [they] will have to explain to [their boards] of directors and their shareholders. You can say to [them] that you are going to act—and this is all we ask—in accordance with those great principles upon which this country was founded: justice, decency, and fair play."

Of the $3 million in total damages that were being sought for Jackson, Baldwin asked the jury to award $2 million against Johns-Manville and $1 million against Raybestos-Manhattan. In the case of Johns-Manville, whose net earnings in 1980 were $80 million, or about $200,000 a day, this was the equivalent of some ten days' earnings. After deliberating for several hours and finding both companies strictly liable and guilty of negligence, the jury awarded total damages of $1,016,500, which included half a million dollars in punitive damages against Johns-Manville and $125,000 in punitive damages against Raybestos-Manhattan—the first punitive damages ever awarded against Raybestos. This was a hefty bite, to be sure, but far bigger bites had been taken out of Johns-Manville in verdicts that had already been returned in the spring of 1982, and the biggest bite of all—punitive and compensatory damages of $2,300,000—was about to be inflicted upon the company by the jury in the Cavett case, in Knoxville, which went to trial two weeks later.

As things turned out, in March, 1984, a three-judge panel led by Chief Judge Charles Clark, of the Fifth Circuit Court of Appeals, threw out the punitive damages in the Jackson case, ruling that punitive awards should not be allowed against asbestos manufacturers because the companies were already struggling to pay compensatory damages. In returning *Jackson* v. *Johns-Manville* to the district court for a new trial, the Fifth Circuit panel also said that testimony about the possibility of cancer because of Jackson's asbestosis should not have been allowed in a case where there was no physical evidence of cancer, and that the Sumner Simpson papers should not have been admitted in evidence because they were too remote in time to be properly considered. In July, 1984, however, the Fifth Circuit decided that instead of returning the case to the district court it would rehear *Jackson* v. *Johns-Manville* en banc (before an entire panel of judges), and on January 21, 1985, by a vote of nine to five, it overturned the ruling of the three-judge panel by upholding the lower court's decision to allow the admission of the Sumner Simpson letters, and by holding that the admissibility of testimony concerning Jackson's increased risk and fear of cancer should be decided by the Mississippi Supreme Court, which should also determine whether punitive damages should be permitted under Mississippi law. In a bitter dissent led by Chief Judge Clark, the five-judge minority issued an unprecedented call for the Supreme Court of the United States to abolish punitive damages in asbestos cases, as well as awards based on the probability or fear of diseases such as cancer. This action encouraged Manville and Raybestos-Manhattan to hope that the Supreme Court would grant their petition for certiorari.

Whatever the ruling may be in the Jackson case, back in the summer of 1982 asbestos litigators throughout the nation were riding the crest of a wave, for some sixteen thousand lawsuits against Johns-Manville and other asbestos manufacturers remained to be settled or tried, and the tide was running strongly in favor of the litigators. The plaintiff attorneys had few, if any, qualms about anticipating good fortune, for, like Ward Stephenson, who had toiled on the Tomplait case for more then seven years before receiving any recompense, men such as Thompson, Gillenwater, Motley, Henderson, Baron, Baldwin, Glasser, Asch, Sweeney, Locks, Levy, and Kilbourne, to name a few, had put in years of effort and, during the early phase of the litigation, had often worked for months on end without remuneration. Indeed, many of them had gone into debt in order to keep their asbestos cases going. Since then, of course, virtually all of them had become rich. Now, confident of continuing high verdicts and big contingency fees, they closed in on Johns-Manville for the kill.

NINE

GOING
FOR BROKE

When the Manville Corporation (formerly the Johns-Manville Corporation) filed for reorganization under Chapter 11 of the federal Bankruptcy Code, on August 26, 1982, the move stunned hundreds of plaintiff lawyers, who were closing in on the company from practically every corner of the country, and dismayed thousands of asbestos-disease victims who had brought claims against it. The move also surprised hundreds of defense attorneys, who had been earning tremendous fees by defending the company from its accusers, and astonished the financial community, which had not expected a company with $2 billion in assets to employ such a stratagem. Manville had been fighting with its back to the wall for several years, however, and had been paying out nearly $2 million a month in defense costs alone since the spring of 1981, when its primary insurer, Travelers, announced that it would no longer defend or indemnify the company and its excess insurers, with one exception, refused to extend its coverage. During that period, moreover, juries around the nation had been granting huge punitive-damage awards—awards of a type for which Manville carried little or no insurance—and the company's troubles had been further compounded by a continuing inability to pin the blame on the federal government for asbestos disease that had developed in several thousand shipyard workers who had filed suit against Manville and other asbestos manufacturers.

The first major attempt to involve the government in the shipyard cases occurred in the spring of 1979, in the United States District Court in Hartford, Connecticut, where about a hundred and fifty present and former employees and relatives and survivors of employees of the General Dynamics Corporation's Electric Boat Division—a maker of nuclear submarines at the company's shipyard in Groton, Connecticut, since 1954—had brought lawsuits against Johns-Manville and eleven other asbestos-insulation manufacturers, as well as against the United States Navy, alleging that they had developed asbestos disease as a result of exposure to the insulation, and that they had not been warned that it was hazardous to their health. Some of the manufacturers, in turn, claimed that the government should bear some of the responsibility for the plaintiffs' injuries because it had sold them raw asbestos from government stockpiles, and had specified the use of asbestos insulation in submarine construction. The manufacturers also claimed that the plaintiff's injuries had been caused by the failure of the Navy and General Dynamics to institute proper precautionary measures for the handling and application of asbestos insulation. (At the time, General Dynamics—a St. Louis–based corporation that is one of the largest military contractors in the nation and has recently come under heavy criticism for cost overruns and improper billings in its contracts with the Defense Department—owned a controlling interest in the Asbestos Corporation, of Thetford Mines, Quebec, which was the largest independent producer of asbestos fiber in Canada; General Dynamics has since transferred control of the Asbestos Corporation to the government of the Province of Quebec.)

The earliest Groton shipyard cases had been filed in 1975 by Stanley J. Levy, of New York City, and Matthew Shafner, an attorney from Groton, who had been helping some of the disabled submarine workers obtain workmen's-compensation benefits. During the summer of that year, Dr. Selikoff, Dr. Ruth Lilis, and a team of physicians and researchers from the Mount Sinai School of Medicine's Environmental Sciences Laboratory had begun to examine 201 active and retired submarine workers at the invitation of the AFL-CIO Metal Trades Council, representing most of the trades in the yard. (These workers included electricians, machinists, welders, riggers, carpenters, and laborers, as well as insulators, and by the time the study was completed, in 1976, Dr. Selikoff and his associates had examined more than a thousand of them, and found that approximately half had developed X-ray evidence of asbestos scarring of the lung, the pleura, or both. This was an alarming discovery, considering the fact that more than a hundred thousand workers are believed to have been exposed to asbestos over the years at the Groton shipyard alone.) As for Electric Boat, which had been making submarines at Groton since 1924, it not only had failed to inform its employees that their chest X-rays showed they were developing asbestosis but also was contesting their efforts to obtain compensation for the disease under the federal Longshoremen's and Harbor Workers' Compensation Act. Some idea of the Navy's attitude toward the problem can be seen from the comments of Captain George M. Lawton, director of the Division of Occupational Health and Preventive Medicine of the Navy's Bureau of Medicine and Surgery, in Washington, D.C. In an interview that was published in *Connecticut Magazine* in 1979, Lawton answered the question of whether the Navy bore any responsibility for working conditions at the Electric Boat shipyard by observing, "If I order an automobile and the way they make automobiles is to throw people into a furnace, I am not responsible for that."

As might be expected, the government's official position on the matter was couched in more circumspect language. The Navy's legal defense in the Groton lawsuits was being handled by Peter A. Nowinski, an attorney with the Department of Justice, which was trying to live down the fact that in 1977 the government had been forced to contribute $5,700,000 to the settlement of a lawsuit involving more than 445 asbestos workers at a plant owned by the Pittsburgh Corning Corporation, in Tyler, Texas. Justice Department officials announced that the Groton shipyard workers were barred from seeking damages against the government because they were already being compensated under the federal Longshoremen's and Harbor Workers' Compensation Act. On June 20, 1979, Federal Judge M. Joseph Blumenfeld, who was presiding over the Groton cases, ruled that the question of whether third parties such as the government and General Dynamics were negligent could not be used by Johns-Manville and its co-defendants to relieve themselves of their own liability. As a result, the government did not participate in a $6,720,000 settlement of the first fifty Groton shipyard cases, which was negotiated by Levy and Shafner in 1981, and it was not a defendant in any of the cases that went to trial at the beginning of 1982.

The Groton settlement involved one of the most imaginative and risky negotiations in the history of asbestos litigation. From the outset, Levy and Shafner took the position that the twelve defendants in the fifty cases should settle at the same time, and that the plaintiffs would refuse to accept any piecemeal or partial settlements. This forced the defendants to negotiate in a group. Late in the discussions, however, when the defendants had offered to settle the cases for $6 million, Raybestos-Manhattan balked at paying its assessed share of $720,000, and withdrew from the group. At that point, Levy told the court that if Raybestos-Manhattan refused to chip in its share, he would accept $5 million as a settlement from the remaining eleven defendants, and proceed to try all fifty cases against Raybestos-Manhattan alone. Levy went on to say that he would propose that if the verdicts in the trial against Raybestos-Manhattan did not make up the $1 million difference, the settling defendants would agree to make a second payment. In return, he would agree that if the verdicts did reach $6 million, the settling defendants would not have to make a second payment. Instead, the plaintiffs would collect every penny of the $1 million difference, plus the $720,000 that Raybestos-Manhattan had balked at paying, from Raybestos-Manhattan. Not surprisingly, when confronted with this proposal, Raybestos-Manhattan agreed to ante up the $720,000.

During 1979, Johns-Manville and ten other asbestos-insulation manufacturers made their next effort to shift responsibility for asbestos disease to the government, this time by bringing a third-party lawsuit against the United States in federal court in Virginia. In their suit, the manufacturers sought to be totally indemnified by the government for a $69,000 settlement they had negotiated with a fifty-nine-year-old former pipe coverer named William B. Glover, who had developed asbestosis in 1975 after working for thirty-five years at the Norfolk Naval Shipyard, and had sued them for negligence, breach of implied warranty, strict liability, and fraudulent misrepresentation and concealment of information about the health hazards of their products. Before settling the case, Johns-Manville and its co-defendants sued the government, claiming that it was liable to them on the basis of noncontractual indemnity, because, as the employer at the shipyard, it had failed to maintain a safe workplace and had thus been guilty of the primary negligence that had caused Glover's disease.

On the face of it, the whole business was bizarre, to say the least, for it placed Johns-Manville and its fellow-manufacturers who would ultimately settle with Glover in the position of having to affirm a case against themselves in order to prove their case against the government —in other words, of having to admit that they were potentially liable to Glover for their failure to warn him of the hazards of their asbestos products, before trying to prove that their liability was superseded by the government's failure to advise Glover on how to handle those products properly and to provide him with a safe place of work. Convoluted as this might seem, *Glover* v. *Johns-Manville* v. *United States of America* was litigated with deadly seriousness, for the simple reason that it bade fair to determine who was going to foot a several-billion-dollar bill for the two thousand shipyard cases that had already been filed and for the thousands of similar claims that were expected to be brought in the future. Indeed, the trial was tantamount to a high-stakes poker game for the asbestos manufacturers and their insurance carriers, as well as for the government.

During week-long proceedings that began on October 10, 1979, attorneys for Johns-Manville introduced evidence to show that Navy safety inspectors had found the Norfolk shipyard to have had some of the worst asbestos-dust conditions of any naval shipyard in the nation, while the government argued that Johns-Manville and the other manufacturers had known for decades that their asbestos products were hazardous to work with, and had done little or nothing to remedy the problem. After two months of deliberation, United States District Judge John MacKenzie ruled that the manufacturers could not claim indemnity against the government, saying that although the United States had "failed to satisfy the duty of care it owed Glover," its liability was limited to payments under the federal Employees' Compensation Act. Johns-Manville appealed MacKenzie's ruling in the Glover case to the Fourth Circuit Court of Appeals, but in the autumn of 1981 the appellate court upheld MacKenzie, agreeing that the manufacturer was more negligent for Glover's asbestosis than the government was.

During 1983 and 1984, Manville filed three lawsuits in the United States Claims Court, in Washington, D.C., charging the government with contractual liability for the asbestos exposure of workers employed in government shipyards, and these cases are still in litigation. Back in 1981, however, Johns-Manville's inability to bring the government into the asbestos litigation as a full-fledged defendant was a bitter blow that isolated the company, driving it into a blind alley, where, deserted by its insurers, harassed by litigators armed with new disclosures about its role in the coverup of asbestos disease, pilloried by juries bent on punishing it for its past deeds, and criticized by the press, it continued not only to fight with tenacity against all comers but also, throughout, to maintain an unruffled public demeanor. In May of that year, in an interview that was published in an investors' report, two of the company's top legal strategists—G. Earl Parker, its senior vice-president for law and public affairs, and Dennis Markusson, the assistant corporate counsel—discussed developments in the asbestos litigation in a manner that was both matter-of-fact and bold-faced. Parker blamed publicity and a litigious society for the sharp increase in asbestos lawsuits during 1980. He said that juries were unable to make consistent judgments on similar facts and could not serve as a means of delivering uniform compensation. As for punitive damages, which had just been awarded against Johns-Manville for the first time, Markusson said that the company intended to raise the issue of whether it was constitutional to assess them more than once for the same thing. "If the notion is to punish, then at some point it goes beyond punishing and becomes an abuse of due process or at least nonsensical," he declared. Parker hastened to add that "We believe no one is at fault in the evolution of asbestos-related disease." He concluded the interview by praising the proposed asbestos health hazards compensation bill—a measure that was widely known as the Johns-Manville bailout bill—which had been introduced during the previous session of Congress by Senator Gary Hart, of Colorado.

The bravura performance put on by Parker and Markusson mirrored an aggressive stance that had been taken at the beginning of the year by John A. McKinney, Johns-Manville's chairman and chief executive officer, who had informed his subordinates that the company would henceforth go to trial whenever practical rather than settle asbestos-disease lawsuits out of court. By then, Johns-Manville had been named as a defendant in more than five thousand lawsuits, and several hundred new cases were being filed against the company each month—a fifty percent increase over the number filed in 1980. As a result, on January 31, 1981, Richard B. Von Wald, Johns-Manville's corporate counsel, was forced to write a letter informing Coopers & Lybrand, the accounting firm that performed Johns-Manville's annual audit, that "the eventual outcome of this litigation cannot be predicted at this time and the ultimate liability to the Company after application of available insurance cannot be estimated with any degree of reliability."

Four days later, Coopers & Lybrand responded by qualifying its report on Johns-Manville's consolidated financial position in 1979 and 1980—an embarrassing development that McKinney was forced to acknowledge in the company's 1980 annual report, which was sent out to the stockholders in March, 1981. "In spite of the uncertainties created by this growth in litigation, we continue to be optimistic about our ability to deal with the problem," he informed the stockholders.

"Since this litigation began, we have won 19 of the 28 cases that have proceeded through trial." He went on to say, "You can be assured that we will continue to be aggressive in asserting our defenses."

As it happens, the nineteen victories in twenty-eight trials had come mostly in cases in which the medical diagnosis of asbestos disease was in serious doubt. Moreover, it was at that time that Travelers was about to inform Johns-Manville that its primary insurance coverage was running out, and that it would no longer undertake to indemnify or defend the company in future asbestos litigation. How, then, was a new policy of going to trial in asbestos lawsuits going to save the company money, since legal fees and the likelihood of adverse jury verdicts made court trials far more costly than settlements and were bound to create a sharp rise in the overall cost of litigation? A possible answer to this question has been suggested by the plaintiff attorneys: by going to trial in the kind of cases that it might have previously settled, Johns-Manville could clog court calendars, and by delaying trial dates, prolonging discovery proceedings, and appealing adverse verdicts it could drastically slow down the payment of compensation to the victims of asbestos disease. In the most optimistic scenario, the resulting strangulation of the court system could persuade Congress to enact legislation that would bail the company out of its legal and financial difficulties. And, at the very least, it would buy time while Johns-Manville devised new strategies for corporate survival.

The first of these strategies emerged in the spring of 1981, when the company's managers worked up a corporate-restructuring plan that provided for the formation of a new parent corporation, called the Manville Corporation. The new corporation would do no other business than hold the stock of five subsidiary companies, which would operate fifty-four second-level subsidiary companies. The five operating subsidiary companies would be the Johns-Manville Corporation, which would manufacture and sell asbestos and asbestos-containing products such as roofing and pipe; the Manville Forest Products Corporation, which would make paper and wood products; the Manville Products Corporation, which would conduct domestic mineral and industrial-specialty operations; and the Manville International Corporation, which would manufacture and sell building and industrial materials through foreign subsidiaries. The key components of the new restructuring scheme were the Johns-Manville Corporation, into which all of Johns-Manville's asbestos mining and asbestos-manufacturing operations would be folded, and the Manville Forest Products Corporation, successor to Olinkraft, Incorporated—a company with 580,000 acres of timberland in Louisiana, Texas, and Arkansas, which Johns-Manville had bought for $600 million (about half its total assets) back in 1978.

Given the legal situation that had developed, one scarcely needed to be a legal or financial wizard to see what lay behind the corporate face-lift. When McKinney described the proposed restructuring to Johns-Manville's board of directors, on July 30, 1981, he said that the purpose of the restructuring was "to remove from Johns-Manville Corporation the non-asbestos-related assets and the people associated with those assets, and thereby insulate them from the negative impact of the asbestos litigation." He also emphasized the need for secrecy in going about this task. "Neither internally nor externally do we intend to say anything more about the reasons for the corporate restructuring and operational reorganization than is stated in the news release and bulletin, or implied by the charts, or will be stated in the letter to shareholders to accompany the proxy statement," he declared. "If asked about any effect on liabilities, we'll say the questioner has to reach his own conclusions about that. We do not wish to precipitate a definitive legal challenge to the new structure."

In the news release that was handed out on the same day, and published in the business sections of newspapers around the country, McKinney explained that consolidation of asbestos operations in the J-M Corporation "will make possible a coordinated policy for successful continuation of the asbestos business." In the letter that was sent with the proxy statement to fifty-two thousand shareholders on September 11, McKinney wrote that "unfavorable publicity and litigation involving the asbestos-related aspects of JM's businesses" necessitated the corporate restructuring. On October 29, the shareholders approved it by an overwhelming margin, and that same day a public announcement was made that it had been accomplished.

In addition to restructuring the company in order to protect its assets from its tort liabilities, Johns-Manville's managers appear to have also begun to toy with the idea of playing the bankruptcy card—a hazardous move, since no one could know whether it would turn out to be an ace in the hole or the joker in the deck. (On the one hand, filing for reorganization under Chapter 11 would result in an automatic stay of all civil litigation and proceedings against the company; on the other hand, it could result in liquidation.) Back in May, company officials had begun to interview outside consultants in order to commission a study that would estimate the future incidence of asbestos disease in the national population and the number of potential claims and law-suits that might be filed against Johns-Manville. This step was highly significant with regard to a future bankruptcy filing, because in the quarterly financial statements (Forms 10-Q and 10-K) that Johns-Manville and other corporations were required to send to the Securities and Exchange Commission, the company was required under Financial Accounting Standards Board Rule 5 (FASB-5) to acknowledge proba-ble losses, such as might result from lawsuits that were pending against it. Under Financial Acounting Board requirements, this liability ac-crual was mandated only when the contingent losses could be reason-ably estimated. If no reasonable estimate could be made, and an appropriate declaration that it could not was noted in the financial statements that are included in Form 10-K, no accrual was required. By the same token, if the contingent losses could be estimated and if the resulting liability was large enough, it could be used to justify a bankruptcy reorganization.

The question of loss contingency had become extremely important at the beginning of 1981, when Von Wald had written to Coopers & Lybrand informing the auditors that the eventual outcome of the asbestos litigation and its ultimate liability to the company could not be estimated with any degree of reliability, because this declaration relieved the company of the burden of having to file an FASB-5 estimation. A few months later, however, after the first punitive dam-ages were awarded, Johns-Manville's strategists appear to have changed their minds about whether they should acknowledge the need for a liability accrual. In any event, by commissioning a study of the future incidence of asbestos disease and the number of potential claims and lawsuits that might be filed, they were taking the first step toward an FASB-5 loss estimation, and also toward a Chapter 11 proceeding. During the first week of June, they met with Dr. Nancy Dreyer, a Ph.D. epidemiologist, who was the president of a consulting group called Epidemiology Resources, Inc., of Brookline, Massachusetts, and a few days later, Epidemiology Resources was hired to undertake the study.

During the next eight weeks, relying almost exclusively upon data supplied by Johns-Manville, Dreyer and her associates estimated that there would be about 230,000 additional cases of asbestos disease by the end of the century—asbestosis as well as cancer—and that this would result in some 49,000 new asbestos-disease lawsuits against the company. The epidemiological part of their equation was certainly open to question, for Dr. Selikoff and his associates at Mount Sinai's Environmental Sciences Laboratory, who were considered to be the world's leading experts on the subject of asbestos disease, were even then completing a study for the Department of Labor in which they estimated that there would be at least 270,000 excess deaths from asbestos-related cancer alone by the year 2010. How, then, could Dreyer and her colleagues at Epidemiology Resources possibly conclude that only 49,000 more people would end up filing asbestos-disease lawsuits against Johns-Manville? The question is answered in part by a caveat they inserted at the beginning of their report. "There are many potential sources of error in these predictions," they wrote. "The actual number of lawsuits might easily be as low as half or as much as twice the number our calculations suggest." In another section, they pointed out that "the zeal of attorneys" in influencing potential plaintiffs to file asbestos-disease lawsuits against Johns-Manville could lead to a 50 percent margin of error in their estimate that only about 21 percent of all the people who developed asbestos disease would sue.

Von Wald and his associates at Johns-Manville were said to be less than happy with the uncertainties expressed in this preliminary report, which was delivered in June, 1981. A report containing such caveats could not, of course, be used to support an FASB-5 estimation of liability accrual, and thus could not be used to justify a bankruptcy filing in the future. However, after mulling things over, the Johns-Manville stratigists directed the Epidemiology Resources people to "refine the estimates" for a March, 1982, deadline, and to "try to lessen the uncertainty" in their study.

It was now September, 1981, and during the previous five months things had taken a bad turn for Johns-Manville in the nation's courtrooms, because juries had awarded punitive damages of more than $1.5 million against the company. But at this gloomy moment Johns-Manville's corporate spirits were lifted when Senator Gary Hart reintroduced his asbestos health hazards compensation bill, which he had first proposed in 1980. To begin with, Hart told his fellow-senators that two million Americans were suffering from occupational diseases, and that the most common of these diseases was caused by breathing asbestos dust. He went on to say that as many as eleven million American men and women had been exposed to asbestos since the beginning of the Second World War, and that more than a million and a half of them were expected to die of asbestos cancer and other asbestos diseases. He then declared that his bill was designed to provide relief for the victims of this terrible tragedy.

In reality, Hart's measure proposed to take away the right of diseased and disabled workers, and the widows and families of workers who had died of asbestos disease, to sue the manufacturers of asbestos insulation and other asbestos products for negligence and failure to warn about the health hazards of asbestos. Thus, it would have eliminated the right of these workers to be compensated for the pain and suffering they had endured as a result of asbestos disease, and would have protected the manufacturers from being judged guilty of outrageous and reckless misconduct, which would justify the awarding of punitive damages. Hart's measure proposed that diseased asbestos workers and their families be compensated for disability and death only by no-fault state and federal workmen's-compensation programs in which they were already entitled to participate, with a minimum 10 percent increase in these programs' meager benefits. It also proposed that minimum standards of compensation be established for total disability or death due to an asbestos-related disease. The minimum, which would be tied to the number of dependents a worker had, would not be less than two-thirds or more than 80 percent of a sick or dead worker's average weekly wage, and would be paid throughout the duration of his disability or his lifetime, or until the remarriage of his widow.

Under Hart's bill, a totally disabled asbestos-insulation worker with a wife and two children, or the widow and two children of an asbestos worker who had died of asbestos disease, would receive an average of $14,000 a year. This would be paid by workmen's-compensation insurance carried by the last employer who exposed him to asbestos. In the case of shipyard workers, the last employer would probably be a private shipyard owner or the United States Navy. In the case of most other plaintiffs, it would probably be a relatively small company engaged in applying asbestos insulation to high-temperature pipes in power plants, chemical factories, and oil refineries.

Johns-Manville officials praised Hart's bill. They had good reason to do so. At the time, the company was a defendant in some seven thousand failure-to-warn lawsuits that had been filed by disabled asbestos workers or the widows and children of asbestos workers, and the bill, which had been written after consultation between Senator Hart's staff and Johns-Manville's Washington lobbyists, proposed to do away with such lawsuits. For this reason, it became known (as had the earlier measure introduced in the House in 1977 by Representative Millicent Fenwick, of New Jersey) as the Johns-Manville bailout bill.

Some of Hart's aides claimed that his bill was backed by the International Association of Heat and Frost Insulators and Asbestos Workers, pointing out that Andrew Haas, president of the seventeen-thousand-member union, who had been trying for years to get Congress to enact legislation to help the victims of asbestos disease, had written Hart a letter of support for the bill in 1980. Other observers have noted that Haas may have been swayed by a provision in the bill that would have prevented disabled union members from suing the union for not having warned them more fully about the hazards of working with asbestos. In any event, Haas's support of Hart's measure was opposed by Roy Steinfurth, the administrator of the union's health hazards program; by many of the union's business agents; and by many of its rank-and-file members, who continued to bring product-liability suits against Johns-Manville and other asbestos manufacturers at an unprecedented rate. Haas himself subsequently developed asbestosis, and retained Robert E. Sweeney, a prominent asbestos litigator from Cleveland, to file a product-liability lawsuit in his behalf—something that Hart's proposed measure would have prevented him from doing if it had been enacted into law.

During the presidential primary campaign of 1984, on the few occasions when Hart was criticized for his asbestos bill, he was quick to use Haas's support to suggest that the bill had had widespread union approval. The fact is, however, that high officials of the AFL-CIO had bitterly denounced the bill. Moreover, on December 10, 1980, Hart and Timothy E. Wirth, the Democrat representative from Colorado's Second Congressional District—home of Johns-Manville's world headquarters—who was thought to be planning to sponsor similar legislation in the House, had been sent a letter by the Oil, Chemical, and Atomic Workers International Union informing them that the measure would result in "institutionalizing cancer" and would remove any inducement for industry to use caution and prevention when dealing with asbestos. In addition, on November 11, 1980, Hart and Wirth had been sent an eleven-page letter by William A. Trine and J. Conard Metcalf, of the Boulder law firm of Williams, Trine, Greenstein & Griffith, which warned them to think twice before sponsoring bailout legislation for the asbestos industry, and informed them about specific details of Johns-Manville's fifty-year coverup of the asbestos hazard, such as the Sumner Simpson papers. At the end of their report, Trine and Metcalf pointed out that while asbestos-disease litigation "may be distressing to Johns-Manville, the truly distressing situation is the man whose lungs are crushed by the wildly aberrant cells of pleural mesothelioma while his wife and children watch helplessly from his bedside." They then told Hart and Wirth bluntly that "bailout legislation is unwarranted and unnecessary," and that in any event no bill should be proposed to bar access to the courts by the victims of asbestos disease.

Hart not only ignored this advice but managed to misconstrue the situation. For example, when he reintroduced his bill in 1981 he tried to persuade his fellow-senators to support it by telling them that in about half of the asbestos cases that had gone to trial the worker or the worker's family had received nothing. The fact was that Johns-Manville and its insurers had settled some two thousand asbestos lawsuits out of court for tens of millions of dollars, and that fewer than forty of the seven thousand lawsuits that were pending against the company had gone to trial. (Most of the twenty or so trials that had been won by Johns-Manville involved cases in which the diagnosis of disease was in doubt, or had occurred before disclosure about the coverup had eroded the company's state-of-the-art defense.) Moreover, Hart did not inform his fellow-senators that in recent months juries had awarded punitive damages of more than $1.5 million against Johns-Manville for outrageous and reckless misconduct after hearing evidence that the company had engaged in the coverup, about which he had been fully informed by Messrs. Trine and Metcalf.

Thanks to the failure of his fellow-senators to support them, neither of Hart's proposed asbestos-compensation bills got out of committee. If either of them had been passed, it would have established a legislative precedent whereby countless other workers—for example, men and women exposed to cancer-producing chemicals—might be similarly deprived of access to the courts in the future. The question is, Why did Hart introduce those bills to begin with? Why did he seek to bail out a company that not only was largely responsible for a tragedy that he himself said would claim the lives of more than one and a half million of his fellow-citizens but also had been found guilty of outrageous and reckless misconduct by juries composed of his fellow-citizens?

The question has not yet been answered in full. What is known from Federal Election Commission records is that Hart accepted contributions from Johns-Manville's political-action committee, including $4,800 for his 1980 Senate reelection campaign. The FEC reports also show that John McKinney, Manville's chairman, gave $999.11 (the maximum an individual can give is $1,000 in each of the primary and general-election campaigns), and that G. Earl Parker, the senior vice-president for law and public affairs, gave $850. These contributions were not extraordinary, of course, and could not explain the fact that Hart's proposed legislation was so favorable to Manville. What many observers of the Colorado political scene believe is that Hart, who first won election to the Senate in 1974, only after he had survived a three-way primary with less than 40 percent of the total vote, and was reelected in 1980 by less than 51 percent of the vote, felt a desperate need to shed the liberal image that had followed him from his days as presidential campaign manager for George McGovern in 1972, and to show business interests in Colorado—particularly the big oil companies, the cattle industry, and the banking community in Denver—that he was not anti-business. Whatever the case, the Johns-Manville bailout bill that he reintroduced in 1981 was nothing that he felt would ever come back to haunt him, for he surely knew that it had little chance of ever being voted out of committee. It was an example of the kind of bill that is not supposed to do its author any real or lasting harm and has the advantage of showing important constituents (in this case, an important corporate constituent) that its author is doing his very best for them. At the time, Hart had no way of knowing that Johns-Manville —a company with $2 billion in assets—was secretly preparing to file for reorganization under Chapter 11, or that within a year and a half McKinney would be required to testify under oath about Johns-Manville's efforts to gain passage of federal legislation that would bail it out of its legal difficulties. When this did come to pass, the stage was set for one of the least-known but most dramatic disclosures in the complex history of asbestos litigation.

During the late autumn of 1981, Manville continued to devise strategy to deal with its growing legal problems. In December, Von Wald got together with nine other attorneys to form an organization called the Litigation Analysis Group, or LAG, whose mission was to investigate these problems and make recommendations with respect to them. Four of LAG's members—Von Wald, Earl Parker, Dennis Markusson, and Christina Bearman—came from inside the company. The six outside members were James W. B. Benkard and Stephen Case, of Davis Polk & Wardwell, a New York City law firm that had handled Johns-Manville's legal affairs since 1928 and one of whose senior partners would become a director of the company the next year; Paul Meyer and James Scarboro, of the Phoenix, Arizona, law firm of Martori, Meyer & Victor, which had been retained to analyze the legal aspects and consequences of Johns-Manville's recent corporate restructuring; Curtis Caton, of Heller, Ehrman, White & McAuliffe, a San Francisco law firm which was representing Johns-Manville in major and protracted insurance litigation in California Superior Court; and Marc Victor (no relation to the Victor of the Phoenix law firm), an attorney who was president of a company called Litigation Risk Analysis, of Menlo Park, California.

As things turned out, Marc Victor played a bizarre role in a complex chain of events that now began to lead toward the filing for bankruptcy, some eight months down the road. A thirty-year-old graduate of Dartmouth, Stanford University School of Law, and Stanford Graduate School of Business, he had worked for six years at the Stanford Research Institute, in Menlo Park, applying decision analysis to legal and other problems, before leaving to start Litigation Risk Analysis, a one-man company that helped map strategy for businesses faced with major lawsuits. In April, 1981, he had been retained by the Heller, Ehrman firm on behalf of Johns-Manville as a consulting attorney in the insurance litigation, and some six months later Von Wald hired him to join the Litigation Analysis Group, which held its first meeting on December 15, and met every month thereafter until Manville filed for bankruptcy.

During the winter of 1982, Victor was assigned to bring his expertise to bear upon the work of the people at Epidemiology Resources, who were refining their estimates of the number of cases of asbestos disease and of asbestos-disease lawsuits against Johns-Manville, in order to meet the March deadline they had been given for their final report. On March 15 and 16, he and several Manville attorneys met at the company's Denver headquarters with Dr. Alexander M. Walker, an associate epidemiologist at Epidemiology Resources, who was in charge of the final-estimation study, to discuss some conclusions that Walker had presented at a LAG meeting in Washington, two weeks earlier.

During the two days in mid-March, Victor, a litigation strategist who was totally without training or experience in epidemiology, was successful in persuading Dr. Walker, a scientist with a doctorate from the Harvard School of Public Health, to reshape some of his assumptions concerning the future incidence of asbestos disease. For example, Walker revised his original estimate in such a way as to lower the projected number of people who might develop lung cancer as a result of exposure to asbestos. (Walker did this by discounting the risk multiplier for lung cancer that had been propounded by Dr. Selikoff, who had found that an asbestos-insulation worker who smokes has five times as much risk of developing lung cancer as cigarette smokers who are not exposed to asbestos, and that an asbestos-insulation worker who doesn't smoke has five times as much risk of developing lung cancer as nonsmokers in the general population. Indeed, when other factors are included, the combination of cigarette smoking and asbestos exposure increases an asbestos insulator's chance of developing lung cancer more than fifty times over the risk incurred by someone who neither smokes nor works with asbestos.) Some idea of what went on at the two-day meeting in Denver can be had from sworn testimony that was subsequently given by Walker in the bankruptcy proceedings.

"Were you requested at any time by Manville or its counsel to make assumptions in your estimates that would result in lower rather than higher resulting numbers?" Walker was asked by Richard Tufero, an attorney for Manville's unsecured creditors.

"I was asked sometime, I believe, during the meeting in Denver, that whenever I had to choose between two equally plausible assumptions, I should choose the assumption which led to a smaller number of cases of disease," Walker replied.

Later, Tufero asked Walker who had given him that intruction. "Marc Victor," Walker replied.

When Tufero asked Walker if he had talked to Victor about why the instruction had been given, Walker said, "I tried to, but he said that he would prefer not to discuss it in any detail."

In an affidavit that was subsequently submitted to the bankruptcy court, lawyers representing the asbestos claimants suggested that the most likely reason for Manville's attorneys to want Walker to keep his assessment of the future incidence of asbestos disease as low as possible was simply that the lower the estimate of disease, the lower the estimate of potential plaintiffs who might bring future lawsuits. As for their desire to downplay the number of future lawsuits, the affidavit suggested that this was necessary in order to come up with an estimate for the company's total financial liability in the asbestos litigation that would be large enough to justify its filing for reorganization, but not so large as to trigger a proceeding that might result in its liquidation. One trouble with all of this was that Manville had been claiming for some time that it had spent only about $25,000 including defense costs, to settle an average asbestos-disease case—a figure that seems very low, and was probably designed to reassure the company's stockholders. Whatever the truth of the matter, the $25,000 figure applied to all the lawsuits that had been settled or tried since 1976, and thus was a historical average that did not take into account the skyrocketing cost of disposing of asbestos cases; that cost rose to an average of more than $40,000 during the first half of 1982, when jurors were awarding huge compensatory and punitive damages, which drove up the price of out-of-court settlement. Low or not, the $25,000 projected cost posed an excruciating dilemma for Manville's attorneys and advisers, who that spring were searching for ways to justify a bankruptcy reorganization under Chapter 11. The nature of this dilemma was subsequently described in the affidavit of the plaintiff attorneys. They pointed out that if there were 200,000 additional lawsuits—a by-no-means impossible number, since approximately 21 million living American men and women (about one in ten of the total population) had been exposed to asbestos in their work between 1940 and 1980, and were therefore estimated to be at some risk of developing asbestos disease—one merely had to multiply the 200,000 potential plaintiffs by Manville's own $25,000 average disposition cost to arrive at a total projected-liability cost of *$5 billion*. If such a figure were to be appended to an FASB-5 estimate for liability accrual, it would undoubtedly have triggered a bankruptcy proceeding under Chapter 7 of the federal code, in which liquidation of Manville would have been the only possible solution. This, of course, was not at all what Manville's attorneys, advisers, and managers had in mind. And so, hung up on their own $25,000 historical-disposition cost, they had no choice but to tinker with the estimates of the future incidence of asbestos disease and of projected lawsuits if they were to arrive at an FASB-5 estimation for a liability accrual that would insure Manville's survival.

To give credit to the people at Epidemiology Resources, they had pointed out back in July, 1981, that there could be a 50 percent margin of error in their estimate of 49,000 additional lawsuits, because of the many uncertainties that were involved in making it. And, to give Dr. Walker his due credit, though he appears to have been influenced by Victor in his estimates of the number of future cases of asbestos disease, he was adamant in expressing his opinion in March, 1982, that the propensity of potential asbestos plaintiffs to sue Manville could not be accurately predicted by any methodology over the long run. As attorneys for the asbestos plaintiffs would later point out, if Manville officials had really wanted to avoid filing for bankruptcy, as they claimed, they would have been delighted with Dr. Walker's opinion, and would have terminated the FASB-5 estimation process forthwith. Instead, as soon as Walker expressed his opinion that propensity to sue was not something that could be predicted, Von Wald's people informed him that he was no longer to concern himself with the projection of lawsuits. This meant that Walker's views on propensity to sue would be excluded from the analysis, and limited him to estimating the future incidence of asbestos disease, which in August of 1982 he did to the satisfaction of the Manville people by predicting in his final report that between 1980 and 2009 there would be 19,000 cases of mesothelioma and 55,000 cases of asbestos-related lung cancer; and that there were at present 65,000 cases of clinically diagnosable asbestosis in the United States. His total of 139,000 cases of asbestos disease between 1980 and 2009 was considerably lower than that of his colleague, Dr. Dreyer, who had estimated that there would be 230,000 cases of asbestos disease by the end of the century, or of Dr. Selikoff and his colleagues at Mount Sinai, who had been studying asbestos disease for more than two decades and had estimated that between 1980 and 2009 as many as 270,000 people would die of asbestos-related cancer alone.

Once Walker had been removed from the propensity-to-sue project, Von Wald and his staff hired two additional sets of experts to perform the analysis. One of these groups discovered that only 25 percent of the people who had developed asbestos disease were filing lawsuits— an extremely low rate compared with other population groups that were filing claims. Its members explained that this was caused by "a low propensity to attribute one's illness to some asbestos exposure dating back many years." Their assessment of the general reluctance to understand the phenomenon of latent disease went a long way toward explaining why asbestos workers and the general public had been so slow to recognize the seriousness of the asbestos hazard.

When neither of the two groups of experts was able to come up with a propensity-to-sue formula that could be used to calculate the number of future lawsuits, Von Wald and some of his associates in LAG proceeded to calculate a propensity-to-sue fraction of their own. They then applied it to the 139,000 cases of future asbestos disease that had been predicted by Dr. Walker and his associates at Epidemiology Resources and came up with the prediction that 52,000 additional lawsuits would be brought against Manville. This seemed to be a case of applying assertion to error, for Walker's assessment of the future incidence of asbestos disease was criticized for its methodology. In a critique that was issued by the Mount Sinai School of Medicine's Environmental Sciences Laboratory in January, 1983, Dr. William J. Nicholson, associate director of the laboratory, pointed out that Walker's estimates were irrelevant because they were based upon data that was not only "statistically unreliable," but did not take into account major exposure to asbestos during a twenty-four-year period on the part of workers in the expanding construction and maintenance industries, especially as a result of asbestos-spraying operations that took place between 1958 and 1972, which exposed virtually the entire construction work force to considerable amounts of asbestos.

When LAG's lawyers applied their arbitrary propensity-to-sue fraction to Walker's estimate—an estimate that Dr. Nicholson says was about a fifth of what it should have been—they were not simply compounding a series of errors but also, by implying that their prediction of 52,000 lawsuits was based upon Walker's assumptions, and by failing to acknowledge that Walker had repeatedly expressed the belief that propensity to sue could not be accurately predicted, they were misleading the readers of the report they would send at the end of July to the members of Manville's board of directors.

In the meantime, the LAG people needed to come up with a third calculation for the FASB-5—an estimate of the disposition costs of future asbestos-disease lawsuits. Von Wald accomplished this by using the $40,600 disposition cost for the quarter immediately preceding Manville's filing for reorganization under Chapter 11. This figure was, of course, far higher than Manville's often-proclaimed historical average disposition cost of $25,000 per case." Be that as it may, when Von Wald and the members of LAG wrote their version of what the various experts had concluded, they managed to imply that the $40,600 future-disposition cost was based on scientific research done by the experts Manville had retained, when, in fact, these experts had never been asked to calculate an average cost for setting future asbestos-disease lawsuits. The total figure that LAG came up with as its disposition-cost projection was $1.9 billion.

On August 4, 1982, Von Wald reviewed LAG's version of the various experts' reports for the twelve members of Manville's board of directors, who met at the company's headquarters, near Denver. In a press release that was issued on the same day, a Manville spokesman announced that the company had reported to its board of directors that it had received studies from outside consultants indicating that asbestos litigation might continue unabated for a number of years, and that the directors had decided not to declare a dividend on the corporation's common stock. He also said that the board had appointed a special committee "to study the potential future impact" on the company of pending and anticipated asbestos-disease cases, and the possible need for the creation of large financial reserves.

The special committee, whose members were chosen by McKinney, was made up of four of the company's ten outside directors. They were John P. Schroeder, a retired vice-chairman of the Morgan Guaranty

Trust Company, of New York, who was named the committee chairman; William F. May, the Dean of New York University's Graduate School of Business Administration, and a former chairman and chief executive officer of the American Can Company, of Greenwich, Connecticut; William D. Tucker, a partner in Davis Polk & Wardwell, the firm that had served as Manville's outside legal counsel for more than fifty years; and Charles J. Zwick, president and chief operating officer of the Southeast Banking Corporation, of Miami, and a trustee of the Rand Corporation, of Santa Monica, California. Three of these men— Schroeder, May, and Zwick—made up an inner sanctum of power within the twelve-man board of directors, whose members also included former Governor John Love, of Colorado, and Robert L. Geddes, Dean of the School of Architecture at Princeton University. On September 1, 1976, acting as representatives of the nine outside directors, these three men had summarily fired W. Richard Goodwin, a former professor at New York University's Graduate School of Business Administration, who had been Johns-Manville's president and chief executive officer for nearly six years. Goodwin had been credited with rejuvenating the corporation by moving its headquarters from an old brick building on East Fortieth Street, in New York City, to a modern multimillion-dollar headquarters building constructed on the ten-thousand-acre Ken-Caryl Ranch, sixteen miles southwest of downtown Denver, which he had bought for $7.5 million. He had also streamlined the company's business structure and raised its net profits 115 percent. He had run afoul of Schroeder and some of the other directors, however, by proposing that Johns-Manville break its old financial tie with Morgan Stanley & Company, which had been its investment banker since 1935 and had been founded by several former partners of J.P. Morgan & Company, and by seeking to increase the number of directors from twelve to fifteen, thus raising fears that he might be trying to pack the board. (On the day after Goodwin was forced to resign, McKinney was nominated and unanimously elected president of Johns-Manville by the full board of directors at a meeting presided over by Schroeder, who was then the vice-chairman of Morgan Guaranty Trust.)

As things turned out, Zwick resigned from the special committee soon after it was appointed, and May was able to attend only half of its meetings. This left Schroeder and Tucker to conduct most of the special committee's work and to formulate its recommendations. On

August 16, 17, 18, and 23, the committee met in New York City at the midtown office of Davis Polk & Wardwell and ate lunch in the dining room of the Fifty-seventh Street offices of Morgan Guaranty.

At the time McKinney appointed the special committee, Manville was looking for an independent public accountant to support the FASB-5 estimation of liability accrual that had been arrived at by Von Wald and the members of LAG. (The company could not very well ask Coopers & Lybrand, its own independent auditors, to perform this undertaking, because Coopers & Lybrand had approved eight successive filings with the SEC stating that Manville's liability in the asbestos litigation could not be reliably estimated.) With Coopers & Lybrand out of the picture, it was decided to ask Robert O. F. Bixby, an audit partner in Price Waterhouse & Company—one of the largest public-accounting firms in the nation—to become an adviser to the special committee, presumably for the purpose of giving his blessing to the FASB-5 estimation. Bixby was first approached by an official of Morgan Guaranty, for which Price Waterhouse was the auditor; then he was approached by Morgan Guaranty's audit partner at Price Waterhouse; and he was hired for the job by Tucker on August 9.

On the face of it, Bixby's task was simply to declare whether or not the proper FASB-5 conditions for the accrual of a liability had been met. By way of preparation, he read the LAG report, which gave the misleading impression that Manville's outside consultants had supplied data to substantiate LAG's disposition-cost projection of $1.9 billion. He was never told that Dr. Walker had serious doubts about the validity of the propensity-to-sue analysis, which was vital to this projection. On August 16, Bixby heard Von Wald and Victor deliver propensity-to-sue and disposition-cost projections to the members of the special committee, who received these projections after Dr. Walker had appeared before them to describe his predictions of the future incidence of asbestos disease. A day later, at another meeting of the special committee, Bixby agreed that the requirements for filing an FASB-5 had been met. Shortly after Bixby left this meeting, Michael J. Crames, a bankruptcy attorney with the New York firm of Levin & Weintraub, appeared before it to explain the benefits of filing for reorganization under Chapter 11. On the next day, August 18, Schroeder and Tucker met with Parker, Von Wald, and several of Manville's financial officers to discuss the pros and cons of a Chapter 11 filing, and at the conclusion of that meeting Parker was authorized to retain

Levin & Weintraub. On August 19, Frederick L. Pundsack, who had retired earlier in the month as president and chief operating officer of Manville, resigned from the company's board of directors, of which he had been a member for nearly six years, and on August 21 he sent a six-page handwritten letter to McKinney urging him not to take Manville into a bankruptcy reorganization. In his letter Pundsack said that Manville's cash flow was adequate for the next three to five years, and told McKinney that he was troubled by the speed with which the decision to file under Chapter 11 was being made. He described the impending action as "wrong for the stockholders, wrong for the employees, wrong for our creditors, wrong for our customers, and wrong for our suppliers."

His other reservations notwithstanding, Pundsack was certainly right about the speed with which Manville was moving toward its bankruptcy petition. On August 25, the members of the special committee signed a report recommending that the board of directors "authorize the immediate filing of a petition in Chapter 11 as the action best calculated to conserve the Company's assets and business and, therefore, the best action to protect the rights of shareholders, creditors, and actual and potential claimants." That same day, the full board of directors sat down to dinner at the Harley of New York Hotel, on East Forty-second Street, to decide what to do in light of this recommendation. Later that evening, foregone conclusion became reality when they voted their unanimous approval of a Chapter 11 filing, and on the next morning, when Manville filed a Chapter 11 petition in the United States Bankruptcy Court for the Southern District of New York, it became the richest and healthiest American corporation ever to do so.

Of the twelve directors on Manville's board, Schroeder, Tucker, and May were far and away the most influential in steering the company toward filing for bankruptcy, because of their membership in the special committee that had been appointed by McKinney. And, of the three, Schroeder appeared to be the dominant one, largely because of a very close fifty-year connection between Johns-Manville and J.P. Morgan & Company and its successor the Morgan Guaranty Trust Company, of New York, where he had spent his entire career. The connection with Morgan had come about in the following manner: In

1925, Thomas Franklyn Manville, a son of Charles B. Manville, one of the founders of the company, died, having been president since 1901, and was succeeded by his brother, Hiram Edward Manville. Thomas Franklyn left a large block of the company's stock to his son and namesake, Thomas Franklyn, Jr., known as Tommy and much publicized as a playboy; his fondness for marrying blond showgirls became the subject of numerous newspaper stories, which invariably described him as "the asbestos heir." The senior Thomas Franklin Manville left another block of stock to his daughter and a third block to the company's several thousand employees. Soon after his brother's death, however, Hiram Edward bought up his nephew's holdings, as well as most of the employees' stock, and in 1927 he sold 400,000 of Johns-Manville's 750,000 outstanding shares to J. P. Morgan & Company for about $50 a share.

J. P. Morgan, which then took over a seat on Johns-Manville's board of directors, had big plans for its new acquisition. To begin with, Morgan brought in a troubleshooting executive named Theodore Frelinghuysen Merseles, who had rescued Montgomery Ward from the depression of 1921, and Merseles brought with him a promising thirty-three-year-old assistant named Lewis Herold Brown. During the next two years, Johns-Manville's annual sales shot up to $62 million and the price of a share of its stock soared to $242. Then, in 1929—the year in which the first negligence lawsuits were filed against the company by employees in New Jersey who had developed asbestosis—Merseles died, the stock market crashed, and the Great Depression began. At that point, Lewis Brown took over the company, which, during the next three years saw its annual sales drop by two-thirds and its stock fall to $10 a share. Moreover, he inherited a serious morale problem, for the house of Morgan was widely detested during the Depression, and the fact that Johns-Manville was known as a "Morgan company" rankled its employees, who bitterly resented the fact that their stock had been sold to the banking firm. In 1933—the year in which Brown was authorized to settle eleven pending asbestosis lawsuits and buy off the plaintiffs' attorney—the Glass-Steagall Banking Act was passed; it prohibited commercial banks from underwriting corporate securities, and J. P. Morgan was forced to transfer its investment-banking activities to Morgan Stanley & Company. Thereafter, Morgan Stanley handled Johns-Manville's investment-banking business, while J. P. Morgan & Company kept the Morgan seat on Johns-

Manville's board of directors. Meanwhile, under the stewardship of Lewis Brown the company regained its financial health. Indeed, by 1939—by then negligence lawsuits had been brought by diseased workers at Johns-Manville's plant in Waukegan, Illinois—*Time* hailed him as an enlightened businessman who had become "one of the chief spokesmen for all Big Business."

By this time, Schroeder, who was born in 1918, in Montclair, New Jersey, had graduated from Exeter Academy and was in his sophomore year at Yale. After graduating from Yale, in 1941, he served for four and a half years in the Navy, and became a lieutenant commander. Upon his discharge, in the fall of 1945, he became a trainee at J.P. Morgan, and began a career that would see him rise through the ranks to executive vice-president in charge of domestic banking, in 1971; to vice-chairman and a seat on the board of directors, in 1976; and, following his retirement, in 1978, to become a member of the bank's directors' advisory council. Along the way, he had become the officer in charge of Johns-Manville's account, and in 1967—the year in which the ravages of asbestos disease were just beginning to receive attention in the press—he was named to the traditional Morgan seat on the board of directors of Johns-Manville, which he holds today.

A tall, dark-haired, and bespectacled man of sixty-six, with a calm and self-assured manner, Schroeder lives in retirement near Damariscotta, Maine. He has exhibited a lifelong penchant for staying out of the limelight (he is not listed in *Who's Who*, for example), and very little has been written about him or his business activities. An exception is an account that appeared in the October, 1976, issue of *Fortune*, which described the firing of Goodwin as follows:

> Schroeder came directly to the point. He told Goodwin that the trio [Schroeder, May, and Zwick] represented the nine outside directors on J-M's twelve-man board, and that they all wanted him to resign.
>
> "Why?" stammered Goodwin, who was caught totally by surprise.
>
> "Under the bylaws of this corporation," replied Schroeder evenly, "we don't have to give you a reason."

Another exception is a two-day-long deposition in which Schroeder testified under oath, on March 15 and 16, 1983, during the bankruptcy proceedings. At that time, he was questioned by Tom Henderson, who zeroed in on what Schroeder had known about asbestos disease and when he had come to know it.

"Did you understand in the late nineteen-sixties that asbestosis was potentially disabling?" Henderson asked.

"Yes," Schroeder replied.

"Did you know in the late nineteen-sixties that asbestosis was potentially fatal?"

"I don't think I did," Schroeder replied.

"When did you first learn that asbestosis was potentially fatal, if ever?"

"I'm not sure that I have yet," Schroeder answered.

"Did you learn in the late nineteen-sixties that asbestos was the principal if not the exclusive cause for malignant mesothelioma?" Henderson asked.

"I don't recall on that point," Schroeder said.

"Do you know now that asbestos is the primary if not the exclusive cause of malignant mesothelioma?"

"My information is that it's at least a fifty-fifty chance that 'meso' is asbestos-related," Schroeder said.

"Who gave you the idea that there is a fifty-fifty chance of mesothelioma being a result of asbestos exposure?" Henderson inquired.

"A number of sources," Schroeder replied.

"Who?"

"Selikoff," Schroeder said. "ERI studies—at least the presentation made to us." Here, Schroeder was referring to the projections and assessments that had been made for Manville by Dr. Walker and his colleagues at Epidemiology Resources, Inc. "The fifty-fifty was an educated guess on the part of people who get paid to make educated guesses."

"When did you first have the information that it was at least a fifty-fifty chance that mesothelioma resulted from asbestos exposure?" Henderson asked.

"I think the first real realization of that on my part was last summer," Schroeder said.

"Last summer?"

"Yes."

"Did you talk to Dr. Selikoff before last summer?"

"I have never met Dr. Selikoff," Schroeder said.

"Did you have the opportunity to read any of what Dr. Selikoff had said in any of his medical and scientific articles?"

"No," Schroeder replied. "I had the opportunity, but I did not do it."

Henderson went on to ask Schroeder whether Manville's board members had ever discussed the allegations of the plaintiffs concerning conspiracy.

"We were concerned, and are concerned, over the doctrine of implicit guilt here," Schroeder said. "We don't think it's fair. We don't think it's accurate. We don't think the record supports it, and we continue to be upset about it."

"What is the doctrine of implicit guilt?" Henderson asked.

"A coverup," Schroeder replied.

"You are saying you don't believe there was any coverup?"

"Absolutely," Schroeder said.

"Did you ever read the so-called Sumner Simpson documents?"

"I have not," Schroeder replied.

"I would invite you to," Henderson said.

Later in the deposition, Henderson asked Schroeder if he had been told about the testimony of Dr. Kenneth W. Smith, the former medical director of Johns-Manville. When Schroeder said he had not, Henderson asked him if he felt he should have been.

"I would assume that management had its own reasons for not telling me," Schroeder replied.

"Would that be the same answer if I told you about the affidavit of one Charles Roemer?" Henderson asked. "Have you had the opportunity to review that affidavit?"

"Not to my knowledge," Schroeder replied.

"Let me see if I can refresh your recollection to see whether or not you might have," Henderson said. "This was an attorney. . . back in the nineteen-forties, who had been told by Vandiver Brown that the Manville employees who were exposed to asbestos sometimes contracted asbestosis, sometimes contracted other diseases, but they just regarded them as another factor in the bottom line, and that they just let them die and paid their claims. Does that ring a bell?"

"No," Schroeder replied.

As it happened, the Roemer affidavit that Schroeder said he did not know about was filed in the bankruptcy proceedings a month after Manville filed its bankruptcy petition, and it provides a fascinating footnote to the assertion of plaintiff lawyers that the company should not be allowed to use Chapter 11 to evade its obligations under the law to the victims of asbestos disease. Charles H. Roemer, a prominent attorney in Paterson, New Jersey, was then in his early eighties, and was living in Fair Lawn, and still practicing law, although he was in frail health. All proceedings pending against Manville had been automatically stayed when Manville filed for bankruptcy, but Judge Burton R. Lifland, who was presiding over the Chapter 11 proceedings in the United States Bankruptcy Court for the Southern District of New York, lifted the stay for the purpose of preserving Roemer's testimony, on being informed by Michael Baumeister, a plaintiff lawyer, that Roemer was "the one living link corroborating all the legal evidence we have compiled which shows that the Manville company knew of the dangers of asbestos at least forty years ago or more," and allowed Roemer to make his statement. In September, 1982, Roemer, in an affidavit that Baumeister later submitted to the court in support of his request to depose him, said that around 1942 or 1943 his cousin Dr. Jacob Roemer had found that workers at the Union Asbestos & Rubber Company's Paterson plant had developed signs of asbestos disease. Charles Roemer went on to say that when he learned of this he immediately informed Robert Cryor, the plant manager (he would later die of mesothelioma), and Edward Shuman, the assistant plant manager, and that they set up an appointment with Vandiver Brown and Lewis Brown, the president of Johns-Manville, at Johns-Manville corporate headquarters, in New York City. Roemer said that he, Cryor, and Shuman asked the Johns-Manville officials whether their physical-examination program had turned up similar findings and, if so, what Johns-Manville was doing about it. According to Roemer, Vandiver Brown admitted that Johns-Manville's physical-examination program had produced X-ray evidence of asbestos disease among workers exposed to asbestos, and that it was Johns-Manville's policy not to do anything and not to tell the employees of the X-ray findings. "Vandiver Brown went on to say that it was foolish for us to be concerned, and that if Johns-Manville's workers were told, they would stop working and file claims against Johns-Manville, and that it was Johns-Manville's policy to let them work until they quit work because of asbestosis or died as a result of asbestos-related diseases," Roemer declared.

At a subsequent deposition taken in April of 1984, Roemer remembered that he had said, "Mr. Brown, do you mean to tell me you would let them work until they dropped dead?" and that Brown had replied, "Yes, we save a lot of money that way."

When he was asked by the attorney who was deposing him if he could recall the time of day the meeting with the Johns-Manville officials took place, Roemer said that it was held before noon. "I remember that distinctly, because I had lunch with them in their board rooms after the meeting," he added.

"I see," the attorney said. "Why do you recall the lunch so vividly?"

"It was the first time in my life I had lobster for lunch," Roemer replied.

As for Schroeder's deposition, during the second day it was concerned partly with his role as chairman of the special committee that had investigated the pros and cons of a bankruptcy filing in August of 1982. Schroeder testified that the members of the special committee had at first resisted the idea of filing under Chapter 11, and had even tried to think of ways that would enable Manville to "tough it out" and survive its legal difficulties, but when Robert Bixby, the Price Waterhouse accountant, came out for an FASB-5 liability accrual, Schroeder said, the committee had been forced to accede to the inevitability of a bankruptcy reorganization. He then talked about what Manville hoped to achieve by going into Chapter 11.

"What we were really doing was buying cash, buying protection, and buying time," he said. "The downside, obviously, is the stigma that's attached in most people's mind [to] a company, any company, filing under a Chapter [11]."

"Did you also consider the downside of a Chapter 7 liquidation?" Henderson asked.

"We never contemplated it," Schroeder replied. "Again, on the going-business theory that our creditors and the diseased people, with whom we have an enormous and real interest, would be benefited the most by our protection as a going business under Chapter 11."

For a moment, Tom Henderson looked at Schroeder without saying anything. At the time of the bankruptcy filing, Henderson had been representing plaintiffs in some 350 asbestos-disease lawsuits that were pending in Maine, Maryland, Pennsylvania, Michigan, New York, and Illinois. Johns-Manville had, of course, been named as a defendant in virtually all of these cases, along with some twelve other asbestos manufacturers that were usually named as defendants in asbestos product-liability lawsuits. Henderson is a mild-mannered, thoughtful man, who is given to neither invective nor overstatement, but, like virtually all of his colleagues, he harbors a profound contempt for the past conduct of most of these companies, and often refers to them in private as "the dirty dozen." Now, after listening to Schroeder try to claim that Manville—the company that Henderson and his colleagues had spent ten years proving was far and away the most culpable of all —had "an enormous and real interest" in the thousands upon thousands of workers who had been afflicted with asbestos disease, none of whom had received a penny of compensation from the company since it filed for bankruptcy seven months earlier, Henderson shook his head in disbelief.

"You will never convince me of that, Mr. Schroeder," he said softly.

In the late spring of 1982—three months before Manville filed for bankruptcy reorganization—the company announced that because of deepening financial problems it was planning to cut a thousand workers from its salaried work force of 8,800 employees. Within a week or so, the company reported that it had lost more than $5 million in the first quarter of the year—its first quarterly loss in half a century. By this time, the executive dining room at the Ken-Caryl Ranch headquarters had been closed; water had been drained from the reflecting pools in front of the headquarters building; hallway lights had been dimmed; and the corporate Grumman G-2 jet had been leased.

Part of Manville's financial woes had been caused by a deep recession in the housing industry, but far and away the biggest cloud hanging over its head was the asbestos litigation, which had made it one of the most often sued companies in history. Manville had by then been named as a defendant in more than ten thousand asbestos-disease lawsuits; its legal costs were approaching $2 million a month; and juries had begun to award huge punitive as well as compensatory damages against it. Nevertheless, the company continued to go to trial in cases that it would formerly have settled out of court. Some plaintiff attorneys theorized that Manville had quit making realistic settlement offers either to avoid cash-flow problems or in the hope that insurance questions would be settled by the time the cases were tried. What they didn't suspect was that the company was taking a hard line in the litigation because it was planning to file for protection under Chapter 11 and take advantage of the federal Bankruptcy Code provision that would provide an automatic stay of all pending civil litigation, including appeals of adverse verdicts.

A sign of what lay ahead appeared at the end of July, when UNR Industries, of Chicago—a steel-fabricating firm that owned UNARCO —filed under Chapter 11, citing the fact that it was a defendant in more than twelve thousand asbestos-disease lawsuits and that the litigation was costing it more than a million dollars a month. Within a few days, Manville and other defendant manufacturers were filing blanket motions to stay all proceedings against them in courts across the nation in a frenzied effort to win a nationwide freeze of all asbestos-disease litigation. For the most part, the scramble to take refuge behind UNR's bankruptcy petition met with failure, although a few courts did grant temporary stays of as much as five months. As far as Manville was concerned, however, the whole question became redundant at 8:56 A.M. on August 26, when the company filed its own petition for reorganization. The filing of the petition gained for the company an automatic stay in some eleven thousand asbestos-disease lawsuits that were pending against it, and gave it a hundred and twenty days in which it had the exclusive right to file a plan for reorganization.

TEN

BANKRUPTCY

In an affadavit that accompanied Manville's bankruptcy petition and was signed by the company's treasurer, James F. Beasley, Manville acknowledged that it had been found liable for punitive damages by juries in ten separate cases that had been decided in 1981 and 1982, and that the average punitive damages that had been awarded against it had come to $616,000 a case. However, in a full-page advertisement-interview explaining Manville's position to the public—it ran on August 27 in the New York *Times,* the Washington *Post,* the *Wall Street Journal,* and other leading newspapers across the nation—McKinney barely mentioned the punitive damages that had been awarded against the company by juries whose members had found Johns-Manville guilty of outrageous and reckless misconduct. Instead, he depicted Manville—a corporation with assets of more than $2 billion—as being unfairly victimized by thousands of unwarranted lawsuits, and he blamed the federal government, the Congress, and Manville's insurance carriers for the company's predicament. He went on to stress that the bankruptcy filing did not signify a financial failure and that Congress should enact "a statutory compensation program for asbestos injuries."

As might be expected, Manville's Chapter 11 filing touched off another scramble by the remaining defendant asbestos manufacturers to file motions for an indefinite stay of claims in every jurisdiction in the nation. By late autumn, however, most judges had ruled that the protection of Chapter 11 applied only to Manville. As for the plaintiff lawyers, who had been caught unawares by Manville's action, they reacted with a mixture of astonishment, fury, and outrage, calling the Chapter 11 filing a fraudulent abuse and perversion of the bankruptcy laws. Early in September, nine trustees of the board of the Asbestos Litigation Group—a consortium of about a hundred and fifty lawyers representing almost 90 percent of the sixteen-thousand-odd asbestos victims who were then suing Manville—met in New York City and announced that they were hiring Robert J. Rosenberg, of Moses & Singer, one of the nation's leading bankruptcy-law firms, to handle plaintiff interests in the bankruptcy proceedings. (The nine trustees included Stanley Levy, Paul Gillenwater, Tom Henderson, Gene Locks, Fred Baron, Ronald Motley, Marlin Thompson, Robert Steinberg, an attorney from Los Angeles, and Kenneth Lynch, an attorney from San Francisco. Among them, they represented clients in more than six thousand asbestos-disease lawsuits.) For its part, Manville had already retained Michael J. Crames, a partner in Levin & Weintraub, and Stephen Case, of Davis Polk & Wardwell.

Meanwhile, the two sides were engaged in a bitter duel over which of them was in the right—a debate that became a favorite topic of newspaper editorial writers, who, for the most part, failed to grasp the meaning and importance of the asbestos lawsuits, probably because during the ten years the litigation had been taking place newspapers across the nation had, by and large, failed to cover the litigation adequately and explain the issues involved. Thus, on August 27, the day after Manville filed for bankruptcy, an editorial writer for the *Times* found himself sufficiently ignorant of the basic evidence in the greatest toxic tort litigation in the history of American jurisprudence to be able to equate the human agony of asbestos disease with Manville's fiscal uncertainties. "Asbestos is a tragedy," he wrote, "most of all for the victims and their families but also for the companies, which are being made to pay the price for decisions made long ago." On the same day, the writer of an editorial that appeared in the Washington *Post* missed the entire point of what had been going on in the nation's courtrooms for a decade by complaining that the asbestos saga was a sad commentary on the effectiveness of the judicial system. A few days later, the *Post* received a comeuppance on public television's *Mac-Neil-Lehrer Report* from Peter Nowinski, the Justice Department attorney, who was lead counsel for the government in the asbestos litigation. After saying that the newspaper's charge of judicial ineffectiveness was based on Manville's contention that too much money was being spent for legal fees and that not enough was going to the plaintiffs, Nowinski pointed out that far and away the largest percentage of those fees was being paid out by Manville and its insurers to resist the claims that were being brought. Nowinski went on to remind his audience that it was the plaintiff attorneys who had exposed Manville's guilt to begin with by bringing the Sumner Simpson papers to light.

Early in September, Cornelius Blackshear, the United States trustee who was handling the administrative details of Manville's bankruptcy, asked Judge Lifland's permission to appoint a committee to represent the interests of claimants with asbestos disease. Several days later, attorneys for the Keene and GAF corporations—companies that had been named as defendants in several thousand asbestos-disease lawsuits—moved to have a committee of asbestos co-defendants appointed so that the interests of asbestos manufacturers who had not filed for bankruptcy reorganization could be looked after. In October, Lifland acceded to Blackshear's request; however, he insisted that a single committee of asbestos-related litigants and creditors be formed, and on October 8 Blackshear appointed seventeen plaintiff attorneys to serve on it, as well as four co-defendant asbestos manufacturers and a shipyard company to serve as ex-officio members. Among the plaintiff attorneys on the committee were Levy, who was elected to be its chairman, Locks, Baron, Gillenwater, Henderson, Motley, Steinberg, and Robert Sweeney. In addition, a committee was formed to represent Manville's unsecured commercial creditors—they included more than a hundred banks and other corporations to which Manville owed money. Its chairman was Albert B. Gordon, a vice-president at Morgan Guaranty. Later on, an equity committee was appointed to represent the shareholders of Manville's common and preferred stock, and an unofficial committee was formed to look after the interests of several thousand schools and school districts that had potential claims against Manville, whose asbestos products had been widely used in the construction of school buildings across the nation. The committees representing the asbestos-disease claimants, the commercial creditors, and the shareholders were given the right to retain legal counsel and the services of other court-approved professionals at Manville's expense.

Soon after it filed for reorganization, Manville took advantage of the shield provided by the Bankruptcy Code to announce that it would stop payment on a $5 million settlement it had reached, back in May, with 141 former employees of the Pearl Harbor Naval Shipyard, in Honolulu, or their widows. The company had already failed to make a payment on a $1.5 million settlement that had been reached in

March with several asbestos plaintiffs in California. Some idea of the human consequences of such defaulting can be seen in a case that was settled out of court by Gillenwater three and a half weeks before Manville filed under Chapter 11. The case involved an asbestos worker in Nashville named James W. Smith, who was suffering from lung cancer and was not expected to live more than thirty days. No doubt mindful of the $2.3 million jury verdict that Gillenwater had won for the dying James O. Cavett a few weeks earlier, Manville offered to settle for $60,000 on the day it went to trial. At that time, Gillenwater visited Smith, who was in the hospital, and told him that he felt the offer was ridiculously low but that a jury award could be delayed on appeal for two or three years. After thinking things over, Smith decided to accept the $60,000 so that his affairs could be settled, and he could be sure his wife would receive some money before he died. On August 16, a draft for $60,000 was received from Manville, along with the usual form releasing the company from any further claim in the matter. The form and the draft were signed by Smith and his wife, Sara, on August 24, and on August 25 Gillenwater deposited the $60,000 draft in a trust account. On August 26, upon learning that Manville had filed under Chapter 11, Gillenwater telephoned the Republic Bank of Brownwood, in Brownwood, Texas—the bank on which the Manville draft was issued—to ask if it would be honored. He was informed that it would not. On August 31, deeply distressed that his wife had received no money and that his claim against Manville was unresolved, Smith died.

A counterattack against the Manville bankruptcy was launched in early November, when a motion to dismiss the bankruptcy proceedings was filed by the Committee of Asbestos-Related Litigants. The motion alleged that Manville was using the bankruptcy law to impair "the constitutionally protected rights of present and future victims of asbestos-related diseases and their survivors . . . to obtain full compensation for personal injuries and wrongful deaths," and that it had filed for Chapter 11 in bad faith.

On November 10, hearings were convened before the Senate Judiciary Committee's Subcommittee on Courts to investigate whether it was proper for a solvent company such as Manville to file for reorganization under the federal Bankruptcy Code. The first witness was G. Earl Parker. He told Senator Bob Dole, the committee chairman, and the other committee members that there had been no way for Manville to know that asbestos insulators and other handlers of finished asbestos products would develop asbestos disease until Dr. Selikoff's 1964 studies. Parker went on to portray Manville as a beleaguered corporation that was "being sued in almost every jurisdiction possible at a rate of three times every business hour of every business day" and had been unfairly abandoned by its insurance carriers. He urged Congress to "legislate a satisfactory solution to the asbestos-health disability dispute," declaring that the personal-injury litigation system was "incapable of providing adequate compensation for disabled workers."

The plaintiffs' side of the story was presented by Robert Steinberg, of the Los Angeles firm of Rose, Klein & Marias. He appeared before the subcommittee in behalf of the Asbestos Litigation Group, which was then urging Congress to make changes in the Bankruptcy Reform Act of 1978. A fifty-three-year-old attorney who had won a jury verdict of $1,200,000 for a client in a 1980 asbestos-disease case, Steinberg told Dole and his colleagues what he and his fellow-attorneys in the plaintiffs' bar thought of Manville. "To us, Manville is more than a legal adversary," he said. "Its corporate actions shake our faith in the free-enterprise system. Too many victims of asbestos disease have died for their survivors and friends to shed a tear for a company that has shown so little compassion for the victims of its willful acts. If Manville is successful in this attempt to misuse the law to evade responsibility for its deliberate, intentional actions, then our faith in the legal system will also be shaken."

Steinberg went on to say that the victims of asbestos disease should not be treated as if they were simply another creditor presenting a due bill. "A paper company can present the bankruptcy court with paper documentation that Manville owes x amount of money for y amount of paper delivered on z date," he declared. "But the victims and their families are people. Dreams, companionship, love, human potential— these are values which measure a society, and, as such, defy objective systems of measurement. The genius of the American judicial system is that such questions are usually left to a jury of human beings, not a computer or a slide rule."

Later in his testimony, Steinberg addressed the crucial and complex issue of future claimants. "The most tragic consequences of Manville's action in filing for Chapter 11 will be suffered by those unknown numbers of individuals who have yet to suffer the ravages of asbestos disease," he said. He went on to warn that these future creditors should not be forced to adhere to an agreement that had been made without their participation.

Further testimony was provided by Mrs. Judy Gentile, of Baltimore, whose father, an asbestos-insulation worker, had developed lung cancer and had died of it a year and a half later. After describing the suffering of her father and the costs borne by her family, Mrs. Gentile posed some tough questions for Senator Dole and his colleagues. "We ask this committee if Johns-Manville is successful in protecting its assets from the people it injured and killed and continues 'business as usual,' then for what purpose did my father die?" she asked. "My mother's life—after nearly thirty-nine years of marriage to a wonderful and gentle man who put her and our family above everything else— is not 'business as usual.' How do we put our lives back together again? How do we live with the knowledge that corporate officers decided to hide the truth and adopt policies that resulted in my father's death?"

By this time, Manville's Chapter 11 filing was causing considerable consternation among its former co-defendants and their insurance carriers, for they were being required in many jurisdictions to continue to defend asbestos-disease lawsuits, and they saw themselves holding the bag as Manville continued to do business under the protection of the bankruptcy laws. On November 19, Arthur Olick, of Anderson, Russell, Kill & Olick—a New York City law firm that represented, among others, the Keene Corporation—asked Judge Lifland to extend the automatic-stay provisions of the Bankruptcy Code to Keene and eight other co-defendant asbestos manufacturers: Owens-Corning, Owens-Illinois, Fibreboard, GAF, Raybestos-Manhattan, Pittsburgh Corning, Celotex, and Eagle-Picher. Olick argued that Manville's absence from the asbestos cases imposed a severe hardship on the co-defendants, who had depended on Manville to supply key documents and expert witnesses in the defense of asbestos-disease lawsuits. He even went as far as to describe the co-defendants as progeny who had been "cast adrift in shark-infested waters."

Judge Lifland reserved decision on Olick's motion, and at the same time authorized Manville's creditors to launch a broad investigation of the company under Rule 205 of the Bankruptcy Code. The Committee of Asbestos-Related Litigants then requested him to order Manville to produce all documents relating to its Chapter 11 filing, and also all notes and records of McKinney and other high-ranking officials which dealt with the corporate restructuring that had taken place in the autumn of 1981. By making this request, the committee acknowledged that its efforts to get Congress to make changes in the Bankruptcy Code had failed, and prepared to do battle with Manville in the intricate arena of Chapter 11.

The insurers for the co-defendants were watching from the sidelines, aware that once the temporary stays were lifted they were going to have to resume paying defense costs and indemnification, and fearful that they would have to pick up some or all of Manville's share of the litigation. As might be expected, these carriers were trying to figure a way out of their legal and financial bind. On September 10, two weeks after Manville's surprise Chapter 11 filing, Leslie Cheek III, vice-president for federal affairs for the Crum & Forster Insurance Companies, of Morris Township, New Jersey—a leading carrier of workmen's-compensation insurance—sent a highly revealing confidential memorandum to Sidney F. Wentz, the president of his company. An experienced observer of the Washington political scene, Cheek had previously written an article for *The National Underwriter* in which he pointed out the "exquisite irony" of the asbestos industry's attempts to cut off the tort rights of asbestos-disease victims against the manufacturers of asbestos products, noting that "this approach is embodied in the bill Johns-Manville persuaded Colorado Senator Gary Hart to introduce this year." In his memo to Wentz, Cheek declared that Manville's bankruptcy petition created a unique opportunity for the insurance industry to solve the problems created by asbestos-disease cases. He went on to recommend that Crum & Forster advocate an amendment to the federal Bankruptcy Act that would authorize the bankruptcy court to take jurisdiction over the interests of the co-defendants in all asbestos-disease claims that were pending against Manville, as well as all insurance claims and counterclaims involving any of the co-defendants in the asbestos cases. According to Cheek, "such an amendment would enable the bankruptcy court to resolve the insurance-coverage disputes in the course of marshalling the assets of the bankrupt, and to consolidate and streamline the processing of the thousands of pending and future asbestos-related disease claims."

In advocating this best of all possible worlds for the insurance carriers, Cheek reminded Wentz that the Bankruptcy Reform Act of

1978 had significantly broadened the powers of bankruptcy judges, granting them jurisdiction over all civil proceedings arising under Chapter 11, or related to cases under Chapter 11. "The statute in its current form would appear to enable a bold bankruptcy judge to assert jurisdiction over all of the asbestos-related disease and insurance claims," he wrote. He was careful to point out, however, that the Supreme Court had recently ruled that those provisions of the 1978 Bankruptcy Act which broadened the powers of bankruptcy judges would be unconstitutional on October 4, 1982, unless Congress gave bankruptcy-court judges the same protection—lifetime tenure and irreducible compensation—given to district-court judges under Article III of the Constitution. Cheek then demonstrated how disdainfully manipulative the insurance industry can be when it comes to dealing with politicians. After reminding Wentz that Senator Dole had described the Manville bankruptcy petition as "dubious," and that Dole was said to be in favor of "clipping the bankruptcy judges' wings," Cheek wrote, "It is entirely possible that the Senator's mind could be changed if he were to be given an opportunity to be a hero to everyone involved in the asbestos mess, including his Congressional colleagues." He then explained his solution to the asbestos problem:

> If Congress were, in the narrow context of the asbestos suits, to reaffirm the authority of the bankruptcy judges to deal with all matters pertaining to claims against and insurance coverage for claims against the various defendants, it would have several salutary effects. First, the reaffirmation of the availability of the bankruptcy shelter might deter still-healthy asbestos defendants from taking the route that Manville and UNR have followed. It would also offer those defendants, as well as Manville and UNR, the prospect of a speedy resolution of the insurance litigation and a more expeditious and less expensive handling of the thousands of claims against them all. A Bankruptcy Court could appoint special masters to handle the insurance matters, and other special masters to divide the claimants into rational classes (asbestosis, mesothelioma and other lung cancer victims) and award compensation. It would vastly reduce legal expenses, in that all defendants could pool their resources in a common defense of individual claims. And, most impor-

tant, the ultimate payout would be reduced to a finite number, pursuant to agreements demanded by the Bankruptcy Court as the price for reorganization of the bankrupt companies.

Thus did Cheek describe the ultimate goal of the insurance industry as one of keeping asbestos-disease litigation out of the tort system so that the bankruptcy court could set a "finite number" (in other words, a set figure that the insurance companies could live with) on the claims of thousands upon thousands of sick, suffering, and dead asbestos workers and their families. It was a goal that fitted in nicely with Schroeder's later explanation of why Manville had filed for reorganization to begin with. "What we were really doing was buying cash, buying protection, and buying time," Schroeder would say in his deposition.

As might be expected, Cheek and his fellow-insurers were not the only people who were attempting to figure out how to use the bankruptcy scenario to best advantage. Many of the co-defendant asbestos manufacturers were trying to decide whether or not to follow Manville's lead and file for reorganization under Chapter 11. (As things turned out, just one of them—the AMATEX Corporation, of Norristown, Pennsylvania, which had been a manufacturer of asbestos cloth for thirty-two years—did file for protection under Chapter 11 on November 1.) And manufacturers of toxic-chemical and other hazardous products, together with their insurers, were keeping a close watch on the bankruptcy proceedings in an effort to determine whether Manville had made a grave miscalculation or pulled off a financial ploy that could serve as a useful model if they should ever be confronted with similar litigation. For their part, the plaintiff attorneys on the Committee of Asbestos-Related Litigants were trying to figure out how best to protect the interests of their sixteen-thousand-odd clients, whose lawsuits against Manville had been stayed, but whose right to a jury trial the plaintiff attorneys had declared they were determined to preserve. The big question was who was looking out for the rights of the future claimants—the tens upon tens of thousands of people who had not yet developed asbestos disease but would surely do so in the future.

From the outset of the Chapter 11 proceedings, these future plaintiffs posed an enormously complex and difficult problem—that was almost without precedent in American jurisprudence. The Manville people dearly wanted to put a dollar value on their claims, in the hope of settling them once and for all (and as cheaply as possible) in bankruptcy court. So did the insurance carriers, who were anxious to get the asbestos claims out of a tort system over which they had little control. As for the plaintiff attorneys, they not only saw themselves as the representatives of the tort system but also claimed to feel an obligation to preserve its role in the solution of the asbestos-disease problem.

"We made it clear to Manville from the start that we were not going to barter away the rights of the future plaintiffs," Stanley Levy said. (At the time, he was with the New York law firm of Kreindler & Kreindler. In the winter of 1985, he left to form the firm of Levy, Phillips & Konigsberg.) "The seventeen of us on that committee had spent years of time and effort bringing Manville to justice for its past actions, and we were not about to take it upon ourselves to discharge the legal rights of more than a hundred thousand people for the convenience of Manville and its insurance carriers. In short, we wanted the Manville people to know that by filing for bankruptcy—a maneuver that we believed had been completely motivated by the desire to escape their legal responsibilities to the victims of asbestos disease— they had chosen a costly alternative."

As the impasse between Manville and the plaintiff lawyers deepened in the fall of 1982, the insurance carriers continued to search for a way out of the dilemma they themselves were facing. In late October, officials of Commercial Union and Travelers agreed that if there was to be any chance at all of achieving a compromise among the plaintiffs, the insurers, and the manufacturers involved in asbestos-disease litigation it would have to be facilitated by someone of national stature.

The insurance people then got in touch with James F. Henry, the president of the Center for Public Resources—a nonprofit research group in New York which was engaged in studying alternative ways of settling potentially litigious disputes—and Henry recommended a dozen or so lawyers connected with either the financial establishment or the business community, who were turned down by the plaintiff attorneys. During its studies, the center had established a judicial panel of prominent figures, including Archibald Cox, the Harvard Law School professor whose conduct as special prosecutor in the Watergate affair had won him widespread acclaim; Elliot Richardson, the Attorney General who had resigned rather than carry out Nixon's order to fire Cox in the so-called Saturday Night Massacre; and Harry Wellington, the Dean of the Yale Law School. Cox was unable to accept the job, and Richardson was rejected by the plaintiff attorneys because he was working for Milbank, Tweed, Hadley & McCloy, a New York City law firm that had been retained as counsel for the committee representing Manville's unsecured creditors. Henry then recommended Wellington for the job of acting as moderator of the asbestos dispute. At that point—in October, 1982—Henry set up a secret meeting, at the Bar Association of the City of New York, which was attended by Wellington, by a dozen leading asbestos-plaintiff lawyers, by an equal number of senior insurance-company executives, and by high officials of a dozen or so of the leading co-defendant asbestos manufacturers. And after further meetings, Wellington was asked to serve as chairman of a group that would attempt to resolve the problem. Wellington accepted the offer.

Under the guidance of Wellington, representatives of the three groups began meeting in secret two or three times a month to see if they could resolve some of their differences, and they continued to meet throughout 1983 and 1984. The negotiations, which soon became known as the Wellington Group talks, had three main goals. To begin with, the leading insurance carriers set out to reach agreement among themselves on how much they were willing to pay to settle the asbestos claims, how they should apportion their individual liability in the claims, and which of them should assume the legal defense of the various co-defendant manufacturers. Second, once the carriers had agreed on a united offer, they would have to negotiate with the asbestos manufacturers to see if they were willing to accept it. The third step of the process would be for the carriers and the manufacturers to establish a voluntary claims-resolution facility, where asbestos claims could be settled or arbitrated, and to win the approval of the plaintiff attorneys. Although it was a condition of the plaintiff attorneys that Manville take no part in these talks, the company obviously had a huge stake in them for the simple reason that agreement between the insurers and the co-defendant manufacturers was vital to any resolution of the asbestos-disease litigation as a whole, and might well be looked upon by Judge Lifland as a way out of the bankruptcy bind into which Manville and its creditors had become locked.

As the Wellington Group talks got under way in the late autumn of 1982, it was becoming clear that Manville was thriving in Chapter 11. Indeed, by December 9 the price of a share of the company's stock had climbed to $9.50 from $4.25 on August 27, the day after Manville filed for bankruptcy. Moreover, Manville reported that it had enjoyed a profit in the third quarter of 1982 of $24,300,000, compared with $12,600,000 a year earlier. By this time, the subject of the asbestos industry's culpability had practically disappeared from the nation's newspapers, and had been replaced by upbeat assessments of the bankruptcy proceedings. Typical was a story by Joann S. Lublin, which appeared on the front page of the *Wall Street Journal* on December 20, under a reassuring headline OCCUPATIONAL DISEASES RECEIVE MORE SCRU-TINY SINCE THE MANVILLE CASE. In her article, Lublin reported that twenty thousand lawsuits had been brought against Manville and other asbestos manufacturers by sick asbestos workers who "often . . . sued because they thought that they couldn't win workers' compensation under state laws." This, of course, was nonsense. Twenty thousand sick asbestos-insulation workers had brought product-liability lawsuits against Manville because workmen's-compensation benefits from their employers amounted to a pittance compared with out-of-court settle-ments and with compensatory damages awarded by juries across the country, who, after hearing evidence of the company's culpability, were also meting out huge punitive damages for outrageous and reck-less misconduct.

Before the end of the year, Federal Judge John E. Sprizzo, of the Southern District of New York, showed what he thought of Manville by informing some of the company's attorneys that their client came to his court with "unclean hands," and could not make use of its equitable powers. On the day before Christmas, however, Bankruptcy Judge Lifland granted Manville a sixty-day extension of the hundred-and-twenty-day period he had already granted it for filing a plan for reorganization under Chapter 11. This was merely the first of the extensions and favorable rulings that Lifland would grant Manville over the next two and a half years to the disappointment and consterna-tion of the plaintiff attorneys, who felt that he was overconcerned with how to facilitate Manville's return to the normal business world. Mean-while, as high-priced bankruptcy attorneys continued to finesse Man-ville's way through the coils of the Bankruptcy Code—Case and Crames had charged the company $200,000 apiece in the three months that followed its Chapter 11 filing—thousands of disabled and uncompensated asbestos workers continued to suffer the agonies of asbestos disease.

By January of 1983, most of the participants in the asbestos drama had begun to resign themselves to a long-drawn-out struggle. On the tenth of the month, Judge Lifland ruled that the automatic stay of litigation against Manville did not apply to the co-defendant asbestos manufacturers, and declared that any future stays must be determined by the courts before which the individual cases were pending. Since many, if not most, courts in the nation had already decided against further stays for the co-defendants, Lifland's decision simply paved the way for resumption of the asbestos litigation in earnest. This was a prospect that was hardly inviting to the co-defendants, for just a month earlier a Philadelphia jury had awarded $1.2 million in damages against, among others, Pittsburgh Corning, Eagle-Picher, Fibreboard, and Keene, in a case involving a shipyard worker who had developed nondisabling thickening of the pleural lining of the lungs.

Toward the end of January, Manville outlined a plan that would reduce its liability in the asbestos-disease litigation by removing the sixteen-thousand-odd lawsuits in which it had been named as a defendant from the courts and submitting them to a form of arbitration. According to Earl Parker, the company wanted the victims of asbestos disease to receive as much from the arbitration process as they had been getting from out-of-court settlements and jury verdicts before Manville's Chapter 11 filing. Yet Manville insisted that this amount should not exceed the average cost of settlements and verdicts since the litigation began, more than a decade earlier. Since this average was nowhere near what an asbestos victim could expect to be awarded at the present time, the proposal was shot down by the plaintiff lawyers almost as quickly as it was launched. Meanwhile, the asbestos manufacturers began to intensify a media campaign to influence public opinion and obtain passage of federal legislation that would help them cope with their legal and financial burdens. For Manville's part, this consisted of spending more than $1 million by the spring of 1984 (with Judge Lifland's approval) to run advertisements in newspapers describing the company's plight, and to hire public-relations and lobbying firms in an attempt to persuade congressmen and senators that it required and deserved federal assistance.

As the winter wore on, lawyer members of the Committee of Asbestos-Related Litigants buckled down to the tedious work of discovery as they prepared to take the depositions of Manville's directors, who were scheduled to testify in March and April. At the same time, a negotiating committee headed by Levy held periodic meetings with Manville people and their attorneys, hoping to reach agreement on a plan of reorganization for the company. However, the two sides were far apart. The plaintiff attorneys were demanding that the 16,500 lawsuits that were pending against Manville at the time of its bankruptcy filing were the only health claims that should be dealt with in the bankruptcy proceedings, but Manville was insisting that the future claims be dealt with first. On February 3, Manville made a dramatic move to break this stalemate by filing a class action under Section 502(c) of the Bankruptcy Code, which asked Judge Lifland to estimate the total number of people who could be expected to develop disease as a result of their exposure to asbestos, as well as the total dollar value of all pending and unfiled asbestos-disease claims against the company, and all claims that might be filed in the future. Manville informed Lifland that until he did this the company would be severely hindered in developing a plan of reorganization and in making payments to its creditors. As for the future claimants, Manville asked Judge Lifland to consider the propensity-to-sue factor in estimating their number and to give weight to the company's contention that the government should be responsible for compensating many of them.

Manville's move placed some extraordinary demands upon Judge Lifland, who was understandably reluctant to decide if the provisions of the Bankruptcy Act could be extended to the future claims of people who had been exposed to asbestos but were not yet manifesting any signs of asbestos disease, and who was wary of taking it upon himself to estimate the dollar value of asbestos-disease cases that had not even been filed—a decision that would surely be appealed. At this point, fully aware that the 502(c) motion could jeopardize any chance of a settlement between the company and its creditors, and hoping to cool things down, he suggested that the negotiators for both sides spend a weekend together at an inn in Connecticut, on the theory that by meeting in a different setting they might be able to reach agreement on some of the issues that were dividing them. Practically everybody was relieved when a severe blizzard forced the weekend meeting to be canceled and rescheduled for March 7 in New York City.

While Manville and its creditors jockeyed for position in the bankruptcy proceedings, asbestos lawsuits against the co-defendant manufacturers went forward in other parts of the country. The outcome of these lawsuits was published in the *Asbestos Litigation Reporter*, a fortnightly journal that had been following the course of the litigation and related events since 1979. During January, five judges began hearing a series of nonjury trials in Philadelphia, where more than fifteen hundred asbestos-disease cases were clogging the courts. (Under the nonjury program, either side in a case could ask for a trial de novo if a judge's verdict was not to its liking.) In February, a lawsuit involving a maintenance supervisor named Carl Hardy, who had worked at a chemical plant in Virginia and had died of mesothelioma at the age of fifty-four, was settled for nearly half a million dollars with Eagle-Picher, GAF, and Pittsburgh Corning. The circumstances were highly unusual: Hardy's wife and son, who was a student at the University of Virginia Medical School, had agreed to have Hardy exhumed and re-autopsied in order to refute the contention of Dr. Harry B. Demopoulos, a pathologist at New York University, who had testified for the defense that Hardy might have died of an undiagnosed tumor of the thyroid. The procedure confirmed an original postmortem finding of mesotheliuma. Meanwhile, in Florida, attorneys for a man who had developed lung cancer after working in a lumberyard, where he sawed asbestos-cement board made by the National Gypsum Company, of Dallas, settled his claim with the corporation for $125,000.

During the first week of March, the seventeen plaintiff attorneys on the Committee of Asbestos-Related Litigants met at Hilton Head, South Carolina, and agreed that their asking price for settling the nearly seventeen thousand asbestos-disease lawsuits that were pending against Manville would be $850,000,000—an average of about $50,000 a case. A few days earlier, Manville's attorneys had distributed an outline for a reorganization plan the company wanted to discuss at the meeting in New York on March 7. The plan proposed that all the pending and future cases of those plaintiffs whose disability could be proved to a medical panel be settled for an average of $13,600. This offer was not only ridiculously low but also unacceptable because it proposed to place a dollar value on future asbestos-disease claims and to take away an injured worker's right to his day in court and a trial by jury. As a result, the plaintiff attorneys boycotted the March 7 meeting. Their determination not to barter away the rights of future victims of asbestos disease received a powerful stimulus on March 25, when United States District Court Judge William T. Hart refused UNR's request to appoint a representative to represent future but unknown asbestos claimants; he said that any such plan would be subject to reversal on the ground of due process, and declared that it was up to Congress to create a solution to the problem of how to deal with future asbestos-disease plaintiffs.

Judge Hart's ruling put increased pressure on Manville to come up with a viable reorganization plan, but because the company insisted on shielding a considerable portion of its assets from future asbestos-disease claims its proposals were rejected by the plaintiff attorneys. Meanwhile, the plaintiff attorneys had begun taking the depositions of Manville directors and other officials of the company to determine the circumstances surrounding the company's Chapter 11 petitions. By far the most extraordinary testimony was given by John McKinney, Manville's chairman and chief executive officer, who was deposed on April 20 and 21 at the downtown office of Davis Polk & Wardwell. During the morning and early afternoon of the first day, McKinney mostly answered questions about Manville's litigation strategy and the sequence of events that led to its bankruptcy filing. Late that afternoon, however, Stanley Levy took over the questioning, and it was then that McKinney made his dramatic statement. Levy asked McKinney about his efforts to generate congressional support for an asbestos-compensation bill. McKinney acknowledged that he had talked with a number of representatives and senators about Manville's legal problems, and that company officials had recommended specific language for Representative Millicent Fenwick's asbestos health hazards compensation bill. He also said that he had spoken with Senator Gary Hart about the asbestos problem, and that Manville's Washington lobbyists had conferred with Hart's aides concerning the asbestos health hazards compensation bill that Hart had introduced in the Senate in 1980 and 1981.

Levy asked McKinney if he had contributed money to Fenwick and to Hart.

"Not to Congresswoman Fenwick," McKinney replied. "I did to Senator Hart."

"Was there an effort made by the company to have senior management make contributions to Congresswoman Fenwick and to Senator Hart?"

"No," McKinney said. "Only to the PAC."

"Which PAC are we talking about?" Levy asked.

"Now called the Manville PAC," McKinney told him.

"Who are the trustees or people who were responsible for administering the PAC?"

"I have forgotten who they are," McKinney said. "There are five of them."

"You don't know any of the five?" Levy asked incredulously.

"I think Hart was on it," McKinney answered. "And Mr. Linke, and Mrs. de Coursey [both were vice-presidents of Manville]. Probably somebody from finance, I would hope. I don't know of anyone—I have forgotten who is on it."

Thus, late in the day—perhaps fatigued after almost seven hours of sworn testimony—did McKinney link Senator Hart with the Manville political action committee, and then try to retract his statement by claiming that he had suddenly forgotten whether a United States senator and two of his own vice-presidents were members of it. But Levy, who was preoccupied with bankruptcy filing, returned to the main subject of the deposition without following up on McKinney's testimony.

In the end, Hart was never confronted by either the press or Mondale with the question of his Manville PAC connection. He claimed that by proposing a bill that would have taken away the legal right of sick and disabled asbestos workers to sue Johns-Manville and other asbestos-insulation manufacturers for damages, in return for slightly improved benefits in state-administered compensation systems in which they were already entitled to participate, he had been only trying to insure that deserving workers would be fairly compensated for their injuries. An examination of the legal record shows, however, that during April, 1983, when McKinney testified about Hart's connection with Manville, workers suffering from asbestosis won verdicts averaging well over $100,000 apiece against Manville's co-defendants in twenty-four of twenty-five nonjury trials that were held in Philadelphia's Court of Common Pleas. Under Hart's proposed bill, these plaintiffs would not have been able to bring suit against the asbestos manufacturers to begin with.

Early in May, Manville's bankruptcy lawyers presented Judge Lifland with a term sheet outlining the basic elements of a reorganization plan that had already been rejected by the plaintiff attorneys. Under the plan, Manville proposed to sell off most of its asbestos operations and to relegate its asbestos-disease liability to a company called M1. It proposed to spin off its nonasbestos operations—they included the fiberglass, forest-products, and roofing divisions, which had produced about three-quarters of Manville's 1982 revenues of 1.8 billion—into a liability-free corporation called M2, whose assets would not be subject to present or future asbestos-disease claims. According to the plan, asbestos litigants would be asked to vote on whether they wanted to be compensated through a no-fault system or through arbitration hearings in bankruptcy court in which no punitive damages would be allowed. The plan anticipated that its provisions would be binding on future as well as present claimants.

In June, the members of the Committee of Asbestos-Related Litigants, voted nine to six against discussing any plan that included the future claimants, or "futures" as they came to be called, on the ground that it would deprive those claimants of due process. By the same margin, they voted to turn down Manville's M1-M2 scheme. Those who were against it questioned the legality of transferring assets without transferring liabilities. Some of them quoted a 1975 California Court of Appeals decision in *Ortiz* v. *South Bend Lathe,* which adopted the theory that a transferee company was liable for torts arising from its predecessor's activities, declaring that "liability attaches to the business like fleas to a dog, where it remains imbedded regardless of changes in ownership of the business."

By the end of May, another serious sticking point had developed in talks that were being conducted between Manville and a newly appointed six-man negotiating committee made up of Levy, Locks, Baron, Motley, Henderson, and Simon. This time, the problem centered on the amount of money that would have to be put together to settle the twenty thousand claims that were by then pending against the company. The plaintiff attorneys had dropped their asking price from $850 million to $700 million, but Manville was holding at $400 million, which came out to an average of about $20,000 a case. According to a company spokesman, the offer was a reasonable one, because six thousand of the twenty thousand cases pending involved no present disability. However, the plaintiff attorneys were quick to point out that $20,000 per case was far below the average amount of the damage awards that were being meted out by juries and judges, or being reached in out-of-court settlements. (Even Manville's own LAG report had acknowledged that dispositions to asbestos plaintiffs during the six months before the company filed under Chapter 11 were averaging almost $30,000 a case.) Exasperated with both sides, Judge Lifland put pressure on the plaintiff lawyers to soften their demands and directed that McKinney and the chief executive officers of the co-defendant companies become directly involved in the negotiations.

As a result, the talks dragged on through the rest of the spring and into summer with almost no progress being made. Toward the end of July, however, some excitement was created by researchers for the Institute for Civil Justice of the Rand Corporation, of Santa Monica, California—a company whose research is supported by the contributions of industry, including several asbestos manufacturers and their insurance carriers—who issued a report of an investigation they had made into the cost of asbestos litigation. The Rand people said that $1 billion had been spent on asbestos lawsuits from the early 1970s through the end of 1982, and that $661 million had been paid by defendant manufacturers and their insurance carriers to close out asbestos-disease claims that either had gone to trial or had been settled out of court. According to the Rand researchers, only 37 percent of that amount had actually gone to compensate the plaintiffs. They went on to report that each asbestos case cost the defendant manufacturers and their insurers about $95,000; that $35,000 of this went to pay for the defense lawyers' fees and expenses; and that out of the $60,000 that remained the average plaintiff paid $25,000 for his attorney fees and expenses, and so was left with an average net compensation of $35,000.

Manville seized on the Rand report to make the point that the difference between its offer of $400 million to settle the pending asbestos lawsuits and the $700 million that was being demanded by the plaintiff attorneys amounted to approximately the plaintiff attorneys' contingent fees and expenses. The Rand report also provided the basis for another Washington *Post* editorial claiming that the tort system was an inefficient way of compensating asbestos victims, and calling on Congress to step in and bail out the defendant asbestos manufacturers. Nowhere did the newspaper point out that far and away the greatest expenses in the asbestos litigation were defense costs resulting from the insistence of each defendant manufacturer to be represented by his own set of lawyers, and the refusal of the defendants to agree to the use of prior testimony. Nor did the *Post* point out that much of the outlay by both sides had been caused by the insistence of the defendant manufacturers and their insurers to relitigate state-of-the-art and other liability issues in practically each and every case, as well as by their insistence to relitigate the medical issue of whether or not asbestos inhalation could cause lung disease in virtually every lawsuit since *Borel,* thus forcing a situation in which high-priced expert witnesses had to be called and refuted in case after case, including most of the cases that were settled before going to trial. Nor did the newspaper mention that when asbestos victims were allowed to use the supposedly inefficient tort system, it appeared to be compensating them at a splendid rate—especially in Rand's home state of California, where a jury in Oakland had recently awarded a total of $865,000 in compensatory damages, and $1.8 million in punitive damages to two asbestotic workers who had been employed in an asbestos factory and the widow of a third.

On August 25, the day before the first anniversary of the filing of Manville's Chapter 11 petitions, the *Times* ran a front-page story by Thomas J. Lueck under a headline MANVILLE THRIVING IN BANKRUPTCY, SHIELDED FROM ASBESTOS LAWSUITS. Lueck said that the company's business had surged since it filed for bankruptcy reorganization, and that its portfolio of securities was worth $215 million—more than twelve times what it had been worth a year earlier. This news was too much for Dr. Selikoff, who fired off a letter to the *Times,* which appeared on September 10. Noting that the bankruptcy judge had given Manville six extensions for filing its reorganization plan, Selikoff took it upon himself to inform Lifland that an immense human tragedy was being played out behind the proceedings over which he was presiding. The letter read, in part:

Death and disease are not held in abeyance by legal writ. The victims are barred from applying for the financial help

needed to ease their difficulties. Men are dying of mesothelioma or lung cancer, unable to seek medical care to ease their
last days, and others are not able to afford the medical surveillance that could save their lives. Still others, short of breath,
with asbestos lung scarring and no longer able to make a living,
can't keep their families together.

It is hard to appreciate the terror of a woman whose husband
has been sent home from a hospital with a tracheostomy tube
in his throat, unable to afford a nurse, resuscitating him at each
emergency, until the final episode. Or widows—of shipyard
workers, steam-locomotive repairmen, construction workers,
power and utility plant personnel and other craftsmen—having
used slowly accumulated retirement dollars for the illness
brought on by asbestos.

Some have written me that they come close to begging in the
streets. Others get along by visiting the children in rotation.
Often, when I write a widow for scientific information, the
reply comes from a trailer park: the house was sold. After a
lifetime of hard work, to die and have his widow live in penury
is a bitter final reward for a worker.

The inexorable progress of asbestos disease continues, while
the lawyerly discussions proceed. The court cannot provide a
legal extension of the lives being endangered or lost.

The human suffering and deprivation described by Selikoff did not,
however, appear to loom large in the deliberations of Judge Lifland,
who had not put any real pressure on Manville during the year since
it had filed for reorganization, or, for that matter, in the deliberations
of the various bankruptcy lawyers, investment bankers, and consultants who had been retained by Manville and the creditors' committees
for the bankruptcy proceedings, and had submitted bills for their
services totaling several million dollars. Indeed, the talks between
Manville and its creditors soon became stalled again—this time over
the issue of jury trials, which the company wished to eliminate in favor
of a "no-fault" arbitration system that would be binding on future as
well as present plaintiffs. Although the reason for Manville's aversion
to the tort system seemed to elude the Washington *Post*, it would have
been apparent to almost anyone who was willing to examine the compensatory damages being awarded to asbestos victims who were able

to bring suit against Manville's co-defendants, and compare them with the relatively meager compensation that Manville was proposing to give. In Seattle, for example, the widow of an asbestos insulator who had died of mesothelioma at the age of fifty-four had recently negotiated a $571,000 out-of-court settlement with twenty co-defendant asbestos manufacturers; in Knoxville, a jury awarded $750,000 in compensatory damages to the estate of a Tennessee pipefitter who had developed asbestosis and lung cancer, and had died at the age of fifty-five; and in Philadelphia a judge in one of the nonjury trials that were taking place in the Court of Common Pleas awarded $725,000 to the widow of a pipefitter who had died of mesothelioma.

While the asbestos litigation against the co-defendants was picking up in August and September, the negotiations with Manville remained at a virtual standstill as Judge Lifland patiently granted the company still another extension for filing its reorganization plan; this one, for thirty days, was the seventh since the proceedings began. Before the extension expired, in the middle of October, Earl Parker announced that Manville intended to file a variation of the M1-M2 plan it had proposed in May. Parker went on to say that Manville would ask the bankruptcy court to regulate the "exorbitant contingent fee arrangements" that existed between the plaintiff attorneys and their clients.

Not surprisingly, the reaction of the plaintiff attorneys to Parker's announcement that Manville would file its M1-M2 plan, not to mention his comments about contingent fees, was something less than cordial, and rumors began floating about that Manville's creditors were talking seriously about liquidating the company. By now, of course, it was clear that Manville would not propose a plan that the attorneys for asbestos-disease claimants could accept and that the present round of settlement talks was bound to fail, and for this reason Robert J. Rosenberg, the bankruptcy attorney for the Committee of Asbestos-Related Litigants, and the members of the committee prepared to launch a legal assault on the company's Chapter 11 petition, on the ground that it was fraudulent. Their chief weapon was a 103-page affidavit in support of a motion to dismiss Manville's petition for bankruptcy reorganization which was submitted to Judge Lifland on November 14 by Stanley Levy, who had pieced together a detailed scenario alleging that during 1981 and 1982 Manville's managers had fraudulently prepared the way for the company to file for bankruptcy reorganization. Levy accused Manville officials of manipulating its

consultants into making improper projections of the incidence of asbestos disease and asbestos-litigation liability, and of deceiving some
of the members of the company's own board of directors. He placed
special emphasis on the concealment from the outside directors of the
letter that had been written by Frederick L. Pundsack, the company's
former president and chief operating officer, who had bitterly protested
the impending bankruptcy filing, on the ground that it was "wrong for
the stockholders, wrong for the employees, wrong for our creditors,
wrong for our customers, and wrong for our suppliers." For its part,
Manville responded to Levy's charges by claiming that he had cited
no evidence to support most of them, including his allegation that
Pundsack's letter had been concealed.

As for Manville's long-awaited reorganization plan, which was filed
with the bankruptcy court on November 21, it proposed to set up a
procedure through which each claimant's physical impairment would
be evaluated on a sliding scale, on the basis of the claimant's age,
degree of disability, personal earnings, and number of dependents, but
that totally eliminated any recovery for pain and suffering, or for loss
of services or consortium. It offered to pay $50,000 to a claimant
suffering from mesothelioma; from $1,500 to $45,000 for lung and
other cancers, depending on the extent to which asbestos was judged
responsible for their development; and from $1,500 to $40,000 for
asbestosis and other nonmalignant impairment. As for future asbestos-
disease victims whose injuries would not be diagnosable at the time
such a plan might be confirmed, they would be enjoined from recovering any damages not only from M2 (Manville's proposed liability-free
operating arm) but even from M1—the nonoperating shell company
through which Manville proposed to deal with its asbestos-disease
liability—unless they first submitted to a still unspecified procedure
for liquidating their claims. In addition, it called on Judge Lifland "to
declare null, void, and unenforceable all prior contingent fee agreements between asbestos claimants and their counsel, and that the
Court determine reasonable fees for such counsel." In an accompanying affidavit, Dennis Markusson cited the Rand report, which said that
approximately $164 million, or 41 percent, of the $400 million that
had been paid out to asbestos claimants by defendant manufacturers
and their insurance carriers had been taken as contingent fees and
expenses by the plaintiff lawyers. (Markusson failed to mention that
defense attorneys hired by the asbestos manufacturers and their insur-

ers had been paid about $236 million in legal fees and costs—a sum approximately equal to the total compensation received by the plaintiffs.)

As might be expected, Manville's position on contingent fees hardly fostered an atmosphere of conciliation with the plaintiff attorneys, who wasted little time in submitting a motion that called on Judge Lifland to reduce the salaries of the company's chief executive officers and the fees of its board of directors. As for Manville's plan of reorganization, the plaintiff lawyers charged that it would destroy the rights of both the present and future claimants and deprive them of due process. By far the most effective rejoinder to Manville's belated reorganization plan, however, was being conducted within the tort system as judges and juries all across the nation heard evidence in cases brought by victims of asbestos disease or their survivors. In Philadelphia, four former shipyard workers suffering from asbestosis —an incurable and often fatal lung disease that Manville proposed to compensate for with a sum ranging from $1,500 to $40,000—won verdicts ranging from $100,000 to $125,000 each; four workers who had developed pleural thickening—a nondisabling condition that may be a precursor of more serious disease, for which Manville had proposed to pay $1,000—won damages of $50,000 apiece; and the widow of a shipyard worker who had died of lung cancer (for which the Manville plan would pay from $1,500 to $45,000) was awarded $550,000. In Marshall, Texas, fourteen asbestos manufacturers settled twenty-eight asbestos-disease cases for $3,470,000, which came to almost $124,000 a case, and in Dallas the widow of a former shipyard worker who had died of mesothelioma reached an out-of-court settlement with six asbestos-insulation manufacturers for $495,000.

During November, judges in the Philadelphia Court of Common Pleas awarded verdicts averaging nearly $170,000 each to five former shipyard workers who were suffering from asbestosis, and a jury in Washington State awarded $183,000 to a former rigger at the Pacific Northwest Shipyard, who had developed the disease. In Virginia, the widows of four former Norfolk Naval Shipyard workers, who had died of either lung cancer or mesothelioma, reached out-of-court settlements that ranged from more than $500,000 to nearly $1 million, and in Dade County, Florida, a jury returned a $500,000 verdict against Eagle-Picher in a case involving an insulation worker who had developed pleural thickening, though the award was subsequently reduced to $300,000. In December, in the first asbestos case ever tried in Arkansas, a federal-court jury awarded $250,000 to a former insulator who had developed asbestosis; in Cleveland, the case of a former insulator who had died of lung cancer was settled for $264,000; and in Baltimore a wrongful-death action brought by relatives of an asbestos worker who had died of lung cancer was settled for more than $300,000. Meanwhile, back in the Philadelphia Court of Common Pleas, the estate and widow of a shipyard worker who had died of lung cancer received a total of more than $910,000—the largest nonjury verdict ever made by that court in an asbestos case.

Clearly, in spite of the claims of Manville, and contrary to the assertions of the editorial writers of the Washington *Post*, who had apparently accepted industry statements without bothering to make an independent check of the legal record, the tort system in 1983 continued not only to dispense justice to diseased asbestos workers and their survivors but, equally important, to serve as a forum in which evidence of the culpability of asbestos manufacturers and of the hardship and suffering of individual claimants could be presented for assessment and action by judges and juries.

The animosity that had been building between the plaintiff attorneys and Manville during the sixteen months since the company had filed for reorganization reached a climax on January 5, 1984, when Judge Lifland heard arguments on motions to dismiss Manville's Chapter 11 petitions. At the hearing, Richard Brewster, of Moses & Singer, accused Manville of rigging the data on which it had based its projection of the number of asbestos-disease claims that would be filed against it, and called on Judge Lifland to terminate its bankruptcy petition, saying that "the integrity of the entire bankruptcy procedure is abused and cheapened." Gordon Harriss, of Davis Polk & Wardwell, told Judge Lifland that Brewster's statements were not sustained by any evidence, and Michael Crames, of Levin & Weintraub, declared that Manville "stands naked before the world," and that the Committee of Asbestos-Related Litigants was seeking to force an inflated settlement of the asbestos-disease claims.

On January 23, Judge Lifland handed down a 49-page decision in which he denied the various motions to dismiss Manville from bankruptcy, saying that there was no question that Manville was eligible to be a debtor under the statutory requirements of the bankruptcy code. "It is only now that negotiations have become seemingly deadlocked that the Asbestos Committee has reverted to its original position of attacking the filing," Lifland declared. "If there was merit in the motion to dismiss on grounds of lack of good faith, it could have been fervently pressed a year ago instead of tolerating this alleged misuse of the courts." (Lifland did not acknowledge that he had played a leading role in the delay, for in order to facilitate a settlement of the asbestos dispute he had brought considerable pressure to bear on the plaintiff attorneys for a year not to litigate their motions to dismiss Manville's bankruptcy petition.) Lifland went on to say that by demanding nearly a billion dollars to settle the sixteen thousand-odd pending asbestos-disease claims the Committee of Asbestos-Related Litigants had belied its own contention that Manville was not financially pressed. He also raised the prospect of still another liability for Manville of anywhere from $500 million to nearly $1.5 billion when he mentioned the numerous individual and class-action lawsuits for property damage that had been filed against the company by, or in behalf of, virtually every public-school district and private school in the United States, as a result of the use of asbestos-containing products, often manufactured by Manville, in the ceilings, walls, piping, and ductwork of school buildings across the nation.

Along with his denial of the motions to dismiss Manville from bankruptcy Judge Lifland handed down another far-reaching decision when he granted a motion by the Keene Corporation to appoint a legal representative for Manville's future asbestos-disease claimants. "From the inception of this case, it has been obvious to all concerned that the very purpose of the initiation of these proceedings is to deal in some fashion with claimants exposed to the ravages of asbestos dust who have not as of the filing date manifested symptoms of asbestos disease," he declared. "Indeed, but for this continually evolving, albeit amorphous constituency, it is clear that an otherwise economically robust Manville would not have commenced these reorganization proceedings." Lifland then took note of the fact that, in responding to a similar motion filed by UNR, Judge Hart had held that future asbestos-disease claims were not dischargeable in bankruptcy, and that Hart's ruling had just been upheld by the Seventh Circuit. He pointed out, however, that his appointment of a legal representative for the future claimants had no direct bearing on whether or not their claims could be discharged in bankruptcy, and was intended only to address the undeniable fact that Manville's reorganization was.of keen interest to these claimants, whom he described as "parties of interest."

As was to be expected, the plaintiff attorneys reacted to Judge Lifland's denial of their motion to dismiss by announcing that they would appeal it, while the Manville people treated it as a major victory. "The judge's rejection of the frivolous contention of the plaintiff attorneys vindicates Manville's position," said McKinney, who predicted confirmation of Manville's reorganization plan. Be that as it may, rumors soon began circulating that some of Manville's trade creditors were once again studying the merits of liquidating the company and the *Wall Street Journal* quoted John Jamieson, dean of the College of William and Mary's School of Business Administration, and the representative on the commercial and trade creditors committee of one of Manville's largest creditors—Goldman, Sachs & Company—as saying, "As time goes by, I think you have to more seriously consider the liquidation scenario."

Jamieson may well have been using the *Journal* as a vehicle to escalate the war of nerves that had been going on between Manville and its creditors for more than a year, because several weeks earlier he had outlined a plan to break the deadlocked negotiations, which was then being given serious consideration by all of the parties in the long-drawn-out dispute. At the heart of the plan was a proposal to establish a settlement trust fund for asbestos-disease victims, which would be directed by independent trustees, who would be given the responsibility of handling asbestos-disease claims and provided with a national claims facility. This trust fund would include an unspecified amount of cash from Manville; all of its product-liability insurance, which was estimated to be at least $600 million; $40 million from the sale of its Canadian asbestos mines; and some $30 million from its overfunded pension plan. In addition, the independent trustees would hold convertible debentures that could be redeemed for a percentage (somewhere between 66⅔ and 75 percent) of the company's stock in the event that asbestos-disease claims exceeded the cash assets that had been made available. This was a crucially important part of Jamieson's plan, because, depending on the percentage of stock involved, Manville's creditors could be placed in a position to take control of the company if circumstances warranted. Another very important aspect of Jamieson's plan was that if a claimant was dissatisfied with the amount he received from the claims facility he would have the right to a jury trial.

In return for these concessions by Manville, Jamieson asked the asbestos creditors to agree not to appeal Judge Lifland's decision against their motion to dismiss Manville from bankruptcy proceedings. The creditors were also asked to agree in principle that all present and future claimants should first seek redress through the settlement trust fund. Finally, they were asked to agree that Manville should be allowed to operate as an independent company, whose assets would be separate from the trust fund. This meant that Manville would be immune from future asbestos-disease claims, or, as the saying among the negotiators went, "bulletproof," while the plaintiff attorneys were given the assurance that if Manville's financial behavior and performance proved to be unsatisfactory they could gain control of the company and, if necessary, liquidate it.

On January 27, the members of the Asbestos Litigation Group held a meeting in Key West and, after hearing Jamieson present his plan in more detailed form, voted overwhelmingly to explore it at greater length, in spite of reservations on the part of some members that it allowed Manville to remain within the confines and protection of a bankruptcy petition that had been filed in bad faith. Thus, the Key West meeting opened the door to a resumption of negotiations, and Jamieson took his proposals to Denver, where he received some qualified support from the Manville people.

On February 6, 1984, the *Times* published a lead editorial entitled "A Glimmer in the Asbestos Gloom," which began by acknowledging that a quarter of a million people were likely to die early because of asbestos disease. The editorial then said that the courts were clogged with twenty-four thousand claims that by this time had been filed by asbestos victims, and that this situation had produced paralysis rather than "a prompt and equitable system of compensation." According to the *Times,* the first step toward creating such a system had been Judge Lifland's decision to allow Manville to stay within Chapter 11; the second step would be for "insurance companies to cease wrangling and start paying up"; and the third step would be for the government "to decide its duty to the thousands heavily exposed to asbestos in the shipyards of World War II."

Thus did the *Times* come out in favor of Manville's long-sought-after goal of getting the American taxpayer to foot a large part of the bill for its asbestos-disease liability—a move that had found little support in Congress and almost none in the nation's courts. In an attempt to make this position palatable to its readers, the *Times* portrayed Manville as a once misguided but now reasonable company, and described the plaintiff attorneys as once the saviors of asbestos victims but now their greedy enemies. "The attorneys who represented the first asbestos claimants built a strong case against the manufacturers," the *Times* said. (The fact was, of course, that the strong case took nearly a decade of painstaking work and discovery to construct.) The newspaper then acknowledged that in upholding a punitive-damage award against Manville an appeals court in New Jersey had declared that the company had withheld information about the asbestos hazard from workers in the 1930s, and that it had "made a conscious, cold-blooded business decision, in utter flagrant disregard of the rights of others, to take no protective or remedial action."

Without describing the relatively paltry payments Manville had proposed to make to the victims of asbestos disease, the *Times* criticized the plaintiff attorneys for trying to preserve their clients' right to a jury trial, suggesting that the lawyers were taking this stand because they stood to lose their contingent fees. The *Times* then stated the case against the judicial process in much the same language that had been used by the spokesmen for Manville and by the editorial writers for the Washington *Post.* "Trials produce long delays and haphazard results, and legal fees bite heavily into any settlement," the newspaper declared, and it went on to support this contention by citing the Rand report.

As it happened, the *Times* was relying on data that were more than six months old. According to a second Rand study that was completed the following month, the average compensation paid for all asbestos-disease claims that began trial between January 1, 1980, and August 26, 1982, was $255,000, and the average total compensation of the 53 percent of the plaintiffs who won their trials was $388,000. Small wonder that plaintiff lawyers whose ethical duty was to their injured clients were loath to advise their clients to give up their right to a jury trial!

As things turned out, the *Times* editorial was grimly and effectively rebutted in a letter to the editor written by James E. Vermeulen, a former asbestos worker suffering from asbestosis, who was the founder and executive director of an organization called Asbestos Victims of America. Judge Lifland had appointed Vermeulen to the Committee of Asbestos-Related Litigants in December, 1983, and his letter was published in the *Times* on February 16. It read, in part:

> Your statement that Manville is not evading its responsibility by filing for bankruptcy (while it continues to rake in the profits) is an insult to the dead and the dying whom Manville has resisted paying for many years. Most trials were protracted and expensive before the bankruptcy because Manville consistently (1) fought any efforts by victims and their attorneys to streamline procedures and (2) refused to make any reasonable settlement offers until the eve of trial, if at all.
>
> The Manville proposal will not automatically compensate victims, and even those managing to qualify for compensation under Manville's rules will receive "benefits" that will not even cover medical bills. Asbestos victims are entitled to just compensation for their injuries. Manville's proposal has only one beneficiary—Manville.
>
> Asbestos victims are entitled to exercise all their rights under our Constitution for their own benefit and for the benefit of the families they will leave behind. Manville cannot be allowed to deprive us of our right to our day in court, aided by the counsel of our choice, the way it has deprived us of our health and peace of mind.
>
> As one of the "Manville Maimed" I say "no" to Manville's proposal.

In January, thirteen of Manville's co-defendant manufacturers, acting through an industry trade group, proposed a no-fault plan for settling asbestos-disease claims, which called for the government to contribute 50 percent to a compensation fund. The move was obviously inspired by the fact that they were taking a terrible beating in the courts and were convinced that they would continue to do so. Indeed, within a few days, the widow of a shipyard sheet-metal worker who had died of lung cancer was awarded $485,000 by a judge in Philadelphia; a jury in the same city awarded $875,000 to a shipyard machinist who had developed pleural thickening and mild asbestosis without any disability; and in Beaumont, three asbestos-cancer lawsuits were settled out of court for $1,147,400.

In February, Chief Justice Warren E. Burger, in his annual State of the Judiciary address at the mid-year meeting of the American Bar Association, in Las Vegas, complained that there was too much tort litigation in the nation, and urged the legal profession to explore new ways of resolving disputes other than going to trial. Two years earlier, in a similar speech, he had advocated moving some lawsuits from the tort system to what he called "administrative processes, like workmen's compensation." Burger apparently had little idea of just how grossly flawed the workmen's-compensation system had proved to be. He could have been enlightened by a study of the compensation paid during 1979 to the widows of 249 men who had died from occupational exposure to asbestos, which had been performed by William G. Johnson, a professor of economics and a senior research associate of the Health Studies Program at Syracuse University's Maxwell School, together with Edward Heler, an assistant professor at the School of Public and Environmental Affairs at Indiana University Northwest, in Gary, Indiana. Johnson and Heler found the workmen's-compensation payments deplorably inadequate, replacing only 36 percent of the losses of those widows for whom it was the only source of income. They also found that those widows who had succeeded in tort suits received far and away the most adequate compensation.

In 1979, juries were beginning to hear the newly uncovered evidence of the coverup that had been engineered by the asbestos industry. As a result, there was a dramatic rise that year in damage awards and out-of-court settlements in asbestos-disease cases, and during the 1980s the tort system began to provide such meaningful compensation to the survivors of dead asbestos workers that relatively few of them bothered to apply for workmen's-compensation benefits. Yet, following Manville's filing for bankruptcy reorganization, virtually everyone involved in the asbestos problem (with the exception, of course, of asbestos-disease victims and their attorneys, whom the *Times* had accused of greed and bias) sought to replace the tort system with some new variation of workmen's compensation that would pay considerably less to the victims and their survivors than what they could expect to win in court. These efforts to circumvent the tort system were usually

characterized as attempts to find alternative methods of handling asbestos-disease claims, and those involved in them often doubted the
ability of the judicial system to cope with the so-called "asbestos-
litigation crisis," and invariably cited the need to reduce the so-called
logjam of asbestos suits in the nation's courts and to cut the overhead
costs of resolving these cases. However, the idea that the nation's court
system was not equipped to handle the asbestos litigation was challenged by a number of leading jurists and legal scholars. Among the
latter is Thomas E. Willging, of the Federal Judicial Center—an organization set up by Congress in 1967 to conduct and stimulate research
on matters of judicial administration—who published a study of asbestos case management in 1985, in which he concluded that "asbestos
cases constitute a relatively small percentage of the civil caseload of
state and federal courts," that they have become "relatively routine,"
and that they can be handled through case consolidation and standard-
ization of pretrial procedures." Meanwhile, during the late winter and
early spring of 1984, judges and jurors of the supposedly inefficient
tort system continued to refuse to allow the asbestos industry and its
insurance carriers to compensate for the loss of lungs and life at
bargain rates. In February, a Knoxville jury awarded half a million
dollars to the widow of a plasterer who had died of mesothelioma after
spraying acoustical plaster containing asbestos in school buildings. Of
the half million, $200,000 was in punitive damages—the first such
punitive award in an asbestos case against National Gypsum. Also in
February, a jury in Detroit awarded $400,000 to an insulator who had
developed asbestosis, and a Pennsylvania judge ordered three suppliers of asbestos materials who had refused to settle out of court to
pay $500,000 in punitive damages to the widow of an asbestos insula-
tor who had died of mesothelioma. During March, in Philadelphia, one
judge awarded $1.5 million to the estate and widow of a former
shipyard electrician who had died of mesothelioma at the age of
sixty-six; a second judge awarded $900,000 to the widow and estate
of an upholsterer who had sewn asbestos cloth at a shipyard during
the 1940s and had died of mesothelioma at the age of fifty-six; a third
judge awarded $673,000 to the estate of a former shipyard electrician
who had died of mesothelioma at the age of seventy-two; and the same
judge awarded $321,000 to the widow of a shipyard electrician who
had died of lung cancer at the age of fify-five. In Seattle, where six
hundred asbestos-disease lawsuits had been filed, the widow of a

former worker at the Puget Sound Naval Shipyard who had died of asbestos disease settled her case against nine insulation manufacturers for $238,750, while eight other shipyard workers who were suffering from various asbestos-related ailments accepted a group settlement of $625,000.

Such awards and settlements undoubtedly acted as a spur to the Wellington Group talks that were taking place among some of the major asbestos insurance carriers—Travelers, Aetna, Hartford, CIGNA, Continental, Fireman's Fund, and Lloyd's among them— which had been bickering for months over who was on the risk and thus liable to provide coverage. They were also a goad to some sixteen major co-defendant asbestos manufacturers who had been squabbling over their respective national market-share percentages in an effort to establish how much each of them should be assessed for settlements and awards. In May, it was announced that the two groups had finally agreed to establish a joint nonprofit asbestos-claims facility to settle asbestos claims out of court, and that they had reached tentative agreement on sharing the cost of doing so from a pool of money that was said to amount to some $7 billion. Many observers hailed the agreement as a way of breaking the asbestos-litigation logjam, because it provided that participation in the claims facility would be voluntary, and it preserved a plaintiff's right to have a jury trial. However, serious misgivings about the Wellington plan were entertained by a number of plaintiff attorneys, who worried that defendant manufacturers might refuse to negotiate with plaintiffs who chose not to use the claims facility, and pointed out that the Wellington plan contained no provision to compensate asbestos plaintiffs who had developed pleural thickening.

Meanwhile, on the first day of spring secret negotiations had resumed between Manville and attorneys representing unsecured creditors with the Jamieson proposal as a structure for their discussion. To begin with, the question of due process for future claimants loomed large in the talks, because both sides were painfully aware that they could spend many more months at the bargaining table only to have future plaintiffs challenge the constitutionality of any settlement they might devise, and, if successful, proceed to litigation against Manville. Soon, however, having been assured that both present and future claimants would have the ultimate right to have their claims determined by a jury, the members of the Committee of Asbestos-Related Litigants backed away from their previous insistence upon strict due process for the futures in the hope of obtaining progress in the negotiations. In the middle of May, at a meeting at the Halloran House, in New York, they voted eighteen to three to authorize their negotiating committee to discuss a settlement plan with Manville that proposed to treat future claimants in the same way that present claimants would be treated. In effect, the members of the committee were able to persuade themselves by a large majority that their primary duty lay with the present claimants, who were their clients, and that they should make no attempt to involve themselves in the interests of future claimants other than to reiterate their previous position that the rights of the futures should not be discharged in bankruptcy proceedings. This conclusion enabled them to agree to a proposal whereby Judge Lifland would grant an injunction that future claims could be brought only against the asbestos-compensation trust fund that was to be set up to compensate the victims of asbestos disease. The idea was that the constitutionality of discharging future claims in Chapter 11 could then be tested in the courts and decided on appeal. As for the outcome of such a test, most of the plaintiff attorneys professed to be convinced that no matter how the issue was decided it could easily be overturned if the day ever came when the trust fund ran dry. The trouble with this rationale was that when all was said and done the fate of future claimants was being left up in the air. Moreover, the precedential issue was simply staggering, for if Manville should be permitted through the simple expediency of a bankruptcy proceeding to deprive people who would develop asbestos disease in the future of their right to a trial by jury what would prevent the chemical industry and other manufacturers of products that cause cancer and latent disease from following this course?

In any event, because of the plaintiff attorneys' change of mind concerning the future claimants the negotiations went better than almost anyone expected. Indeed, by the end of May Manville and its creditors, who had been at loggerheads for more than twenty months, seemed close to agreement on the broad outlines of a plan for reorganizing the company. Among other things, Manville agreed to scrap its controversial benefits-payment schedule in favor of a scheme in which an effort would be made by the claimant's attorney and a representative of the trust fund to negotiate a settlement. If this failed, some kind of nonbinding arbitration would be attempted. And if that failed, a dissatisfied claimant would have the right to a jury trial. As for the independent trustees, they would be given control of a large percentage of Manville's common stock—the creditors were asking for 80 percent, Manville was offering 66 ⅔ percent, and the final figure was the subject of intense bargaining—with the idea that the creditors would be in a position to take over, and even liquidate, the company if the fund was not sufficient to compensate victims of asbestos disease. In addition to an initial $100 million payment by Manville, the trust fund would be financed by annual payments of $20 million over a period of ten to twenty years by Manville's operating arm and a minimum of $600 million of product-liability insurance that was expected to be provided by the twenty-seven carriers with which Manville had been in litigation since 1980.

Of course, many problems remained to be solved. The plaintiff lawyers were calling on Manville to pay their clients $100,000 for nondisabling pleural thickening, $150,000 for asbestosis, $300,000 for lung cancer, and $450,000 for mesothelioma—compensation that was roughly equivalent to what the victims of such diseases were receiving in cases that were going to trial against Manville's co-defendants. It was all very well for them to issue such calls, but the calls were unlikely to be answered; after all, to many observers Manville's chief reason for entering into bankruptcy proceedings to begin with was to allow the company, which had not paid a single penny to any asbestos-disease claimant since the day it had filed for reorganization, to settle claims for far less than they were worth in tort litigation.

An additional irony was the fact that even as it worked to deprive asbestos victims of just compensation, the bankruptcy system was providing a bonanza of staggering proportions for most of the bankruptcy attorneys who had become involved in it. (The expenses of the plaintiff attorneys were being paid but they were not being reimbursed for the time they spent on bankruptcy matters.) In the year and a half following Manville's Chapter 11 filing, the bankruptcy lawyers had billed the company for more than $27 million in legal fees and expenses. This came to about $1.5 million a month—75 percent of what Manville had been paying in 1982 for defending asbestos lawsuits, which it claimed was one of the costs that drove it to file for bankruptcy reorganization. Between August 26, 1982, and January 30, 1984, Heller, Ehrman, White & McAuliffe—the San Francisco law firm that was handling Manville's insurance litigation—charged more than $6 million; Davis Polk & Wardwell, Manville's principal outside counsel for more than fifty years, had charged nearly $3.5 million; Milbank, Tweed, Hadley & McCloy, the New York firm that represented the company's commercial creditors, had charged Manville nearly $1.7 million; Moses & Singer had billed the firm for slightly more than $1.5 million; and Levin & Weintraub (by now Levin & Weintraub & Cranes) had charged Manville slightly more than $1.3 million. Small wonder that in an article in the *Times* which appeared on June 12, Tamar Lewis, who had been following the bankruptcy proceedings from the beginning, called it "a lawyers' feeding frenzy."

A week or so earlier, the asbestos issue had been introduced into the Democratic primary campaign. This occurred when Walter Mondale made a two-hour stopover in Manville, New Jersey, where he met with a number of asbestos-disease victims and promised that (unlike Hart) he would seek to preserve their right to sue the asbestos manufacturers whose products had made them sick. The meeting received extensive media coverage and gave Mondale's campaign in the New Jersey Democratic primary—a contest he had to win if he was going to avoid a deadlocked convention in July—a much-needed lift. By this time, many observers—particularly environmentalists—were wondering why Mondale had waited so long to try to take political advantage of Hart's link to Manville and his sponsorship of an asbestos-compensation bill that would have bailed the asbestos industry out of its legal difficulties. (Mondale had brought the subject up only briefly in a debate with Hart in Philadelphia, and in passing on another occasion in Texas.) As it happened, there were at least two political reasons that could explain Mondale's reluctance to deal with the matter. The first was that some officials of the AFL-CIO, which had thrown its support to him even before the primary campaign began, were known to be embarrassed by Haas's espousal of Hart's proposed asbestos bill and reluctant to have it become public knowledge—something that was bound to happen if Mondale made a political issue of it. Second, and more important, perhaps, was the fact the three of Mondale's closest campaign advisers—people with unrestricted access to the candidate—worked for firms that represented either Manville or other asbestos manufacturers. Michael Berman, the Mondale campaign treasurer and trusted colleague from Minnesota who would be named to help run the Democratic National Committee after the convention, was a registered lobbyist for the H. K. Porter Company, of Pittsburgh, which over the years had acquired several companies that manufactured asbestos products, and was a defendant in thousands of asbestos lawsuits. Anne Wexler, a longtime political adviser to Mondale, and a former assistant to the President for public liaison during the Carter-Mondale Administration, who would be named to Geraldine Ferraro's staff after the convention, was the chairman of a Washington consulting firm that had been retained by Manville since July, 1983, at an annual fee of $300,000, to provide lobbying services for proposed and pending legislation affecting the company. And Richard Moe, a senior political adviser to the Mondale campaign, who had been Mondale's chief of staff during his Vice-Presidency, was not only a member of Davis Polk & Wardwell, Manville's principal outside counsel over the years, but had lobbied in behalf of Manville in the Congress when changes in the Bankruptcy Reform Act were being considered in the winter and spring of 1984. During the course of the spring primary campaign, there was said to have been considerable discussion in the Mondale camp over whether to use the asbestos issue against Hart, especially in key industrial states such as Massachusetts, Pennsylvania, Illinois, and New York, where the two candidates were engaged in crucial contests. Caution prevailed, however, and the entire matter—an issue that not only emphasized a major difference between the candidates but could profoundly affect tens of thousands of voters—was allowed to lie dormant until a desperate Mondale decided to raise it at the eleventh hour in New Jersey.

Toward the end of May, part of the bitter four-year controversy over Manville's insurance coverage was apparently resolved when the Manville people, who had been negotiating in secret for nearly six months with the company's primary insurer, Travelers, and with its two major excess carriers—the Home Insurance Company and a group of syndicates connected with Lloyd's of London—announced that the three carriers had agreed to pay a total of nearly $315 million to settle the claims that Manville had brought against them in the California insurance litigation. Coming on the heels of the announcement that Manville and its creditors were close to agreement on a Chapter 11 reorganization plan, news of the proposed insurance settlement raised the hopes of many observers of the bankruptcy proceedings. Within a few days, however, the plaintiff attorneys, who had requested in vain that they be kept informed of the insurance negotiations, learned that the deal between Manville and the three insurers—it called for Travelers to pay Manville $85 million; for the Lloyd's syndicates to pay almost $110 million; and for Home to contribute $120 million— contained a provision that the asbestos-compensation trust fund, which was supposed to indemnify asbestos-disease victims, would also be expected to indemnify the three insurers against any and all future claims that might be asserted for any reason against the insurance policies in question by other excess carriers or reinsurers, or, for that matter, by almost anyone, including the schools and school districts throughout the country that were sure to bring claims involving coverage of hundreds of millions of dollars' worth of property damage. Not surprisingly, the plaintiff lawyers found this provision totally unacceptable, calling it a walkaway deal that shielded the insurance carriers and Manville at the expense of their afflicted clients. As a result, the settlement talks that had been under full sail suddenly came dead in the water.

ELEVEN

RESOLUTION
AND
REFLECTION

The new turn of events threatened to make a mockery of the bankruptcy proceedings over which Judge Lifland had been presiding for twenty-one months. Yet Lifland, sanguine as ever, remarked that if the talks were becalmed all they needed was some wind, and at a hearing on July 26 he continued all pending matters until early September, when he planned to conduct a fairness hearing on the controversial insurance agreement. By now, Lifland seemed to be simply going through the legal motions and playing for time until the participants in the shabby drama being staged in his courtroom got sufficiently tired of the endeavor to make the compromises that would be necessary to achieve a settlement.

As for the attorneys on the Committee of Asbestos-Related Litigants, who had gone along with the bankruptcy charade in the hope of achieving just compensation for their clients, and had bartered away at least some of their moral and ethical position in doing so, they filed a belated petition for writ of mandamus in the United States Court of Appeals for the Second Circuit, seeking to have Manville dismissed from bankruptcy. In its petition, the committee asked for a full district-court review of the propriety of Manville's bankruptcy filing, pointing out that it had been undertaken in bad faith, and that Lifland had "simply swallowed the Manville story whole." Many observers felt, however, that the committee had been badly outmaneuvered in the proceedings, that the time for requesting that Manville be thrown out of bankruptcy was long past, and that the petition was a question of too little and too late.

In the middle of August, Judge Lifland appointed Leon Silverman, a sixty-three-year-old attorney who is co-chairman of the New York firm of Fried, Frank, Harris, Shriver & Jacobson, to represent the future claimants. Silverman, who had recently directed a special investigation into the alleged racketeering connections of Labor Secretary

Raymond J. Donovan, was given the same powers as those enjoyed by any of the creditors' committees. It appeared that he would need even more than that, for—in theory, at least—he was assuming the well-nigh impossible task of assessing the potential asbestos-disease claims that would be brought against Manville and of assuring payment to the claimants. It was a task that would soon be complicated by the announcement of the Environmental Protection Agency that asbestos could be expected to be found in more than 700,000 government, residential, and commercial buildings, and in about 31,000 schools attended by some 15 million students and staffed by 1.4 million teachers and other employees. Silverman's task would also soon be complicated by the astonishing news that 200,000 private homes in Orange County, California, had been found to contain forced-air heating-and-cooling systems whose ducts were made of asbestos, and by a report issued by members of the American Society of Home Inspectors, who found asbestos in nearly 30 percent of 670 homes they surveyed in the eastern United States.

A couple of weeks after Silverman's appointment, the second anniversary of Manville's filing for bankruptcy reorganization came and went with scarcely a mention in the nation's press, which appeared to have lost interest in the whole affair. By this time, it seemed clear that Manville's objectives in filing for bankruptcy reorganization—buying protection, buying cash, and buying time—had been achieved. It also seemed likely that serious negotiations between Manville and its creditors would not be resumed for some time. (None did take place in the course of the next nine months.) During the autumn, the bankruptcy proceedings moved along at an even more leisurely pace than usual, with Manville officials assuring Judge Lifland that they were engaged in sensitive negotiations aimed at resolving insurance-coverage disputes with other excess carriers, and with Lifland twice postponing arguments concerning the fairness of Manville's $315 million settlement with Travelers, Home, and the London syndicates. As for the plaintiff lawyers, they pointed out that the open-ended indemnity clause in the settlement would not only bar third-party claims against the three insurers but might require Manville to assume defense costs and other liabilities that could wipe out the entire $315 million without leaving a dime for compensating the victims of asbestos disease. Judge Lifland, however, would not allow them to conduct discovery or take depositions to determine whether the insurance settlement was indeed a fair one, and he refused to hold a full-fledged hearing with testimony on the matter. Meanwhile, on the other side of the Atlantic the Lloyd's people voiced displeasure with the underwriting policies of their colleagues in the United States. "We can no longer accept the volume of poor risks that the American insurers have been assuming in their mad quest to fatten their books and raise their cash flow," said the chairman of one of Lloyd's leading member groups. He added that "asbestos claims will prove to be the most expensive burden on insurers in history."

As might be expected, this burden was increasing by leaps and bounds as more asbestos cases went to trial and more juries heard the evidence that had been compiled against the defendant asbestos manufacturers. In October, a jury in the Philadelphia Court of Common Pleas awarded about $315,000 to a shipyard insulator who had developed nondisabling pleural thickening, and in Galveston, Texas, a United States District Court jury awarded a total of $1.95 million to three insulators who had developed asbestosis. The Galveston verdict was dwarfed within a few weeks, when a jury in Marshall, Texas, that had been scheduled to hear a total of thirty asbestos lawsuits voted against the state-of-the-art defense and proceeded to award three insulators who were suffering from asbestosis, together with the widow of a fourth insulator, who had died of the disease, a whopping $7.9 million, including $1 million each in punitive damages. Not surprisingly, this judgment spurred settlement talks and by the first week in December, the remaining twenty-six cases—about half of them involved plaintiffs who had developed nondisabling pleural thickening —and also the four cases that had been tried, since in these no final verdict had been entered, were settled for $12 million by the ten defendants: Pittsburgh Corning, Raymark (formerly Raybestos-Manhattan), Owens-Illinois, Nicolet, Celotex, Eagle-Picher, Keene, Fibreboard, Standard Asbestos, and Armstrong Cork. The fact that each of the thirty plaintiffs would have received $400,000 if the $12 million settlement had been split evenly among them gave some indication of how steeply the disposition price of asbestos-disease claims had risen since 1968, when Ward Stephenson, the pioneering attorney from Orange, Texas, settled the case of Claude Tomplait, the insulator who had developed asbestosis, for $75,000. The Marshall settlement was also interesting in view of the fact that five of the ten defendant manufacturers had been defendants in the landmark case of *Borel* v.

Fibreboard, which Stephenson had won in 1971, when a jury in Beaumont awarded $68,000 to the widow of Clarence Borel, the asbestos insulator who had died of mesothelioma.

Since the sharp rise in verdicts in Texas reflected a trend that had been developing elsewhere in the nation, the co-defendant manufacturers and their insurers, who had been bearing the brunt of the asbestos litigation over the two years and more since Manville had filed for bankruptcy reorganization, redoubled their efforts to find a way out of their predicament. Some of them sought to shift the blame to the United States under the government-specification defense, which alleged that as contractors they had merely complied with the government's decision to specify the use of asbestos insulation in U.S. Navy ships during the Second World War. Others banked heavily upon the Wellington plan, under which a number of them had reached tentative agreement with some of their insurers to establish a national asbestos-claims facility that would operate to settle asbestos lawsuits out of court, using alternative dispute-resolution techniques. Since it had first been announced, in May, the Wellington plan had encountered trouble attracting enough subscribers, especially among excess insurance and reinsurance carriers, who had not expected that they would ever be on the risk for the asbestos coverage they had sold, and had little inclination to acknowledge that they might be. Moreover, many leading plaintiff attorneys were threatening to boycott the proposed claims facility because the manufacturers and their insurers had proposed ground rules that would bar compensation for asbestos claimants who suffered from pleural thickening or pleural plaques. In spite of these problems, Dean Wellington, the chairman of the plan, remained optimistic. "I am convinced the facility will succeed," he said in a statement that was published in a fortnightly digest called *Mealey's Litigation Reports: Asbestos.* "The time has come for traditional and expensive courtroom warfare to give way to a private and equitable settlement of the asbestos tragedy."

Wellington left little doubt that the private, no-fault solution he was proposing to the asbestos problem was designed to discourage jury trials, which he described as "complicated, time-consuming, and expensive." Even before he made his statement, however, the nonjury approach to asbestos litigation was running into trouble in the Philadelphia Court of Common Pleas, where a nonjury program that had been in effect for nearly two years had been suspended because more than half of the 234 verdicts that had been handed down by judges had resulted in appeals by either plaintiffs or defendants for a trial de novo. As for the no-fault aspect of the Wellington plan, it would probably discourage the discovery and disclosure of any further evidence concerning the conduct of the nation's asbestos manufacturers. Moreover, because many of its backers were touting the Wellington plan's proposed national claims facility as a model for dealing with future mass toxic-tort litigation, such as the avalanche of lawsuits expected to result from the chemical contamination of the nation's groundwater supplies, it was not hard to see how the whole scheme might be put to work to discourage the uncovering of evidence concerning culpability on the part of certain chemical companies.

As it turned out, a fine example of the kind of information that might never see the light of day if the Wellington plan were to become a legal reality occurred a week or so before Wellington issued his statement. At that time, government attorneys who were searching through the National Archives during the course of discovery in an asbestos lawsuit came upon a report showing that Eagle-Picher Industries, Inc., of Cincinnati—a manufacturer of asbestos insulation since 1930 and a defendant in asbestos product-liability lawsuits since 1966—had been warned about the asbestos hazard more than fifty years ago. The report described the results of an industrial-hygiene survey of an Eagle-Picher rock-wool plant in Joplin, Missouri, which had been conducted back in September of 1931 by a physician of the United States Bureau of Mines; he found that lung scarring had developed in three of four men who had been employed part-time for less than two years in the plant's mixing room, where mineral wool containing a high percentage of silica was combined with asbestos and made into bricks used to insulate buildings and furnaces. In his report, which was forwarded to Eagle-Picher on a confidential basis in March, 1932, the Bureau of Mines physician warned that the mixing room "is a particularly dusty place," that in combination with fused silica dust "asbestos dust is one of the most dangerous dusts to which man is exposed," and that "it is reasonable to conclude that the men [working there] will get extensive fibrotic changes in a relatively short period of time." At the time the report came to light, a leading plaintiff attorney described its fifty-three-year-old warning as "the strongest piece of punitive-damage evidence" that had yet been unearthed against Eagle-Picher, and some observers predicted that it could prove damaging to the company's legal defense in the twenty-thousand-odd asbestos lawsuits that had been brought against it throughout the nation.

At the beginning of December, there was another call to put an end to asbestos litigation as it was being conducted. This one came from Stephen Case, an attorney and partner in Davis Polk & Wardwell, who wrote an article in the business section of the New York *Times* that ran under the headline "LAWYERS OFTEN ARE GROSSLY OVERPAID." In his article Case criticized plaintiff attorneys for charging contingent fees in asbestos cases and other mass torts, saying that this practice constituted an "unprofessional orgy of greed." He went on to suggest that "all lawyers in mass torts should accept expedited dispute resolution procedures and compensation based on hourly rates." Case's article did not mention the fact that in 1981 and 1982 he had been a member of LAG, Manville's Litigation Analysis Group, which had calculated the FASB-5 estimation of liability accrual that paved the way for Manville to file for bankruptcy reorganization under Chapter 11. Nor did his article mention that Davis Polk & Wardwell had been Manville's principal outside counsel for more than fifty years, and also its co-counsel during the twenty-seven-month-long bankruptcy proceedings. During the first seventeen months of the bankruptcy, the firm had reportedly billed Manville's Chapter 11 estate nearly $3.5 million dollars for its services—at hourly rates, to be sure—and then, for the four-month ending on September 30, 1984, it had run up a bill of more than $1 million in fees and expenses. (During this same four-month period, some sixty law firms, investment counselors, and other consultants involved in the bankruptcy, including firms that represented the Committee of Asbestos-Related Litigants, had submitted bills reflecting hourly fees and expenses totaling more than $8 million.)

On December 4, two days after Case's article appeared in the Sunday *Times*, headlines across the nation and throughout the world were dominated by news of the ghastly accident in Bhopal, India, where methyl-isocyanate gas leaking from a chemical pesticide plant owned by the Union Carbide Company, of Danbury, Connecticut, killed an estimated 1,700 people within a few hours and injured as many as 200,000. During the next several weeks, complaints seeking billions of dollars in compensatory and punitive damages were filed against Union Carbide in the United States by American attorneys who had gone to Bhopal after the accident and signed up thousands of its injured residents and relatives of the dead as their clients. As might be expected, this engendered intense speculation in the press about the potential liability of Union Carbide, as well as criticism of the plaintiff lawyers, who were castigated by some editorialists as international ambulance chasers seeking to make a killing in contingent fees. Few newspapers—the *Wall Street Journal*, being the chief exception—pointed out that under Indian law plaintiffs in tort cases are required to pay a nonrefundable filing fee of up to 5 percent of the total damages sought—a prohibitive expense for most of the impoverished victims of the Bhopal tragedy—and that the chaotic court system in India was so backlogged with cases that lawsuits brought there on behalf of these victims might take decades to litigate and decide on appeal. For these reasons, no doubt, a number of prominent Indian lawyers and jurists, including the chief justice of India's Supreme Court, strongly advocated that the Bhopal accident cases be tried in the United States, since its contingent-fee system affords poor people an opportunity of suing wealthy and powerful corporations. In April, 1985, the Indian government, after hiring American counsel, brought suit against Union Carbide in the district court in New York on behalf of all the dead and injured citizens of the stricken city. Eight days later, Federal District Judge John F. Keenan, who is presiding over the case, announced that he would name a three-lawyer committee—it would consist of one attorney representing the Indian government and two attorneys from among the dozens of personal-injury attorneys who had filed complaints in behalf of groups of Bhopal victims—to coordinate the litigation. During the next two months, settlement talks between the Indian government and Union Carbide reached an impasse when Union Carbide offered to settle all claims arising from the Bhopal accident for $230 million, and the Indian government demanded at least $1 billion. Meanwhile, as the cases in the United States proceeded toward trial, two thousand lawsuits had been filed in the Bhopal District Court. According to some American lawyers, Union Carbide was challenging many of these lawsuits on technicalities. According to the mayor of Bhopal, ten thousand residents of the city were suffering from severe lung damage.

Some months earlier, plaintiff lawyers representing a chemical worker who was suing Union Carbide in Little Rock, Arkansas—he alleged that he had developed asbestos disease after being exposed to asbestos that had been mined by the company in Coalinga, California, and used as a reinforcing agent in the manufacture of plastic bags—

introduced as evidence in the case a report entitled "Asbestos as a Health Hazard in the United Kingdom," which had been written in 1967 by a researcher at one of Union Carbide's British subsidiaries and presumably sent to the corporate home office in New York. In his report, the British researcher warned that "we are not entitled under any circumstances to state that our material [Coalinga asbestos] is not a health hazard." He went on to declare that "if it is believed that a potential customer would use our material 'dangerously,' and that he is unaware of the toxicity question, then it must surely be our duty to caution him and point out means whereby he can hold the asbestos air float concentration to a minimum." Up until the time this report was introduced in the Arkansas case, Union Carbide had not been a substantial defendant in the asbestos litigation—in fact, relatively few asbestos-disease lawsuits had been filed against it—but as a result of the new disclosure, plaintiff lawyers expected that the number of complaints against the company would increase.

Early in January, 1985, *Fortune* published the results of its annual survey of two hundred and fifty of the nation's large corporations. The survey had been conducted in the autumn of 1984, before the tragedy at Bhopal took place, and it ranked Manville last for community and environmental responsibility and among the three least-admired firms in the country for quality of management and ability to attract, develop, and keep talented people. During the same week, lawyers for the Committee of Asbestos-Related Litigants, the Committee of Equity Security Holders, and a potential future plaintiff filed briefs in the United States District Court for the Southern District of New York, asking for the overturn of Judge Lifland's August appointment of Leon Silverman to represent future asbestos-disease victims who might have claims against Manville. The brief for the Committee of Asbestos-Related Litigants declared "No other conclusion can be drawn but that the Bankruptcy Judge intends that a plan of reorganization in this proceeding will affect the rights of Future Claimants, binding them and perhaps even discharging their claims, and that the legal representative appointed in the Decision on appeal will be the instrument to carry out this intention." The plaintiff attorneys went on to point out that the Fifth Amendment requires that " 'due process of law" be accorded before a person's rights can be affected," and that "the bankruptcy power, like other great substantive powers of Congress, is subject to the Fifth Amendment."

This was a significant argument, of course, but Lifland's appointment of Silverman was buttressed in late February when the bankruptcy judge in UNR's Chapter 11 proceedings authorized the appointment of a legal representative for future asbestos-disease claimants, and when the Third Circuit Court of Appeals reversed a lower court denial of the AMATEX Corporation's motion to appoint a guardian for future claimants in its Chapter 11 proceedings. Meanwhile, it had become apparent to many observers of the long-drawn-out bankruptcy proceedings that with Judge Lifland's tacit approval, Silverman had not only begun to play a leading role in formulating a plan for reorganizing Manville but had become the principal architect of and chief behind-the-scenes negotiator for such a plan.

In February, Manville announced that it had settled its insurance-coverage disputes with three of its excess carriers—the Insurance Company of North America (INA), the Midland Insurance Company, and the Allstate Insurance Company. They had agreed to provide almost $112 million toward settling asbestos-disease claims once the $315 million in coverage from Manville's prior settlement with Travelers, Home, and the Lloyd's syndicates was exhausted and certain other conditions were met. The agreement provided that if the settlement were approved by the bankruptcy court, and if either Manville or the three settling insurers should subscribe to the Wellington claims facility, the $112 million in coverage would be dispensed under the Wellington plan. It also provided that this insurance coverage would be triggered during the period beginning with the date of a claimant's first exposure to asbestos and ending on the date on which the claimant first manifested symptoms of asbestos disease, or on which asbestos disease was diagnosed. For its part, Manville agreed to dismiss without prejudice the actions it had brought against INA, Midland, and Allstate in the huge insurance-coverage lawsuit it had filed in San Francisco Superior Court in 1980 naming twenty-seven of its insurers as defendants. At the same time, Manville announced that it was continuing to negotiate with the twenty-one other insurance carriers against whom it remained in litigation in California, and that it was seeking some $200 million of additional coverage from them.

Preparations for the California insurance-coverage trial had been under way all winter. The case—one of the most complex and potentially expensive insurance claim disputes in history, with alleged damages running into the billions of dollars—was a consolidation of Manville's 1980 lawsuit against its twenty-seven insurers and lawsuits that had been brought against many of these same insurers and forty or so additional carriers by four additional asbestos-insulation manufacturers: Armstrong World Industries, Inc. (formerly the Armstrong Cork Company), GAF Corporation, Fibreboard, and Nicolet. At issue was whether billions of dollars in asbestos-disease claims should be paid by the insurer whose policies were in effect during the time a claimant was exposed to asbestos or by the insurer whose policies were in effect when asbestos disease first manifested itself in the claimant or, under a triple-trigger approach, by both. The logistics of trying the case were staggering: attorneys from some sixty law firms, who represented the five asbestos manufacturers and the more than seventy insurance carriers involved in the case, were scheduled to present arguments and introduce in evidence about a hundred thousand exhibits and documents totaling approximately a million pages in a marathon trial that was expected to be conducted in several phases and to last at least a year and a half. In order to handle all the legal activity and paperwork, an elaborate sound and intercom system, together with a $200,000 computer system capable of storing all of the exhibits and documents and of producing a two-hundred-page daily transcript of the proceedings, were installed in Nourse Auditorium, a sixty-two-year-old, thousand-seat theater hall with rococo wall sculptures, Greek pediments, a gilded ceiling, and huge chandeliers, which had been leased for a year and remodeled at a cost of more than $200,000. Among the renovations and additions were a white-oak judge's bench that had been installed at stage center; a white-oak jury box at stage left; twenty-six oak-topped attorneys' tables arranged in an arc on new flooring and carpeting that had been laid down over the orchestra pit; and air-conditioned judge's chambers lined with bookshelves and equipped with a private toilet, which had been converted from a ladies' dressing room. Presiding over this magisterial scene was Superior Court Judge Ira A. Brown, Jr., an opera-loving jurist who acknowledged that he had been a character actor in his college days, and that he had later "gravitated to trial work, which is about as theatrical as you can get in the law."

On March 4, 1985, the day the trial began, the newly renovated interior of Nourse Auditorium was jammed with attorneys, spectators, television camera crews, and reporters from newspapers, magazines, and law journals all across the nation. On the sidewalk, a dozen or so former asbestos workers who were suffering from asbestos-lung disease held a demonstration to protest the fact that asbestos victims would continue to go uncompensated while Manville spent millions of dollars in attorneys' fees on the insurance litigation. They were led by James Vermeulen, who carried a portable oxygen tank to help him breathe.

Meanwhile, during the two-week period before the huge insurance trial got under way, three of the major defendant carriers in the litigation—Fireman's Fund, the Home Insurance Company, and CNA Insurance companies had signed up conditionally to join the Wellington plan and its proposed asbestos claims facility. This prompted some proponents of the plan, whose conditional subscribers now numbered thirty-three asbestos manufacturers and twenty-two insurance companies—to push ahead for final binding signups. Some of the attorneys who were involved in the California insurance litigation predicted that if the Wellington settlement could be completed and its claims facility set up during the summer the companies involved in the huge lawsuit would dismiss their claims against one another. In any event, almost no one believed that the insurance case would be litigated to the bitter end, not the least of the reasons being that the evidence the manufacturers and the insurance carriers had dug up on each other over the years might be used against them in future cases by lawyers for asbestos-disease plaintiffs.

As for the plaintiff attorneys, some of them who had supported the basic concept of the Wellington plan now began to express concern that it might be used against their clients. At a hearing held before the Senate Labor and Human Resources Committee's Subcommittee on Labor on March 19, an attorney for the AFL-CIO pointed out that the Wellington agreement was essentially a peace treaty between asbestos manufacturers and their primary insurers, and asked whether the claims facility would offer fair and timely compensation to asbestos-disease victims, or whether the manufacturers and insurers would "use their new-found harmony to wage a unified war of attrition against the victims who seek compensation." At the outset of the hearing, Dean Wellington, who said that he was there to testify as "the neutral moderator of a private group of major asbestos producers and their insurers," declared that "asbestos litigation in America has reached truly epidemic proportions. . . ." (He could, of course, have said the same thing about asbestos disease.) Referring to the Rand report that had been used by the Washington *Post* to support its contention that the tort system was an inefficient way to compensate asbestos victims, Wellington said that it was unacceptable that almost two-thirds of the judgments or settlements in asbestos cases were going to lawyers, and that asbestos-disease claimants were "getting only 37 cents of each dollar awarded." At that point, Senator Howard K. Metzenbaum, Democrat of Ohio, asked Wellington if he had "taken a look at the report itself to determine impartially that it is objectively done." Referring to a copy of the report that he had brought with him, Metzenbaum then pointed out that asbestos-disease claimants in tort litigation were actually getting 59 cents on the dollar. After acknowledging that he could not testify to the validity of the figures in the Rand report, and apologizing for any confusion he may have caused, Wellington proceeded to criticize the way asbestos-disease claims were being handled by the tort system, saying that "even when a company is judged blameless, it still incurs large legal expenses," and pointing out that workers claiming similar injuries might be awarded widely different damages if they filed their claims in different legal jurisdictions. Later in his testimony, after informing Metzenbaum that key questions about how the claims facility would work to compensate asbestos-disease victims could be answered only after the facility was in operation, Wellington declared that it was "an obscenity" to have twenty teams of defense lawyers in each asbestos case when one would suffice, and assured his listeners that the claims facility proposed under the Wellington plan would have only one. The fact is, of course, that the manufacturers and their insurers could have pooled their defenses at any time during the long-drawn-out asbestos litigation, and saved millions of dollars in legal fees in doing so; instead, they had forced attorneys for sick and dying plaintiffs to litigate the same issues of medical causation and liability over and over again in a calculated effort to wear the plaintiffs down and force them to agree to cheaper settlements.

Among the witnesses at the March 19 hearing who favored establishing the claims facility were the president and chief executive officer of the Pittsburgh Corning Corporation, who declared that "asbestos litigation is a burden on our companies," and the chairman and chief executive officer of the Hartford Insurance Group, who said that "the money that is being dissipated by the endless legal wrangles threatens the economic foundations of both asbestos producers and insurance companies." Also testifying in favor of the facility was Robin A. G. Jackson, a director of Merrett Syndicates, Ltd., a major underwriting agent of Lloyd's. Jackson was the chief negotiator for the London reinsurance market in the Wellington talks, and was appearing at the hearing in his capacity as chairman of the London Asbestos Working Party, a group of insurers and reinsurers that had been formed in 1980 to deal with problems posed by asbestos-disease claims. He told the hearing, "What has really distressed all of us in London so much is the grim reality that, on current performance, many of those suffering will not live to receive their damages and for many others compensation will come too late to provide any real relief." (What would soon be additionally distressing to the people back in London was that five hundred member investors of two of Lloyd's other underwriting syndicates—most members are nonprofessional investors known as "names," and are often prominent and wealthy people—who were heavily on the risk for asbestos-product-liability and Agent Orange disease claims in the United States, and were facing losses that could exceed $165 million, not only were refusing to pay up but were threatening to sue the managers of the syndicates for irregularities and fraud, and pressing Lloyd's to compensate them for at least some of their losses, claiming that Lloyd's should assume a more vigilant role in monitoring its $5 billion insurance market.) Later in his testimony, Jackson told the hearing, "The sooner the spirit of compromise prevails over producers, insurers, and reinsurers alike, and they unanimously adopt the Asbestos Claims Facility, the sooner we can start defusing this social and economic time bomb." Jackson soon took a step to defuse any future insurance time bombs. On the day after he testified at the hearing, he wrote a letter to another syndicate member of Lloyd's, saying that his syndicate would henceforth "exclude absolutely all pollution coverages."

On June 19, thirty-four asbestos manufacturers and sixteen insurance companies signed a final, binding agreement that will make the Wellington plan and its proposed claims facility a reality. Missing from the manufacturer signatories were Manville, UNR, AMATEX, and Forty-Eight—the asbestos producers that had filed for bankruptcy

reorganization—as well as such major defendants in the ongoing asbestos litigation as Raymark Corporation (formerly Raybestos-Manhattan), GAF, and Nicolet. At least half a dozen of the manufacturers who
signed the final agreement were relatively minor participants in the
litigation. Among the insurers who declined to sign it were Travelers,
Home, and CNA. Home and CNA, which had earlier been conditional
signers, had significant liability for excess asbestos-insurance coverage. Home was reportedly having problems with its reinsurers, which
refused to endorse its participation in the Wellington plan.

As for how the Wellington plan will fare, a major question is
whether the manufacturers and their insurers will be able to agree on
how to deal with the tens of billions of dollars in property-damage
claims that have been filed by schools, cities, counties, government
agencies, businesses, and individuals that have discovered friable asbestos products in their buildings. Up to now, the problem has loomed
so large that most of the Wellington-plan negotiators have been reluctant to discuss it in public. For example, neither Wellington nor
anyone else who testified in favor of the proposed claims facility at the
March 19 hearing had anything to say about the property-damage
claims. These claims had been looming for some time as a second tidal
wave of asbestos litigation, and following Judge Lifland's recognition
of an unofficial creditors' committee for asbestos-related property-
damage school claimants, in 1983, they had begun to be an issue in
Manville's Chapter 11 proceedings. Still, the true extent of the potential problems that these claims posed for Manville did not become
apparent until the summer of 1984, when Lifland, in yet another
demonstration of the astonishing powers that are vested in bankruptcy
judges, set an October 31 deadline for filing them. This, naturally,
occasioned a dramatic rise in the number of property-damage claims
being brought by schools and school districts, by local and state
government agencies, and by private property owners who had found
asbestos in their office buildings. The surge of claims was further
encouraged when the Environmental Protection Agency (EPA) announced, on October 12, that friable asbestos might be found in
31,000 of the nation's school buildings and in 20 percent of the
nation's commercial, residential-apartment, and federal buildings—an
estimated 733,000 buildings in all.

Whatever the validity of these estimates, the EPA's efforts to deal
with the hazard of asbestos in schools had been inept and ineffective

from the start. When Congress passed the Asbestos School Hazard Abatement Act in 1984, it authorized the EPA to oversee a program of inspecting the nation's schools for asbestos and to allocate $600 million in loans and grants over the next six years for the purpose of removing asbestos from the schools in which it was found. However, thanks to bureaucratic foot-dragging within the EPA, both the inspection program and the removal process soon fell far behind schedule. Schools were supposed to have been inspected for the presence of asbestos, and notices about the findings of the inspections sent out to parents, teachers, and school employees by June of 1983. This was not accomplished in many, if not most, of the nation's schools, in spite of EPA assurances to the contrary. (Indeed, in December of 1984, an EPA official admitted that at least two-thirds of the schools in New Jersey were not in compliance with the inspection program.) To make matters worse, EPA safety regulations designed to protect the health of pupils, teachers, and school employees while asbestos-removal projects were in progress have not been implemented. According to some observers, this negligence came about because of concern among officials of the Reagan administration's Office of Management and Budget (OMB) that EPA regulation of asbestos-removal in schools might cause additional pressure to be brought upon the government to help pay for the claims of workers who have developed asbestos disease as a result of their employment in government-owned or government-sponsored shipyards during the Second World War. (Such assessments gained credence in April, 1985, when EPA officials admitted in testimony before the Oversight and Investigations Subcommittee of the House Energy and Commerce Committee that they had, in fact, been pressured by the OMB to weigh the dollar value of human life in considering how to regulate asbestos.) Be that as it may, the EPA's failure to implement safety regulations for asbestos-abatement projects has allowed many fly-by-night contractors with poorly equipped and poorly trained workers to undertake asbestos removal without instituting proper precautions or procedures and, by so doing, to stir up asbestos-dust levels far greater and more hazardous than those they were supposed to be abating. As a result, almost all insurance companies have refused to issue liability policies to asbestos-removal contractors, and this, in turn, has brought abatement of the asbestos hazard in schools to a virtual standstill. At the same time, some insurance carriers were refusing to issue liability policies to schools that have not undertaken asbestos removal, thus compounding the problem being faced by school boards and school districts across the nation.

Because of this unholy mess, it is not surprising that efforts to deal with the asbestos hazard in schools have moved into the legal arena. In September, 1984, a federal judge in the Eastern District of Pennsylvania certified a national-plaintiff class of some fourteen thousand schools and school districts across the nation in a class-action lawsuit that had been brought against more than fifty manufacturers of asbestos-containing products that had been used in the construction of school buildings throughout the United States, and also a number of mining companies that had supplied the raw asbestos used in these products. Among the defendants in the class action were the National Gypsum Company, of Dallas; the United States Gypsum Company, of Chicago; and W.R. Grace & Company, of New York City—major manufacturers of sprayed-on asbestos acoustical ceiling material—as well as Owens-Illinois, Owens-Corning, Pittsburgh Corning, and Celotex, all of whom made asbestos insulation that had been used to cover pipes and boilers in school buildings. During the last two weeks of September, the State of Maryland filed a lawsuit against forty-seven manufacturers and distributors of asbestos products, seeking $500 million to clean up asbestos in three thousand public schools, and the City of Baltimore filed a $225 million lawsuit against fifty-five asbestos companies. In mid-October, because of complaints by many states, counties, municipalities, and other agencies that they had received insufficient notice, Judge Lifland was obliged to extend the filing deadline to January 31, 1985. During the next ninety days or so, an avalanche of additional claims was filed against Manville and other asbestos manufacturers. Among them were a $250 million claim by New York City and its board of education; separate $400 million claims by Oregon, Nebraska, and the District of Columbia; a $650 million claim by the National Association of Counties in behalf of approximately two thousand county governments; a claim for nearly $2 billion by Michigan; a $10 billion class-action claim by a California school district in behalf of public schools across the nation; and a $10 billion claim by the City of San Leandro, California, in behalf of other municipalities in the country.

Early in April, Manville announced that as of March 1, it had been named in some eleven thousand property-damage claims seeking approximately $50 billion. Because the damages sought in many of these are believed to be inflated, and because the claims include those made against other manufacturers of asbestos products that have been used in the construction of schools and buildings, it is difficult to assess how seriously they may affect Manville's attempt to deal with its asbestos-litigation problems in Chapter 11. Some attorneys estimate that the justifiable combined property-damage claims against Manville and other manufacturers may amount to between $10 billion and $15 billion, though most observers believe that the total bill that the producers and their insurers will end up paying will be far less. Other attorneys say that Manville's own potential liability could be enormous—perhaps running to several hundred million dollars—because the company not only made and sold asbestos-insulation products, but also mined and sold much of the raw asbestos used by other manufacturers in making such products, which had found their way into hundreds of thousands of government, commercial, and residential buildings, and schools. Still others predict that co-defendant manufacturers seeking to hold Manville liable for supplying them with raw asbestos may find it extremely difficult to substantiate this position in court.

As for the biological consequences of asbestos in the nation's schools, one thing is indisputable: because of exposure to low levels of asbestos, millions of children have been and are still being placed at potential risk of developing malignant mesothelioma—the invariably fatal tumor that is almost always associated with some, even if slight, inhalation of asbestos, and that can occur from twenty to forty or more years after first exposure to the mineral. In addition, hundreds of thousands of teachers and other school employees—particularly maintenance personnel—are at even greater risk because of longer and more intimate exposure to asbestos. It is not known, nor can it be accurately predicted, just how many of these people will develop cancer as a result. What is known is that asbestos levels in schools with asbestos-containing ceilings that have been badly damaged are similar to those measured in the homes of asbestos workers, and that, according to a study by Herbert Seidman of the Department of Epidemiology and Statistics of the American Cancer Society, the wives and children of asbestos workers have been shown to be at greater risk of developing cancer than people in the general population. Indeed, a study conducted by Dr. Henry A. Anderson and Dr. Selikoff and their associates at Mount Sinai shows that mesothelioma caused five out of approximately four hundred deaths that occurred twenty or more years after first exposure to asbestos among members of the households of workers at an asbestos factory in Paterson, New Jersey, and other studies conducted by them show that the chest X-rays of fully 30 percent of the wives and children of asbestos insulators and factory workers reveal asbestos-related abnormalities. Thus, it should come as no surprise that cases of mesothelioma are now beginning to be reported among teachers, custodians, and former pupils, at schools containing friable asbestos products, which constituted their only known exposure to asbestos.

For their part, asbestos manufacturers have denied that asbestos levels in the ambient air of schools are hazardous, claiming that they are far too low to cause disease. Be that as it may, on April 9, 1984, School District Five of Lexington County, South Carolina, reached a $675,000 out-of-court settlement with United States Gypsum in the nation's first school-asbestos lawsuit to go to trial. However, the asbestos manufacturers have no doubt been encouraged by jury verdicts that were won in March and August of 1985 by United States Gypsum and National Gypsum, the defendants in the second and third school-asbestos cases to go to trial. The second lawsuit had been brought against the two companies by Anderson County, Tennessee, and during the course of the trial, defense lawyers told the jury that asbestos-fiber counts in air samples collected in the county schools were so low that it would take a thousand years for a pupil to develop cancer as a result of exposure to them. Another factor in the outcome of the case was that the defendants were able to erect a state-of-the-art defense based upon the claim that the medical and scientific community had no knowledge about the hazard of low-level exposure to asbestos until the early 1970s. This, of course, was reminiscent of a similar and subsequently discredited defense raised in cases involving asbestos insulators, when the manufacturers claimed that the medical and scientific community had no knowledge of the hazard posed by asbestos to insulators until Dr. Selikoff published his epidemiological studies of mortality among asbestos insulators in 1964. In the third lawsuit, which was brought against United States Gypsum and National Gypsum by a school district in Spartanburg County, South Carolina, the defense attorneys were also successful in claiming that the levels of exposure were not high enough to constitute a health hazard. While most lawyers were cautious in appraising the verdict in the Anderson

County case (the County's motion for a new trial was subsequently denied), and in the Spartanburg County case, the outcome appeared to indicate that the litigation over asbestos-property-damage claims would turn out to be as protracted and hard-fought as the personal-injury lawsuits had been.

Meanwhile, the Manville bankruptcy proceedings continued to limp along as Judge Lifland postponed for the third time a fairness hearing on Manville's ten-month-old insurance settlement with Travelers, Home, and the underwriters' syndicates at Lloyd's of London. The reason given for the latest delay was that Leon Silverman was in the process of fashioning a plan for Manville's reorganization and would soon be presenting it to the company's creditors. Nothing could delay the continuing time of reckoning for some of Manville's co-defendants, however, and during the late winter and early spring several important verdicts were handed down in asbestos-disease cases that went to trial across the nation. On February 22, 1985, a federal court jury in Hawaii awarded $230,000 in compensatory damages and $500,000 in punitive damages against Raymark Industries to the survivors of a worker at the Pearl Harbor Naval Shipyard, who had died of lung cancer at the age of sixty-six. However, the presiding judge dismissed the verdict because the state has a two-year statute of limitations, and the jury had found that the dead man knew or should have known that he had developed asbestos disease two years and twenty-three days before he filed his lawsuit. On February 27, a circuit-court jury in Cook County, Illinois, returned an $804,000 verdict—including $174,000 in punitive damages—against Forty-Eight Insulations, of Aurora, Illinois, on behalf of a pipe coverer who had become disabled by asbestosis and lung cancer. (Less than two months later, Forty-Eight became the fourth asbestos-insulation manufacturer to file for reorganization under Chapter 11.) In late February, a San Francisco longshoreman suffering from mesothelioma, who was represented by Steven Kazan, of Oakland, reached an out-of-court settlement of slightly more than $1 million with ten defendant manufacturers. In March, a jury in the Philadelphia Court of Common Pleas awarded the unusually large sum of $500,000 to a shipyard worker who had developed pleural plaques and pleural thickening, in a trial de novo that was requested by the plaintiff after a judge in a nonjury trial had returned a verdict for the defense. And on April 22, a federal jury in Hawaii came back with a staggering award of $5.3 million in compensatory damages, plus $3 million in punitive damages, against Raymark in behalf of the family of Lawrence Kaowili, a ship-fitter at the Pearl Harbor Naval Shipyard from 1959 to 1978, who had developed asbestosis and died of lung cancer in 1979, at the age of forty-five, leaving a widow and five minor children. Because Kaowili had been a cigarette smoker, the jury found that he was contributorily negligent and one-third responsible for his injuries, and for this reason the presiding judge was obliged to lower the compensatory damages by about $1.8 million. (The $3 million punitive verdict was allowed to stand.) Two and a half weeks later, a California Superior Court jury in Los Angeles added to Raymark's woes when it returned a $2 million compensatory verdict against the company in favor of an eighty-one-year-old former garage mechanic who had developed mesothelioma and claimed that it had been caused by his inhaling asbestos fibers from brake linings manufactured by Raybestos-Manhattan. This was the first plaintiff verdict in a brake-lining case—the plaintiff was represented by Aaron Simon—and it bode especially ill for Raymark, a major manufacturer of brake linings, because, back in 1981, Dr. Selikoff and William Nicholson had predicted that there would be twenty thousand excess deaths from asbestos-related cancer among automobile mechanics in the United States within the next forty years.

As for the Kaowili case, it had an ironical aftermath. Following the trial, it was learned that all of the other twenty-odd defendants in the action had previously settled out of court for a total of $775,000. (Even so, the jury found that two of these defendants, Johns-Manville and H. K. Porter, had a share of responsibility for Kaowili's injuries worth $1.4 million, and, under Hawaii law, this amount was credited to Raymark, further reducing the company's obligation to $2.1 million.) As it happened, Kaowili's family, which was represented by a plaintiff attorney named Gary Galiher, of Honolulu, had been willing to settle with Raymark for $425,000, but the company had refused, offering only $50,000. At a subsequent hearing, Galiher called this a "nuisance-value offer," pointing out that it was less than the attorney fees Raymark had incurred in litigating the case, and on May 14 the presiding judge added slightly more than $1 million in prejudgment interest to the compensatory damages awarded to the Kaowili family. Another ironical twist occurred on April 23, the day after the initial jury verdict, when Frederick J. Ross, the president and chief executive officer of Raymark, told a House labor subcommittee that the current asbestos litigation was a "grossly inadequate means" of providing compensation for asbestos workers, and urged Congress to "instruct the government to contribute its fair share" to this end. Ross was testifying in support of a proposed bill to compensate asbestos victims, which was being sponsored by the subcommittee chairman, Representative Austin J. Murphy, a Democrat of Pennsylvania. Like the Fenwick and Hart bills that preceded it, Murphy's measure, which carried the unfortunate title the Asbestos Workers' Recovery Act, sought to involve the nation's taxpayers in bailing the asbestos industry out of its legal and financial difficulties. It proposed that the federal government and the industry create a joint fund to compensate asbestos victims, with the government paying half of all benefits awarded up to an annual federal cap of $150 million.

By now it should have been obvious to almost anyone following the asbestos litigation that was taking place in the nation that asbestos-insulation manufacturers who chose to go to trial in asbestos-disease cases, rather than settle out of court, ran an increasing risk of incurring punitive-damage verdicts, which were no longer merely a feared phenomenon but fast becoming a dreaded probability. For this reason, one of the most interesting and potentially controversial provisions of the long-awaited reorganization plan that Silverman outlined for Manville's creditors on April 3, at a meeting held in the downtown offices of Fried, Frank, Harris, Shriver & Jacobson, was that while asbestos-disease victims with claims against Manville should retain their right to have a jury trial, the question of whether they should be able to collect punitive damages against the company was left deliberately vague. This was undoubtedly done to encourage asbestos-disease victims to take their claims to the all-inclusive claims-handling facility that Silverman's proposed reorganization plan required Manville to join, and seemed to indicate that Silverman expected Manville to join the claims facility that was being set up under the Wellington plan.

The slippery issue of whether it was constitutional for the claims of future asbestos-disease victims to be dealt with in bankruptcy proceedings was one that Silverman sidestepped at the outset of his presentation, announcing that he intended to serve as a guardian of their interests without taking a position in the matter. In this connection, he said that he would work as a negotiator to put together a settlement vehicle that would provide fair and equitable compensation for present asbestos-disease claimants, and that would accommodate future claimants as their need arose. Silverman's proposals for financing this settlement vehicle turned out to be considerably more demanding of Manville's resources than any that had previously been considered by the company's creditors. In addition to the $615 million in insurance coverage that Manville was said to possess, he called for the company to provide $100 million in cash immediately upon confirmation of the settlement plan for the purpose of compensating the victims of asbestos disease. He went on to propose that Manville pay $37.5 million a year for seven years, in order to continue financing the settlement vehicle, and increase these payments to $75 million a year for the next eighteen years. Moreover, he proposed that if Manville's chief operating company should prove to be financially successful, additional funds as required would be provided to the settlement vehicle based upon an earnings formula.

In order to insure further that all present and future asbestos-disease claims would be compensated, Silverman called for the settlement vehicle to own 90 percent of the stock of Manville's chief operating company and for the holders of common stock and the holders of preferred stock to receive 7 percent and 3 percent, respectively, of the remaining 10 percent. (As might be expected, this proposed stock dilution was opposed by members of the shareholders' committee in the bankruptcy proceedings, who felt it was excessive.) Silverman went on to say that Manville's other creditors should also be prepared to make sacrifices if his plan was to have any chance of succeeding. First, he called upon the banks and other trade creditors, to whom Manville owed some $300 million, to forgo payment of the interest that they claimed had been accruing on this debt since the company had filed for reorganization. (In making this request, he was undoubtedly hoping to achieve some compromise in the matter.) Second, he called upon the plaintiff attorneys to be prepared to discuss the question of their contingent fees, undoubtedly expecting these fees to be lowered. And, finally, he suggested that the co-defendant asbestos manufacturers put up a guarantee that if the Manville settlement vehicle should run out of money they would step in and continue to finance it.

In addition to the sidestepped question of whether it was constitutional to deal with future asbestos-disease claimants in bankruptcy court, Silverman's proposed settlement plan contained at least one serious potential defect: this was his unexplained and undocumented assumption that the property-damage claims against Manville, which totalled some $50 billion, could somehow be settled in bankruptcy court for a mere $50 million. (Silverman apparently believed that Judge Lifland might accomplish this by issuing a non-appealable bankruptcy reorganization order.) Nevertheless, his ideas for reorganizing Manville were fairly well received by the company's other creditors— except for the representatives of the property-damage claimants and of the shareholders—for they felt that he had put together the broad outlines of a settlement plan upon which everyone except Manville might be able to agree, and they were hoping that Judge Lifland, whose confidence Silverman appeared to enjoy, would end up forcing Manville to accept it.

As things turned out, this proved to be substantially the case. During June, intensive negotiations began between Silverman and top officials of Manville—the first serious talks in the bankruptcy proceedings in more than eight months. Toward the end of July, however, the negotiations were on the verge of breaking down, chiefly because of Manville's unwillingness to commit future profits to a settlement trust fund if additional money were needed to pay off asbestos-disease claims, and its refusal to offer what Silverman considered to be a sufficient amount of its common stock to finance the trust fund. Silverman then contacted the leaders of other creditor groups and suggested that he would join with them in forcing a nonconsensual reorganization plan down Manville's throat. On July 25, Judge Lifland, who had made it clear earlier in the month that he did not want the bankruptcy case to extend beyond its third anniversary without substantial progress toward a settlement, abandoned his previous position of acquiescing to Manville's delaying tactics, and tightened the screws on the company by adjourning until July 29 a request from Manville for approval to spend $28 million on a platinum-mining venture in Montana. At this point, Manville's managers apparently saw the writing on the wall and decided that it was time to make a deal. On July 28, three high officials of the company flew to New York from Denver and, together with their lawyers from Davis Polk & Wardwell and their bankruptcy attorneys from Levin & Weintraub & Crames, met for eight hours with Silverman and his associates in the offices of Fried, Frank, Harris, Shriver & Jacobson. By the end of the day, they had agreed in principle to a reorganization plan that was similar to the one Silverman had outlined almost four months earlier. On the following day, the agreement was announced to Judge Lifland, and on August 2, it was approved by Manville's board of directors.

Under the terms of the plan, which would not go into effect until December 31, 1986, Manville's operating business arm would be protected by an injunction issued by the bankruptcy court against any future asbestos-disease claims, and a settlement trust would be set up to assume all liabilities for present and future asbestos claims. The settlement trust would dispose of such claims either through negotiation or by going to trial, and would be funded initially by an estimated $846.5 million—$315 million in cash from the insurance settlement that had been made with Travelers, Home, and the Lloyd's syndicates; $31.5 million in interest from this settlement; $300 million in cash or other insurance coverage yet to be settled; and $200 million in cash and other assets from Manville's operating arm. The settlement trust would also receive 50 percent of the outstanding shares of Manville's common stock, as well as shares of the company's preferred stock which could be converted to another 30 percent of common stock if this were needed to pay off asbestos claims, thus creating a situation in which the settlement trust could own as much as 80 percent of Manville's common stock. In addition, Manville would be required to contribute $75 million each year to the settlement trust from the fourth through the twenty-fifth years after final approval of the reorganization plan, and, beginning in the fifth year, to contribute up to 20 percent of its annual profits if they should be needed to pay for future asbestos-disease claims. The plan called for the settlement trust to join the Wellington claims-handling facility, or to operate its own claims-handling facility; it proposed to pay off any punitive-damage claims against the settlement trust with a one-time $5 million contribution to the trust; and it stipulated that the $80 billion in property-damage claims that had by now been brought against Manville be resolved by a final order of the bankruptcy court, which would cap them at $50 million. When all was said and done, Manville was agreeing to pay out some $2.5 billion over the next twenty-five years to settle some thirty thousand asbestos-disease claims that had already been brought, as well as the tens of thousands of additional cases that would be brought against it in the future.

As might be expected, reaction to the proposed reorganization plan was varied. Some observers praised Manville for agreeing to settle with the asbestos victims; others pointed out that the company's bankruptcy strategy had not only backfired, but had resulted in a drastic dilution of its stockholders' investment; and even Manville officials acknowledged that the company would emerge from bankruptcy in a financially weaker condition than when it had entered. However, many participants in the bankruptcy proceedings were strongly opposed to one or more of the plan's provisions. The court-appointed representative for the holders of Manville's common and preferred stock bitterly assailed the proposed stock dilution, claiming that "The corporate shares are not Manville's property," and that the company should not be allowed "to make a present of them to Mr. Silverman." (Be that as it may, hardship inflicted upon Manville's stockholders could have a beneficial effect if it served to make the shareholders of other companies with suspect policies and records regarding occupational and environmental health—for example, some of the nation's leading chemical manufacturers—sit up and take notice of the conduct and policies of the managers of these corporations.) Attorneys for the property-damage claimants objected to the provision that would enable Manville to deal with these claims for a fraction of what their clients were seeking. Plaintiff attorneys opposed the proposed injunction to protect Manville's operating arm against future asbestos-disease claims, pointing out that if the number of future asbestos victims were underestimated and the settlement trust were to run out of money, future claimants might be deprived of due process and compensation. The plaintiff attorneys also objected to Manville's attempt to insulate the settlement trust from punitive-damage claims with a contribution of only $5 million, pointing out that ten juries had awarded some $6 million in punitive damages against the company in 1981 and 1982 alone, after finding Manville guilty of outrageous and reckless misconduct.

Other aspects of the reorganization plan were expected to be the subject of intense bargaining during the rest of 1985. Among them was the thorny question of how the proposed asbestos-claims-handling facility would operate to compensate asbestos victims, and how much it would pay for various asbestos-related diseases, as well as the complex and unresolved question of how much insurance coverage Manville really had. (The figure of $615 million has been bandied about for years, but it has never been verified and some knowledgeable observers believe that Manville's actual coverage may be two to three times that amount.) For all these reasons, it appeared that before a final reorganization plan could be approved, there would be many more months of negotiating and of backing and filling in bankruptcy court, and perhaps as much as a year or two of litigation, depending upon how many appeals were made. However, the agreement reached between Manville and Silverman also indicated that sooner or later a resolution of the long-drawn-out dispute would be achieved and set out on paper in properly laborious legal terminology. Once that had come about, everyone concerned would no doubt proclaim the triumph of common sense and compromise, and, echoed by the nation's newspapers, hail the resolution of a great national tragedy. The real resolution of the asbestos tragedy would go largely unmentioned, however, because it would be something entirely different. The real resolution would be the terminal despair and suffering of tens of thousands of disabled asbestos workers who were dying or would die of asbestosis, of lung cancer, and of malignant mesothelioma.

One obvious lesson to be learned from the fifty-year asbestos-disease saga is that a society that cannot summon up the sense to protect the lungs and the lives of its workers cannot hope to protect the lungs and lives of its other citizens, including its children. Specifically, if we had been able to muster up the courage and the conviction to safeguard the health of our asbestos workers back in the 1930s and 1940s, when the first serious warnings about the asbestos-disease hazard were issued, we would surely not have allowed asbestos to be used in thousands of school buildings that were constructed in the United States between 1959 and 1972, and would thus not be faced today with the prospect of spending billions of dollars to decontaminate these schools of asbestos, or with the anxiety of wondering what past asbestos exposure will mean for the future well-being of the millions of children who have been attending them. The same holds true, of course, with regard to the nation's chemical workers. If we had seen fit to protect them from the ravages of carcinogenic chemicals back in the 1950s and early 1960s, when pioneers such as W. C. Hueper and Rachel Carson were warning of the hazard, we would scarcely have allowed these chemicals to be sprayed indiscriminately on our croplands and dumped into our landfills, so that they could one day find their way into our drinking water. That we did allow this to happen not only reflects our societal callousness toward the well-being of workers but also attests to a profound failure of imagination, which rendered us unable to understand that the poorly controlled manufacture and use of toxic substances in the workplace was bound to come back to haunt us, for the simple reason that workers make things that the rest of us either use directly, or are exposed to indirectly when they are used, or discarded, by our neighbors. In the case of asbestos—an indestructible mineral that is an ingredient of several thousand products and industrial applications, and has found its way into almost every building, factory, school, home, and farm across the land, as well as into every automobile, airplane, train, ship, and missile that is produced in the nation—our callousness and unimaginativeness have had some unique and ironic ethical consequences. The health hazard posed by this ubiquitous and invisible fiber of stone has not only sifted into the far corners of our society but has called into question the conduct of a huge cross-section of the institutions that make up the private-enterprise system, including many of its manufacturing corporations, insurance companies, investment houses, law firms, trade unions, and governmental regulatory agencies, as well as many members of the medical and legal professions, the scientific community, and Congress. Indeed, such are the ramifications of the asbestos-disease issue that it has called into serious question the conduct of a leading contender for the Democratic nomination for the Presidency.

Whether our society can learn from the hideous example of asbestos disease is open to conjecture. On June 14, 1985, Judge Ronald J.P. Banks, of the Cook County Circuit Court, in Chicago, found three officials of a company engaged in reclaiming silver from old film guilty of murder in the death of a plant employee from exposure to hydrogen cyanide fumes that resulted from the reclamation process. In a landmark decision, the judge said that "the conditions under which workers performed their duties were totally unsafe, " and that the convicted officials were "totally knowledgeable" of the hazardous conditions in the plant. Richard M. Daley, the Cook County State's Attorney, who prosecuted the case, said that the verdicts meant that employers who knowingly exposed their workers to dangerous conditions could be held "criminally responsible" for their actions. On July 1, Judge Banks sentenced each of the three officials to twenty-five years in prison and fined each of them $10,000. These developments notwithstanding, it also seems likely that, rather than reform the private-enterprise system in order to stem the onslaught of environmental pollution and accompanying illness, we will fulfill the ethical bankruptcy prophesied by Anthony J. Mazzochi, the outspoken former legislative director of the Oil, Chemical, and Atomic Workers International Union. "History shows that the lawsuit is the only adequate preventive measure against occupational and environmental cancer," Mazzochi has said. "Take away the lawsuit, replace it with a compensation schedule or some other administrative scheme, and you pave the way for cancer to become just another commodity to be costed out. The solution now being negotiated for the asbestos problem can then be applied across the board to future problems, such as the widespread contamination of the nation's drinking water supplies with cancer-producing chemicals. In this manner, you can institutionalize occupational and environmental cancer as a way of life."

The fact is that as a result of bills like Senator Hart's and the reluctance of the public and influential officials like Chief Justice Burger to understand that the asbestos litigation was a triumph of justice which is now being betrayed by the thickets of the Bankruptcy Code, the foundation for this institutionalization has already been laid. As a result, not only may Manville escape the full measure of its liability for the horror of asbestos disease, but corporations that are found guilty of similar misconduct in the future may similarly escape responsibility.

Another escape hatch may well be the proposed Uniform Product Liability Act, several versions of which have been introduced in the Senate since 1982 by Senator Robert W. Kasten, Jr., Republican of Wisconsin, who is chairman of the Senate Commerce Committee's Consumer Subcommittee. If enacted, Kasten's bill could help to facilitate the production of carcinogenic chemicals and toxic substances, for it proposes, in effect, to do away with the concept of strict liability, and to shift the burden of proof from the manufacturers and distributors of hazardous products to the consumers. This measure is supported by the Reagan administration and by two large business coalitions—the Product Liability Alliance and the Coalition for Uniform Product Liability Law. These two organizations are made up of some three hundred manufacturing corporations, insurance companies, and trade associations (the alliance includes the National Association of Manufacturers, the Business Roundtable, and the American Insurance Association), and, according to Robert J. Malott, chairman of the board and chief executive office of the FMC Corporation, a Chicago-based manufacturer of, among other items, insecticides, fungicides, and herbicides, they are considered to be "the most broadly based coalition of business groups ever assembled to support a specific cause."

Among other provisions, Kasten's bill would prevent anyone who is injured by a defective product from recovering damages from its manufacturer unless he can prove that the manufacturer knew or should have known to begin with that the product was defective. It would prevent anyone from recovering damages against the manufacturer of a capital good—one selling for a thousand dollars or more—if the defective product that caused the injury was more than twenty-five years old. It would prevent anyone from bringing a product-liability lawsuit against the manufacturer of a harmful product more than two years after the claimant discovered, or should have discovered, the injury and its cause. Under certain circumstances, it would allow a manufacturer to avoid liability for a defective product by warning an intermediate seller or employer, who would then be expected to warn the user or consumer about its hazard. It would do away with the important concept of market-share liability, as stated in 1980 in *Sindell* v. *Abbott Laboratories,* by requiring a claimant to prove that the product that injured him was manufactured by the defendant; that is, it would negate the rule of law under which drug manufacturers were held liable for injuries caused by DES, on the ground that it was impossible for the daughter of a woman who had been given the drug to identify its particular manufacturer. In addition, the bill proposed by Kasten would make it more difficult for juries to award punitive damages against corporations manufacturing defective products by raising the criteria for their award from a preponderance of evidence showing reckless disregard on the part of a manufacturer to "clear and convincing evidence" of such disregard. Moreover, Kasten's measure proposes that judges, not juries, would henceforth decide the amount of punitive damages to be awarded. The 1984 version of his bill would have protected a company from having to pay punitive damages to more than one defendant, and thus would destroy the concept of punitive damages as a deterrent to future misconduct, but widespread opposition to this provision forced Kasten to delete it when he reintroduced his measure before the Senate in January of 1985.

Opponents of Kasten's bill point out that it has been designed to limit the legal rights of the three hundred thousand Americans who are permanently disabled each year by product-related injuries, and of the survivors of the eighty thousand people who die each year of such injuries. In March, 1982, in testimony before Kasten's Consumer Subcommittee, David I. Greenberg, the legislative director of the Consumer Federation of America, said that agitation for a federal product-liability law was being spearheaded by the nation's insurance carriers. He went on to say that if the legislation were enacted it would "force too many innocent victims to thread a legal needle while providing too many defendants with a legal hole large enough to drive a truck through."

In an Op-Ed piece that was published in the New York *Times* in the spring of 1983, Jay Angoff, an attorney with the Public Citizen's Congress Watch—a public-interest group founded by Ralph Nader—put the problem of Kasten's bill in a nutshell. "The existing private litigation system is the primary self-protection tool consumers have," he wrote. "It compensates victims of defective products and encourages manufacturers to do safety research, since they know they will be held liable. The Kasten bill discourages manufacturers from doing such research, because if manufacturers don't know about a defect, they can't be liable for injury it causes."

A year later, Congress Watch reported that the political action committees of members of the Product Liability Alliance and the Coalition for Uniform Product Liability Law had made campaign contributions totaling almost $900,000 to members of the Senate Commerce Committee since January 1, 1979. According to Congress Watch, more than $130,000 of this went to Senator Paul S. Trible, Jr., Republican of Virginia, who introduced an amendment to the Kasten bill that would limit punitive damages against corporations making defective products. A spokesman for Trible admitted that the senator had introduced the amendment after being approached by the A. H. Robins Company, of Richmond, Virginia, makers of the Dalkon Shield intrauterine device. Robins had sold nearly three million Dalkon Shields in the United States between 1971 and 1974, and since 1972 it has been the target of more than twelve thousand lawsuits and claims brought by women who alleged that they had been injured by the device, and were seeking damages because Robins had failed to warn them that it could be hazardous to their health. The company, whose attorneys combated some of the lawsuits by demanding that claimants reveal details of their sex lives, has settled with almost nine thousand plaintiffs for more then $300 million, and, as of March,

1984, had been found guilty of outrageous and reckless misconduct by the members of seven juries, who returned punitive awards against it totaling more than $13 million. In July, 1984, a former attorney for Robins testified in a federal court in Minneapolis that the company's vice-president and general counsel had ordered him to arrange for the destruction of hundreds of documents relating to the safety of the Dalkon Shield, and that some papers were burned in early February. This was just before a jury in Wichita made the first award of punitive damages to users of the device. That October, Robins filed a motion in United States District Court in Richmond, asking that all punitive-damage cases be consolidated into one class action, and urged women who were still using the Dalkon Shield to have it removed. In April of 1985, company officials announced that they had set aside a $615 million reserve fund to pay for compensatory damages and legal expenses, but they acknowledged that this would not cover punitive damages for lawsuits brought by women in foreign countries who had used the Dalkon Shield.

Congress Watch reported that other senators on the Commerce Committee had also received PAC contributions from members of the Product Liability Alliance and the Coalition for Uniform Product Liability Law. In addition to Kasten, who received nearly $70,000, they included the committee chairman, Bob Packwood, Republican of Oregon; John C. Danforth, Republican of Missouri; Russell B. Long, Democrat of Louisiana; Barry M. Goldwater, Republican of Arizona; Ted Stevens, Republican of Alaska; Ernest F. Hollings, Democrat of South Carolina; Howell Heflin, Democrat of Alabama; J. James Exon, Democrat of Nebraska; Wendell H. Ford, Democrat of Kentucky; Larry Pressler, Republican of South Dakota; Slade Gorton, Republican of Washington; Donald W. Riegle, Jr., Democrat of Michigan; Daniel K. Inouye, Democrat of Hawaii; Nancy L. Kassebaum, Republican of Kansas; and Frank Lautenberg, Democrat of New Jersey. (Ironically, Hollings, Heflin, and Riegle have been leading opponents of Kasten's proposed bill. Indeed, Hollings has described the measure as "the snake oil of our day," claiming that it is "anti-consumer" and "probably unconstitutional.")

Considering the kind of money that was spread around the Commerce Committee, it should come as no surprise that its members voted to report a version of Kasten's bill out of committee in March of 1984. (Senators Packwood, Hollings, Riegle, Heflin, and Lautenberg voted not to report the bill out.) During the autumn of 1984, Hollings and other opponents prevented it from coming to a floor vote by threatening to hold a filibuster, and in May of this year, an eight-to-eight tie vote prevented it from being reported out of committee. It will no doubt be reintroduced and another close battle is expected in 1986. By drastically curtailing the present legal remedies of the victims of toxic substances, such as asbestos and DES, the bill would have the effect of institutionalizing the production of hazardous and defective products. In this way, it supplements the proposal of Senator Hart to deny asbestos victims their day in court, and complements the attempt of Manville and its insurers to employ the Bankruptcy Code as a convenient tool for compensating these victims at bargain rates for loss of their health and their lives. Thus, sweeping efforts to weaken the tort system and in effect grant immunity to manufacturers of toxic substances are gathering force in a land whose inhabitants, though they are supposedly more aware than ever of the dimensions of the occupational-and-environmental-disease problem, seem incapable of insisting that the present predicament become a national priority. As a result, the American people bid fair to repeat an ironic disaster of history—the one that is said to have overtaken the latter-day Romans, who continued to use lead vessels in the making of wine even after they had been warned that they might be poisoning themselves by doing so. In our case, it seems clear, we are being asked not only to ignore the warnings we have received about occupational and environmental cancer and other disease but to sanction an act of callousness followed by a perverse and stupid exercise in participatory democracy. We are being solicited by the private-enterprise system, as it is now constituted, to deny just compensation to tens upon tens of thousands of its victims, our fellow-citizens, and to become its accomplices in the destruction of the public health and, therefore, of our own.

AFTERWORD

In describing the dimensions of the immense disaster that has befallen the nation's asbestos workers, it is easy to use statistics. As someone once said, however, statistics are human beings with the tears wiped off. It becomes something else to try to imagine the agonizing human consequences of the asbestos tragedy. Harry T. Ahrens, a journeyman with the International Association of Heat and Frost Insulators of New York, addressed this question in a letter that was published in the *National Law Journal* in November of 1981. In his letter, Ahrens criticized an article that had appeared in the *Journal* about the "boom in asbestos litigation," saying that it was like other articles he had read in which practically everyone who was involved in the asbestos litigation had been interviewed except the victims. "No need to speak to workers or their widows," Ahrens wrote bitterly. "It's more interesting to gaze at Johns-Manville's billion-and-a-half-dollar structure than the individual bricks of which it was built—life by life, over the years."

As it happens, Dr. Irving J. Selikoff and his colleagues at the Mount Sinai Medical School's Environmental Sciences Laboratory have got in touch with hundreds of asbestos workers' widows over the past decade in order to obtain information about their husbands' illnesses and permission to have their husbands' medical records released, so that these data could be incorporated into continuing studies of the causes of mortality among asbestos workers. What follows is a collage of sentences that have been taken from thirty or so of the letters that were written by the widows in reply:

I remember very well the pathologist coming into the room and asking my husband if he had ever been around asbestos . . . He had oxygen for the last two years of his life, which made him hallucinate and act paranoid . . . They told me that his death was due to industrially incurred disease from asbestos particles in the lungs, but my appeal for burial and medical expenses was turned down due to statutes of limitations . . . He went through all kinds of tests at the hospital, and then another doctor operated on him and sewed him right up, and came down and told me he had just two months to live . . . Each day he ate less and lived for the hypos to kill the pain . . . He died with carcinoma of the lungs and metastatic lesions all through his body caused by asbestosis of the lung, and the bones in his legs were as though they were moth-eaten . . . To go to sleep at night was terrifying for him because he feared that his oxygen mask would fall off and he would die in his sleep . . . I knew my husband knew it but wouldn't tell me, so when I found out I didn't mention it to him either . . . When he worked in close places where he couldn't get air, down in the hull of ships, was where he fared badly . . . Most of the clothes he used to work in were left on the job, but what he wore home would be so heavy with asbestos dust that it would stop the washer, even after they were shook and aired outside . . . He came home daily covered in white and held his young ones as they greeted him . . . In my case, I was still grief-stricken and have a mentally ill daughter, and the prospect of maybe not being able to provide for her and maybe lose everything if I went through a court trial prompted me to accept the pittance I got . . . I first noticed in 1961 that my husband was able to do very little physical exertion . . . June of 1969 is when his stomach started to swell, and this was hard to understand because he started to lose his appetite in March and was losing weight . . . The last words he said were to his brother; he jerked the oxygen out of his nose and said, "John, this is hell" . . . At least half of the last twenty years of his life, he could sleep only in a sitting position . . . It got so bad he couldn't walk and talk at the same time . . . I slept on the Chesterfield so I could pound his back and give him oxygen treatments . . . In the end he was choking on the pills he had to take because he couldn't take in enough air to hold his breath while he took the pill . . . The doctor came back from the operating room and told me his intestines were completely grown together with tumors and that it was just a matter of time . . . He had told me about getting a test for asbestosis, but he told me he was all right, 'cause I worried so . . . When his brother, who also worked with asbestos, came to visit from Port Arthur, Texas, he said it was too bad John had died so long ago because lots of people there were suing for asbestos and I could have sued too had I known back then . . . Why, when the kids were little, a couple of families would all go over to the priest's house on a Saturday to put asbestos on the boilers . . . So they wouldn't accept the autopsy, and I settled out of court for $6,000 . . . Earl had a lawyer who was going to get him the money, but when they went down to the Compensation Board they were told he couldn't get it because he had been a day late to the examination . . . One widow got $7,000; it sounded big at the time . . . The Social Security doctor said he was 90 percent disabled, but the doctor from the Industrial Board said he was only 50 percent disabled, so he didn't get it . . . The doctor who operated said he found asbestos fibers in the cancer, but he wouldn't say one way or the other whether the cancer was actually caused by asbestos or not because he didn't want to get involved in a court case . . . He died the night he came home from the hospital. He came home and sat up. He even got on his feet. The doctors shook their heads. They couldn't believe it. He tried to get well. He loved life and he wanted to live for me and the kids. He laid down and when his last breath went out, he called me and said, "Honey, I'm dying." Then he died.

INDEX

Attorney's Textbook of Medicine (Gray),
201–2
Auerbach, Oscar, 226, 240
Auribault, M., 12, 13
Austin, Charles Lee and Edna, 108
Austin v. Johns-Manville, 108, 121–23,
142

Baldwin, Scott, 83–93, 215, 223,
241–43
Ball, Herbert Morton, 166
Banks, Ronald J. P., 349–50
Barnett, Gordon Luther, 138, 140,
142, 147, 233
Baron, Frederick M., 81–93, 158,
172–73, 215, 216, 284, 285, 300
Bath Iron Works Yard, 203
Baumeister, Michael, 276
Baumgardner, William, 136–37
Bean, Jackie, 27, 40, 43, 44–45, 62,
63–65, 69–70
Bearman, Christina, 263
Beasley, James F., 283
Bell Asbestos Mines, Ltd., 108, 222
Benkard, James W. B., 263
Berlin, N.J., Kaylo manufactured in,
149, 150, 151, 153
Berman, Michael, 318
Bernays, Richard, 85
Bhopal, India, toxic chemicals in, 184,
328–29
Binder, Otto L., 171, 173
Bixby, Robert O. F., 270, 277
Blackshear, Cornelius, 285
Blagden, Augustus S., 204
Blatt, Solomon, 135
Blatt, Solomon, Jr., 135
Blatt & Fales, 135–36, 231, 234
Blue, Lisa, 172–73
Blumenfeld, M. Joseph, 251
*Bob Alan Speake v. Johns-Manville
Corp. et al.*, 168, 170–77, 226
Boeschenstein, Harold, 152
Borel, Clarence:
death of, 41, 215, 217, 326
symptoms of, 39, 40, 52–53
work history of, 40, 46, 48, 52–53,
56
Borel, Thelma, 41, 45, 54–55, 63, 64,
65, 326
*Borel v. Fibreboard Paper Products
Corporation, et al.*, 39–70, 73–77,

82, 97, 98, 100, 106, 107, 121,
128, 146, 153, 165, 167, 169,
170, 180, 211, 215, 217, 224,
226, 227, 237, 325–26
Bowes, U. E., 150
Brach, William L., 165–67
Braun, Daniel C., 126, 179, 236
Brewster, Richard, 307
British Journal of Radiology, 47
British Medical Journal, 13, 120
Britt, David, 172, 173
Brittingham, Russell, 87
bronchitis, 226, 229
Brooklyn Navy Yard, 237
Brooks-Fisher insulation company,
128, 131
Brown, Ira A., Jr., 332
Brown, Lewis Herold, 176, 272–73,
276–77
Brown, Vandiver, 18, 103, 111–20,
147, 235, 239, 242, 275, 276
mystery of, 170–74
Browner, Harold, 159, 160
"bucket shops," 86
Buckley, Robert E., 87, 92
Budd, Larner, Kent, Gross, Picillo &
Rosenbaum, 142
Burger, Warren E., 313, 350

Cadwalader, Wickersham & Taft, 127
calcium hydroxide, 148
calcium silicate, 31, 148, 151
Califano, Joseph A., Jr., 140
California, asbestosis lawsuits in,
157–62, 167–77, 218
California Industrial Accident
Commission, 139, 140, 160–61,
162
Calvados, France, asbestos disease in,
12
cancer:
asbestos as cause of, 6, 30, 50, 53,
77, 80, 90, 93, 98, 125–26, 141,
203, 227, 230, 258, 259, 264,
266–67, 313, 339, 342, 357
asbestosis and, 125–26, 178, 206,
223, 233, 238, 241
bone, 69
bronchial, 236
deaths caused by, 30–31, 50,
69–70, 77, 90, 258, 267, 342
DES and, 191

ABOUT THE AUTHOR

Paul Brodeur, a staff writer on *The New Yorker,* specializes in environmental and occupational medicine and has spent some twenty years covering the asbestos story. He is the author of three highly acclaimed nonfiction books, *Expendable Americans, The Zapping of America,* and *Restitution;* two novels, *The Stunt Man* and *The Sick Fox;* and a collection of short stories entitled *Downstream.* The articles upon which this book is based first appeared in *The New Yorker* and were awarded the 1985 Association of Trial Lawyers of America Special Literary–Public Service Award. His previous articles have won the Sidney Hillman Foundation Award, Columbia University's National Magazine Award, an American Association for the Advancement of Science–Westinghouse Science Writing Award, and an American Bar Association Award. He lives on Cape Cod.